SAINTS OF THE ROMA

SAINTS
OF THE ROMAN CALENDAR

Including Feasts Proper to the English-Speaking World

Enzo Lodi

Translated and Adapted by
JORDAN AUMANN, OP

ALBA • HOUSE NEW • YORK
SOCIETY OF ST. PAUL, 2187 VICTORY BLVD., STATEN ISLAND, NY 10314

Library of Congress Cataloging-in-Publication Data

Lodi, Enzo.
        [I santi del calendario romano.   English]
        Saints of the Roman calendar : including feasts proper to the
    English-Speaking world / Enzo Lodi ; translated and adapted by
    Jordan Aumann.
            p.   cm.
        Translation of: I santi del calendario romano.
        ISBN 0-8189-0652-9
        1. Christian saints — Biography.   2. Catholic Church — Liturgy.
    I. Title.
    BX4655.2.L63513   1992   92-20261
    263'.98 — dc20   CIP

Nihil Obstat:
    Dennis R. Zusy, O.P.
    Socius and Vicar Provincial

Imprimi Potest:
    Donald J. Goergen, O.P.
    Prior Provincial

Designed, printed and bound in the United States of
America by the Fathers and Brothers of the
Society of St. Paul, 2187 Victory Boulevard,
Staten Island, New York 10314, as part of their
communications apostolate.

PRINTING INFORMATION:

Current Printing - first digit   3   4   5   6   7   8   9   10   11   12

Year of Current Printing - first year shown

                                                                          1999

AUTHOR'S PREFACE

The title of this book, *Saints of the Roman Calendar*, will undoubtedly appear to be somewhat pretentious. To show the relevance of the saints of the entire Roman Calendar presupposes a profound knowledge of each and every saint in order to describe the spirituality of the saints in the context of their time and to show their relevance to contemporary Christians.

The purpose of this book is predominantly liturgical and pastoral, namely, to provide the faithful and the celebrants of the Eucharist with an explanation of the liturgical formularies in honor of the saints as found in the Sacramentary and in the Liturgy of the Hours. Accordingly, I have tried to present the most significant aspects of their life and spirituality.

The method used is essentially hermeneutical and liturgical. It has its limitations, however, and first of all because the historical and biographical details had to be severely restricted in a one-volume work. Secondly, references to the readings from Sacred Scripture are limited to those cases in which the readings are proper to the feast and contain significant material. Normally, however, the readings for the feast of a saint are taken from the weekday readings. In many cases the revised liturgy has "personalized" the various prayers, and especially the Opening Prayer of the Mass, which normally makes a reference to some characteristic trait of the saint in question.

This book is not written in the traditional panegyric style that focuses on the extraordinary phenomena and the miraculous in the lives of the saints. The liturgy is much more reserved; it portrays the holiness of the saints as particular manifestations of the all-inclusive holiness of Christ. The prayer formulas of the Mass do not give biographical details as a rule, but when a feast has a proper Preface, it will usually give a synthesis of the life and mission of that particular saint. The Office of Readings also is an excellent source of information, especially if the second reading contains biographical or autobiographical material.

The method used in this book is twofold. First of all, the "historico-liturgical note" usually traces the origin and development of the cult of the saint and notes any changes in the dates for the celebration of the feast of the saint in question. There is also a brief summary of the life of the saint.

Secondly, as regards the "message and relevance" of the saint, this is based on the prayers of the Mass and the prayers and readings of the Liturgy of the Hours. These not only depict the life and spirituality of the saint but they also serve as a basis for discovering in what way a particular saint has any relevance to contemporary Christian life. It is not always easy to show how a saint who lived centuries ago, in a different culture and historical setting, is of any significance to Christians today. Nevertheless, in spite of these differences, the saints are not simply heroes from an age that is past. Since they attained to the perfection of charity in the particular circumstances of their lives, they can always be put forward as models and exemplars of the Christian life in any age.

This book offers nothing original as regards the common hagiographical sources, but it should prove a helpful source book for homilies for the celebrant of the liturgy and for sermons on the saints during novenas and tridua. Moreover, in the hands of the faithful it will provide useful material for spiritual reading and meditation. In this way the particular devotions of the faithful can be based on and inspired by the liturgy. This is in keeping with the teaching of the Second Vatican Council, which stated that the liturgy is "the primary and indispensable source from which the faithful are to derive the true Christian spirit" (*Sacrosanctum Concilium*, no. 14).

It is my hope that these pages will serve to fill the vacuum that has existed after the Second Vatican Council because the revision of the liturgy has rendered useless the works of Abbot B. Baur and Pius Parsch. May these pages provide light and inspiration for our Christian communities as they celebrate and pray in the liturgy.

ENZO LODI

TRANSLATOR'S NOTE

This is not an exact translation of *I Santi del Calendario Romano* by Enzo Lodi. First of all, since the book was originally written with Italian readers in mind, it was necessary to adapt the translation with a view to English-speaking readers.

Secondly, some of the material is of interest only to Italian readers or to professional liturgists. Consequently, we have not hesitated to make deletions where necessary or to add material that would be of interest to English-speaking readers. For example, we have inserted the feast days that are proper to the United States.

Finally, it should be noted that the author frequently referred to the official Latin text of liturgical formularies whenever the Italian translation omitted important details. We have done the same when the English version of the formularies differs noticeably from the Latin. The author has also provided numerous Prefaces that are proper to certain saints, but are not found in the Sacramentary used in the United States. We have either located the official translations of those Prefaces in the Sacramentaries of various religious institutes or have made our own translation.

This book should be a welcome addition to the ever-increasing number of books that treat of the lives of the saints. It is offered to the English-speaking public in the hope that it will foster greater devotion to the saintly men and women who are not only historical figures worthy of veneration but models worthy of our imitation.

JORDAN AUMANN, O.P.

TABLE OF CONTENTS

MARCH

APRIL

MAY

JUNE

JULY

AUGUST

SEPTEMBER

OCTOBER

NOVEMBER

DECEMBER

INTRODUCTION

In recent years there has been a revival of interest in the cult of the saints, as is evident from the ever-increasing number of books that deal with the biographies, spirituality and writings of the saints. In the search for new forms and models of holiness in our pluralistic and multicultural society, one cannot ignore the great figures who throughout the centuries have given vivid witness to the holiness of the Church. Neither can one ignore the socio-anthropological influence of the saints, since the choice of heroes, models and leaders can have a lasting effect on the development of one's personality. Of course, the hero and model *par excellence* is Jesus Christ, and the Christian life consists essentially in the following and imitation of Christ.

The cult of the saints began with the veneration of the early martyrs, who followed Christ to the point of sharing in his bloody sacrifice on Calvary. Then, when the persecutions of the Church came to an end, the ascetics replaced the martyrs as exemplars of the perfection of charity. The veneration of the saints had as its primary purpose to provide models of the Christian life, in accordance with the dictum of St. Ambrose: "The life of the saints is the norm of life for all others." However, in the early Church the veneration of the martyrs was primarily for the purpose of intercession. Consequently, many of the faithful looked to the saints as protectors in times of calamity or helpers in times of prosperity. Thus, one would usually hear of a long list of miracles that occurred at the tombs or shrines of the saints. This eventually led to certain superstitious practices that were vehemently denounced by the Protestant reformers. They did not deny the exemplary value of the saints as models for imitation; but they did deny the saints' power of intercession. Consequently, the Council of Trent advised bishops as follows: "They should instruct the faithful carefully concerning the intercession and the invocation of the saints, the honor due to their relics, and the lawful use of images; they should teach the faithful that the saints, reigning together with Christ, pray to God for men; it is a good and useful thing to invoke the saints humbly and to have recourse to their prayers and to their efficacious help to obtain favors from God through his Son Jesus Christ our Lord who alone is our Redeemer and Savior" (Session XXV).

Even if the Scriptural basis for the cult of the saints should prove to be of little weight, it is certainly a doctrine of faith that we profess in the Credo: "I believe in the communion of saints." In the Byzantine eucharistic liturgy the celebrant says "holy things to the saints." Moreover, tradition attests to the fact that devotion to the saints was practiced in the early Church in the second century, when Christians visited the tombs of the martyrs on the anniversary day of their death. That cult comprised three elements: (1) the gathering of the local Christian community; (2) on the anniversary day of the martyrdom (*dies natalis*) or burial (*depositio*); (3) the celebration of the Eucharist. But the cult of the saints was never allowed to obscure the absolute primacy of the paschal mystery of Christ. Hence we read in Vatican II's document on the liturgy: "The Church has also included memorial days of the martyrs and other saints in the annual cycle. . . . By celebrating their anniversaries, the Church proclaims the achievement of the paschal mystery in the saints who have suffered and have been glorified with Christ. She proposes them to the faithful as examples who draw all men to the Father through Christ, and through their merits she begs for God's favor" (*Sacrosanctum Concilium*, n. 104). In fact, Scripture states that all those who are called "saints are called to share in the holiness of God" (Heb 12:10); for that reason St. Paul could say: "You are fellow citizens of the saints and members of the household of God" (Ep 2:19). According to the traditional teaching of the Church, the People of God should be the *holy* People of God, and the Second Vatican Council reiterated this teaching (cf. *Lumen Gentium*, nos. 40-41).

The saints are also, in a certain sense, a prolongation of

the sacred humanity of Christ because they "fill up what is lacking in the sufferings of Christ for the sake of his body, the Church" (Col 1:24). All together they represent the total Christ, for although Christ's human nature is perfect and inimitable, it is nevertheless limited in manifesting the entire infinite mystery of the Word that was made flesh. Like ourselves, the saints belong to the Mystical Body of Christ, and in union with them we offer the eucharistic sacrifice (In union with the whole Church," says the Roman Canon of the Mass). Having gone before us in this life, they can help us unite ourselves to Christ, as was affirmed by the Second Vatican Council: "Exactly as Christian communion between men on their earthly pilgrimage brings us closer to Christ, so our community with the saints joins us to Christ. . . . It is most fitting, therefore, that we love those friends and coheirs of Jesus Christ who are also our brothers and sisters and outstanding benefactors, and that we give due thanks to God for them. . . . Every authentic witness of love, indeed, offered by us to those who are in heaven tends to and terminates in Christ, 'the crown of all the saints,' and through him in God who is wonderful in his saints and is glorified in them" (*Lumen Gentium*, no. 50).

Our modern secularistic culture has lost the clear concept of the holy in relation to the sacred. In fact, some persons would call ours a "post-sacred" age. The reason for the confusion is that the word "holy," which is intimately related to the paschal mystery of Christ, has been identified with the mysterious and esoteric or the numinous aspect of the sacred as found in some religions. The concept of the sacred that is limited to the reaction of individual persons to God and in total opposition to the profane has never been accepted in Catholic teaching.

The religious vacuum that has been created in modern society is compensated for by a new sacralization, namely, that of the great myths of the social collectivity. In any case, there is an interest in and a search for the sacred, and that can serve as a disposition for accepting the faith. Eventually it can open the way to an authentic sanctity which is nothing more or less than the total and free acceptance of the divine message.

In making the saints relevant it is therefore necessary to avoid thinking of their message as something definitive, completed and static. Their participation in the divine holiness manifests a tension in respect to Christ, the perfect model, and an unlimited openness to ever greater perfection. The calendar of the saints is a book that is always subject to the contradictions of human history, but it is at the same time a reflection of the one true "Saint" who is resplendent in every epoch and in all conditions. In the first Preface for Holy Men and Women we read: "In their lives on earth you give us an example. In our communion with them you give us their friendship. In their prayer for the Church you give us strength and protection."

THE TYPOLOGY OF THE SAINTS

The saints are classified under various titles or typologies in the liturgy and it may be helpful as well as interesting to see the basis for this classification.

Martyrs. Martyrdom is never presented as an act of heroism, an example of courage or even as the firmness of one's faith. Rather, it is a sign of the plan of God that is realized through suffering; first, that of the just who were persecuted in the Old Testament and then in the Messiah, the Suffering Servant of God. Thus, Jesus said: "I solemnly assure you, unless the grain of wheat falls to the earth and dies, it remains just a grain of wheat. But if it dies, it produces much fruit" (Jn 12:24-26). To suffer persecution is part of the mission of the People of God; it is a sign of their truth and a condition for their efficacy. Moreover, the trials and tribulations of life are an extension of martyrdom and a sign of one's sharing in the paschal mystery of Christ with its threefold certitude: after the cross comes the victory of the resurrection; no persecutor can destroy the true life; Christ should be loved above all things, even at the cost of one's life.

Pastors. The pastoral ministry is a choice made by God because God alone leads his people to salvation. He is the true Shepherd. Human pastors are never such by delegation but by the mystery of sharing in the pastoral care of God and of Christ (Ezk 34:11-16; Jn 10:11-16). The pastoral ministry is a manifestation of the authority of Christ himself, as we see in his commission of the apostles: "Full authority has been given to me both in heaven and on earth; go, therefore, and make disciples of all the nations" (Mt 28:18-19). God himself determines the limits, the purpose and the efficacy of those who are sent by him. The apostle is completely subordinate to the Gospel (2 Cor 4:1-7) and to the word of God (Ac 20:17-36). Consequently, pastoral service comprises three elements: the communitarian character of this ministry, which is manifested in a diversity of ministries and charisms with the participation of the entire community; the establishment of the Church (Lk 10:1-24), which requires poverty, freedom, detachment and humility; and the connection between earthly service and a sharing in the eschatological dimension (Lk 22:24-30).

Doctors. The glorification of the wisdom of the Doctors of the Church has its origin in the inculturation of God's revelation to the Jews, thus introducing human experience into revelation itself. But sapiential reflection is linked to poverty of spirit because this wisdom comes from God and not from the human person; it is a gift to be welcomed. In the Gospel, wisdom is not theoretical or philosophical knowledge; it is the capacity to transform life through good works (Mt 5:13-19; Lk 6:43-45). In the light of the paschal mystery, wisdom is the recognition of the salvific value of the cross (1 Cor 1:17-19).

Virgins. The Christian exaltation of virginity does not imply a disdain for human sexuality nor is it simply an expression of personal perfection. It is the symbolic manifestation of the Church offering herself as a bride to Christ the Bridegroom. The virgin is free from every other love because she is the spouse of Christ (2 Cor 11:1-2). Moreover, there is an eschatological aspect in the sense that virginal love is necessary in order to discover the relation of everything to Christ (cf. 1 Cor 7:29; Mt 19:3-12).

Men and Women Saints. Sanctity is presented in the biblical texts with a Trinitarian dimension, as the fruit of the love of the Father and the Son through the action of the Holy Spirit who dwells in us. It is also a vital union with the holiness of Christ, as is evident from the allegory of the vine and the branches (Jn 15:1-8). Finally, holiness is the perfection of the virtue of charity (Jn 15:9-18), and it is expressed in works of mercy for the little ones who are especially loved by Christ (Mt 25: 31-40). This demands a radical dedication that leads to a childlike spirit (Mk 9:35).

LITURGICAL FORMULARIES

The prayers in honor of the saints are always addressed to God the Father, who has sanctified the faithful who witnessed to him during their lifetime. Now in the state of glory, they have received the reward for the merits of their virtues and we honor them as intercessors and patrons. In ancient times St. Cyprian taught that "we pray for the saints as we pray for the deceased." He said that "we offer sacrifices for them each time we celebrate their anniversary days or the memorial of martyrs" (Letter 39). On the other hand, St. Augustine taught that we do not pray for the saints but for the other deceased, for it would be an insult to pray for a martyr; we should rather recommend ourselves to their prayers (cf. Sermon 159).

The Eucharist celebrated in memory of a saint is distinct from the Sunday Eucharist, but it is not different. The *Constitution on the Sacred Liturgy* of Vatican Council II states: "By celebrating their anniversaries, the Church proclaims the achievement of the paschal mystery in the saints who have suffered and have been glorified" (no. 104).

The selection of saints in the general calendar and the transfer of memorials of local interest to particular calendars was based not only on a qualitative basis, that is, to honor saints of greater importance, but also for geographical reasons, so that the calendar would have a more universal appeal. There was also an attempt to select saints from various periods of history, as well as a regard for popular devotion. Two other criteria were used, namely, a reduction of the number of devotional feasts and a more rigorous examination of the cult of a given saint.

For all 206 feasts of saints in the present Roman Calendar the prayers of the Mass had to be selected from the abundant texts in the Liturgy of the Hours. There are no longer any negative titles of the saints, e.g. "not a virgin" or "not a martyr." There are four classes of celebrations: solemnity, feast, obligatory memorial, and optional memorial.

BRIEF HISTORY OF THE ROMAN CALENDAR

The most ancient Roman Calendar dates back to the year 354. It was called the *Depositio Martyrum* and the *Depositio Episcoporum.* It contained 23 feasts of saints, but only 14 of those feasts have been retained. In the sixth century 19 feasts were added, of which only 13 remain. Between the eleventh and the sixteenth centuries the Gregorian reform introduced more feasts: 28 popes (today there are 18), 49 non-Roman martyrs (today there are 18).

In promulgating the reform commanded by the Council of Trent (1568), the Dominican Pope Pius V composed a new Calendar. As a result there were 65 feastdays of saints, of which approximately 48 were martyrs. At the beginning of the seventeenth century, numerous feasts of the saints were raised to a higher class; in fact, there was a danger that the sanctoral feasts would replace the liturgical cycle. This situation was remedied somewhat by Pope Pius X, who reestablished the priority of the Sunday liturgy, both as regards the Mass and the Liturgy of the Hours. Nevertheless, by the twentieth century there were more than 200 feastdays of saints, as compared with 65 at the time of the Council of Trent (1568). In addition to feasts of the saints, there were numerous feasts introduced to honor the Blessed Virgin Mary: between the fourteenth and the sixteenth century: the Visitation, the Transfiguration and the Holy Rosary; from the seventeenth century onward: the Holy Name of Mary (1683), the Seven Sorrows of Mary (1814), Our Lady of Mount Carmel (1726), the Immaculate Conception (1879), Our Lady of Lourdes (1907), the Maternity of Mary (1931), Mary, Queen (1955).

In 1969 the Roman Calendar was again revised. The revision was carried out in two phases: the first schema between 1964 and 1966, and the final revision in 1969. The obligatory memorials were doubled, from 36 to 66; the optional memorials were reduced, from 122 to 96.

This brief survey of the Roman Calendar raises a question: Will the saints of today and the future be modelled on the saints of yesterday? If, as Bernanos said, "the life of every saint is a new flowering," we can suppose that the working of the Holy Spirit is unpredictable. Nevertheless, the prototype of sanctity is always the same; it is Christ, of whom we say "You alone are holy." Therefore the saint that we honor in the liturgy today is always a saint who comes out of a tradition that is constantly being renewed. It is easier to say what the saints were than what they will be, but we can always be certain about what a saint could never be.

The saint that we await will always be different from our plans, our predictions or the expectation of our changing times. But he or she will certainly be a saint for all times, because he or she will be an imitator of Christ, although in a new way in accordance with his or her historical and cultural context. If, as St. Irenaeus says, "Life in man is the glory of God; the life of man is the vision of God" (*Against the Heresies*, IV, 20, 5-7), the saint of the future will always be one who, even in our technological age, is a personification of the divine intervention, a radiant presence in the world, though he or she is not of this world (cf. Jn 8:16).

The statement of St. Bernard in the Office of Readings for the feast of All Saints is always relevant: "The saints have no need of honor from us; neither does our devotion add the slightest thing to what is theirs. Clearly, if we venerate their memory, it serves us, not them. But I tell you, when I think of them, I feel myself inflamed by a tremendous yearning" (Sermon 2).

ENZO LODI

JANUARY

January 1
SOLEMNITY OF MARY, Mother of God

HISTORICO-LITURGICAL NOTE

The solemnity of the Mother of God, which now coincides with the octave-day of Christmas and the beginning of the new year, was probably assigned this day because of the influence of the Byzantine Church, which celebrates the synapsis of the most holy Theotokos on December 26. This is in accordance with the Eastern practice of honoring secondary persons on the day after the feast of the principal personage (in this case, the birth of Christ). The Coptic Church celebrates this feast on January 16, but in the West, as early as the fifth century, the feast was celebrated on the Sunday before Christmas, although in France it was celebrated on January 18 and in Spain on December 18. Even before Pope Sergius introduced four Marian feasts in the seventh century (the Birth of Mary, the Annunciation, the Purification and the Assumption), the octave day of Christmas was celebrated in Rome in honor of the Maternity of Mary. Later, in the thirteenth and fourteenth centuries, the feast of the Circumcision was added, although it had been introduced into Spain and France at the end of the sixth century and was later included in the Missal of Pope St. Pius V. The recent liturgical reform has restored the original Roman practice, which replaced the pagan feast of the New Year, dedicated to the god Janus, with this feast honoring the Mother of God.

A popular movement began in Portugal in the eighteenth

century for a feast honoring Mary's maternity, and in 1914 the date of the feast was fixed at October 11. It was extended to the entire Latin Church in 1931, the fifteenth centenary of the Council of Ephesus. The restoration of the feast to January 1, which falls in the Christmas season and has an ecumenical significance, coincides with other anniversaries; for example, the octave day of Christmas, the circumcision of the Infant Jesus (assigned to the first Sunday of January); the feast of the Holy Name of Jesus (which dates back to 1721); and the day for peace, introduced by Pope Paul VI.

In the encyclical *Marialis Cultus* (1974) Pope Paul VI states: "This celebration, assigned to January 1 in conformity with the ancient liturgy of the city of Rome, is meant to commemorate the part played by Mary in this mystery of salvation. It is meant also to exalt the singular dignity which this mystery brings to the 'holy Mother . . . through whom we were found worthy . . . to receive the Author of life.' It is likewise a fitting occasion for renewed adoration of the newborn Prince of Peace, for listening once more to the glad tidings of the angels, and for imploring from God, through the Queen of Peace, the supreme gift of peace. For this reason . . . we have instituted the World Day of Peace, an observance that is gaining increasing support and is already bringing forth fruits of peace in the hearts of many" (no. 5).

MESSAGE AND RELEVANCE

The Opening Prayer of the Mass is addressed to "God, who has given to mankind the blessings of salvation through the fruitful virginity of Mary" and it asks that we may "experience the intercession of her through whom we have received the Author of life." The faith of the Church is already expressed in the Apostles' Creed with the assertion that Christ "was conceived by the power of the Holy Spirit and born of the Virgin Mary." The Council of Ephesus (431) used this statement to defend Mary's title as "Theotokos," not in the sense that the nature of the Word and his divinity had their origin in the Virgin Mary, but that the Word, the second Person of the Trinity, was born of her according to the flesh. What was born of her was the humanity to which the Word is united hypostatically.

The mystery of Mary's maternity is expressed in the Entrance Antiphon of the Mass: "Hail, holy Mother! The child to whom you gave birth is the King of heaven and earth for ever." This implies God's choice of her who is "full of grace" (Lk 1:28) as well as her voluntary consent: "Let it be done to me as you say" (Lk 1:38). The word "conceive" applies not only to the body but also to the spirit, as was stated by the Second Vatican Council: "The Virgin Mary, who at the message of the angel received the word of God in her heart and in her body . . . is acknowledged and honored as being truly the Mother of God and of the Redeemer. . . . Rightly, therefore, the Fathers see Mary not merely as passively engaged by God, but as freely cooperating in the work of man's salvation through faith and obedience" (*Lumen Gentium*, nos. 53 and 56).

The theme of motherhood should be associated with that of "fruitful virginity," which is preferable today because it is one of the proofs of the divinity of Christ and because it is an example of the way in which God uses lowly and weak means for our salvation.

The Prayer over the Gifts reminds us that in this Christmas season we celebrate "the beginning of our salvation." Hence this feast fits in very well with the beginning of the new year. "On this feast of Mary, the Mother of God, we ask that our salvation will be brought to its fulfillment."

The Preface of the Mass states the reason for this solemn feast: "Through the power of the Holy Spirit, she became the virgin mother of your only Son, our Lord Jesus Christ, who is for ever the light of the world." Mary represents, as it were, the maternal aspect of God, not only because her Son is also the Son of the Father, but because the Holy Spirit, through whose power she conceived, took up his dwelling in the Word made flesh. This mysterious relationship between Mary and the Holy Spirit, who made her virginity fruitful, manifests another maternal aspect of the Father, namely, his merciful love. The maternity of Mary is not therefore something purely functional; she is an authentic icon of the mystery of the Trinity. As the Father from all eternity generates the Son in the love of the Holy Spirit, so Mary, in the flesh, generated the same eternal Word by the power of the Holy Spirit.

The antiphon for the Canticle of Zechariah beautifully summarizes the dogma of the Incarnation: "Marvelous is the mystery proclaimed today: human nature is made new as God becomes man; he remains what he was and becomes what he was not. Yet each nature stays distinct and for ever undivided." The significance of this feast is found especially in the Prayer after Communion: "We proclaim the Virgin Mary to be the mother of Christ and the mother of the Church."

> Prayer after Communion: *Father, as we proclaim the Virgin Mary to be the Mother of Christ and the Mother of the Church, may our communion with her Son bring us to salvation.*

January 2
ST. BASIL (330-379) and
ST. GREGORY NAZIANZEN (329/30-389/90)

HISTORICO-LITURGICAL NOTE

In the revised Roman Calendar of 1969 this feast of two great saints of Cappadocia (now in Turkey) was assigned the date closest to the day of the death of St. Basil (January 1) because that of St. Gregory Nazianzen (January 25) falls on the feast of the Conversion of St. Paul.

Basil was born in 330 of a deeply Christian family (of the ten children, three became bishops: Basil, Gregory of Nyssa and Peter of Sebaste). His grandmother, Macrina, his parents and his eldest sister are all honored as saints. He received an excellent education: at Caesarea (where he became a close friend of Gregory Nazianzen), at Constantinople, and later at Athens. After his baptism (358?) he entered the monastic life and visited numerous monasteries in the East. Later he founded a new cenobitic monastery where the monks dedicated themselves to prayer, intellectual pursuits and manual labor. He wrote two Rules for monastic life; one containing general legislation, which has been recognized by the Church as the basic Rule for monastic life in the East, and the other a collection of exhortations. He is therefore the primary legislator for Eastern monasticism. He became bishop of Caesarea (in central Turkey) in 370 and was a strong defender of the faith against the Arians. He was the champion of orthodoxy after the death of St. Athanasius in 373, concentrating especially on the dogmas of the Trinity and the Incarnation. He was a gentle, prudent bishop and the organizer of charitable works.

Gregory Nazianzen also came from a very Christian family that produced numerous saints. After completing his studies in company with St. Basil, he reluctantly consented to be ordained to the priesthood by his father, St. Gregory Nazianzen the Elder, and ten years later, with equal reluctance and at the insistence of Basil, he was ordained bishop. Being of a contemplative and monastic disposition, he escaped from administrative duties into solitude as often as possible. He did, however, preside for a time over the First Ecumenical Council of Constantinople (381), but when the legitimacy of his transfer to Constantinople was contested, he resigned for the sake of peace and unity. His eloquent discourses on the Trinity earned him the title "the theologian." He spent the last years of his life in relative seclusion.

MESSAGE AND RELEVANCE

The Opening Prayer of the Mass in honor of these two Doctors of the Church contains the message of their spirituality. It resembles the Prayer after Communion in the Mass for St. Francis of Assisi in the Franciscan Missal: "In humility may we come to know your truth." Basil stands out as the Doctor of the theology of the Holy Spirit; in fact, the second reading for the ferial Liturgy of the Hours on January 2 is taken from his treatise on the Holy Spirit. It is also from this treatise that the liturgical formula of the Trinitarian doxology was taken, but to emphasize the equality of the Holy Spirit, the phrase "in the Spirit" was replaced with "and to the Holy Spirit."

St. Gregory Nazianzen was also a great seeker after truth, especially in his discourses on the divine nature, the Holy Spirit and the Trinity, and the divinity of Christ. But the doctrinal preeminence of both Basil and Gregory was accompanied by a deep humility. Rufinus said of Gregory, for example: "There has never been seen a life more simple or more irreproachable, an eloquence more vivid or more brilliant, a faith more pure or more orthodox, a knowledge more perfect and exhaustive. He was the only one whose faith could not be questioned even by the opposing factions. Consequently, not to agree with Gregory on the faith was sufficient to be guilty of a sin against the Catholic faith."

The significance of the spiritual message for this feast can be found in the Opening Prayer of the Mass which, in accordance with St. Paul's statement, "Let us profess the truth in love" (Ep 4:15), reminds us that charity is inseparable from truth and humility. Moreover, St. Basil shows us how to reconcile the contemplative life with solicitude for the poor, and both of these saints illustrate the great help that comes from fraternal friendship. "Our single object and ambition," says St. Gregory, "was virtue, and a life of hope in the blessings that are to come. . . . We followed the guidance of God's law and spurred each other on to virtue. If it is not too boastful to say, we found in each other a standard and rule for discerning right from wrong" (Office of Readings).

> Opening Prayer: *God our Father, you inspired the Church with the example and teaching of your saints Basil and Gregory. In humility may we come to know your truth and put it into action with faith and love.*

January 4 (United States)
ST. ELIZABETH ANN SETON (1774-1821)

HISTORICO-LITURGICAL NOTE

This wife, mother and foundress of a religious congregation was born Elizabeth Ann Bayley on August 28, 1774 in New York City, the daughter of an eminent physician and professor at what is now Columbia University. Brought up as an Episcopalian, she received an excellent education, and from her early years she manifested an unusual concern for the poor. In 1794 Elizabeth married William Seton, with whom she had five children. The loss of their fortune so affected William's health that in 1803 Elizabeth and William went to stay with Catholic friends at Livorno, Italy. William died six weeks after their arrival, and when Elizabeth returned to New York City some six months later, she was already a convinced Catholic. She met with stern opposition from her Episcopalian friends but was baptized a Catholic on March 4, 1805.

Abandoned by her friends and relatives, Elizabeth was invited by the superior of the Sulpicians in Baltimore to found a school for girls in that city. The school prospered, and eventually the Sulpician superior, with the approval of Bishop Carroll, gave Elizabeth and her assistants a rule of life. They were also permitted to make religious profession and to wear a religious habit. In 1809 Elizabeth moved her young community to Emmitsburg, Maryland, where she adopted as a rule of life an adaptation of the rule observed by the Sisters of Charity, founded by St. Vincent de Paul. Although she did not neglect the ministry to the poor, and especially to Negroes, she actually laid the foundation for what became the American parochial school system. She trained teachers and prepared textbooks for use in the schools; she also opened orphanages in Philadelphia and New York City. She died at Emmitsburg on January 4, 1821, was beatified by Pope John XXIII in 1963, and was canonized by Pope Paul VI in 1975.

MESSAGE AND RELEVANCE

The life and work of St. Elizabeth Ann Seton are of special significance to the Catholics of the United States. The Opening Prayer of the Mass summarizes the principal phases of her life and spirituality: wife and mother, educator and foundress of the first religious congregation of women to have its origin in the United States. Eventually the congregation multiplied into seven distinct branches. St. Elizabeth Ann Seton dedicated her efforts especially to the care of the poor and to the Catholic education of youth.

In the Office of Readings there is an inspiring excerpt from one of St. Elizabeth's conferences to her Sisters of Charity: "What was the first rule of our dear Savior's life? You know it was to do his Father's will. Well, then, the first end I propose in our daily work is to do the will of God; secondly, to do it in the manner he wills; and thirdly, to do it because it is his will. I know what is his will by those who direct me; whatever they bid me do, if it is ever so small in itself, is the will of God for me. Then, do it in the manner he wills it."

Opening Prayer: *Lord God, you blessed Elizabeth Seton with gifts of grace as wife and mother, educator and foundress, so that she might spend her life in service to your people. Through her example and prayers may we learn to express our love for you in love for our fellow men and women.*

January 5 (United States)
ST. JOHN NEUMANN (1811-1860)

HISTORICO-LITURGICAL NOTE

Born on March 28, 1811 in Prachatitz, Bohemia (now in the Czech Republic), John Neumann realized a long cherished dream when he came to the United States and was ordained a priest in New York City in 1836. Four years later he joined the Redemptorists and subsequently labored in Maryland, Pennsylvania, Ohio and the American frontier. He was the first Redemptorist to make religious profession in the United States. In 1852, at the age of 41, he was ordained bishop of Philadelphia, where he worked zealously for the establishment of parochial schools and of parishes for immigrants from Europe. He also inaugurated the Forty Hours Devotion in the United States. Possessing special skill in languages, by the end of his life he had mastered twelve. He composed two catechisms in German and a Bible History for use in the parochial schools. Bishop Neumann had a special love for children, the Sisters and the immigrants. He is the first bishop from the United States to be canonized a saint. This was done by Pope Paul VI in 1977.

MESSAGE AND RELEVANCE

The Opening Prayer of the Mass states that God "called St. John Neumann to labor for the gospel among the people of the New World." He ministered not only to the numerous immigrants from Europe, but also to the native Indians in northern New York. His entire life as a priest and a bishop was dedicated to the tireless service of others. It is likely that when he collapsed on a Philadelphia street and died before reaching the hospital, it was from sheer exhaustion.

At one time Bishop Neumann had offered to leave Philadelphia and be transferred to a different, newly erected diocese. In his letter, quoted in the Office of Readings, he says: "If, however, it should be displeasing to His Holiness to divide the diocese, I am, indeed, prepared either to remain in the same condition in which I am at present, or if God so inspires His Holiness to give the whole administration of the diocese to Most Reverend James Wood, I am equally prepared to resign from the episcopate and to go where I may more securely prepare myself for death and for the account which must be rendered to the Divine Justice" (October, 1858).

Opening Prayer: *Father, you called St. John Neumann to labor for the gospel among the people of the New World. His ministry strengthened many others in the Christian faith: through his prayers may faith grow strong in this land.*

January 6 (United States)
BLESSED ANDRÉ BESSETTE (1845-1937)

HISTORICO-LITURGICAL NOTE

This Holy Cross Brother, known as "Frére André," has been credited with thousands of cures. He was the founder of St. Joseph's Oratory in Montreal, Canada, perhaps the world's principal shrine in honor of St. Joseph. When he died at the age of 91, it was estimated that close to a million people came to the Oratory to pay their last respects. He was beatified in 1982.

André was the eighth child in a family of 12 and at baptism he was given the name Alfred. Orphaned at the age of 12, he tried his hand at various trades but was not successful in any of them. He could barely read and write and was sickly most of his life. At the age of 15 he became a Brother of Holy Cross but was rejected at the end of the novitiate. At the insistence of the bishop of Montreal, however, Brother André was allowed to make religious profession. For forty years he worked as porter at the College of Notre Dame, until he was needed full time at the shrine of St. Joseph. People from all over Canada came to him for cures or for spiritual direction. The Oratory that he built in honor of St. Joseph was solemnly dedicated in 1955 and raised to the rank of a minor basilica.

MESSAGE AND RELEVANCE

The Opening Prayer of the Mass describes two character- istics of the spirituality of Brother André: his deep devotion to

St. Joseph and his "commitment to the poor and afflicted." For many years he gathered funds to replace the primitive chapel with a suitable church, even cutting the hair of the students at five cents each. His concern for those who needed spiritual healing and support led him to spend 8 to 10 hours a day receiving clients. He became so well known that secretaries had to be assigned to answer the 80,000 letters he received annually.

If one were to seek the outstanding virtue of Brother André one would have to say that it was his humility. He once said: "I am ignorant. If there were anyone more ignorant, the good God would choose him in my place." And when the power of healing was attributed to him, he responded: "It is St. Joseph who cures. I am only his little dog."

The significance of the life and works of Brother André for today's Christian is the fact that this humble Brother, who could scarcely read or write, was chosen by God as an instrument for good. As we read in the Preface for Martyrs, God reveals his power shining through our human weakness.

> Opening Prayer: *Lord our God, friend of the lowly, you gave your servant, Brother André, a great devotion to St. Joseph and a special commitment to the poor and afflicted. Through his intercession help us to follow his example of prayer and love and so come to share with him in your glory.*

January 7
ST. RAYMOND OF PENYAFORT
(1175/80-1275)

HISTORICO-LITURGICAL NOTE

A renowned expert in canon and civil law, St. Raymond also worked assiduously for the formation of priests and the evangelization of Jews and Muslims. He encouraged missionaries to learn Arabic and to study the Koran in order to enter into dialogue with Islam.

Born at Penyafort, near Barcelona, Spain, sometime between 1175 and 1180, he took his early studies at the cathedral school in Barcelona and then proceeded to Bologna, where he became an outstanding professor of canon law. He was at that time a diocesan priest, but after coming into contact with the newly founded Order of Preachers, he joined the Dominicans in 1218. He composed a *Summa* of canon law with a pastoral orientation and was later called to Rome by Pope Gregory IX to be the papal penitentiary and to edit the *Decretals* issued by that same Pope (1234). In 1238 Raymond was elected third Master General of the Dominican Order, succeeding Jordan of Saxony in that post. He resigned two years later and returned to Spain.

For the rest of his life Raymond dedicated himself to the direction of souls as a confessor and to the promotion of evangelization among the Jews and Muslims of North Africa. He encouraged Thomas Aquinas to write the *Summa contra Gentiles* and at the request of St. Peter Nolasco he drafted the Rule for the Mercedarians, an order founded for the redemption of Christian captives held by the Muslims in North Africa. He died at Barcelona on January 6, 1275, almost a centenarian.

MESSAGE AND RELEVANCE

The revised Opening Prayer for this feast is based on texts taken from three suppressed feasts: St. Thomas of Villanova, St. Peter Nolasco and St. Raymond Nonnatus. It recalls Raymond's ministry to sinners (especially in the sacrament of penance). The Dominican Missal offers a choice of Opening Prayers: the first one refers to Raymond's compassion for sinners, and the second one to his profound knowledge of the law.

The relevance of the spirituality and teaching of Raymond of Penyafort for our day is multiple. First of all, his ministry as a confessor, by which he freed sinners from the "slavery to sin" so that they could "love and serve God in liberty" (Opening Prayer), reminds the faithful today of the importance of this sacrament of reconciliation. Secondly, his missionary zeal and ecumenical spirit should prompt us to dialogue with non-Christians and to engage in the re-evangelization of Christians. Finally, his letter to the Dominican cloistered nuns (Office of Readings) states that "all who want to live righteously in Christ will suffer persecution. . . . The only exception to this general statement is, I think, the person who either neglects or does not know how to live temperately, justly and righteously in this world."

Opening Prayer: *Lord, you gave St. Raymond the gift of compassion in his ministry to sinners. May his prayers free us from the slavery of sin and help us to love and serve you in liberty.*

January 13
ST. HILARY (315-367)

HISTORICO-LITURGICAL NOTE

St. Hilary was called the "Athanasius of the West" and was declared a Doctor of the Church by Pope Pius IX. The cult of this saint became widespread in France only in the ninth century and in Italy in the eleventh and twelfth centuries.

Converted from paganism after reading the Scriptures, and especially the Prologue to St. John's Gospel, this married man and father of one daughter later became a gifted interpreter of the Psalms and the Gospel according to St. Matthew. While still a layman he was elected bishop of Poitiers, France, in 350. But because he fought strenuously against the semi-Arians, who were supported by the emperor, he was sent into exile. The point at issue was the consubstantiality of the Son with the Father (of the same nature), which had been defended by St. Athanasius in the East. In his treatise on the Trinity (in twelve books) Hilary became the first theologian of the Latin Church to combat the Arian heresy and to introduce into the language of the West the precisions of Catholic doctrine and Greek thought. He also helped St. Martin of Tours promote the monastic life and he composed several liturgical hymns.

MESSAGE AND RELEVANCE

The Opening Prayer of the Mass comes from the Parisian Missal of 1684 and is inspired by the ancient Gelasian Sacramentary, but with this difference: the phrase "proclaimed the dignity of the Word" has been replaced by "defended the divinity of Christ your Son." Hilary had in fact fought unsuccessfully in defence of the orthodox faith. He was unable to convince his opponents of their error, largely because of his inflexibility. He expressed great sorrow at the betrayal of his own peers from the East, who by their silence had practically conceded to the opposition.

Hilary himself showed prudence and moderation amid the hostility of the rigorists and the weakness of the concordists. Bishops who repented of their past errors were allowed to remain in office. Sulpicius Severus wrote of him: "The whole world ought to recognize that our French nation was freed from the sin of heresy through the intervention of Bishop Hilary." After his return from exile, Hilary had the courage to protest vigorously against the emperor's unwarranted intervention in religious matters. In fact, it was under Hilary that the clergy recognized more and more that even in a Christian state the Church must be separate and independent.

The relevance of Hilary's message can be deduced from the Opening Prayer of the Mass, in which we ask God to "give us a deeper understanding of the divinity of Christ and help us to profess it in all truth" against the rationalism of our day. Moreover, in his treatise on the Trinity (Office of Readings) he exhorts us to be faithful to the teaching of Sacred Scripture: "Impart to us the meaning of the words of Scripture and the light to understand it." Finally, it is interesting to note that in a letter to his daughter, Abra, he urged her to renounce marriage and remain a virgin.

> Opening Prayer: *All-powerful God, as St. Hilary defended the divinity of Christ your Son, give us a deeper understanding of this mystery and help us to profess it in all truth.*

January 17
ST. ANTHONY (251-356)

HISTORICO-LITURGICAL NOTE

This feast in honor of Anthony, who died in the desert of Egypt at the age of 105, has been celebrated on January 17 since the beginning of the fifth century in the Syriac, Coptic and Byzantine liturgies. In the West, however, his cult began only in the ninth century, and in Rome in the eleventh and twelfth centuries.

The life of Anthony was written by St. Athanasius shortly after the death of this saintly hermit. Not only did it make St. Anthony known, but it contributed to the conversion of many individuals, including St. Augustine and St. Martin. The widespread cult of St. Anthony is due in great measure to the fact that the "unbloody martyrdom" of his long life became a model and exemplar of the Christian's journey to God.

At the age of twenty, Anthony, an orphan, took to heart the words that were read in his church: "If you seek perfection, go, sell your possessions, and give to the poor. You will then have treasure in heaven" (Mt 19:21). Anthony immediately sold all his goods and contributed the money to the education of his young sister and other virgins. He then embraced the ascetical life and had to endure terrifying struggles with the

Devil and violent temptations of the flesh. He later retired to live among the tombs in the cemetery, which was always considered the habitat of the Devil (Mk 5:2-5). There the diabolical assaults continued and the Devil often appeared to him in terrifying forms. But Anthony was also consoled by a vision of the Lord.

Anthony's next move was to the desert, to fight the Devil in his own stronghold, and once again he emerged victorious. By this time his manner of life had attracted so many followers that he was considered the father of the monastic life. Meanwhile, Anthony had developed an intense desire for martyrdom, so he left his seclusion and went to Alexandria, where the Christians were being persecuted. He was spared, however, so he returned to an even more remote part of the desert.

His seclusion was interrupted again in 312, when he returned to Alexandria to combat the Arian heresy, after which he resumed his solitary life in the desert, where he died in 356.

MESSAGE AND RELEVANCE

The spiritual message of Anthony is contained in the three prayers and two antiphons of the Mass for his feastday. The Communion Antiphon (Mt 19:21) recalls the cost of the following of Christ based on trust in the word of the Lord. The Entrance Antiphon — "The just man will flourish like the palm tree" — refers to Anthony's sojourn in the desert. In the Opening Prayer of the Mass we ask that "we may learn to deny ourselves and to love God above all things." The Prayer over the Gifts continues the same theme: "May no earthly attractions keep us from loving you."

The Prayer after Communion reminds us that in this life we are engaged in a "struggle with evil." But as God "helped St. Anthony conquer the powers of darkness," he will also assist us if we enter the spiritual desert of self-renunciation. Then, like St. Anthony, we shall be called "the friend of God" (Office of Readings).

Preface: *Father, we offer you this sacrifice of praise on the feast of the abbot St. Anthony. Inflamed with love of you, he was able to accept the invitation of the gospel with total commitment and profound joy. Inspired by your grace to follow Christ with a free and pure heart, he gave all his possessions to the poor. Overcoming the weakness of the flesh by the strength of his spirit, he lived in perfect communion with you, Father, in the austere solitude of the desert.*

January 20
ST. FABIAN (+250) and ST. SEBASTIAN (+288)

HISTORICO-LITURGICAL NOTE

These two saints are honored on the same day because their names are linked together in the Calendar of 354. However, the two feasts were celebrated separately until the twelfth century, when a common Mass was composed, with the prayers in honor of St. Fabian and the readings in honor of St. Sebastian. Another reason for the change was that the relics of St. Fabian were transferred to the basilica of St. Sebastian. Now the revised Calendar has restored the original separation of the two feasts, although Fabian and Sebastian are still mentioned together in the Litany of the Saints.

Pope Fabian was a victim of the persecution of the Church by Decius (249-251), as we know from a letter written by St. Cyprian a few weeks after Fabian's martyrdom. According to the account by Eusebius, Fabian was elected pope as a result of a sign from heaven. During the conclave a dove appeared and rested on his head. Fabian was the first layman to be elected pope.

His accomplishments as pope can be summarized as follows: the division of seven ecclesiastical regions under the government of seven regional deacons; works done on the catacombs; the transfer of the body of St. Pontian from

Sardinia; support of Origen against accusations of heterodoxy; the commissioning of several renowned bishops for the evangelization of the Gauls. His epitaph in the catacomb of St. Callistus reads: "Fabian, bishop, martyr."

St. Sebastian is much more widely known and venerated than St. Fabian. The record of his martyrdom is one of the best literary compositions of the fifth and sixth centuries. It describes Sebastian, a native of Milan and born of Christian parents, as a model soldier. Although he was not interested in a military career, he was drafted into the army and eventually became a captain in the guard of Maximian at Rome. In this way he was able to help Christians who were arrested during the persecution of Diocletian. The record of his life and martyrdom, written by a monk before the end of the fifth century, is not historically reliable, but it does give the names of numerous martyrs who were exhorted to final perseverance by Sebastian.

Eventually the moment of truth arrived also for this courageous Christian soldier. Diocletian turned him over to the archers and after they had pierced his body with numerous arrows, they left him for dead. According to the legend, a Christian widow named Irene had him carried to her home, where she nursed him back to health. But the brave soldier of Christ again confronted the emperor and denounced the cruelty of the persecution. The enraged emperor had Sebastian beaten to death and his body thrown into the common sewer. Shortly after his death, Sebastian appeared in a vision to a lady named Lucina, asking that his body be recovered and buried in the catacomb where the basilica of St. Sebastian now stands. During an outbreak of the plague in 680 his relics were carried in solemn procession. The cessation of the epidemic led to his being acclaimed patron of victims of the plague.

MESSAGE AND RELEVANCE

The Opening Prayer of the Mass in honor of St. Fabian is of Roman, or at least Italian, origin. It expresses the theme of the feast when it calls us "to share his faith and offer God loving service." St. Cyprian says in his letter (Office of Readings) that "it is helpful and encouraging when a bishop offers himself as a model for his brothers by the constancy of his faith." Cyprian then reminds the priests and deacons of Rome: "Widows, the destitute who cannot support themselves, and those who are in prison or who have been evicted from their homes should surely have someone to help them."

The Opening Prayer of the Mass in honor of St. Sebastian presents him as a model of martyrs because of his "spirit of courage." It also reminds us of the admonition of St. Peter in Acts 5:29: "Better for us to obey God than men." Finally, the mention of Sebastian by St. Ambrose in the Office of Readings invites us today to live the "secret martyrdom" which is the lot of "all those who wish to live a holy life in Christ Jesus."

Opening Prayer (St. Fabian): *God our Father, glory of your priests, may the prayers of your martyr Fabian help us to share his faith and offer you loving service.*

Opening Prayer (St. Sebastian): *Lord, fill us with that spirit of courage which gave your martyr Sebastian strength to offer his life in faithful witness. Help us to learn from him to cherish your law and to obey you rather than men.*

January 21
ST. AGNES (+304)

HISTORICO-LITURGICAL NOTE

The feast of this young girl, martyred at the age of twelve on January 21, is attested by the most ancient Roman Calendar (354) and the early Roman Sacramentaries. It is also mentioned by some of the Fathers of the Church: St. Ambrose (who described her martyrdom and wrote a hymn in her honor), Prudentius, St. Jerome and St. Augustine. The reasons for the widespread cult in her honor are: her extreme youth and her purity (the name Agnes in Greek means chaste); her heroic Christian witness in the midst of terrible torture (including fire, from which she emerged unscathed); and finally her spontaneity in going to her martyrdom with full awareness.

In the Greek tradition since the fifth century, there are some details that do not correspond to the tradition of Pope Damasus and St. Ambrose. This may be due to the confusion between two different martyrs named Agnes. In the fourth century the daughter of the emperor Constantine had a basilica built in honor of St. Agnes.

Agnes is one of the most illustrious martyrs of the Church; she is mentioned in the Roman Canon of the Mass and in the Greek Calendar of saints.

MESSAGE AND RELEVANCE

The Opening Prayer of the Mass comes from the ancient Gelasian Sacramentary and it states that God chooses "what the world considers weak to put the worldly powers to shame." We then ask that we may remain loyal to the faith that Agnes professed. Her steadfast fidelity is exalted by St. Ambrose in the Office of Readings: "The cruelty that did not spare her youth shows all the more clearly the power of faith in finding one so young to bear it witness. . . . She is too young to know of death, yet is ready to face it. . . . She shows herself a master in valor despite the handicap of youth. . . . One victim, but a twin martyrdom, to modesty and to religion; Agnes preserved her virginity, and gained a martyr's crown."

In her vibrant declarations — "I am espoused to him whom the angels serve. . . . For him alone I keep my fidelity intact" — we see the model of espousal with Christ that is born of chastity, and not only consecrated chastity, but of all Christians called to tend towards Christ with the same ardor as this young girl. So we read in the antiphon for the Canticle of Mary:

"Holy Father, hear me. I am coming to you whom I have loved, whom I have sought and always desired." Virginity of heart is for all Christians, even for those who do not observe bodily virginity. In contemporary society this witness to a love that transcends age or sex is urgently needed.

> Opening Prayer: *Almighty, eternal God, you choose what the world considers weak to put the worldly power to shame. May we who celebrate the birth of St. Agnes into eternal joy be loyal to the faith she professed.*

January 22
ST. VINCENT (+304)

HISTORICO-LITURGICAL NOTE

The early Church honored three martyred deacons from three different localities: Stephen (Palestine), Lawrence (Rome) and Vincent (Spain). Vincent was mentioned by the poet Prudentius and by St. Augustine, who several times preached on the feast of St. Vincent. According to Augustine, this feast "is celebrated throughout the Roman Empire and wherever you find the name Christian." The Gregorian Sacramentary and the Roman Lectionary of the seventh century had a liturgy in Vincent's honor.

He was martyred at Valencia, Spain, during the persecution by Diocletian and Maximian. The *Acts of the Martyrs* described his torments in some detail and recorded Vincent's speech to Dacian, governor of Spain: "The more I witness your fury, Dacian, the greater is my pleasure. Do not lessen in any way the sufferings you prepare for me so that I can make my victory shine more resplendently."

In the face of the indomitable courage of the martyr the prefect had to admit his defeat: "It is useless to struggle any longer; take him to a bed so that he can be revived and cured."

But Vincent refused to accept this concession. As a soldier fighting for the glory of God, he had no reason to live if he could not continue to give witness to Christ. After enduring tortures that went beyond all human expectations, his soul went to God on January 22, 304. He is venerated in the church of St. Germain in Paris because it is said that in 531 either his tunic or his stole was placed in that church.

MESSAGE AND RELEVANCE

The Opening Prayer of this Mass is taken from a Spanish Sacramentary. It highlights the courage of St. Vincent in enduring torture and death and asks God to "fill us with your Spirit and strengthen us in your love." This reminds us of the Gospel teaching: "When they hand you over, do not worry about what you will say or how you will say it. When the hour comes, you will be given what you are to say. You yourselves will not be the speakers; the Spirit of your Father will be speaking in you" (Mt 10:19-20).

The foregoing passage explains the strength of the martyrs in enduring painful torture and in desiring to suffer death in witness to their faith. In the Office of Readings St. Augustine quotes the same text and then says: "Thus it was Vincent's body that suffered, but the Spirit who spoke."

This feast falls in the week assigned for prayers for Christian unity. As the power of the Holy Spirit sustained the most celebrated martyr of the Iberian Peninsula, so we also can hope to overcome the seemingly insurmountable obstacles that stand in the way of unity in faith and charity. For that reason we ask God to "fill us with your Spirit and strengthen us in your love."

> Opening Prayer: *Eternal Father, you gave St. Vincent the courage to endure torture and death for the gospel: fill us with your Spirit and strengthen us in your love.*

January 24
ST. FRANCIS DE SALES (1567-1622)

HISTORICO-LITURGICAL NOTE

The life of this outstanding and highly influential bishop, spiritual director, author and preacher spans the turbulent decades following the Protestant Reformation. Born at Savoy in France in 1567, he studied at Annecy, then under the Jesuits at Paris, and finally at Padua, Italy, where he obtained a doctorate in both civil and canon law. He refused the political office as senator from Chambery and instead entered the service of the Church. He was ordained priest at Annecy in 1593 and immediately dedicated himself to the re-evangelization of Chablais, which had become almost entirely Calvinistic. Between 1595 and 1598 he won many converts to the Catholic Church by his persuasive preaching but at the same time he was often in danger of his life at the hands of the hostile Calvinists. Later on, the notes that he used during this period were gathered together in a book entitled *Book of Controversies*, which holds a high place in the field of apologetics.

At the age of 32 Francis was ordained auxiliary bishop and three years later he was installed as bishop of Geneva. For 20 years he labored zealously for the conversion of the Calvinists, but also found the time to write spiritual books that immediately became best sellers among the laity: *The Introduction to the Devout Life* and the *Treatise on the Love of God*. In addition, he was co-founder, with St. Jane Frances de Chantal, of the Visitation nuns. Canonized in 1665, he was declared a Doctor of the Church by Pope Pius IX in 1887, the first Frenchman to receive this honor. Pope Pius XI named him patron saint of journalists.

MESSAGE AND RELEVANCE

The Opening Prayer of the Mass synthesizes the spirituality of St. Francis de Sales, who knew how to promote an authentically Christian humanism — a humanism of hope — to replace the naturalistic or even pagan humanism rampant in his time. The text of the prayer mentions two outstanding characteristics of Francis de Sales: "gentle love" and "compassion for all men on the way to salvation." First mentioned is the apostolic love of Francis by which he was able to be "all things to all men" (1 Cor 9:19-23). He had stated in his *Introduction to the Devout Life*: "Inasmuch as divine love adorns the soul, it is called grace, which makes us pleasing to his Divine Majesty. Inasmuch as it strengthens us to do good, it is called charity" (Part I, 1). Then, in his *Treatise on the Love of God*, he says: "In holy Church all is by love, in love, for love and of love" (Preface). The Opening Prayer speaks of the horizontal dimension of love and asks that we may manifest God's love "in the service of our fellow men." Love is thus the source from which everything else irradiates.

Another concept in the Opening Prayer is "gentle love," and that summarizes perfectly the spirituality of the meek and gentle Francis de Sales. It is also a characteristic of the devout and optimistic humanism that he promoted, a humanism that opened a new dimension to the culture of his day. In the *Treatise on the Love of God* we read that "human nature has in fact received greater graces by the redemption wrought by its Savior than it would ever have received from Adam's innocence even if he had persevered therein" (Bk. 2, chap. 5).

The same theme of "love and service" is found in the Prayer after Communion, although the Latin version has the phrase "charity and meekness" rather than "love and service." And in the Prayer over the Gifts reference is made to "the divine fire of your Holy Spirit, which burned in the gentle heart of Francis de Sales." In a letter to Jane Frances de Chantal, Francis said that "if the soul is all gold through charity, all myrrh through mortification, and all incense through prayer, then the action of the Holy Spirit likewise influences the entire body of the Church of which we are living members."

In the Office of Readings we have a selection from the *Introduction to the Devout Life*, containing another element of Salesian spirituality that is applicable to people of our time. "Devotion must be exercised in different ways by the gentleman, the laborer, the servant, the prince, the widow, the young girl, and the married woman. Not only is this true, but the practice of devotion must also be adapted to the strength, activities, and duties of each particular person. . . . It is an error, or rather a heresy, to wish to banish the devout life from the regiment of soldiers, the mechanic's shop, the court of princes, or the home of married people. . . . Purely contemplative, monastic, and religious devotion cannot be exercised in such states of life. However, there are several others adapted to bring perfection to those living in the secular state" (Part 1, 3).

> Opening Prayer: *Father, you gave St. Francis de Sales the spirit of compassion to befriend all men on the way to salvation. By his example, lead us to show your gentle love in the service of our fellow men.*

January 25
CONVERSION of ST. PAUL

HISTORICO-LITURGICAL NOTE

This feast originated in France at the end of the sixth century, when some relics of the apostle were transferred there. It was not celebrated in Rome until the eleventh century, perhaps in connection with the feast of the Chair of St. Peter, celebrated in France on January 18. The importance of the conversion of the "Apostle to the Gentiles" is evident from the three accounts given in the Acts of the Apostles (9:1-30; 22:3-21; 26:9-20). It is evident also from the prayers in the Mass and in the Liturgy of the Hours.

The biblical account of what happened to Paul on the road to Damascus describes the radical change that took place: "He who was formerly persecuting us is now preaching the faith he tried to destroy" (Gal 1:23). The apostle himself always contrasts that experience on the road to Damascus with what had preceded it (Gal 1:11-24). "In legal observance I was a Pharisee, and so zealous that I persecuted the Church. I was above reproach when it came to justice based on the law. But those things I used to consider gain I have now reappraised as loss in the light of Christ" (Ph 3:5-7).

But it is not simply a matter of conversion as a personal experience of Paul; it is also a phase of development in the history of the Church, as recorded in the Acts. St. Luke states: "All except the apostles scattered throughout the countryside of Judea and Samaria. After that, Saul began to harass the Church. He entered house after house, dragged men and women out, and threw them into jail" (Ac 8:1-4).

MESSAGE AND RELEVANCE

The Opening Prayer of the Mass is derived from the French Missal and it contains two interrelated themes. The first one presents the dynamics of Paul's conversion and following of Christ. Some have tried to use psychological principles to explain his conversion experience. St. Luke does not describe events in a chronological order, but although it was a case of sudden divine intervention, its meaning was revealed gradually. Thus, in the first account (Ac 9:15-16) the incident is made known only to Ananias; in the second account (Ac 22:17-21) its significance is revealed to Paul indirectly, through Ananias, and in vague terms; only in the third account (Ac 26:15-18) does the Risen Christ reveal to Paul the nature and extent of his mission.

The second theme of the Opening Prayer is contained in the phrase "bearing witness to your truth." But to be a witness to the truth of Christ, like St. Paul, requires that we discover the meaning of the faith in the events and experiences of life, both individual and ecclesial. Paul himself, after the dazzling experience on the road to Damascus, spent three years in Arabia, southeast of Damascus, in order to grasp fully the specific dimensions of his vocation (Gal 1:17).

A second line of reflection can be found in the Prayer over the Gifts, which invokes upon us the light of the Holy Spirit, "who helped Paul the apostle to preach your power and glory." We read in the antiphon for the Canticle of Zechariah: "He was transformed from being a persecutor of Christ into a vessel of his grace." He saw the close relationship between his own particular calling and that of the prophets of the Old Testament (cf. Gal 1:15 and Jr 1:5). For Paul, the preaching of the Gospel was not a cause for boasting but a duty (cf. 1 Cor 9:16 and Am 3:8). For us also evangelization should be the fruit of the light of the Holy Spirit who sustains and illumines our faith.

In the Prayer over the Gifts we pray that the Holy Spirit will "fill us with the light of faith," and in the Prayer after Communion that faith is manifested by St. Paul in his "love for all the churches." In St. Paul, therefore, the ecumenical motif finds a valid model.

There is yet another theme in this Pauline spirituality, and it appears especially in the Communion Antiphon, the third antiphon for Evening Prayer, and in the Office of Readings (Gal 1:11-24): Christ is the focal point and center of the life of St. Paul. His contact with Christ on the road to Damascus was not only a transforming and crucial experience; it became a primary point of reference for all of his apostolic ministry. Thus, we read in the third antiphon for Evening Prayer: "For me, life is Christ, and death is gain" (Ph 1:21); and in the Communion Antiphon: "I live by faith in the Son of God." That transformation on the road to Damascus, which was always in the forefront of his mind, was the source of Paul's theology and spirituality. We also should say with him: "I know whom I have believed" (2 Tm 1:12; the Entrance Antiphon). The letter of St. John Chrysostom in the Office of Readings is not only a lyrical tribute; it is a fascinating reconstruction of the spiritual typology of St. Paul, for whom "to enjoy the love of Christ was his life, his whole world, his future, everything."

> Preface: *Father, in order to reveal to the apostle Paul the marvels of your grace, you chose him with loving providence from his mother's womb so that he would announce to the nations redemption by your Son. First an unbeliever and persecutor, he later became such an intrepid and faithful apostle that Jesus Christ was able to manifest in him the fulfillment of his Passion for the benefit of believers. Now from heaven Paul, the untiring messenger of salvation, exhorts and impels us to proclaim your mercy, O Father, and with the angels and the saints we unite our hymn of praise.*

January 26
ST. TIMOTHY and ST. TITUS

HISTORICO-LITURGICAL NOTE

The feast of these two companions of St. Paul the Apostle is now assigned to January 26, but previously, in the twelfth century, the feast of St. Timothy was celebrated on January 24, the vigil of the feast of the Conversion of St. Paul. The prayer formulas, which are now common to both saints, were formerly proper to the feast of St. Titus (February 6) and were introduced into the Roman Calendar in 1854.

Timothy, favorite disciple of St. Paul, was born of a Greek father and a Jewish mother who eventually converted to Christianity (cf. 2 Tm 1:5). St. Paul states that from his infancy Timothy was educated in the Scriptures by his mother, Eunice, and his grandmother, Lois (2 Tm 3:14-15). He was converted to Christianity by St. Paul on his first missionary journey and accompanied Paul on his second and third journeys, highly recommended by the Christian community at Lystra. From the

Acts of the Apostles (chaps. 16 to 20) and from references in the First Letter of Paul to the Corinthians, we learn that Timothy was sent by Paul to Macedonia, Thessalonica and Corinth. On two occasions, when Paul was imprisoned, Timothy was near to give him support. It is not known when Timothy received Holy Orders but he had the care of the Church at Ephesus and it is likely that he died there.

Titus came from a pagan family and he also converted to Christianity during Paul's first missionary journey. He accompanied Paul and Barnabas to the Council at Jerusalem, where Paul received official approbation as an apostle to the Gentiles (Gal 2:9). In his Second Letter to the Corinthians (7:5-7; 8:16-24), Paul expresses his great trust in Titus as an intermediary to establish peace between Paul and the Church of Corinth. Later he assigned Titus as head of the Church in Crete (Tt 1:4-5), where he died at an advanced age. St. Titus is especially venerated in Croatia.

MESSAGE AND RELEVANCE

The Opening Prayer of the Mass recalls the apostolic zeal of these two co-workers with St. Paul. The exhortations given by Paul to Timothy so that he would be a faithful and courageous preacher of the gospel in the midst of doctrinal deviations and divisions in the Church, demonstrate Paul's interest in the ministry of his favorite disciple. The antiphon for the Canticle of Zechariah in the Liturgy of the Hours quotes the phrase from 2 Timothy 4:2: "Proclaim the message, insist on it in season and out of season, refute falsehood, correct error, call to obedience, but do all with patience and sound doctrine." These virtues are still necessary for pastors and for all who serve the Christian community. They must all be vigilant and teach Christ's doctrine without weakness or compromise.

The second part of the Opening Prayer and the antiphon for the Canticle of Mary contain a sentence from Paul's Letter to Titus; it presents the eschatological aspect of the Christian life: "We must live temperately, justly, and devoutly in this age as we await our blessed hope, the appearing of the great God and of our Savior Jesus Christ" (2:12-13). The emphasis on the eschatological aspect gives Christian morality a mystical tone rather than one that is purely legalistic and pragmatic. Finally, if we can live in the joyful hope of reaching heaven, "our true home" (Collect), that will transform the commandments into a sweet and gentle yoke.

Preface: *God, our Father, it is truly right and just to praise you, all-powerful and eternal God. Through the mystery of your grace, which you have bestowed on us in Christ with infinite mercy, you have called and led us to the kingdom of freedom and of life. You have revealed to us the inscrutable design of your wisdom in the gospel of salvation, of which St. Timothy and St. Titus were the preachers and teachers. Today we unite ourselves to your blessed servants whom we honor today and to the choirs of angels to sing the hymn of your glory.*

January 27
ST. ANGELA MERICI (1474-1540)

HISTORICO-LITURGICAL NOTE

Today we honor a saint who lived at a time when the Church was in need of reform. Born in Brescia, northern Italy, in 1474, a time of strife, pestilence and famine, Angela was left an orphan at the age of fifteen. She gave up her patrimony and joined the Franciscan Tertiaries in order to live in poverty. She attracted a group of devout laity, members of the nobility and persons of a humble station in life, and in 1535 she founded a religious institute under the patronage of St. Ursula (Ursulines). She wanted them to be consecrated to God and dedicated to the service of their neighbor, but remaining in the world and living a celibate life in their own homes. She thus anticipated the secular institutes that have flourished in modern times.

Angela had made a pilgrimage to the Holy Land in 1524, then to Rome in 1525, and later to Mantua to pray at the tomb of the Dominican Tertiary, Blessed Hosanna, for light and inspiration regarding her own foundation. Pope Clement VII asked Angela to collaborate in the work of the charitable institutes under the title of Divine Love, but Angela preferred to remain at Brescia, where she could counsel and guide the Ursulines. When she died at Brescia on January 27, 1540, there were some 24 branches of the Company of St. Ursula serving the Church. She was not canonized until 1807, largely because some persons opposed her ideas, which they considered too progressive. In fact, in 1566, more than 25 years after the death of Angela, the cloister and choral Office were imposed on the Ursulines, and they were required to wear a religious habit.

MESSAGE AND RELEVANCE

The new Opening Prayer for the Mass presents Angela as a model of "charity and wisdom." These qualities were manifested especially in her role as a foundress because the Rule she composed for the Ursulines was flexible enough to be adapted to every time and place. This explains the numerous changes in the lifestyle of the Ursulines through the centuries. The Rule was approved by Pope Paul III in 1544, and in reading it we find that the Ursulines were not only to practice both vocal and mental prayer, but were to be affiliated to their own parish church. St. Angela also insisted on obedience to the Church, the bishop, the spiritual director, the superior and council of the Company, one's parents, all the laws and statutes, and especially the inspirations of the Holy Spirit.

The last-mentioned item — obedience to the inspirations of the Holy Spirit — reveals the courage of St. Angela Merici. Even St. Charles Borromeo was a bit dubious about placing this legislation in the Rule. However, this particular item should serve to remind us that the Holy Spirit has not been replaced by the hierarchy or any other authority in the Church. He still animates and guides the Church and is given to all for the good of the entire Christian community.

In the Office of Readings, taken from her *Spiritual Testament*, St. Angela cautions educators of young people that they should not function in a purely professional manner, but should be truly spiritual mothers. Moreover, they should respect the freedom of the young students and avoid any kind of coercive measures. They are to treat the students with love, not with harshness and severity.

The petition in the Opening Prayer, in which we ask "to be faithful to your teaching and to follow it in our lives," reminds us that today also we should be obedient to the Church and to the Holy Spirit who guides the Church. This is a fundamental principle in the spiritual teaching of St. Angela Merici. Thus, she writes in her recommendations for visitators: "Hold to the ancient way and tradition of the Church, ordained and confirmed by numerous saints under the inspiration of the Holy Spirit. Make a new life. . . . But pray and make others pray so that God will not abandon his Church, but will reform it as he wills and as he sees what is best for us and for his greater glory." These words are always relevant in every age.

> Opening Prayer: *Lord, may St. Angela commend us to your mercy; may her charity and wisdom help us to be faithful to your teaching and to follow it in our lives.*

January 28
ST. THOMAS AQUINAS (1225-1274)

HISTORICO-LITURGICAL NOTE

Son of the Count of Aquino and a mother who was of German descent (it is said that she was related to the

Barbarossa family), Thomas was born at the castle of Roccasecca, near Montecassino, Italy. As a child he was educated there by the Benedictines and from his earliest years he had a thirst for knowledge and truth. He later studied at the University of Naples, where he came into contact with the Dominicans and joined their ranks at the age of 18. His father was bitterly opposed to this choice and arranged to have Thomas kidnapped and held prisoner in the tower of the castle for fifteen months. Liberated with the help of his sisters, Thomas proceeded to Paris for further studies (1245); then to Cologne, where he studied under St. Albert the Great, and finally back to Paris (1256), where he became a Master of Sacred Theology at the age of 31. Together with St. Bonaventure, he defended the right of the friars to teach at the University against the opposition of the diocesan clergy.

Between 1259 and 1269 he was in Italy, at the service of Pope Urban IV, and during that time he wrote the *Catena Aurea* to help the clergy better understand the word of God, the *Summa contra Gentiles* (at the request of Raymond of Penyafort) to provide doctrinal material for missionaries to the Muslims, and the Divine Office for the feast of *Corpus Christi*. From 1269 to 1272 he was once again in Paris to defend the rights of the friars and to justify the use of Aristotle's philosophy in the study of theology. During this period he wrote his commentaries on various works of Aristotle and the greater part of his famous *Summa Theologiae*.

In 1272 Thomas was back in Naples to found a theological studium, and to preach, teach and write. On December 6, 1273, while celebrating Mass, he received an interior inspiration to cease writing and teaching. Nevertheless, he did accept the invitation of Pope Gregory X to assist at the Council of Lyons. On the way to France he died at the Cistercian monastery at Fossanova, Italy, on March 7, 1274.

Thomas Aquinas was canonized by Pope John XXII in 1323. Pope Pius V proclaimed him a Doctor of the Church and in 1880 Pope Leo XIII declared him patron of all Catholic schools. Since the sixteenth century he has been called "the Angelic Doctor," and this for two reasons, as is stated in the

Preface of the Mass: the purity of his life and the loftiness of his doctrine. Later he was given the title *Doctor Communis* because of the depth and breadth of his teaching. His feast is celebrated on January 28 because on that day in 1368 his relics were transferred to Toulouse, France, by order of Pope Urban V.

MESSAGE AND RELEVANCE

The first part of the Opening Prayer of the Mass expresses the two outstanding characteristics of St. Thomas Aquinas: his holiness and his learning. Totally dedicated to the ministry of the word, he nourished this ministry by a life of prayer and mortification. In the Office of Readings the second lesson is taken from a conference by Thomas Aquinas on the *Credo* in which he proposes Christ crucified as the exemplar of love. It is said that towards the end of his life, while praying before a crucifix, a voice asked Thomas what reward he wanted for all his labors. He replied: "None but yourself, O Lord."

The antiphon for the Canticle of Zechariah in the Dominican Liturgy of the Hours states: "Blessed be the Lord, out of love for whom the blessed Thomas studied, kept vigil and labored." The responsorial for the Office of Readings is taken from the Book of Wisdom: "I prayed, and prudence was given me; I pleaded, and the spirit of wisdom came to me" (7:7-8). Our petition in the Opening Prayer is that we "may grow in wisdom by his teaching, and in holiness by imitating his faith." St. Thomas Aquinas is still the *Doctor Communis* of the Church, since the revised *Code of Canon Law* states that St. Thomas Aquinas "in particular" should be the teacher of seminarians preparing for the priesthood (canon 252, #3).

The antiphon for the Canticle of Mary sums up very well the message and the relevance of St. Thomas Aquinas: "The Lord God has given him wisdom in great abundance, and he has communicated it to others without pretense and without envy." His message to us today is "to seek the truth in charity."

Preface (Dominican Missal): *You raised up in your Church the blessed Thomas, a doctor angelic in the integrity of his life and in the loftiness of his mind. You raised him up to strengthen your Church with his salutary and solid doctrine, and to enlighten her as a sun; his wisdom, extolled by all, commands the admiration of the whole world.*

January 31
ST. JOHN BOSCO (1815-1888)

HISTORICO-LITURGICAL NOTE

John Bosco was born near Castelnuovo in the archdiocese of Turin, Italy, in 1815. His father died when John was only two years old and it was his mother Margaret who provided him with a good humanistic and Christian education. His early years were financially difficult but at the age of twenty he entered the major seminary, thanks to the financial help received from Louis Guala, founder and rector of the ecclesiastical residence St. Francis of Assisi in Turin. John Bosco was ordained a priest on June 5, 1846, and with the help of John Borel he founded the oratory of St. Francis de Sales.

At this time the city of Turin was on the threshold of the industrial revolution and as a result there were many challenges and problems, especially for young men. Gifted as he was as an educator and a leader, Don Bosco formulated a system of education based on "reason, religion and kindness." In spite of the criticism and violent attacks of the anti-clericals, he conducted workshops for the tradesmen and manual laborers, schools of arts and sciences for young workers, and schools of the liberal arts for those preparing for the priesthood. In 1868 there were 800 students involved in this educational system. To ensure the continuation of his work, Don Bosco founded the Society of St. Francis de Sales

(Salesians), which was approved in 1869. Also, with the help of Sister Mary Dominic Mazzarello, he founded the Institute of the Daughters of Mary Auxiliatrix.

In 1875 a wave of emigration to Latin America began, and this prompted the inauguration of the Salesian missionary apostolate. Don Bosco became a traveller throughout Europe, seeking funds for the missions. Some of the reports referred to him as "the new St. Vincent de Paul." He also found time to write popular catechetical pamphlets, which were distributed throughout Italy, as was his *Salesian Bulletin.* This great apostle of youth died on January 31, 1888, and was canonized by Pope Pius XI in 1934. Pope John Paul II named him "teacher and father to the young."

MESSAGE AND RELEVANCE

It is as "teacher and father to the young," as stated in the Opening Prayer of the Mass, that St. John Bosco's life is best summarized. He himself had said in his old age: "I promised God that until my last breath I would live for my poor youth." This sense of fatherhood for his boys caused him to proclaim: "Remember: whatever I am, I am all for you, day and night, morning and evening, at every moment."

His own awareness of the fatherhood of God was extremely vivid. He was convinced that without a sense of intimacy with God, it is impossible to be an educator. "Education," he said, "is something from the heart, and God alone is its master; we cannot succeed in anything unless God gives us the key to these hearts." And he asserted that only a Catholic can successfully apply the Salesian educational method.

Of the three qualities that Don Bosco required in teachers, kindness was of particular importance. In the Office of Readings he advises educators to love the young as they would love their own sons. It goes without saying that this also applies to parents as educators; indeed, parents should be the prototype of teachers. Moreover, the document on education issued by the Second Vatican Council defends the absolute priority of parents in the education of their children. Others perform this function only by way of delegation.

In a famous letter written from Rome in 1884, Don Bosco said: "But are not my youth loved enough? You know that I love them. You know how much I have suffered and endured for them in the course of forty years, and how much I would suffer and endure for them even now." The Responsorial for the Office of Readings, "Let the little children come to me," reminds us of another statement of Christ regarding children: "Whoever welcomes one such child for my sake, welcomes me" (Mt 18:5). That summarizes well the spiritual fatherhood of Don Bosco and it also explains why he promoted devotion to Mary under the title of Help of Christians. He looked on Mary as a mother who pardons all and covers all with her mantle.

Another characteristic of Don Bosco was described by an anti-clerical writer: "He knew how to create an impressive system of education by bringing the Church back into contact with the masses, which the Church was losing. . . . For us who are outside the Church and outside every church, he is really a hero, the hero of preventive education and of the family-school. His followers can be proud."

As its name indicates, "preventive pedagogy" aims at preventing evils, at protecting youth by means of comprehensive understanding that respects their freedom but at the same time inculcates moral values. An outstanding example of the success of Don Bosco's system of education is seen in St. Dominic Savio, who once said to a companion: "Here we make holiness consist in being very happy and in performing our duties as perfectly as possible." As Don Bosco put it: "The young should know that they are loved."

In the Opening Prayer of the Mass we ask God to give us a love like that of St. John Bosco so that we may "give ourselves completely to your service and to the salvation of mankind." Don Bosco especially liked the statement: "Jesus began to do before he began to teach." He was truly prophetic in bringing to souls a spirituality based on the apostolate and an asceticism based on work. "I do not recommend penance and the discipline," he said, "but work, work, work."

Opening Prayer: *Lord, you called John Bosco to be a teacher and father to the young. Fill us with love like his: may we give ourselves completely to your service and to the salvation of mankind.*

FEBRUARY

February 3
ST. BLASE (+316?)

HISTORICO-LITURGICAL NOTE

According to the Latin Martyrology, the feast of St. Blase is celebrated on the day of his death. His feast is found in the Calendar of Naples in the ninth century and in Rome in the tenth century. His cult became widespread in the eleventh and twelfth centuries, especially in Germany, where he was considered a helper in need. The feast has been retained in spite of the historico-critical difficulties.

Blase, the bishop of Sebaste in Armenia, is the only representative of the Armenian Church in the Roman liturgy. Biographical details are very scarce and therefore legend has embellished his life with many prodigious events that made him one of the most popular saints in the Middle Ages. The first representation of the legend of St. Blase is found in the lower church of the basilica of St. Clement in Rome, dating back to the ninth century. His relics were distributed widely, which is evidence of his popularity.

It is said that during the persecution of Christians by Licinius (320-324), the governor of Cappadocia imprisoned the saintly bishop in a cave outside Sebaste and that wild beasts came to him to be cured. It is also said that a mother came to the bishop, asking him to cure her son who was choking on a fish bone stuck in his throat, and the bishop saved the lad with a prayer and the sign of the cross. For that reason St. Blase is venerated as patron of those suffering from diseases of the throat. He was eventually condemned to death and was beheaded in 316. He is venerated in the East on February 11 and in the West on February 3.

In many churches of the Latin rite two blessed candles are tied or held together in the form of a St. Andrew's cross and applied to the throat as the priest pronounces a special invocation to St. Blase to protect the individual against diseases of the throat. During the fifteenth and sixteenth centuries in Germany, St. Blase was invoked in cases of hemorrhage and ulcers.

MESSAGE AND RELEVANCE

In the Opening Prayer of the Mass we ask God, through the intercession of St. Blase, to give us the joy of his peace in this life and eternal happiness in heaven. In the Italian Missal the request is for "peace and health," thus recognizing the widespread confidence in St. Blase as a healer.

The Office of Readings contains an excerpt from a sermon by St. Augustine on the anniversary of his episcopal ordination. He reminds his hearers of the words of Christ: "I have not come to be served, but to serve," and then Augustine says: "We, too, have a duty to contribute our meager offerings to his members, for we have become his members. He is the head; we are the body."

If St. Blase is invoked as a powerful intercessor for the health of the body, it is because he was a martyr for the Church; he gave witness to the sufferings of Christ. As a bishop, he also, like St. Peter, heard the words of Christ: "Feed my sheep," meaning, sacrifice yourself for my sheep. The relevance of this feast can be found in the fact that it falls in the middle of winter, as if to remind us that there is no redemption or healing of the body that is not effected through sacrifice.

Collect: *Lord, hear the prayers of your martyr Blase. Give us the joy of your peace in this life and help us to gain the happiness that will never end.*

February 3
ST. ANSGAR (801-865)

HISTORICO-LITURGICAL NOTE

In the new Calendar St. Ansgar is associated with four other saintly apostles who represent northern Europe and the Slav countries: St. Augustine of Canterbury, St. Boniface, and Sts. Cyril and Methodius.

Born at Corbie, near Amiens, France, he became a Benedictine monk and was for a time the master of the monastic school. After the baptism of King Harold of Denmark in 826, Ansgar went to that country to preach the gospel. A few years later he was invited by King Bjorg to preach the gospel in Sweden. In 831 he was named the first archbishop of Hamburg and papal legate for all of Scandinavia and northern Germany. In 845 the pagan Norsemen destroyed Hamburg, and Denmark and Sweden relapsed into idolatry. Later, Pope Nicholas I united Hamburg with Bremen and appointed Ansgar over both. Ansgar made a second apostolic voyage to Scandinavia and his work was greatly aided by the conversion of King Olaf of Sweden in 852. Unfortunately, after the death of Bishop Ansgar, Sweden once again relapsed into paganism and remained in that condition until the eleventh century, when St. Sigfrid of England evangelized the country. All his life St. Ansgar had desired martyrdom, but he died from natural causes on February 3, at the age of 64.

MESSAGE AND RELEVANCE

In the Opening Prayer of the Mass, taken from a French Mass in honor of St. Ansgar, we ask that through the intercession of this apostle to the Scandinavian countries we may "walk in the light of your truth." This petition is especially relevant in our day, when the light of truth is often obscured by the paganism of modern society. Today we are keenly aware of the need for a re-evangelization of our secularized society. The Office of Readings contains an excerpt from the Vatican II document on missionary activity: "Every disciple of Christ is responsible in his own measure for the spread of the faith." The feast of St. Ansgar invites all the faithful to respond to this missionary vocation by perfecting their understanding of the faith through a systematic catechesis and a more dedicated collaboration in the work of evangelization and re-evangelization.

> Opening Prayer: *Father, you sent St. Ansgar to bring the light of Christ to many nations. May his prayers help us to walk in the light of your truth.*

February 5
ST. AGATHA (+250)

HISTORICO-LITURGICAL NOTE

Agatha suffered martyrdom at Catania, Sicily, in the year 250 and was venerated at Milan, Rome and Ravenna, and also in the East. Although the account of her martyrdom is of little historical value, it was the source for the antiphons and responsorials in the former Breviary.

The cult of St. Agatha is very ancient. A church was constructed in her honor at Rome in the fifth century and, at the beginning of the sixth century, Pope Symmacus introduced her feast into the liturgy at Rome and dedicated a basilica in her honor. The inclusion of her name in the Roman Canon of the Mass is attributed to St. Gregory the Great.

The devotion of numerous popes to St. Agatha is possibly based on the legend that St. Peter appeared to her to console and heal her. She had been tortured on the rack and her breasts had been cut off. A few days later she was rolled naked over burning coals. Her last prayer to Christ was "Receive my soul," after which she breathed her last. It is believed that through St. Agatha's intercession Catania was miraculously saved from an eruption of Mount Etna. Consequently, she is invoked against any outbreak of fire.

MESSAGE AND RELEVANCE

The Opening Prayer of the Mass is taken from the two prayers contained in the Gregorian Sacramentary and it emphasizes the glory associated with virginity and martyrdom. The Latin text distinguishes these two realities by referring to the "power" of martyrdom and the "merit" of chastity. Martyrdom reveals the power of God that triumphs over the weakness of creatures through the operation of the gift of fortitude; the merit of chastity derives from the cooperation of the individual person with the grace of God.

The Office of Readings is taken from a homily by St. Methodius, a native of Syracuse in Sicily and Patriarch of Constantinople. He describes St. Agatha as a bride and a virgin: "To use the analogy of Paul, she is the bride who has been betrothed to one husband, Christ. A true virgin, she wore the glow of a pure conscience and the crimson of the Lamb's blood for her cosmetics."

In the same homily St. Methodius says: "Agatha, the name of our saint, means 'good' . . . Agatha, her goodness coincides with her name and way of life. She won a good name by her noble deeds, and by her name she points to the nobility of those deeds. Agatha, her mere name wins all men over to her company. She teaches them by her example to hasten with her to the true Good, God alone."

In the face of the modern sexual revolution, this feast has special significance in stressing the importance of the virtue of chastity for every state of life. This is readily seen in the "unbloody martyrdom" of consecrated virginity, which is especially meritorious. However, all Christians, even if they are married, should practice chastity in accordance with their condition and state of life. Finally, as in the Middle Ages, St. Agatha should be invoked by those women who are suffering from diseases of the breast.

> Opening Prayer: *Lord, let your forgiveness be won for us by the pleading of St. Agatha, who found favor with you by her chastity and by her courage in suffering death for the gospel.*

February 6
ST. PAUL MIKI and COMPANIONS (1564/6-1597)

HISTORICO-LITURGICAL NOTE

This group of 26 Christians suffered martyrdom on February 5, 1597, near Nagasaki, Japan. The group was made up of 6 Franciscans (from Spain, Mexico and India), 3 Japanese Jesuit catechists (including Paul Miki), and 17 Japanese lay Catholics. They were all crucified by being attached to crosses with ropes and chains and then put to death by the thrust of a lance.

The Office of Readings contains an account of their martyrdom, written by a contemporary witness. He focuses especially on the heroism of St. Paul Miki: "Our brother, Paul Miki, saw himself standing now in the noblest pulpit he had ever filled. To his 'congregation' he now began by proclaiming himself a Japanese and a Jesuit. He was dying for the gospel he preached. He gave thanks to God for this wonderful blessing and he ended his 'sermon' with these words: 'As I come to this supreme moment of my life, I am sure none of you would suppose that I want to deceive you. And so I tell you plainly: there is no way to be saved except the Christian way'.'" These 26 martyrs for Christ were canonized in 1862.

MESSAGE AND RELEVANCE

The Opening Prayer of the Mass states that Paul Miki and companions entered the joy of eternal life "through the suffering of the cross." The first part of the prayer is taken from the Sacramentary of Verona: "God our Father, source of strength for all your saints." Martyrdom is presented as a superhuman act, in the sense that only God can give one the courage to undergo torments and give one's life for him. This is all the more true when we realize that in the group there were three young boys, ranging in ages from 12 to 14. The prayer then goes on to ask perseverance in the faith for ourselves so that we may be "loyal until death."

In the Office of Readings the description of the martyrdom resembles the choral Office, with one of the martyrs reciting Psalm 112, another reciting the Our Father and the Hail Mary, and others repeating "Jesus! Mary!" Their example shows that we can give witness to our faith through the simplest and most elementary prayers. They may seem to be small and insignificant, but if recited with fervor and an awareness of their relation to what we profess in our faith, they can constitute an authentic Christian witness. On this feast of the Japanese martyrs we should ask for the grace of a truly Christian death. It is also an occasion to pray for the Japanese people, who seem so impervious to the Christian teaching.

Opening Prayer: *God our Father, source of strength for all your saints, you led Paul Miki and his companions through the suffering of the cross to the joy of eternal life. May their prayers give us the courage to be loyal until death in professing our faith.*

February 8
ST. JEROME EMILIANI (1486-1537)

HISTORICO-LITURGICAL NOTE

This feast is assigned to the day on which Jerome Emiliani died at Somasca (Bergamo), Italy, where he had founded a congregation of clerks regular. He is a model of conversion from a dissolute life to a life of total dedication to the care of the sick, abandoned children and women converts.

Born in Venice of a noble family, he entered the military service when the city was defending itself against the troops of Maximilian I. He was imprisoned for a time but is said to have been liberated through the intercession of the Blessed Virgin, as a result of which he made a vow to dedicate himself to her service. For three years he prepared himself for his future apostolate by performing works of charity. While nursing the sick during the epidemic in 1528 he himself fell ill, and when he recovered he began to gather orphans into his home. His motto was: "Anyone who does not work should not eat" (2 Th 3:10). His apostolate gradually extended beyond the area of Venice, to Brescia, Milan and especially to Bergamo, where he founded the Company of Servants of the Poor, clerks regular approved by Pope Paul III in 1540. He died of the plague in 1537 with the names of Jesus and Mary on his lips. He was canonized in 1767 and in 1928 Pope Pius XI named him patron of orphans and abandoned infants.

MESSAGE AND RELEVANCE

The Opening Prayer of the Mass contains two themes. The first is the merciful fatherhood of God, who raised up this saint to be "a father and friend of orphans." Today there are many who do not know the meaning of true fatherhood, not only in a natural and juridical sense, but in an affective sense as well. There is an ever-increasing number of children who are "psychological orphans," who are not affirmed with love. They are deprived of that bond of love that comes, not so much from social institutions, but from a reflection of the divine fatherhood.

The second theme of the prayer is the spirit of adoption by which we are called, and truly are, children of God (1 Jn 3:1-2). A deep awareness of the transcendent and mysterious reality of our adoptive filiation leads us into the mystery of the Trinity. We are sons in the Son. This supernatural dignity is the basis of our trust in God, even in the midst of tribulation. Thus, St. Jerome Emiliani wrote in a letter two years before his death: "This is the way God has dealt with all his saints. . . . If then you remain constant in faith in the face of trial, the Lord will give you peace and rest for a time in this world, and for ever in the next" (Office of Readings).

Our dignity as children of God ought to give us a sense of solidarity and responsibility towards every person, but especially towards those who suffer from loneliness, abandonment, or the lack of parental love and care.

> Opening Prayer: *God of mercy, you chose Jerome Emiliani to be a father and friend of orphans. May his prayers keep us faithful to the Spirit we have received, who makes us your children.*

February 10
ST. SCHOLASTICA (480-547)

HISTORICO-LITURGICAL NOTE

Scholastica, the twin sister of St. Benedict, was born at Norcia, which is at the border between Umbria and Sabina. She consecrated herself to God from her earliest years and remained at home with her father, while Benedict went off to Rome for his education. According to the *Dialogues* of St.

Gregory the Great — the only source we have concerning Benedict and Scholastica — it is likely that while Benedict was at Subiaco, Scholastica was at a monastery nearby. Later, in order to stay close to her brother, Scholastica followed him to Montecassino and entered a monastery at Piumarola. There she died in 547.

According to the Benedictine Calendar at the end of the eighth century, the feast of St. Scholastica was celebrated on February 10. By the ninth century it was celebrated throughout the monastic world and reached its widest diffusion between the eleventh and thirteenth centuries. By the end of the eighteenth century her feast is found in the Roman liturgical books. We have no historical details concerning the translation of her relics to Le Mans, France, in the seventh century or from the archaeological investigation of her tomb at Montecassino in 1950.

MESSAGE AND RELEVANCE

The former Opening Prayer of the Mass, which gave details of her death, based on the account of St. Gregory the Great, has been replaced by the present one. Its theme is the two loves, human and divine, that are at the center of every consecrated life and every Christian life. In the Latin version of the prayer we ask that we may "love and serve God with purity of heart" so that we may experience the joy of his friendship. When our love of God is pure, it produces abundant and joyous fruits that can transform the network of human relations, including our friendships.

The Office of Readings describes the annual visit between Benedict and Scholastica, which took place in a house separate from the monastery. On one occasion Scholastica wanted Benedict to wait until the following day to return to his monastery, but Benedict refused. Then, as St. Gregory reports, Scholastica prayed to God, and such a violent thunderstorm arose that Benedict and his companions could not leave the house. "What have you done?" asked Benedict.

She answered: "I asked you, and you would not listen; so I asked my God and he did listen."

The lesson for us is summarized in the comment of St. Gregory the Great: "Since, as John says, God is love, then surely he can do more who loves more." This statement is used as the responsory for the Office of Readings, together with Psalm 133:1.

> Preface (Monastic Supplement to the Roman Missal): *Father, to clothe your Church in virginal beauty, you adorned St. Scholastica with the jewels of innocence and made her more acceptable to you with the simplicity of a dove. Sister of our glorious Father St. Benedict, she was also associated with him in sanctity, and under his guidance, seeking you alone above everything else, she produced abundant fruits of grace and has merited to enjoy your love for all eternity.*

February 11
OUR LADY OF LOURDES

HISTORICO-LITURGICAL NOTE

February 11 was approved for the diocese of Tarbes, France, by Pope Leo XIII in 1890 to commemorate the first apparition at Lourdes. Later, in 1908, Pope Pius X included it in the Roman Calendar. The feast is based on the apparitions to Bernadette Soubirous (1844-1879) at the grotto of Massabielle from February 11, 1858, until July 16 of that same year, a total of 18 apparitions. The Blessed Virgin Mary identified herself as the Immaculate Conception and asked that a shrine be built there. These visions and messages were the occasion for renewed devotion to Mary Immaculate, and hence the focal point of the feast is not the events at Lourdes, but the Immaculate Conception.

MESSAGE AND RELEVANCE

In the Opening Prayer of the Mass we ask that Mary's prayers will "help us to rise above our human weakness." That weakness may be understood as the moral weakness caused by our sins or the physical weakness resulting from any kind of bodily illness or affliction. In the Latin version we pray "that we may rise from sin to a new life." This is the key to the significance of Lourdes, namely, that after admitting our human frailty, we ask for the life of grace, which in Mary's case was received at her Immaculate Conception in view of her divine maternity.

The Office of Readings is taken from a letter written by Bernadette, in which she gives a straightforward account of the message received. In addition to asking that a shrine be built on that spot, the Virgin Mary told Bernadette to pray for the conversion of sinners. She also suggested the recitation of the Rosary, which provides material for meditation on the salvific events in the life of Christ.

The relevance of the feast of Our Lady of Lourdes does not rest on the numerous miracles that have occurred there but on the "prolonged miracle" of the effects of the paschal mystery on our physical, moral or spiritual weakness. To bathe in the waters of Lourdes is to return, as it were, to the font of our baptism and to rise from sin to a new life. Rightly therefore did the Second Vatican Council urge "that the cult, especially the liturgical cult, of the Blessed Virgin be generously fostered and that the practices and exercises of devotion towards her, recommended by the teaching authority of the Church in the course of centuries, be highly esteemed" (*Lumen Gentium*, no. 67).

> Collect: *God of mercy, we celebrate the feast of Mary, the sinless Mother of God. May her prayers help us to rise above our human weakness.*

February 14
ST. CYRIL (827-869) and ST. METHODIUS (815-885)

HISTORICO-LITURGICAL NOTE

These two saints were proclaimed co-patrons of Europe, together with St. Benedict, by Pope John Paul II on December 31, 1980. The feast itself is on the date of the death of Cyril (baptized Constantine), the blood brother of Methodius (baptized Michael). They were born at Thessalonica, Greece, and became apostles to the Slav nations of Moravia, Bohemia and Bulgaria. Their feast has been celebrated universally in the Church since 1880.

St. Cyril was ordained a priest at Constantinople and taught philosophy there. His older brother Michael, after being governor of a Slav province, became a monk and took the name Methodius. In 862 Rostislav, prince of Moravia, asked for missionaries who could speak the language of his country. The two brothers, Cyril and Methodius, were selected for the task. They differed greatly from the Latin-Rite missionaries from Germany because they were able to adapt to the people they were evangelizing. For example, they created a Slav alphabet and they translated the Bible and the liturgy into the Slav language (hence the characters were called "Cyrillic").

As could be expected, the methods of inculturation used by Cyril and Methodius were severely criticized, especially by the missionaries of the Latin Rite. However, when they brought the alleged relics of St. Clement to Rome, Pope Adrian II received them warmly. Not only did he approve the use of the Slavonic language in the liturgy but he named them bishops. However, it is not certain that Constantine was ever ordained a bishop, since he died at Rome on February 14, 869, after having made monastic profession, taking the name of Cyril. He is buried in the basilica of St. Clement in Rome.

After being ordained bishop, Methodius returned to the East as papal legate to the Slav nations. But the unsettled political situation and the opposition of the German bishops of the Latin Rite greatly impeded his ministry. Pope John VIII defended Methodius but he did for a time suspend the use of the Slavonic language in the liturgy and he restricted the jurisdiction of Methodius. During the last four years of his life St. Methodius dedicated himself to the translation of the Bible and other works into Slavonic. He died on April 6, 884 or 885, and the funeral liturgy was conducted in the Greek, Latin and Slavonic Rites.

MESSAGE AND RELEVANCE

The first part of the Opening Prayer of the Mass recalls the great merit of the two brothers as missionaries who "brought the light of the gospel to the Slavic nations." Those countries rightly consider Cyril and Methodius as their fathers in the Christian faith. By introducing new languages into the liturgy of the Church, they revived "the prodigy of the early Church."

The two missionaries not only made the Church resplendent by their work of evangelization, but they are models for the adaptation of the faith to various cultures. They understood the points of reference to the culture of the people and they knew how to promote unity without imposing rigid uniformity. Because they laid the foundation for a truly Christian popular culture, Cyril and Methodius can also serve as reliable guides in the ecumenical movement.

In the Opening Prayer of the Mass the petition that we may become "one in faith and praise" echoes the sentiments expressed by St. Cyril on his deathbed (Office of Readings). "Build up your Church," he prayed, "and gather all into unity. Make your people known for the unity and profession of their faith. . . . May all praise and glorify your name, the Father, Son and Holy Spirit." These two elements — unity and profession of the faith — are the guaranty of an authentic and fruitful evangelization. The use of a common language promotes unity among the People of God because there is no longer a division between what they understand in their minds and what they profess with their lips in the liturgy.

The Prayer after Communion invokes "the Father of all nations who, through the one bread and the one Spirit has made us companions and heirs of the eternal banquet." We then ask that he will "grant that all his children, united in the same faith, will be in full agreement in promoting justice and peace."

All the cultures of the Slavic nations owe their beginnings and development to Sts. Cyril and Methodius, whether it was the creation of their alphabet or the translation of the liturgical books into the language of the people. That Slavonic language is used even today in the liturgy of the Eastern Church, both Catholic and Orthodox, in eastern and southeastern Europe, and in the Roman liturgy of Croatia. Consequently, as Pope John Paul II points out in his apostolic letter *Slavorum Apostoli*, the work of these two co-patrons of Europe was an outstanding contribution to the common Christian foundation of Europe.

> Opening Prayer: *Father, you brought the light of the gospel to the Slavic nations through St. Cyril and his brother St. Methodius. Open our hearts to understand your teaching and help us to become one in faith and praise.*

February 17
SEVEN FOUNDERS of the SERVITE ORDER (1245-1310)

HISTORICO-LITURGICAL NOTE

According to tradition, the date for this feast is the anniversary of the death of the best known of the Seven

Founders, Alex Falconieri (+ 1310). The seven men in question were from prominent families in the city of Florence and they were all members of the Confraternity of the Blessed Virgin Mary. As they progressed in the spiritual life, they became more and more detached from the world. With permission of the bishop they moved to a location outside the city of Florence with the intention of leading an austere eremitical life. In due time there were so many visitors that the seven founders moved to a much more solitary and wild location. They refused to accept any new members at that time.

When he visited the group, the bishop of Florence told them that their life was too rugged and their asceticism too severe. Moreover, they should admit those who wished to join them. They took the bishop's advice and in 1240 they donned a black habit and adopted the Rule of St. Augustine. Their style of life also changed; with less emphasis on the eremitical observances, they came to resemble the mendicant friars, with great emphasis on poverty. In due time all but one of the original seven founders were ordained to the priesthood. They adopted the name Servants of Mary and are popularly known as Servites. However, they were not approved by the Holy See until 1259 and it was not until 1304 that they were canonically approved.

The seven founders were canonized in 1888 by Pope Leo XIII. The one and the same sepulcher on Mount Senario contains the relics of those who in this life were united by the bond of fraternal charity.

MESSAGE AND RELEVANCE

In the Opening Prayer proper to the Servite Order we are told that the seven holy founders were "fraternally united in devoted service to Mary, the Mother of God," and that they "revived the faith of the Christian people." What is first emphasized is the singular fraternal love of these men who lived in a time of war and division. They succeeded in living a community life and devoted themselves to the promulgation of devotion to Mary.

Today also, when in many places there is tension and division between the Church and civil society, community life in fraternal charity is a challenge to form new patterns of social life based on Christian principles. The word *communio* has become a password since Vatican Council II, and those holy men who formed the first community of the Servants of Mary have left us a remarkable example of fraternal charity, which is the most essential element in *communio*.

A second lesson can be taken from their devotion to Mary as Mediatrix in the light of the two fundamental Christian mysteries: the Incarnation and the Redemption. In the first of these mysteries we contemplate the humility of Mary; in the second, we are prompted to draw near with Mary to the crosses of our brothers and sisters.

The Office of Readings gives us an account of the founding of the Servite Order and describes the humility, unanimity and poverty of the seven holy founders. They were able to synchronize, as it were, the urban life of the city, where the need for solidarity and fraternal charity is so acute, and the isolation of the mountains, which is so conducive to prayerful contemplation.

Preface (Servite Missal): *Father, in a wonderful manner you called the seven holy founders to the service of the holy Mother of God so that, faithfully associated with her at the foot of the Cross, they could lead your people to the copious fountain of salvation that gushes forth from the wounds of Christ. Moreover, O Father, by the sublime charity that united them, you sent them forth as apostles of union and peace among the Christian people so that, resolving every conflict, they could gather people together in fraternal concord.*

February 21
ST. PETER DAMIAN (1007-1072)

HISTORICO-LITURGICAL NOTE

This feast was placed in the liturgical calendar and Peter Damian was declared a Doctor of the Church only in 1828. Born at Ravenna, Italy, and after manifesting unusual intellectual gifts, he began to teach in the university at the age of 21. Seven years later he retired to the solitude of Fonte Avellana to live a penitential life. There he composed the Rule for the Camaldolese hermits and was elected prior. However, he was called out of the eremitical life by Emperor Henry III and by Pope Stephen X, who made him bishop of Ostia and a cardinal. He resigned from the see of Ostia in 1067 after failing to reconcile the papacy and the empire. At various times he served as papal legate in France, Germany and numerous places in Italy. In addition to his theological treatises, he is the author of the life of St. Romuald, founder of the Camaldolese hermits. He worked zealously to overcome the two principal vices of the clergy of his time: simony and immorality.

As a peacemaker and reformer, Peter Damian was a forerunner of the reform instituted by Pope Gregory VII. He died on February 22, 1072, and his cult was popular in the area of Ravenna and in the Camaldolese Order. In the *Divine Comedy* Dante places St. Peter Damian in the seventh heaven, among the contemplatives.

MESSAGE AND RELEVANCE

The first part of the Opening Prayer of the Mass presents Peter Damian as a teacher and model of the Christian life; the second part urges us to imitate the saint "by making Christ and the service of his Church the first love of our lives." The first part refers to the masterly leadership of Peter Damian during a sad period in the Church. In one of his works he stated:

"Monastic discipline is lax and far removed from its customary perfection; the majority of the clergy live mundane lives and the laity fight and plunder one another." His denunciation of the vices of the day increased the hostility of his adversaries. Peter was coldly rebuffed by Pope Leo IX, who had capitulated to the very persons that Peter was denouncing. Today as well we need persons who will follow the courageous example of Peter Damian and pass judgment on the decadence of public morality. We must never compromise the gospel.

The second point for our imitation is Peter Damian's dedicated service to the Church. Out of love for the Church he left his beloved solitude at Fonte Avellana to travel extensively as a peacemaker in the name of the Holy Father. Vatican Council II and Pope John Paul II have stressed the urgent need for the faithful to sacrifice personal interests and individual preferences for the good of the Church, whether on the diocesan or parish level. For Peter Damian every Christian is a "little church," capable of realizing in himself or herself the relationship of Christ to his Church. In the Office of Readings St. Peter Damian exhorts us not to give in to bitterness and discouragement under the "lashes of the heavenly discipline" (the various trials of life).

Finally, the Latin version of the Opening Prayer quotes a phrase from the Rule of St. Benedict: "Do not prefer anything to the love of Christ." This is not only an ideal for the monastic life but an imperative for every true Christian who lives according to the gospel. We can summarize the entire life of this great saint in three phrases contained in the Office of Readings: "Let the serenity of your spirit shine through your face. Let the joy of your mind burst forth. Let words of thanks break from your lips."

Opening Prayer: *All-powerful God, help us to follow the teachings and example of Peter Damian. By making Christ and the service of his Church the first love of our lives, may we come to the joys of eternal light.*

February 22
CHAIR of ST. PETER

HISTORICO-LITURGICAL NOTE

This feast is found in the oldest Roman Calendar of 394, assigned to February 22, the day on which the Romans commemorated the deceased. At one time there were two feasts of the chair of St. Peter: one on January 18, celebrated in France in the eighth century, and one on February 22 to commemorate the chair of St. Peter at Antioch, for he had been there before going to Rome. The most ancient date for the celebration of this feast in St. Peter's Basilica in Rome is the middle of the fifth century, and it was preceded by a night vigil over which the pope presided. Soon thereafter the cult spread throughout Europe; then, for some inexplicable reason, there was silence in the seventh and eighth centuries. Finally it was again revived in the eleventh and twelfth centuries.

MESSAGE AND RELEVANCE

The texts for the Mass and the Liturgy of the Hours serve as an excellent catechesis on the role of the apostle Peter at a time when there are ecumenical discussions concerning the mission of Peter and his successors. This is a crucial difficulty in the promotion of Christian unity.

The Entrance Antiphon quotes Luke: "The Lord said to Simon Peter: I have prayed that your faith may not fail; and you in your turn must strengthen your brothers" (Lk 22:32). The prayers of the Mass then describe the mission of Peter.

The Opening Prayer is taken from the Gelasian Sacramentary for June 29 and portrays a central characteristic of St. Peter: "You have built your Church on the rock of St. Peter's confession of faith." Peter is thus the rock of the community of Christ, as is stated in the Communion Antiphon: "You are Peter, the rock on which I will build my Church."

Because of Peter's confession, "You are the Christ, the Son of the living God," the "jaws of death" (meaning the attacks of evil) will not prevail against the Church (Mt 16:18). It is by the power of God ("No mere man has revealed this to you, but my heavenly Father" Mt 16:17) and not by his personal strength — much less because he had experienced the weakness of a believer — that Peter is constituted the sure point of reference for our apostolic faith and serves as a motive for fidelity to the word of God. In the numerous texts referring to St. Peter in the Liturgy of the Hours we find references to Christ's promise that Peter would have the primacy.

Another theme for catechesis is found in the Prayer over the Gifts: "With St. Peter as our shepherd, keep us true to the faith he taught and bring us to your eternal kingdom." The certitude of the apostolic faith is linked to his integrity, and precisely because he is the shepherd of the People of God.

In the Prayer after Communion it is interesting to note the mention of the Eucharist, which is the sacrament of unity and peace. The liturgy thus links Peter, the visible sign of unity in the Church, with the effects of the eucharistic sacrifice. Ultimately it is Christ, acting through this supreme sacrament, who guarantees the ministry of visible unity in the faith, but St. Leo says in the Office of Readings: "It is not without reason that the authority bestowed on all the apostles is entrusted to one. For Peter received it separately in trust because he is the prototype set before all the rulers of the Church."

Preface: *It is truly right and just to give you thanks, almighty and everlasting God, and to admire your greatness, especially in the saints that you raised up for the support of your Church. With remarkable wisdom the Church was prefigured in the Old Testament, and when the time was fulfilled, you established it on the foundation of the apostles. From among them you chose Peter, who was the first to recognize the divinity of Christ, and you made him the solid rock on which your Church would be built. You have constituted him as guide and custodian of your entire flock so that throughout the centuries he could strengthen his brethren. Your Son, our Lord Jesus Christ, gave him the keys of the kingdom so that whatever he decided on earth, you, O Father, would ratify in heaven. Today we devoutly celebrate the singular and provident charge that was committed to the head of the apostles, as we join the choirs of angels and sing a hymn to your glory.*

February 23
ST. POLYCARP (75/82-155)

HISTORICO-LITURGICAL NOTE

The date for this feast, mentioned in the letter from the Church of Smyrna and inscribed in the Martyrology of Nicomedia (361), is celebrated by the Syrians, the Byzantines and the Copts. In the Western Church his cult goes back to the sixth century and became widely diffused in the thirteenth century. His feast was previously celebrated on January 26.

Polycarp, bishop of Smyrna, was born of Christian parents sometime between the years 75 and 80. According to St. Irenaeus, in his preaching he constantly referred to the teaching of St. John the Evangelist and the other eye-witnesses of the life of Christ. He is therefore a link with the Church of apostolic times. When Ignatius, together with Zosimus and Rufus, was on his way to Rome, where he suffered martyrdom, he met Polycarp and entrusted to him the care of the church at Antioch because he considered Polycarp to be an apostolic man and a true pastor. The only other detail we know about St. Polycarp before his martyrdom is that he visited Rome in order to discuss the problem of the date for Easter with Pope Anicetus. Since they could reach no agreement, the pope decided to let matters stand as they were. Polycarp's letter to the Philippians (still extant) was so excellent that it was read publicly in the churches in the time of St. Jerome.

Polycarp's martyrdom is usually dated in the year 155, although some have given the year 167.

MESSAGE AND RELEVANCE

The Opening Prayer of the Mass is based on Polycarp's prayer at the site of his martyrdom. and it reveals two traits of this saintly bishop. First of all, he was a witness to the faith by his martyrdom; secondly, he was a perfect imitator of the divine Victim who drank the cup of suffering during his passion. The antiphon for the Canticle of Mary refers explicitly to these two traits in the words of St. Polycarp: "Almighty God, I give you praise, for you have counted me worthy to be among your martyrs, who drink of the cup of Christ's sufferings." The antiphon for the Canticle of Zechariah also quotes the exact words of St. Polycarp: "For eighty-six years I have served Jesus Christ and he has never abandoned me. How could I curse my blessed King and Savior?"

The details of the martyrdom in the Office of Readings show that St. Polycarp imitated Christ to the very end. The prayer of the saintly bishop has all the solemnity of a Preface of the Mass. It is a eucharistic prayer, in the sense of a thanksgiving prayer: "Lord, almighty God, Father of your beloved and blessed Son Jesus Christ, through whom we have come to the knowledge of yourself, God of angels, of powers, of all creation, of all the race of saints who live in your sight, I bless you for judging me worthy of this day, this hour, so that in the company of the martyrs I may share the cup of Christ, your anointed one, and so rise again to eternal life in soul and body, immortal through the power of the Holy Spirit."

Opening Prayer: *God of all creation, you gave your bishop Polycarp the privilege of being counted among the saints who gave their lives in faithful witness to the gospel. May his prayers give us the courage to share with him the cup of suffering and to rise to eternal glory.*

MARCH

March 3 (United States)
BLESSED KATHARINE DREXEL
(1858-1955)

HISTORICO-LITURGICAL NOTE

This Philadelphia heiress and founder of the Sisters of the Blessed Sacrament for Indians and Colored People was beatified in 1988.

She was the daughter of a wealthy banker and was raised by a loving step-mother, since her own mother died when Katharine was still an infant. She travelled extensively and was well educated. After the Third Plenary Council of Baltimore her family was asked to contribute to the missions that served the Indians and Negroes. Katharine became involved in this apostolate and later, when she had an audience with Pope Leo XIII, he urged her to be a missionary to those deserving people.

Katharine entered the novitiate of the Sisters of Mercy in Pittsburgh and in 1891 she founded her own religious congregation. In 1915 she established Xavier University for the colored people in New Orleans. It is estimated that during her lifetime she spent approximately 12 million dollars on the apostolate to Indians and Negroes.

MESSAGE AND RELEVANCE

Coming as she did from the highest level of Philadelphia society, Katharine's total dedication to the needs of the Indians and Negroes was made possible by her willingness to use the wealth of her inheritance for a good cause. She is an example of poverty of spirit and detachment from the goods of this world.

Katharine Drexel is especially relevant to contemporary American society, in which unemployment, homelessness and racial injustice are still a burden for the native Indians and the Negroes. The span of her life extended to 1955 and for that reason her example and her apostolate are especially relevant to contemporary society. Hence the petition in the Opening Prayer is significant. We ask God to "enable us to work for justice among the poor and the oppressed." It is noteworthy that this prayer refers to the Eucharist as the focal point of unity in the Church.

> Opening Prayer: *Ever-loving God, you called Blessed Katharine Drexel to teach the message of the gospel and to bring the life of the Eucharist to the African American and Native American peoples. By her prayers and example, enable us to work for justice among the poor and the oppressed, and keep us undivided in love in the eucharistic community of your Church.*

March 4
ST. CASIMIR (1458-1484)

HISTORICO-LITURGICAL NOTE

This saintly Polish prince, who died in his twenty-sixth year on March 4, 1484, after a life lived according to the gospel and in virginal chastity, is a patron saint for Poland and Lithuania. He received his religious education from his mother, Elizabeth of Austria, and after an adolescence of great piety and austerity, he was elected king of Hungary at the age of thirteen as a rival to the monarch Matthias Corvino. But after the Hungarians were reconciled to their own king, Casimir renounced the throne and accepted the office of regent of Poland while his father was in Lithuania. In that office, in spite of his youthfulness, he exemplified great prudence and virtue. He refused marriage with the daughter of the emperor of Germany, Henry III, and in 1483 became vice-chancellor in Lithuania, but shortly thereafter he died of tuberculosis and was buried under the altar of the Blessed Virgin in the castle at Vilna. There was a popular devotion to him and he was canonized in 1521 by Pope Leo X. To this day the Lithuanians and Poles honor him. After the Reform of 1602 Pope Clement VIII reissued the bull of canonization of Pope Leo X, which had never reached Poland.

MESSAGE AND RELEVANCE

The Opening Prayer of the Mass begins with the phrase: "to serve you is to reign," and it is still a valid reminder because power can easily be used for selfish reasons. Only through self-denial can one overcome that tendency and dedicate oneself to the service of others. Consequently, the virtues mentioned in this prayer are "holiness and justice."

The Office of Readings contains an excerpt from the life of St. Casimir, written by the papal legate, Zaccaria Ferreri, some thirty years after the death of Casimir. It is a tribute to his life of charity and chastity in the midst of the corruption of the royal court. Every day Casimir recited the lengthy hymn composed perhaps by St. Bernard in honor of the Blessed Virgin Mary, *Omni die dic Mariae*, of which the English version is entitled "Daily, daily sing to Mary." He had made a copy of this hymn and it was found under his head when his tomb was opened in 1604. The words of his biographer are a repetition of the teaching of Christ himself and are still relevant today: "He always preferred to be counted among the meek and poor of spirit, among those who are promised the kingdom of heaven, rather than among the famous and powerful men of this world."

Opening Prayer: *All-powerful God, to serve you is to reign: by the prayers of St. Casimir, help us to serve you in holiness and justice.*

March 7
ST. PERPETUA and ST. FELICITY (+202/3)

HISTORICO-LITURGICAL NOTE

These two saints faced martyrdom hand in hand at Carthage in North Africa during the persecution of Septimus Severus. The account of their deaths was probably written by Tertullian. The account was so highly esteemed that in the fourth century it was read publicly in the churches of northern Africa.

Perpetua, 22 years of age, was the daughter of a pagan nobleman and she was the mother of an infant still in swaddling clothes. Felicity, a slave, gave birth to a child prematurely while in prison. Three other catechumens were imprisoned with Perpetua and Felicity, and they were soon joined by their teacher, Saturus. They were baptized while in prison, prior to their death in the amphitheater. The detailed account of their martyrdom is one of the greatest literary treasures that have come down to us from the early Church.

MESSAGE AND RELEVANCE

The Opening Prayer is taken from the Proper of a Mass that was celebrated in North Africa: "Your love gave the saints Perpetua and Felicity courage to suffer a cruel martyrdom." The petition in the prayer reads as follows: "Help us to grow in love of you."

The Office of Readings is taken from the account of their martyrdom and it highlights the intensity of their love of God, which gave them the courage to endure the torments of martyrdom, and their maternal love for their children, one newly born and the other still a nursing infant. The response given by Felicity when a prison guard begged her to avoid martyrdom for the sake of her unborn child, even as she was going through the pains of labor, can serve today as a protest against the widespread slaughter of the unborn through legalized abortion. Only her love of God could enable her to transcend one of the most powerful of human loves, that of a mother for her own child. "Today it is I who suffer in giving birth, but then it will be Another who will suffer in me, because I shall suffer for him." Another statement that is relevant today is found in Perpetua's account of their imprisonment: "The Spirit inspired me to ask from the water of her baptism nothing more than constancy of the flesh" [in the face of martyrdom.]

> Opening Prayer: *Father, your love gave the saints Perpetua and Felicity courage to suffer a cruel martyrdom. By their prayers, help us to grow in love of you.*

March 8
ST. JOHN OF GOD (1495-1550)

HISTORICO-LITURGICAL NOTE

John of God is so called, it is said, because the people did not know his real name. He was born in Portugal, and until the age of 40 he lived an adventurous life: a soldier who fought against the Turks in the defense of Vienna, a shepherd in Spain, a manual laborer in North Africa, and finally a seller of religious articles in Granada, Spain. It was in Granada that he was converted after listening to a sermon by the famous preacher, St. John of Avila. John then began to roam the streets in an abstracted manner, sometimes shouting and beating his breast. As a result of this strange behavior he was confined to an asylum for the insane. Through the intervention of St. John of Avila he was pacified and released.

Having witnessed the harsh treatment given to the inmates of the asylum, John decided to found a hospital in which he could care for the sick and wretched. With two companions he laid the foundation of what eventually became the religious institute of Brothers Hospitalers (known in Italy as Fatebenefratelli since the days of Pope Sixtus V). However, the rules governing the institute were not written until 6 years after the death of St. John of God, and the members did not take religious vows until 20 years after his death. He was canonized in 1690, and in 1886 Pope Leo XIII named him patron of hospitals and the sick, together with St. Camillus de Lellis. In 1930 Pope Pius XI placed all nurses under his patronage.

MESSAGE AND RELEVANCE

The Opening Prayer of the Mass mentions St. John's apostolate of charity: "Father, you gave John of God love and compassion for others." His apostolate to the sick and suffering is described in the Office of Readings in the words of St. John himself: "If we look forward to receiving God's mercy, we can never fail to do good so long as we have the strength. For if we share with the poor, out of love for God, whatever he has given to us, we shall receive, according to his promise, a hundredfold in eternal happiness. . . . Whenever I see so many poor brothers and neighbors of mine suffering beyond their strength and overwhelmed with so many physical or mental ills which I cannot alleviate, then I become exceedingly sorrowful; but I trust in Christ, who knows my heart." Today we are also invited to practice charity "by doing good for others."

St. John of God is a precursor of modern methods of mental therapy and the care of the sick. He endeavored first of all to heal the mind and spirit before treating the physical symptoms of the body. He also separated persons suffering from infectious diseases from the other patients. His loving care was always directed to the individual and prudently adapted to the needs of each one. This type of universal and individualized charity reminds us today of the primacy of the individual person, who is often overlooked in institutional care. Moreover, in serving our needy brothers and sisters we should always see in them the face of Christ.

> Opening Prayer: *Father, you gave John of God love and compassion for others. Grant that by doing good for others we may be counted among the saints in your kingdom.*

March 9
ST. FRANCES OF ROME (1384-1440)

HISTORICO-LITURGICAL NOTE

Francesca Busso was born in Rome in 1384 of a noble family and at the age of 13 was married to Lorenzo Ponziani. They had three children, Evangelista, Battista and Agnes. Since the family was well off financially, Frances was able to perform many works of charity, especially during the time of famine and the plague. She also helped the poor and needy when Ladislaus of Naples invaded Rome and took the anti-pope John XXIII prisoner. Her husband was commander of the pontifical troops and was wounded in battle. Frances courageously endured the subsequent disability of her husband and the loss of two of her children to the plague. In order the better to provide for the various almshouses, she founded the Olivetan Oblates of Santa Maria Nuova. Following the death of her husband in 1436, after 40 years of marriage, she entered the religious congregation she had helped to found and she eventually became superior. During her life she was given the grace of contemplative prayer and received numerous extraordinary mystical gifts as well. She died while reciting the Office of the

Blessed Virgin on March 9, 1440. After her canonization in 1608, the church of Santa Maria Nuova was named St. Frances of Rome. The bull of her canonization states that by her prayers and sufferings she helped bring the Western Schism (1378-1449) as well as the residence of the popes at Avignon, France to an end.

MESSAGE AND RELEVANCE

The Opening Prayer describes St. Frances of Rome as "a unique example of love in marriage as well as in religious life." In a city plagued with moral decadence, the example of this wife and mother aroused admiration, wonderment and some criticism as well. Beneath the costly dresses that her social condition required, she wore rough undergarments and sackcloth. She dedicated herself generously to the education of her children.

Today also one can reconcile the duties of family life with an intense ascetical life if one imitates her example of patience and constancy. This is what we ask for in the petition of this prayer: "Help us to see and follow you in all the aspects of life." That St. Frances achieved this in her own life is noted in the biography written by the superior of the Oblates: "No one ever observed in her a tendency toward impatience. She never exhibited any displeasure when she complied with an order, no matter how foolish" (Office of Readings).

What should be noted especially in the life of St. Frances of Rome is the harmonious fusion of married life with asceticism and a lofty mysticism. At a time when daily Communion was not permitted, and especially not for married persons, a priest once marvelled that she was receiving Communion several times a week (with permission of her confessor). Her life as an Oblate was simply a prolongation of the practice of virtue that had characterized her married life. But it is especially as a wife and mother who practiced heroic virtue that she is a model and exemplar for all married people.

Opening Prayer: *Merciful Father, in Frances of Rome you have given us a unique example of love in marriage as well as in religious life. Keep us faithful in your service, and help us to see and follow you in all the aspects of life.*

March 17
ST. PATRICK (385-461)

HISTORICO-LITURGICAL NOTE

The Apostle of Ireland was born in Britain, possibly in Wales, the son of Calpurnius Sucatus, a municipal official. At the age of sixteen he was kidnapped by pirates and sold into slavery in Ireland, where he was assigned to the care of the flock as a shepherd. There also he learned the Celtic language and was converted to the Catholic faith. Later he fled to France, where he became a disciple of St. Germain of Auxerre and visited the monastery on the isle of Lerins, near Cannes (412-415).

Returning to Auxerre, where he spent the next 15 years, Patrick was ordained a priest. Some time thereafter Pope Celestine I sent Palladius as a missionary to Ireland, but he died there within a year. Consequently, St. Germain ordained Patrick bishop so that he could pick up the work started by Palladius. Patrick arrived in Ireland in 432. He converted some of the indigenous chieftains and was very successful in adapting the gospel to the Irish culture. Ireland is the only country in western Europe in which the Church was established without martyrdom.

A few years before his death, Patrick convoked a synod and turned over the government of the church in Ireland to other bishops. It is not true, however, that he spent the last years of his life as abbot in the monastery at Glastonbury. It is believed that he died on March 17, 461, and was buried at Saul on Strangford Lough, where he had built his first church. Although he was venerated in Ireland and England for many centuries, his feast was not listed in the Roman Calendar until 1632.

MESSAGE AND RELEVANCE

The first part of the Opening Prayer of the Mass is new; it states that God sent St. Patrick to preach the gospel to the people of Ireland. Patrick had always considered that mission as a great gift from God. In his *Confession*, which was written to defend himself against calumny and false accusations, he says: "How did so great and salutary a gift come to me, the gift of knowing and loving God, though at the cost of homeland and family? I came to the Irish peoples to preach the gospel and endure the taunts of unbelievers, putting up with reproaches about my earthly pilgrimage, suffering many persecutions, even bondage, and losing my birthright of freedom, for the benefit of others" (Office of Readings).

In the second part of the Opening Prayer we ask that all Christians may proclaim God's love to all men. The Italian version also asks that we may rediscover the missionary aspect of the faith, and the Latin text asks "that we may glory in the name Christian." Some persons are not sufficiently conscious of this if they come from nations that have been Christian for many centuries. Like St. Patrick, we should be grateful for our Christian heritage and strive to share with others the joy of our faith.

Opening Prayer: *God our Father, you sent St. Patrick to preach your glory to the people of Ireland. By the help of his prayers, may all Christians proclaim your love to all men.*

Alternate Opening Prayer: *Father in heaven, you sent the great bishop Patrick to the people of Ireland to*

share his faith and to spend his life in loving service.
May our lives bear witness to the faith we profess and
our love bring others to the peace and joy of your gospel.

March 18
ST. CYRIL OF JERUSALEM (313/15-386/7)

HISTORICO-LITURGICAL NOTE

This great bishop was born in Jerusalem and after receiving a Christian education he was ordained a priest and dedicated himself to the preparation of catechumens for baptism. He became well known through the publication of his 24 catechetical lessons, which were taken down by a secretary. They are also the basis for his being named Doctor of the Church by Pope Leo XIII.

As bishop of Jerusalem he had a primacy of honor over the other bishops, but he came into conflict with the Arian bishop, Acacius of Caesarea, and was exiled from Jerusalem. The same thing happened twice more, as the bitter conflict continued, but Cyril finally was reinstated and spent the last 8 years of his life as primate of Jerusalem. In 381 he took part in the Second Ecumenical Council of Constantinople, which recognized the legitimacy of his office and promulgated the official version of the Nicene Creed. He signed the document condemning the semi-Arians and the Macedonians, who denied the divinity of Christ and the Holy Spirit. St. Cyril died at Jerusalem after more than 35 years as a bishop, of which 16 were spent in exile. His feast is assigned to March 18 in the Eastern Calendar of saints and in the Armenian Lectionary of the fifth century.

MESSAGE AND RELEVANCE

The new Opening Prayer of the Mass contains two themes. The first refers to Cyril as a teacher and author who led the Church to "a deeper understanding of the mysteries of salvation." An example of his teaching is found in the Office of Readings, where he speaks of the seal of the Holy Spirit that will be impressed on the souls of the catechumens at their baptism. This is a good example of Cyril's catechesis, which is more detailed than the Nicene Creed recited in the liturgy. It is the type of catechesis proposed by the Second Vatican Council: "The Church, therefore, earnestly desires that Christ's faithful, when present at this mystery of faith, should not be there as strangers or silent spectators. On the contrary, through a good understanding of the rites and prayers they should take part in the sacred action, conscious of what they are doing, with devotion and full collaboration" (*Sacrosanctum Concilium*, no. 48).

In the second part of the Opening Prayer reference is made to the orthodox teaching of St. Cyril, who tempered his love of truth with the law of charity. He was, as Theodoret said, a "zealous defender of doctrine," and St. Cyril himself had said: "Error has many forms but truth has only one face."

The late date of St. Cyril's cult at Rome (under Pope Leo XIII in 1882) is due to the uncertainty about the orthodoxy of some of his doctrine. In defending the faith of the Council of Nicea, he seems to have avoided the expression "consubstantial with the Father" (*homoousios*) in referring to the Son, preferring the semi-Arian term "similar to the Father." But in a letter written to Pope Damasus in 382, the Fathers of the Council of Constantinople supported "the venerable and devout" Cyril because he had in various places engaged in numerous combats against the Arians. We could apply to him the statement made by St. Athanasius, who said that some of those who disagree "mean what we mean but differ only about the terminology." Cyril's motto is still relevant for us today: "The Christian is a bearer of Christ."

Opening Prayer: *Father, through Cyril of Jerusalem you led your Church to a deeper understanding of the mysteries of salvation. Let his prayers help us to know your Son better and to have eternal life in all its fullness.*

March 19
ST. JOSEPH,
Spouse of the Blessed Virgin Mary

HISTORICO-LITURGICAL NOTE

The feast of St. Joseph on March 19, which appears around the year 800 in a French Calendar, did not become widespread until the fourteenth or fifteenth century. There was a feast in honor of St. Joseph in the Roman Breviary published in 1482, but the first Mass celebrated in his honor at Rome was in 1505. Certain saints and spiritual writers were especially devoted to St. Joseph: St. Margaret of Cortona, St. Bridget of Sweden, St. Vincent Ferrer, St. Bernardine of Siena and John Gerson of Paris. Finally, the Carmelite friars recognized his feast and included it in the calendar of their Order in 1498. In the East, however, the feast was celebrated as early as the fifth century according to the Coptic Calendar, but on a different date. In 1621 Pope Gregory XV made the feast of St. Joseph a holy day of obligation, but that is no longer universally observed. Moreover, the feast may be transferred out of Lent if a National Bishops' Conference so desires.

The genealogy of St. Joseph is given in the gospels of St. Matthew and St. Luke. We also know from the gospel that he was a carpenter, and very likely Jesus learned that trade from his foster-father. Joseph and Mary were poor, as is evidenced by the fact that at Mary's purification in the Temple they offered a pair of turtle-doves. The tribute paid to him in Scripture is that he was a just man. On several crucial occasions, such as Mary's pregnancy, the flight into Egypt and the return to Palestine, Joseph was instructed by an angel. Pope Pius IX proclaimed St. Joseph the patron of the Universal Church.

MESSAGE AND RELEVANCE

The wealth of material in the prayers of the Mass and in the Office of Readings provides a variety of themes that can be synthesized as follows.

The Opening Prayer of the Mass states that the Father entrusted our Savior to the care of St. Joseph. In this statement we have the first theme, namely, the fidelity of St. Joseph in fulfilling his role as spouse of Mary and foster-father of Jesus. He supported them by his daily work as a carpenter and was their protector during the flight into Egypt and their return to Palestine. The Preface for the feast refers to St. Joseph in this context: "He is that just man, that wise and loyal servant, whom you placed at the head of your family."

The second theme pertains to St. Joseph's role as the foster-father of Jesus. Again, we read in the Preface: "With fatherly care he watched over Jesus Christ your Son, conceived by the power of the Holy Spirit." The second responsory in the Office of Readings quotes the text from Genesis 45:8, which refers to Joseph of the Old Testament: "God has made me father to the king and master of all his household." Then, in the Office of Readings we have an excerpt from a sermon by the Franciscan St. Bernardine of Siena who, together with John Gerson of Paris, was a principal promoter of devotion to St. Joseph. "In him the Old Testament finds its fitting close. He brought the noble line of patriarchs and prophets to its promised fulfillment. What the divine goodness had offered as a promise to them, he held in his arms."

The third theme refers to St. Joseph's prompt obedience, springing from a faith that was truly extraordinary, since the events that were unfolding were contrary to all the messianic expectations. We have no record of any words spoken by St.

Joseph. St. Matthew tells us in his gospel only that "Joseph did as the angel of the Lord directed him" (1:24). At the Annunciation, Mary conversed with the angel; the silent obedience of Joseph is more eloquent than words.

A fourth theme for this feast pertains to the relationship between Joseph and Mary. The phrase coined by St. Bernard, *Omnia per Mariam* (All through Mary), applies to St. Joseph as much as to all the faithful. As he became the head of the Holy Family and foster-father of Jesus through Mary, it is also through her and second to her that he is the guardian of the Mystical Body of Christ and universal patron of the Church.

Finally, in accordance with a long-standing tradition of popular devotion, St. Joseph is venerated as the patron of a happy death. Thus, the hymn for Evening Prayer I of the Liturgy of the Hours asks him to "direct our way to heaven. St. Joseph, be our guide!"

In the Prayer over the Gifts we proclaim: "With unselfish love St. Joseph cared for your Son." We then ask: "May we also serve you at your altar with pure hearts." St. Joseph's unselfish love was especially manifested in the promptness of his obedience to the instructions from the angel: "Joseph got up and took the child and his mother and left that night for Egypt" (Mt 2:14); "He got up, took the child and his mother, and returned to the land of Israel" (Mt 2:21).

In the Prayer after Communion two phrases are especially noteworthy: "Protect your Church always and in your love watch over the gifts you have given us." Joseph was the guardian of Christ and his Virgin Mother, the two greatest gifts that God has given to his Church. As universal patron of the Church he exercises a spiritual fatherhood in relation to all the faithful. We are also called upon to be guardians and protectors of the sacred realities because of a mission we have received from God through our baptism.

> Preface: *Father, all-powerful and ever-living God, we do well always and everywhere to give you thanks, as we honor St. Joseph. He is that just man, that wise and loyal servant, whom you placed at the head of your*

family. With a husband's love he cherished Mary, the virgin Mother of God. With fatherly care he watched over Jesus Christ, your Son, conceived by the power of the Holy Spirit. Through Christ the choirs of angels and all the powers of heaven praise and worship your glory.

March 23

ST. TURIBIUS OF MONGROVEJO (1538-1606)

HISTORICO-LITURGICAL NOTE

Turibius Alfonso was born in Leon, Spain, studied law at the University of Salamanca, and became a professor there. He was so brilliant that he attracted the attention of King Philip II, who named him chief judge in the court of the Inquisition. When the archbishopric of Lima, Peru, became vacant, Turibius, though a layman, was named to that post. He received all the holy orders and sailed for Peru in 1580. The archdiocese extended from Panama to Argentina and the new archbishop worked assiduously for the formation of the clergy and the moral uplifting of the people. He died while on a pastoral visitation in an Indian village and was canonized in 1726. Four other saints lived in Lima under the jurisdiction of St. Turibius: St. Rose of Lima, St. Martin de Porres, St. John Macias (all Dominicans) and the Franciscan St. Francis Solano.

MESSAGE AND RELEVANCE

The Opening Prayer of the Mass expounds two themes, of which the first is the indefatigable apostolic zeal of the saintly archbishop. The scandals of the time made his work much more difficult, as did the resistance on the part of the colonial government and some religious orders. He was criticized for being away from Lima on pastoral visitations, and when he tried to correct abuses, he was told that the established customs had the force of law. His response was: "Christ called himself the truth, not custom." Hence the second theme in the Opening Prayer is "his unwavering love of truth."

The petition of the Opening Prayer is that the People of God may "continue to grow in faith and holiness." Thanks to numerous councils and synods, St. Turibius was able to restore in great part the authentic ecclesiastical discipline. Pope Benedict XIV compared him to St. Charles Borromeo because of his dedication to his flock and his efforts to help them grow in faith and holiness.

The Office of Readings presents an excerpt from the decree of Vatican Council II on the pastoral office of bishops. It lists the characteristics of good evangelization: clarity of doctrine, gentleness in dialogue, prudence in action, unlimited trust and a special love for the poor and needy. All of these qualities were manifested in St. Turibius to an eminent degree, both in his dealings with the Spanish colonists and the native Indians.

Opening Prayer: *Lord, through the apostolic work of St. Turibius and his unwavering love of truth, you helped your Church to grow. May your chosen people continue to grow in faith and holiness.*

APRIL

ST. FRANCIS OF PAOLA (1436-1507)

HISTORICO-LITURGICAL NOTE

Born in Calabria, Italy, Francis entered the Franciscan Order at the age of 13 because of a vow his parents had made to St. Francis of Assisi. Two years later he retired to the life of a hermit. In due time he attracted followers who shared his ascetical fervor and later he founded the Order of Hermits of St. Francis of Assisi (1456). Later the name was changed to the Order of Minims (little ones) and was approved by the Holy See in 1506.

The observances of the Minims were stricter than those of any other religious order at the time, for they not only observed a perpetual fast, but they abstained from eggs and milk as well as meat. Impressed by Francis' fame as a wonder-worker and a man of extraordinary spiritual gifts, Pope Sixtus IV sent him to France to serve at the court of King Louis XI. After the death of the king, Francis remained as spiritual director of Charles VIII and to serve King Louis XII. Because of his influence at court, he was also successful as a peacemaker. St. Francis spent 25 years in France, founding numerous monasteries, and he died there on Good Friday, 1507. He was canonized in 1519 and named patron of seafarers in 1943.

MESSAGE AND RELEVANCE

The Opening Prayer of the Mass begins with an invocation that refers to the charism of this holy founder who, out of humility, never advanced to the priesthood: "Father of the lowly, you raised St. Francis of Paola to the glory of your saints." The petition of the prayer is that we may "come to the rewards you have promised the humble."

The life of this miracle-working and austere hermit, who vowed to observe the Lenten fast throughout the entire year, was something truly extraordinary in a society that was so averse to any ascetical practices. His example is significant for us in the light of St. Paul's statement that summarizes the spirituality of St. Francis of Paola: "The love of Christ impels us" (2 Cor 5:14). His rigorous austerity was sustained by his meditation on the passion and death of Christ. This is evident in the letter he wrote to the procurator of the hermitage at Cosenza, Italy: "Fix your minds, then, on the passion of our Lord Jesus Christ. Inflamed with love for us, he came down from heaven to redeem us. For our sake he endured every torment of body and soul and shrank from no bodily pain. He himself gave us an example of perfect patience and love."

We could say that humility was the outstanding virtue practiced by St. Francis of Paola; it was humility that caused him to refuse to be ordained a priest. True humility is difficult to attain, and especially for us today, but it is nevertheless true that our greatness in the eyes of God and men consists in the recognition of our littleness. We can make his deathbed prayer our own: "Beloved Jesus, preserve the just; justify sinners; have compassion on all the faithful, living and dead; be merciful to me, although I am nothing more than an unworthy sinner."

Opening Prayer: *Father of the lowly, you raised St. Francis of Paola to the glory of your saints. By his example and prayers, may we come to the rewards you have promised the humble.*

April 4
ST. ISIDORE (556-636)

HISTORICO-LITURGICAL NOTE

This saintly bishop of Seville, Spain, was from a noble family that was probably of Roman origin. Two of his brothers, Leander and Fulgentius, are saints, as is his sister Florentina. It is almost certain that Isidore never became a monk, although he had a great respect for the monastic life and composed a rule that was observed throughout Spain. He followed his brother Leander as bishop of Seville and during his forty years as bishop he succeeded in converting the Visigoths from Arianism to Catholicism. An outstanding educator, he founded an institute at Seville for the formation of the clergy and the laity and was its first master. The school became famous throughout Spain, and the Fourth Council of Toledo (633) made it mandatory to establish similar schools. These centers of learning were the forerunners of the famous universities.

Isidore was a prodigious writer and an erudite scholar of the literature of the Eastern Church. He was a great admirer of Origen and among his works the two most significant ones are *History of the Goths* and the *Book of Etymologies*. The latter work was greatly appreciated in the Middle Ages as an encyclopedia of all human knowledge. He completed the composition of the Mozarabic Missal and Breviary that had been started by his brother Leander. The Mozarabic liturgy is still in use in Toledo, Spain. This great scholar and educator ranks on a par with St. Gregory the Great, Cassiodorus and Boethius. He was named a Doctor of the Church in 1722 and his name is included in the Canon of the Mass in the Mozarabic rite.

MESSAGE AND RELEVANCE

The Opening Prayer of the Mass is somewhat general, perhaps because it was so difficult to characterize the spirituality of a man who is remembered especially for his encyclopedic knowledge of theology, canon law and liturgy, as well as his role as counselor to princes and kings. In fact, the text of the Opening Prayer asks that the Church may "learn from his teaching." The relevance of this Doctor of the Church, who has been called the "Schoolmaster of the Middle Ages," is found not so much in his extensive knowledge as in his commentaries on Sacred Scripture.

In the Office of Readings there is an excerpt from St. Isidore's *Book of Sentences*, which treats of dogmatic and moral theology. His advice is still applicable to our post-Vatican II age: "Reading the Holy Scriptures confers two benefits. It trains the mind to understand them; it turns man's attention from the follies of this world and leads him to the love of God. Two kinds of study are called for here. We must first learn how the Scriptures are to be understood, and then see how to expound them with profit and in a manner worthy of them. A man must first be eager to understand what he is reading before he is fit to proclaim what he has learned. The conscientious reader will be more concerned to carry out what he has read than merely to acquire knowledge of it."

> Opening Prayer: *Lord, hear the prayers we offer in commemoration of St. Isidore. May your Church learn from his teaching and benefit from his intercession.*

April 5
ST. VINCENT FERRER (1350-1419)

HISTORICO-LITURGICAL NOTE

The zealous Dominican preacher, Vincent Ferrer, lived in one of the most turbulent periods in the history of the Church. It was the time of the Western Schism and the residence of the pope at Avignon, France. Vincent was born at

Valencia, Spain. He entered the Dominican Order at the age of 15 and was ordained a priest in 1378. All his life he felt that he was called to carry the gospel not only to Christians but also to the Jews, the Muslims and the heretical sects of the Cathari and Waldensians. In 1390 Vincent became the official theologian for the papal legate, Cardinal Peter de Luna, and accompanied him on trips throughout Spain. When the cardinal became pope, taking the name of Benedict XIII, he called Vincent to Avignon as confessor. Vincent naturally supported this pope and persuaded the courts in France, Aragon and Castile to do likewise. Later, when he saw the stubborn resistance of the pope in perpetuating the Schism, he changed his mind and announced that the kings of Aragon, Castile and Navarre should refuse to obey the pope at Avignon.

St. Vincent preached not only in Spain and France but also in Italy, Switzerland and the Netherlands. He is reputed to have received the gift of tongues and was renowned as a healer. During a preaching mission at Lyons, France, in 1404 he organized the large number of people who accepted his teaching and followed him wherever he preached. They were called the *flagellantes* or penitents. They dressed in the black and white colors of the Dominican habit and carried the staff of a pilgrim.

The high point of St. Vincent's preaching mission was between the years 1412 and 1419. He died at Vannes, France, while on a preaching mission in which he tried to put an end to the Hundred Years War between France and England. He was canonized in 1455 and is highly venerated to this day not only in Spain and Latin America but also in the Philippines.

MESSAGE AND RELEVANCE

The Opening Prayer of the Mass states that God "called St. Vincent Ferrer to preach the gospel of the last judgment." He urged his hearers to perform acts of repentance in view of the final days, a practice that is still relevant today. Vincent called himself Christ's legate and he believed that the Blessed Virgin had obtained from her divine Son the assurance that the world would exist until the mission of St. Dominic and St. Francis of Assisi would be completed. He felt that in view of the increasing corruption of morals and the large number of conversions yet to be made, God had given him the special vocation and mission to preach on the four last things. Many persons considered him a second John the Baptist, preaching penance unto conversion.

St. Vincent's sermons on the coming of the Angel of the Apocalypse made a strong impression in those days of schism and moral decadence. In fact, up to the present time the artists in Spain portray St. Vincent with the wings of the Angel of the Apocalypse. His preaching was accompanied by numerous miracles and prophecies.

The petition in the Evening Prayer of the Dominican Liturgy of the Hours retains the eschatological note. We ask that we shall see reigning in heaven him whom Vincent preached as the judge who is to come.

The Office of Readings is taken from St. Vincent's *Treatise on the Spiritual Life* and it contains his advice on preaching and hearing confessions. His counsel is still applicable, especially the following statements: "Each sinner in your congregation should feel moved as though you were preaching to him alone. Your words should sound as if they were coming, not from a proud or angry soul, but from a charitable and loving heart. . . . This way of preaching has proven profitable to congregations, for an abstract discourse on the virtues and vices hardly inspires those who listen."

Opening Prayer: *Father, you called St. Vincent Ferrer to preach the gospel of the last judgment. Through his prayers may we come with joy to meet your Son in the kingdom of heaven, where he lives and reigns with you and the Holy Spirit, one God for ever and ever.*

April 7
ST. JOHN BAPTIST DE LA SALLE
(1651-1719)

HISTORICO-LITURGICAL NOTE

John Baptist de la Salle was born in 1651 at Rheims in France and belongs to what is known as the French school of spirituality. He studied at the major seminary in that city and was ordained to the priesthood in 1678. He was at first a canon but renounced that office in order to dedicate himself to the education of poor youth. Out of this grew the Congregation of the Brothers of the Christian Schools, popularly known as the Christian Brothers. In 1684 his first twelve followers made temporary profession and placed the Congregation under the special patronage of the Blessed Virgin Mary. However, in 1700 the first difficulties arose in regard to the teaching methods introduced by the founder. For example, those who charged tuition in their schools were opposed to the free schools founded by John Baptist de la Salle. Moreover, the Sulpicians reacted coldly to him because John Baptist did away with outdated traditional methods of teaching and insisted on the use of French rather than Latin. Although his original intention was to conduct only free schools for poor youth, in 1698, at the request of King James II of England, he opened the first school for boys of the aristocracy. The Congregation and its work prospered in spite of numerous trials and difficulties. St. John Baptist resigned as superior in 1717 and dedicated himself to the instruction of novices and the publication of some books, including a method of mental prayer. He died on Good Friday of 1719, was canonized in 1900, and declared patron of teachers by Pope Pius XII in 1950.

MESSAGE AND RELEVANCE

The Opening Prayer speaks of this saint as one chosen by God "to give young people a Christian education." The apostolic work of this aristocratic priest inspired teachers to dedicate themselves entirely to the work of teaching. His truly paternal spirit was born of his love of Christ and enabled him to overcome many of the barriers that separated the various social classes in his day. His pedagogical methods led to the establishment of institutes of study for graduates, the organization of Sunday classes, and trade schools for students from ages 7 to 20.

The Office of Readings contains a meditation composed by St. John Baptist de la Salle. After stating with St. Paul that there is a variety of ministries but the same Holy Spirit, he continues: "Therefore you should not doubt that you have been given the same kind of grace to teach boys, to instruct them in the gospel, and to form them in religion. . . . In your teaching, the boys in your charge must see by the way you teach that you are true ministers of God, full of true charity and sincere in carrying out your task. . . . Let your students be moved by your untiring care for them and feel as though God were encouraging them through you, because you perform your duties as ambassadors of Christ."

John Baptist was humiliated by his own disciples, who criticized him for being too much committed to students from the lower classes, and by the aristocrats, who accused him of dishonoring his status as a canon. He often encountered open hostility from some of the clergy and insubordination from some of the Brothers of the Congregation. In spite of all of these trials, the saintly educator could say on his deathbed: "I adore God's manner of acting in all things in my regard."

Opening Prayer: *"Father, you chose St. John Baptist de la Salle to give young people a Christian education. Give your Church teachers who will devote themselves to helping your children grow as Christian men and women."*

April 11
ST. STANISLAUS (1030-1079)

HISTORICO-LITURGICAL NOTE

Born in the outskirts of Cracow, Poland, of parents advanced in age, Stanislaus was ordained to the priesthood after studying in Paris and designated as a canon and preacher. In 1072, much against his will, he was ordained bishop of Cracow. He ruled as a good shepherd, having a special concern for the poor and making frequent pastoral visitations of the clergy. The king of Poland at the time was Boleslaus II, a courageous man who won a glorious victory against the Russians at Kiev, but was morally corrupt and unfaithful. Like another John the Baptist, Stanislaus rebuked him and even reached the point of excommunicating him. As a result, Boleslaus ordered the bishop's assassination, but when the soldiers failed three times to carry out the order, the king himself killed Stanislaus as he was celebrating Mass on April 11, 1079. He was buried in the church of St. Michael in Kalka and was canonized by Pope Innocent IV in 1253. Stanislaus is the first Polish saint to be officially recognized as a martyr.

MESSAGE AND RELEVANCE

The Opening Prayer of the Mass states that St. Stanislaus "faced martyrdom with courage." He also had the courage to condemn the public scandal of a king who had kidnapped a beautiful married woman and lodged her in his palace. In doing so, Stanislaus acted like another John the Baptist and he suffered the same fate. Eventually the king fell from power and went into exile in Hungary. He later became a lay brother in the Benedictine monastery at Osjak, where he is buried.

In the petition of the Opening Prayer we ask God to "keep us strong and loyal in our faith until death." Perseverance in the faith is also the theme of the excerpt from a letter of St.

Cyprian in the Office of Readings. It can be read with direct reference to St. Stanislaus, who fought the good fight and received a martyr's crown. St. Cyprian also refers to the Eucharist, which sustains the courage of the martyr. This concept of the Eucharist, not only as the nourishment of the spiritual life, but as a source of courage in professing the faith, should be used in catechesis today.

> Opening Prayer: *Father, to honor you, St. Stanislaus faced martyrdom with courage. Keep us strong and loyal in our faith until death.*

April 13
ST. MARTIN I (+655)

HISTORICO-LITURGICAL NOTE

According to a biography written in Greek and the date given in the Byzantine Calendar, St. Martin I died at Kherson in the Crimea on April 13, 655. Born in Umbria, Italy, he became pope in 649, after serving in Constantinople. Shortly after his election as pope, he called a Council at the Lateran in Rome in order to condemn the heretics who denied that Christ had a human will. The same Council condemned a document promulgated by the emperor Constans II. Infuriated, he sent emissaries to kidnap the pope and take him back to Constantinople. On arrival Martin was thrown into prison and, though seriously ill, was later exiled to the Crimea. The emperor had actually condemned Pope Martin I to death, but his life was spared through the intervention of Paul, Patriarch of Constantinople. Since he had been condemned to death and spent the last few years of his life in such misery and want, he is venerated as a martyr. He is, in fact, the last pope to be honored as a martyr.

MESSAGE AND RELEVANCE

In the Opening Prayer of the Mass, taken from the Paris Missal of 1738, we ask that "through our faith" God will give us "the courage to endure whatever sufferings the world may inflict upon us." In the Office of Readings there is an excerpt from several of the letters written by St. Martin I to a friend in Constantinople. The pope groans under the weight of his affliction to the point of saying: "Behold, we are deprived of our very life." He then adds: "But God wishes all men to be saved and to come to a knowledge of the truth through the prayers of Peter. Hence I pray that God will strengthen their hearts in the orthodox faith, help them to stand firm against every heretic and enemy of the Church, and guard them unshaken."

The people in the Crimea were pagans, and the Christians who lived there had taken on pagan ways. St. Martin says: "Indeed, I have been amazed and continue to be amazed at the lack of perception and the callousness of those who were once connected with me, both my friends and my relatives. They have all completely forgotten about my unhappy state, and do not care to know where I am, whether I am alive or dead." This constituted the moral martyrdom suffered by Pope Martin I and it is still relevant in some parts of the world today. The example of his steadfast courage can be an inspiration to all: "Even if they cut me into pieces, I can never accept union with the Church of Constantinople."

Opening Prayer: *Merciful God, our Father, neither hardship, pain, nor the threat of death could weaken the faith of St. Martin. Through our faith, give us courage to endure whatever sufferings the world may inflict upon us.*

April 21
ST. ANSELM (1033-1109)

HISTORICO-LITURGICAL NOTE

St. Anselm, a Benedictine monk who became a bishop, was declared a Doctor of the Church in 1720 and has been called "the Father of Scholasticism." Born in Piedmont, Italy, he first entered the Benedictine monastery at Aosta, Italy, but under pressure from his father he had to leave the monastic life. After an unsettled period, the youth fled to France and entered the Benedictine monastery at Bec (1059), where he eventually became abbot and gained renown as a preacher and a reformer of the monastic life. During this period he wrote his best theological works, which exerted a powerful influence and established him as a theological master in the late Middle Ages. Eventually he became archbishop of Canterbury in England and was involved in the struggle over lay investiture with King William II, who refused to recognize Pope Urban II. Twice Anselm went into exile (1097 and 1103) but finally he was able to return to his see, where he died on April 21, 1109.

MESSAGE AND RELEVANCE

The Opening Prayer of the Mass presents the characteristic traits of the spirituality of St. Anselm: "to study and teach the sublime truths" of revelation. His definition of theology was "faith seeking understanding." He contributed greatly to the development of systematic theology but always with an emphasis on the contemplative and spiritual dimension. St. Anselm's theological heritage became the patrimony of Scholasticism. We should note the primacy that Anselm gives to wisdom in the study and teaching of theology, which is the point of greatest convergence between St. Anselm and St. Thomas Aquinas.

The excerpt from the *Proslogion* in the Office of Readings is an example of the manner in which St. Anselm did theology. For him it was not mere intellectual research or logical deduction from principles. "My soul," he asks, "have you found what you are looking for? You were looking for God, and you have discovered that he is the supreme being, and that you could not possibly imagine anything more perfect. You have discovered that this supreme being is life itself, light, wisdom, goodness, eternal blessedness and blessed eternity. He is everywhere and he is timeless." His other works include a treatise entitled *Cur Deus Homo?*, a marvelous theological investigation of the Incarnation. He also defended the orthodox doctrine on the *Filioque* when he attended the Council of Bari (Italy) in 1102.

Today also we should strive for a deeper understanding of our faith so that we can love the truth we have studied, as is stated in the Opening Prayer: "Let your gift of faith come to the aid of our understanding and open our hearts to your truth." The famous axiom, *Credo ut intelligam* (I believe in order that I may understand) reminds us that we should be guided by the light of faith and not by the light of reason alone. Otherwise, if we rely too much on human knowledge, there is a danger of weakening our faith.

> Opening Prayer: *Father, you called St. Anselm to study and teach the sublime truths you have revealed. Let your gift of faith come to the aid of our understanding and open our hearts to your truth.*

April 23
ST. GEORGE (+303?)

HISTORICO-LITURGICAL NOTE

The Greek Church venerates St. George as the greatest of the martyrs and his feast is also celebrated on this day in the

Byzantine Church. In the middle of the fourth century a church was constructed over his tomb at Lydda, Palestine, where he suffered martyrdom. The account of his death was judged to be apocryphal by the Gelasian Decree in the sixth century and was placed on the Index of forbidden books; nevertheless, Pope Leo II (683) dedicated a basilica in his honor at Velabro, Italy, and the feast of St. George was celebrated at Rome.

Legend states that St. George was born at Cappadocia and instructed in the Christian religion by his mother. He became a soldier in the Roman army and confronted Diocletian, the cruel persecutor of Christians. As a result, George was handed over to the torturers, who tried every means to put him to death. He was beaten with clubs, tortured with red-hot irons, given poison to drink, crushed between two spiked wheels, thrown into a caldron of molten lead, but came through all the tortures unscathed. Then, pretending that he was willing to offer sacrifice to the idols, when all the people had assembled, George prayed, and fire coming down from heaven killed all the pagan priests and people. In the end, St. George was beheaded. So much for the legend.

There is every reason to believe that St. George was a martyr and it is possible that his cult was propagated in Europe by the crusaders, who considered him their patron. He was venerated not only in Georgia (which bears his name), but also in Spain, Portugal, Italy, Lithuania and England. He was named patron of England in 1222 during the reign of Henry III and was proclaimed protector of the kingdom by Pope Benedict XIV. Until 1778 the feast of St. George was a holy day of obligation for English Catholics. In iconography, St. George is portrayed as the conqueror of the dragon.

MESSAGE AND RELEVANCE

The Opening Prayer of the Mass, which is derived from the ancient Gelasian Sacramentary, recalls that "St. George was ready to follow Christ in suffering and in death." The Latin version states that he was an "imitator of the Lord's passion," because the feast falls in the Easter season. Moreover, Vatican Council II states in the document on the liturgy that we should always celebrate the paschal mystery of Christ on the feasts of the saints (*Sacrosanctum Concilium*, no. 104).

The extract from the sermon of St. Peter Damian in the Office of Readings harmonizes very well with the petition in the Latin version of the Opening Prayer of the Mass: "Make your power shine on us and sustain us in our weakness." The same sentiment is expressed in the Preface for a martyr: "His (her) death reveals your power shining through our human weakness." St. Peter Damian says: "Dear brothers, our joy in today's feast is heightened by our joy in the glory of Easter. . . . Anyone who wishes to offer himself to God in the tent of Christ, which is the Church, must first bathe in the spring of holy baptism; then he must put on the various garments of the virtues. . . . Truly, we must be cleansed of the stains of our past sins and be resplendent in the virtue of our new way of life. Then we can be confident of celebrating Easter worthily and of truly following the example of the blessed martyrs."

> Opening Prayer: *Lord, hear the prayers of those who praise your mighty power. As St. George was ready to follow Christ in suffering and death, so may he be ready to help us in our weakness.*

April 24
ST. FIDELIS OF SIGMARINGEN (1578-1622)

HISTORICO-LITURGICAL NOTE

Born in Sigmaringen, Germany, Mark Roy studied at Freiburg-im-Breisgau and received doctorates in law and in philosophy. After practicing law at Colmar, he entered the Capuchin Order and received the name of Fidelis. He dedicated himself to preaching and ministering to the Austrian troops. Then he was appointed by the Propagation of the Faith to a preaching ministry among the Protestants, and especially among the Calvinists. When an edict was promulgated against the Calvinist sect in a canton of Switzerland in which the Austrians were in power, it provoked a violent reaction among the citizens. Fidelis was asked to join the Calvinist sect, to which he replied: "I have come to combat heresy, not to embrace it." He was canonized by Pope Benedict XIV in 1746.

MESSAGE AND RELEVANCE

In the Opening Prayer of the Mass reference is made to "the fire of love" that "gave him the privilege of dying that the faith might live." It is also this love that Pope Benedict XIV recalls in the Office of Readings: "He practiced the fullness of charity in bringing consolation and relief to his neighbors as well as strangers. With a father's love he embraced all those who were in trouble. . . . In addition to this charity, he was faithful in truth as well as in name. His zeal for defending the Catholic faith was unsurpassed and he preached it tirelessly."

The petition in the Opening Prayer makes a reference to "the power of Christ's resurrection" because the feast falls in the Easter season. Therefore, with the Easter faith that overcomes the world, we also can experience the power of love that inspired St. Fidelis to pray for an entire year for the grace of martyrdom. "Although I am unworthy," he said, "I know for certain that God has granted this to me."

Opening Prayer: *Father, you filled St. Fidelis with the fire of your love and gave him the privilege of dying that the faith might live. Let his prayers keep us firmly grounded in your love, and help us to come to know the power of Christ's resurrection.*

April 25
ST. MARK

HISTORICO-LITURGICAL NOTE

The feast of St. Mark is celebrated on this day by the Copts, the Syrians and the Byzantines. In the West it has been celebrated since the ninth century. Although, as Papias said in the second century, Mark did not follow Christ with the other apostles, he was a disciple of St. Peter and the author of the Second Gospel. This we learn from the Acts of the Apostles (12:12). We likewise know that he accompanied St. Paul on a mission to Cyprus (Ac 13:5), after going from Jerusalem to Antioch with Paul and Barnabas (12:25).

For some unexplained reason he returned to Jerusalem (Ac 13:13) and embarked once again for Cyprus in the company of Barnabas, his kinsman (Col 4:10). There had been some kind of disagreement between Paul and Mark but eventually they were reconciled, because Paul speaks of Mark as his collaborator and his consoler during his imprisonment in Rome (Col 4:10; 2 Tm 4:11).

St. Mark was also closely associated with St. Peter, as is testified by Clement of Alexandria, Irenaeus and Papias. St. Peter refers to Mark as "my son," which could mean that Mark had been baptized by Peter. According to the historian Eusebius and the prologue to the ancient Latin version of St. Mark's Gospel, Mark ended his days as bishop of Alexandria. He is the patron of the city of Venice, Italy, which claims to have his relics, which were brought there from Alexandria in the ninth century. His symbol is the head of a lion, taken from the four creatures mentioned in Revelation 4:7-8.

MESSAGE AND RELEVANCE

The texts of the prayers in the Mass, of which only the Opening Prayer is based on the previous prayer formulas, describe the characteristics of St. Mark. We read in the Opening Prayer that God "gave St. Mark the privilege of proclaiming your gospel." Tradition considers St. Mark to be the interpreter and mouthpiece of St. Peter, for which reason Mark's Gospel has sometimes been called the "Gospel of St. Peter." Evidently, since Mark was not an eyewitness to the actions and teaching of Christ, he must have learned the details from St. Peter. His Gospel is a compendium of the entire life and activity of Jesus, from Bethlehem to Calvary. Its purpose is to proclaim to the Gentiles that Jesus Christ is the Son of God.

The Entrance Antiphon, like the Gospel of the Mass, recalls the missionary apostolate mandated by Christ: "Go out to the whole world, and preach the gospel to all creation" (Mk 16:15). Then the petition in the Opening Prayer explicitly links the following of Christ with knowledge of the gospel. Mark, therefore, wrote his Gospel not simply to give historical documentation concerning the life of Christ, but to urge the followers of Christ to be so committed to him that they would be willing to lay down their life for the sake of the good news (Mk 8:35-38).

The Prayer over the Gifts asks that the "Church may always be faithful to the preaching of the gospel." Similarly, the Prayer after Communion asks that the gifts received at the altar will "make us holy and strengthen us in the faith of the gospel preached by St. Mark."

The Office of Readings gives a synthesis of Christian doctrine taken from the treatise of St. Irenaeus against heresies. After stating the basic beliefs of the Catholic faith, he says: "The faith and the tradition of the churches founded in Germany are no different from those founded among the Spanish and the Celts, in the East, in Egypt, in Libya and elsewhere in the Mediterranean world."

Another thing to be noted about the Gospel according to St. Mark is that it does not narrate the events in the life of Christ in a strict chronological order. It is a theological narrative of the life of Christ that terminates, after the passion and death, with a revelation of the identity of the Son of God. Yet,

Mark's Gospel is not triumphalistic, focusing only on the resurrection. Therefore the responsory for the Office of Readings states: "To us who are on the way to salvation the cross of Christ is the proof of God's power" (1 Cor 1:17-18). The two themes of this feast — the cross and missionary preaching — are always relevant for all times and places.

> Preface: *Father, you have willed that the holy mysteries of Christ your Son, the source of redemption and of life, should be made known through the Sacred Scriptures, the work of men illumined by the Holy Spirit. In this way the words and deeds of the Savior, contained in the immortal pages of the Gospels, are entrusted to the Church and become a fecund seed that brings forth fruits of grace and glory throughout the centuries.*

April 28
ST. PETER CHANEL (1803-1841)

HISTORICO-LITURGICAL NOTE

This first martyr of Oceania and of the Society of Mary (Marists) was canonized in 1954 by Pope Pius XII. Born in the diocese of Belley in France, he was ordained a priest in 1827 and served as a parish priest in a church near Geneva. After a few years he entered the newly founded Society of Mary. In 1836, the year in which Pope Gregory XVI approved the new religious institute, he was sent to the missions in Oceania, and specifically to Polynesia, which had been entrusted to the Marists. In 1837 he went with a companion to the island of Futuna, west of Tahiti. He met with early success in his evangelization, but when the king's son asked to be baptized, the king turned against the missionary. He sent a group of warriors to kill St. Peter. As he was dying, he said: "My death is a great blessing for me." Within a short time the entire population embraced the Catholic faith, a proof that the blood of martyrs is truly the seed of the Church.

MESSAGE AND RELEVANCE

The Opening Prayer of the Mass states that God "called St. Peter Chanel to work for your Church and gave him the crown of martyrdom." His whole life had been a preparation for that final act. Before he had learned the language of the natives and found it difficult to preach to them, he said: "Since we cannot make Jesus Christ loved through our instructions, let us glorify him through fidelity to our Rule. In that way we shall draw down graces upon our dear savages. In such a difficult mission it is necessary that we be saints. The greater our spirit of sacrifice, the more success we shall have in desperate situations." These sentiments are echoed in the Office of Readings, which is taken from the memoirs of a Marist Brother who was a companion of St. Peter Chanel.

The conclusion of the Opening Prayer makes reference to the Easter season in which this feast is celebrated, asking that we also, in our celebration of Christ's death and resurrection, may be "faithful witnesses to the new life he brings." This request was realized in the case of St. Peter Chanel, who has been named patron of the islands of the South Pacific. After his death numerous healings took place at his tomb and the entire population of the island of Futuna was converted. Full participation in the paschal mystery always brings new and unexpected fruits.

> Opening Prayer: *Father, you called St. Peter Chanel to work for your Church and gave him the crown of martyrdom. May our celebration of Christ's death and resurrection make us faithful witnesses to the new life he brings.*

April 29
ST. CATHERINE OF SIENA (1347-1380)

HISTORICO-LITURGICAL NOTE

This popular saint was proclaimed co-patroness of Italy, together with St. Francis of Assisi, in 1939 and she was named a Doctor of the Church in 1970. She lived in the fourteenth century, the period of schism in the Church and the residence of the pope in Avignon, France.

Born at Siena, Italy, the youngest of 25 children of the Benincasa family, she was drawn to a life of prayer from her earliest years. She had her first vision of Christ at the age of 6. As a teenager she strongly resisted her mother's insistence that she prepare for marriage. Instead, at the age of 15 she joined the Dominican Tertiaries, known as the *Mantellate*, and donned the Dominican habit: a white tunic and veil and a black mantle. As a lay Dominican she continued to live at home and to perform various works of charity, but soon she was drawn into political and religious activities. Her predominant concerns were the reform of the Church, including the clergy, and the return of the pope from France to Rome. She soon attracted a following of both men and women and embarked upon an apostolate that necessitated much travelling to various parts of Italy. She was summoned to the General Chapter of the Dominican Order in 1374 to explain her apostolate and travels and then the Chapter assigned the Dominican Raymond of Capua as her spiritual director. In her last years she lived in Rome with some of her followers, near the Dominican church of Santa Maria sopra Minerva, where her body was placed under the main altar after her death in 1380. She was canonized in 1461.

MESSAGE AND RELEVANCE

The Opening Prayer of the Mass touches on several characteristics of the spirituality of St. Catherine of Siena: her meditation on the sufferings of Christ, her ardent love and her service to the Church. Her life was filled with extraordinary mystical phenomena such as visions and revelations, infused knowledge, raptures, the mystical espousal and mystical marriage, and the stigmata, which appeared on her body only after her death.

Her writings consisted of 382 letters, various prayers, and the *Dialogue of Divine Providence*, which she dictated to secretaries, often in a state of ecstasy. The Office of Readings contains an extract from the *Dialogue*, addressed to the Trinity. "You are a mystery as deep as the sea;" she says, "the more I search, the more I find, and the more I find, the more I search for you. But I can never be satisfied; what I receive will ever leave me desiring more. When you fill my soul, I have an even greater hunger, and I grow more famished for your light."

The antiphon for the Canticle of Mary states: "Always and everywhere Catherine sought and found God. Through the strength of her love she entered into union with him." The intimacy of her union with God reached such a high point that, at her mystical espousal, Christ exchanged hearts with her. But Catherine's spirituality is ultimately an apostolic one, as we read in the Responsory in the Office of Readings: "Go forth from the quiet of contemplation and courageously bear witness to my truth."

The antiphon for the Canticle of Zechariah refers to Catherine's devotion to the Church: "The holy virgin Catherine steadfastly begged the Lord to restore peace to his holy Church." She wrote numerous letters of admonition and pleading to the pope at Avignon, begging him to return to Rome. She did not hesitate to speak with authority and even to reprimand cardinals and legates. Catherine of Siena is one of those saints who has a universal appeal, and both her spirituality and her mission in the Church are of perennial relevance.

> Preface (Dominican Missal): *Father, all-powerful and ever-living God, we do well always and everywhere to give you thanks. We praise you today because you revealed to St. Catherine the unsearchable mysteries of*

your own life and gave her a special love for your Church. She contemplated you in constant prayer and pleaded that discord might give way to unity. Obedient and humble, she challenged the Church of Christ to be mindful of its mission and be a faithful spouse of Christ, holy and spotless until the end of time.

April 30
ST. PIUS V (1504-1572)

HISTORICO-LITURGICAL NOTE

This great pope of the Counter-Reformation died in Rome on May 1, 1572, but his feast is celebrated today because May 1 is the feast of St. Joseph the Worker. He was born with the name Michael Ghislieri at Bosco Marengo in northern Italy. He entered the Dominican Order at the age of fourteen and was ordained to the priesthood at Bologna in 1528. During the next sixteen years he served as professor, provincial, and finally as commissary general of the Roman Inquisition. In 1556 he was ordained bishop and in 1558 Pope Paul IV named him a cardinal and appointed him Inquisitor General of the entire Catholic world. Despite his unwillingness, he was elected pope in 1566, thanks in great part to the influence of St. Charles Borromeo.

Pope Pius V immediately began the work of reforming the Church. He showed great compassion for the poor and lowly, but insisted on strict justice in dealing with the powerful. His success in enforcing liturgical and moral reform was due in large part to the respect that the people had for his personal holiness. His two major concerns were the spread of Protestantism and the threat of the Turks. In his efforts to combat Lutheranism he soon came into conflict with the German emperor, Maximilian II. As a result of his support of Mary Stuart, Queen Elizabeth I launched a severe persecution of

Catholics in England. This in turn led Pope Pius V to excommunicate Elizabeth in 1570. He did, however, succeed in forming an alliance between Spain and Venice which ultimately led to the defeat of the Muslims at Lepanto (October 7, 1571). In gratitude Pope Pius V instituted the feast of Our Lady of Victory, later named Our Lady of the Rosary. Moreover, the invocation "Mary, Help of Christians" was added to the Litany of Loreto.

Pope Pius V was not only a reformer; he was also an innovator. Thus, he published a new Breviary and a new Missal; he deleted some of the extravagant details in the lives of the saints; he authorized a critical edition of the works of St. Thomas Aquinas and proclaimed him a Doctor of the Church. The *Catechism* of the Council of Trent was completed during his pontificate; he insisted on the catechetical teaching of the young as a duty of all parish priests and he called for adequate instruction prior to the baptism of adults.

Pope Pius V was canonized in 1712 and was the last pope to be declared a saint prior to Pope Pius X.

MESSAGE AND RELEVANCE

The Opening Prayer of the Mass is a modification of the one used since 1672 and it highlights two activities of St. Pius V. First, it states that God chose this pope for the defense of the faith. His efforts to convert heretics and his refusal to compromise on matters of the faith made him a champion of the truth. The publication of the *Roman Catechism* of the Council of Trent in 1566 and the sending of missionaries to India and the Orient are evidences of his zeal.

Secondly, the prayer mentions his reform of the liturgy. In the Office of Readings St. Augustine states that "the apostle Peter, because of the primacy of his apostleship, stood as a symbol of the entire Church." As a successor to St. Peter, Pope Pius V used his authority to promote a badly needed reform of the liturgy so that the Church throughout the Catholic world would offer God "more fitting worship" (Opening Prayer). The centrality of the liturgy in Catholic life and worship has been highlighted by Vatican Council II in its document on the liturgy.

In the second part of the Opening Prayer we ask that we may "celebrate your holy mysteries with a living faith and an effective love." It suggests that we should make the liturgical reforms of the Second Vatican Council as vital and fruitful as St. Pius V did in promoting the reforms of the Council of Trent. There were, of course, many other reforms put into motion by St. Pius V: against simony in the Roman Curia and the practice of nepotism, rules concerning the residence of bishops and parish priests, regulations on cloister for religious, celibacy of the clergy, and the use of the *Summa Theologiae* of St. Thomas Aquinas as the basic text for theology.

As he was dying, Pope Pius V said to the cardinals in attendance: "I recommend to you the Church that I have always loved. Try to elect as my successor a zealous man who will seek nothing but the glory of the Savior and will have no other interest here below than the honor of the Apostolic See and the good of Christianity."

Opening Prayer: *Father, you chose St. Pius V as pope of your Church to protect the faith and give you more fitting worship. By his prayers help us to celebrate your holy mysteries with a living faith and effective love.*

MAY

ST. JOSEPH the WORKER

HISTORICO-LITURGICAL NOTE

"May Day" has long been dedicated to labor and the working man. The feast in honor of St. Joseph the Worker was instituted by Pope Pius XII in 1955. It falls on the first day of the month that is dedicated to the Blessed Virgin Mary. Pope Pius XII expressed the hope that this feast would accentuate the dignity of labor and would bring a spiritual dimension to labor unions. It is eminently fitting that St. Joseph, a working man who became the foster-father of Christ and patron of the universal Church, should be honored on this day.

MESSAGE AND RELEVANCE

The texts of the Mass and the Liturgy of the Hours provide a catechetical synthesis of the significance of human labor seen in the light of faith. The Opening Prayer states that God, the creator and ruler of the universe, has called men and women in every age to develop and use their talents for the good of others. The Office of Readings, taken from the document of the Second Vatican Council on the Church in the modern world, develops this idea. In every type of labor we are obeying the command of God given in Genesis 2:15 and repeated in the responsory for the Office of Readings. The responsory for the Canticle of Zechariah says that "St. Joseph faithfully practiced the carpenter's trade. He is a shining example for all workers." Then, in the second part of the Opening Prayer, we ask that we may do the work that God has asked of us and come to the rewards he has promised. In the Prayer after Communion we ask: "May our lives manifest your love; may we rejoice for ever in your peace."

The liturgy for this feast vindicates the right to work, and this is a message that needs to be heard and heeded in our modern society. In many of the documents issued by Pope John XXIII, Pope Paul VI, the Second Vatican Council and Pope John Paul II, reference is made to the Christian spirit that should permeate one's work, after the example of St. Joseph. In addition to this, there is a special dignity and value to the work done in caring for the family. The Office of Readings contains an excerpt from the Vatican II document on the modern world: "Where men and women, in the course of gaining a livelihood for themselves and their families, offer appropriate service to society, they can be confident that their personal efforts promote the work of the Creator, confer benefits on their fellowmen, and help to realize God's plan in history" (no. 34).

> Preface: *Father, in your provident love you have chosen St. Joseph to be the custodian of your Son made man, to surround him with fatherly love and to give us an example of working for a livelihood. Though a descendant of the royal stock of David, he earned his daily bread by the sweat of his brow. Encouraged and consoled by living with Jesus and Mary, he ennobled human toil; practicing his trade with zeal and remarkable virtue, he became the teacher of work to Christ the Lord, who did not disdain to be called the son of a carpenter.*

May 2
ST. ATHANASIUS (295-373)

HISTORICO-LITURGICAL NOTE

The feast of this great bishop of Alexandria in Egypt was celebrated by the Copts and Byzantines on this day to honor one of the four great doctors of the Eastern Church. It was introduced at Rome only in the sixteenth century, though it had been celebrated in France since the twelfth century.

He was born at Alexandria of Christian parents and received an excellent education, eventually becoming an expert in Sacred Scripture. He was ordained a deacon at the age of 21. A year later a heretic by the name of Arius began to teach that the Word (the second Person of the Trinity) is not eternal but was created in time by God the Father. As theologian to his bishop, Athanasius attended the Council of Nicea, which condemned the heretical teaching, excommunicated Arius and promulgated the Nicene Creed. Three years later Athanasius succeeded Alexander as patriarch and dedicated his efforts to implementing the decrees of the Council of Nicea. From the very beginning he met with opposition, and to such an extent that five times he was banished from his see. He spent a total of 17 years in exile. He was accused of every kind of evil, from treason and murder to embezzlement and sacrilege. Purified by these trials and thus atoning for any excessive intransigence in the name of orthodoxy, he died at Alexandria in 373. His *Life of St. Anthony* is his masterpiece and for many centuries it served as a model for hagiography and the eremitical life.

MESSAGE AND RELEVANCE

The prayers of the Mass describe this "outstanding defender of the truth of Christ's divinity." In his three major treatises he firmly established the basic tenet of Christianity, namely, the consubstantiality of the Incarnate Word with the Father, thus defending the divinity of Christ. In the Prayer after Communion "we join St. Athanasius in professing our belief in the true divinity of Christ your Son."

The Office of Readings contains an excerpt from a discourse by St. Athanasius. In it he discusses the incarnation of the Word, and in so doing he explains the consequences of this doctrine, not only so far as it relates to the Trinity, but also to our very destiny. The purpose of the loving plan of God was to restore mankind to justification after it had fallen into sin and corruption. "The immortal Son of God," says St. Athanasius, "united with all men by likeness of nature, thus fulfilled all justice in restoring mankind to immortality by the promise of the resurrection." Faith in our justification through Christ, the incarnate Son of God, helps us grow in the knowledge and love of God, as we ask in the Opening Prayer.

> Opening Prayer: *Father, you raised up St. Athanasius to be an outstanding defender of the truth of Christ's divinity. By his teaching and protection may we grow in your knowledge and love.*

May 3
ST. PHILIP and ST. JAMES

HISTORICO-LITURGICAL NOTE

This feast dates from the sixth century and was formerly celebrated on May 1 to commemorate the dedication of the basilica of the holy apostles (560), where the relics of Philip and James were preserved.

The apostle Philip, sometimes confused with the deacon by the same name (Ac 21:8), was born at Bethsaida in Galilee (Jn 1:44). His name is mentioned several times in St. John's

Gospel, where we learn that Philip was called by Christ the day
after he had called Peter and Andrew. Philip responded immediately to the call, convinced that Jesus was the promised
Messiah. He even approached his friend Nathanael with the
announcement that he had found the one of whom Moses and
the prophets spoke (Jn 12:20-22). Before the multiplication of
the loaves and fishes, it was Philip whom Jesus addressed, and
at the Last Supper it was Philip to whom Jesus said: "He who
sees me sees the Father also" (Jn 14:8-11). Philip later
preached the gospel in Phrygia, and possibly in Greece. He
was martyred at Hierapolis and was buried there until his
relics were transferred to Rome.

James, the son of Alpheus and "brother" (first cousin) of
the Lord (Mk 15:40), is also known as St. James the Less.
When he became head of the church at Jerusalem he was
known as James the Just. During the Council of Jerusalem he
spoke in favor of St. Peter's decision in the discussion about
Gentile converts and the Jewish observances. He was so successful in winning converts to Christianity that the Scribes and
Pharisees plotted his death. According to one account, he was
thrown from the pinnacle of the Temple, and since he was not
yet dead, he was stoned; finally he was dispatched by a blow to
the head with a club. His martyrdom took place in the year 62.
There is much discussion about the authorship of the Epistle of
St. James.

MESSAGE AND RELEVANCE

The Opening Prayer of the Mass asks that we may "share
in the suffering, death and resurrection of your only Son." The
last phrase in this prayer, "to come to the eternal vision of your
glory," reminds us of Philip's request "to see the Father" (Jn
14:8), which is explicitly stated in the Communion Antiphon.
For us too the desire to see the Father will be fulfilled if we
know how, through faith, to unite Jesus to the Father, seeing
the Father in the divine power and attributes of Jesus. Hence,

in the Prayer after Communion we ask: "With the apostles Philip and James may we see you in your Son."

The antiphon for the Canticle of Zechariah presents Philip as a model for the apostolate. He does not attempt to force Nathanael to meet Jesus; he simply says: "Come and see."

The Prayer over the Gifts contains the only reference to the Letter of James, asking for a "religion pure and undefiled" (Jm 1:27). The description of religion in this context, reminiscent of the Old Testament, reminds us that the apostle James, who was able to reconcile tradition with the new Christian religion, is the prototype of the authentic Christian Jew. The message for us today is that we have sometimes separated the Old Testament from the New Testament to such an extent that we forget the Jewish roots and origins that are necessary for understanding the message of Jesus and the apostles (Ac 21:17-26).

In the Office of Readings the text from Tertullian states that the unity of the Church rests on the fact that the Church is apostolic. "Every family can be traced back to its origins. That is why we can say that all these great churches constitute that one original Church of the apostles, for it is from them that they all come. They are all primitive, all apostolic, because they are all one. They bear witness to this unity by the peace in which they all live, the brotherhood which is their name, the fellowship to which they are pledged."

> Preface: *It is truly right and just, almighty God, to honor and praise you on the feast of the apostles Philip and James. Having heard the voice that made them disciples of Christ, they followed his life and teaching with such fidelity that they were able to know you, O Father, and to contemplate your face openly. Confirmed in their faith in the resurrection of the Master, they became eloquent and faithful witnesses of the gospel. Our assembly also, gathered here in your*

*name and for your glory, is inspired by their teaching
and by the redemption that your everlasting love has
offered to the human race.*

May 12
ST. NEREUS and ST. ACHILLEUS (+304?)

HISTORICO-LITURGICAL NOTE

The cult of these two martyrs goes back to the fourth century, when Pope Siricius constructed a church in their honor in the cemetery of Domitilla (398). In the sixth century a church was constructed in their honor near the Baths of Caracalla in Rome. In the sixteenth century the relics of the two saints were transferred there and united with those of St. Domitilla. Originally, this feast was celebrated in honor of all three saints, but Domitilla's name is found only in the legendary accounts.

The so-called "acts" of their martyrdom state that Nereus and Achilleus were Praetorian soldiers during the reign of Trajan and they were beheaded after being exiled to the island of Terracina. All we know for certain about them is taken from the inscription composed in their honor by Pope Damasus at the end of the fourth century. It states that the two soldiers had at one time "exercised the cruel office of carrying out the orders of the tyrant, being ever ready through the constraint of fear to obey his will. O miracle of faith! Suddenly they cease from their fury, they become converted, they fly from the camp of their wicked leader; they throw away their shields, their armor and their blood-stained javelins. Confessing the faith of Christ, they rejoice to bear testimony to its triumph."

MESSAGE AND RELEVANCE

The Opening Prayer of the Mass states that we honor these two saints "for their courage in dying to profess their faith in Christ." As models of fortitude they have a lesson for those who do not really understand what it means to be members of Christ. In this context St. Augustine says: "If then you are among the members of Christ, whoever you are who hear this, whatever you suffer at the hands of those who are not among the members of Christ was lacking to the suffering of Christ. . . . Do not then imagine, brethren, that all the just who suffered persecution at the hands of the wicked, even those who were sent to foretell the coming of the Lord before he came, did not belong to the members of Christ."

> Opening Prayer: *Father, we honor Saints Nereus and Achilleus for their courage in dying to profess their faith in Christ. May we experience the help of their prayers at the throne of your mercy.*

May 12
ST. PANCRAS (+304?)

HISTORICO-LITURGICAL NOTE

This saint, whose Latin name is Pancratius, was born in Phrygia or Syria and was taken by an uncle to Rome as an orphan. There, they both converted to Christianity. Pancras was martyred by decapitation at the tender age of fourteen, perhaps on the same day as Sts. Nereus and Achilleus. In fact, their feasts at one time were celebrated on the same day. In 514 Pope Symmacus erected a basilica in his honor and St. Augustine of Canterbury dedicated in his honor the first church he erected in that city. Later, when Pope St. Vitalian (672) sent relics of St. Pancras to the king of Northumberland, the cult of the saint became firmly established in England. In the late Middle Ages he was listed among the saints who had special powers of intercession.

MESSAGE AND RELEVANCE

The Opening Prayer of the Mass asks God to "give your Church joy and confidence through the prayers of St. Pancras." In the Office of Readings St. Bernard comments on Psalm 90:15: "I am with him in tribulation." He says: "It is good for me to be sad, O Lord, as long as you are with me, rather than to be a king apart from you, to feast without you. . . . It is better for me to embrace you in tribulation than to be without you in heaven. . . . 'Gold is tested in the furnace, and the just by the trial of tribulation.' There, yes, there, you are present with them, Lord."

Opening Prayer: *God of mercy, give your Church joy and confidence through the prayers of St. Pancras. Keep us faithful to you and steadfast in your service.*

May 14
ST. MATTHIAS

HISTORICO-LITURGICAL NOTE

This feast is placed in the period between the Ascension of the Lord and the feast of Pentecost because it was during that time, according to the Acts of the Apostles, that Matthias was chosen to replace Judas Iscariot. St. Peter had announced that the new apostle should be one who "was of our company while the Lord Jesus moved among us, from the baptism of John until he was taken up from us" (Ac 1:21-22). After praying, they cast lots and the choice fell on Matthias. He first preached in Judea and it is said that later he evangelized Cappadocia and the area around the Caspian Sea. We know nothing about the details of his martyrdom; legend says that he was either crucified or beheaded. It is said that his relics were preserved at Jerusalem until St. Helen had them brought to Rome. His cult did not begin in Rome until the ninth century; at first his feast was celebrated on February 24.

MESSAGE AND RELEVANCE

In the Latin version of the Opening Prayer of the Mass we read that God willed to inscribe St. Matthias in the "college of the apostles." The same phrase was used by the Second Vatican Council, referring to the bishops. The account of St. Peter's discourse in the First Reading in the Mass and repeated in the responsory for the Canticle of Zechariah invites us to acknowledge the apostolicity of the Church. This is all the more significant because it is in the Acts of the Apostles that we learn about life in the early Church.

In addition to the qualifications for an apostle listed by St. Peter, the number twelve was also important because it symbolized the twelve tribes of Israel. All bishops, who are the successors of the apostles, receive the same power and authority that were conferred by the Lord on the apostles. This feast reminds us again that the Church is apostolic.

Moreover, the feast of St. Matthias has yet another theme, that of "election." In the Opening Prayer we ask that we may be "counted among those you have chosen." This feast therefore prompts us to give thanks to God that out of millions of people we have been chosen to receive the apostolic faith. And since faith is a free gift of God, we should respond with gratitude and the gift of self to God.

Preface: *Father, in order that the number of the apostles would be complete, you cast a special glance of love on Matthias, who was already introduced to the following of Christ and to his mysteries. His voice was in accord with that of the other eleven witnesses of the Lord and he announced to all the world that Jesus of Nazareth is truly risen and the kingdom of heaven has been proclaimed to all men.*

May 15 (United States)
ST. ISIDORE (1070-1130)

HISTORICO-LITURGICAL NOTE

Not to be confused with St. Isidore of Seville (+636), this saint was born in Madrid, Spain, in 1070 and spent his whole life working as a farm laborer for the same landowner, John de Vergas. He married a girl as poor and as holy as himself and after their one son died in infancy, they lived the rest of their married life in perfect chastity. Isidore was a man of intense prayer and his life was marked by numerous miracles and supernatural interventions. His wife survived him for several years and they are both venerated as saints in Spain. Isidore was formally canonized in 1622, together with St. Ignatius, St. Teresa of Avila, St. Francis Xavier and St. Philip Neri. The body of St. Isidore is still intact.

MESSAGE AND RELEVANCE

The feast of St. Isidore is celebrated in the United States and he has been named patron of the National Catholic Rural Life Conference. He is, however, not only a patron for farmers, but he is as well a model of the spirituality of the laity. He shows how persons living and occupied in the world, and especially those doing manual labor, can be united with God in prayer even as they perform their daily duties. His charity toward the poor and needy and his respect for God's creation are of special significance to those living in our modern consumer society. Finally, he is a reminder to all lay persons in the Church that they are called by God to sanctify the temporal order in this world.

Opening Prayer: *Lord God, all creation is yours, and you call us to serve you by caring for the gifts that*

*surround us. May the example of St. Isidore urge us to
share our food with the hungry and to work for the
salvation of all mankind.*

May 18
ST. JOHN I (+526)

HISTORICO-LITURGICAL NOTE

This pope died of starvation and thirst in jail at Ravenna,
Italy, as a result of imprisonment by the Arian king Theodoric.
Born in Tuscany, Italy, he joined the Roman clergy as an
archdeacon and was elected pope in 523. He governed the
Church for only three and a half years (523-526). He convoked
several Church councils, among them the famous Council of
Orange, which settled the arguments about grace. The king
sent him to Constantinople to plead the cause of the Arians in
the East, who were being persecuted. While there, he crowned
Justin as emperor (526), thus provoking the wrath of
Theodoric, who accused the pope of high treason. Consequently, when Pope John I returned to Italy, Theodoric imprisoned him, and shortly thereafter the pope died. The inscription
on his tomb reads: "Victim for Christ because of a forced
journey."

MESSAGE AND RELEVANCE

The Opening Prayer of the Mass derives from the Missal
of the Lateran of the twelfth century. It recognizes the merits of
this pope who sealed his apostolic service with martyrdom.
Two pastoral accomplishments deserve special mention: the
definitive fixing of the date for Easter, based on the research
done by Dionysius the Little, and his promotion of the Roman

chant, which led to the development of Gregorian chant. He also regulated the instructions prior to baptism.

In the Office of Readings the extract from a letter by St. John of Avila (1569) refers to constancy in the faith, which was exemplified by Pope John I. For that reason the Latin version of the Opening Prayer of the Mass has us ask, with the sentiments of St. Paul, that "we may be delivered to death for Jesus' sake so that the life of Jesus may be revealed in us" (2 Cor 4:11). Today also this martyred pope exemplifies the type of believer who can be victorious simply by suffering.

Opening Prayer: *God, our Father, rewarder of all who believe, hear our prayers as we celebrate the martyrdom of Pope John. Help us to follow him in loyalty to the faith.*

May 20
ST. BERNARDINE OF SIENA (1380-1444)

HISTORICO-LITURGICAL NOTE

This great popular preacher and promoter of devotion to the Holy Name of Jesus died at Aquila in Italy in 1444 and was canonized six years later. Born at Massa Marittima, near Siena, he lost both parents before he was 7 years old. He was a handsome, affable youth and on several occasions older men tried to seduce him but he vehemently rejected their advances. After completing his studies at the University of Siena, he entered the Franciscan Order at the age of 22. His first 12 years as a Franciscan were spent mostly in retirement and prayer, but in 1417 he began his ministry as a preacher. From 1438 to 1443 he was commissioned to reform the Franciscan Order, but he succeeded only partially in reconciling the "conventuals" with the "spirituals." He also worked as a peacemaker between feuding cities, and in 1427 Pope Martin V asked him to accept the bishopric of Siena, but Bernardine refused. Then, from 1430 until 1442 he returned to the task of reforming the Franciscans, and with great success. He died at Aquila on the vigil of the Ascension in 1444 while en route to the kingdom of Naples. He was canonized six years after his death.

MESSAGE AND RELEVANCE

The Latin version of the Opening Prayer of the Mass focuses on the particular traits of St. Bernardine as a reformer, preacher and writer. In the English translation, however, the theme is St. Bernardine's "special love for the Holy Name of Jesus." Then we ask that we may "always be alive with the spirit of your love."

To appreciate the importance of devotion to the Holy Name of Jesus, it suffices to read the excerpt in the Office of Readings. Bernardine considered the name of Jesus to be a compendium of Scripture and a symbol of unity. He invented the logo IHS, meaning *Iesus hominum Salvator* (Jesus, Savior of mankind), and he had it painted on a board which he would hold aloft in the pulpit. Some persons accused him of superstitious practices because of this, but he was exonerated after an investigation by a team of theologians.

Pope Nicholas V stated in the bull of canonization that Bernardine "served and followed Christ." We do well to remember St. Bernardine's statement, made like a true Franciscan: "If you speak of God, speak with love. If you speak of yourself, speak with love. Take care that there is nothing in you but love, love, love."

Opening Prayer: *Father, you gave St. Bernardine a special love for the Holy Name of Jesus. By the help of his prayers, may we always be alive with the spirit of your love.*

May 25
ST. BEDE the VENERABLE (672/3-735)

HISTORICO-LITURGICAL NOTE

This Benedictine monk has been called "the father of English erudition." He died at the monastery at Jarrow, England, and was named a Doctor of the Church in 1879, the only Englishman so honored. His autobiography is found at the end of his great work, *Ecclesiastical History of the English People* (731). There we learn that Bede was born in the region of the monastery and was educated there from the age of 7. He spent his whole life in that monastery, dedicating himself to the study of Sacred Scripture and the Fathers. He was a grammarian, naturalist, poet, and theologian. He also composed the first historical martyrology. Throughout the Carolingian Renaissance he was considered the outstanding ecclesiastical author of the time and was described by St. Boniface as "a light of the Church lit by the Holy Spirit." The title "Venerable" was bestowed on him by the Council of Aachen.

MESSAGE AND RELEVANCE

The Opening Prayer, which dates from 1899, states that the Lord has "enlightened the Church with the learning of St. Bede." He was in fact not only an erudite scholar, but all of his study was directed to a better understanding of Scripture, knowledge of the Church and participation in its mystery. He said: "The pagan authors are acorns on which the pigs feed. . . . The philosophers are the fathers of heretics." His love for Scripture also included its dissemination, as when he wrote his commentary on the Gospel of St. Luke to replace that of St. Ambrose, which was too difficult to understand.

The second part of the Opening Prayer asks that "your people may learn from his wisdom." The Latin version speaks of "the wisdom of the Fathers and the charity of the saints."

Bede considered the wisdom of the Fathers of the Church to be a veritable treasure and he was so faithful in using their works and commenting on them that he was considered an authentic transmitter of the ancient tradition of the Church. To the very end of his life he continued to teach and dictate. As regards the charity of the saints, see Cuthbert's account in the Office of Readings. St. Bede had declared in his martyrology that it does not suffice merely to record the dates, but to describe how the martyrs conquered the world.

His death was peaceful, and before he died he distributed little gifts to the monks in accordance with monastic poverty. He was, as Cardinal Newman said, the model of a true Benedictine. "And so Bede, as he lay upon the floor of his cell, sang: 'Glory be to the Father, and to the Son, and to the Holy Spirit.' And when he had named the Holy Spirit, he breathed his last breath" (Office of Readings). For us today, Bede's own words can be a source of inspiration: "It has ever been my delight to learn, to teach, or to write."

Opening Prayer: *Lord, you have enlightened your Church with the learning of St. Bede. In your love may your people learn from his wisdom and benefit from his prayers.*

May 25
ST. GREGORY VII (1020-1085)

HISTORICO-LITURGICAL NOTE

Pope Gregory VII died at Salerno, Italy, while the troops of Henry IV and Robert of Guiscard, the Norman duke of Calabria, were confronting each other in Rome. He was canonized in 1606 and was listed in the Roman Calendar in 1728, much to the chagrin of the Gallican prelates in France.

Born in Tuscany, Italy, he received the name Hilde-brand. He was sent to Rome to be under the care of an uncle who was superior of the monastery of St. Mary on the Aventine. He studied at the Lateran, where one of his teachers ultimately became Pope Gregory VI and, as such, named Hildebrand as his secretary. After the death of Pope Gregory, Hildebrand also served under the next five popes and eventually he himself was elected pope (1073) by acclamation, taking the name Gregory VII. He instituted what came to be known as the "Gregorian Reform," which was aimed at abolishing simony, immorality of the clergy, and lay investiture. He also tried to end the schism of the Eastern Churches (1054) and to launch a Crusade to free Jerusalem from the hands of the Turks (1070).

During the Roman Councils between 1078 and 1079 he succeeded in reconciling Berengarius, who had denied the real presence of Christ in the Eucharist. He also supported the conquest of England by William the Conqueror (1066). Fi-nally, he inspired and promoted the compilation of canon law by Peter Damian, Anselm of Lucca and Deusdedit.

He opposed Henry IV of Germany concerning the investi-ture of the see of Milan and the dispute over the investiture of bishops by the laity. When 24 bishops gathered together at Worms in 1076 at the instigation of Henry IV and refused to obey his sovereignty, he reacted by excommunicating Henry IV and dispensing his subjects from the oath of loyalty. Henry then did the only thing he could do: he met the pope at Canossa and received absolution, but within a few years he once again besieged Rome and finally took it (1084). Pope Gregory VII once more excommunicated Henry and took refuge in the Castel Sant'Angelo. He was rescued by Robert Guiscard and fled to Salerno. Henry then connived for the election of the anti-pope, Clement XIII, and Pope Gregory VII made a last appeal from Salerno. He died there in 1085, alone and abandoned, forgiving all his enemies and lifting all excom-munications except those against Henry IV and the anti-pope.

MESSAGE AND RELEVANCE

The new Opening Prayer of the Mass for this great defender of the freedom of the Church is based on the last words of the dying pope: "I loved justice and hated wickedness; therefore I die in exile" (Ps 45:8). The prayer states that "the spirit of courage and love for justice" distinguished Pope Gregory VII. His courage was manifested in the reform of the clergy, in spite of all opposition, his removal of prelates who had obtained their offices by simony or bribery, and his suspension of all priests who were guilty of concubinage. In addition, he fought against the investiture of ecclesiastical benefices by temporal rulers. Therefore the second part of the Opening Prayer asks: "Make us courageous in condemning evil and free us to pursue justice with love."

In the Office of Readings, which is taken from a letter of the pope, we find this clear assertion: "All those throughout the world who are numbered as Christians and who truly acknowledge the Christian faith know and believe that the Blessed Peter, the prince of the apostles, is the father of all Christians and, after Christ, the first shepherd, and that the holy Roman Church is the mother and teacher of all." The responsory then states that "the Lord glorified him in the sight of kings, and gave him commandments for his people."

The concept of a total separation of Church and State was inconceivable in the Middle Ages, because they were considered to be united but unequal. This worked sometimes to the advantage of an emperor or king and sometimes to the advantage of a pope. However, Pope Gregory VII never claimed that the papal primacy gave him absolute power over temporal rulers, as was done later, unfortunately, by Innocent III and Boniface VIII. Gregory held that the two supreme powers, that of the emperor and that of the pope, are like the two eyes in the human body. His view, with adaptations by Yves of Chartres and St. Thomas Aquinas, became the *Magna Carta* of medieval Christianity. It serves as a stimulus for us today to make full use of our freedom in the service of the good. We should not forget that Gregory's energetic defense of the prerogatives of the papacy did not prevent him from loving and forgiving his enemies.

> Opening Prayer: *Lord, give your Church the spirit of courage and love for justice which distinguished Pope Gregory. Make us courageous in condemning evil and free us to pursue justice with love.*

May 25
ST. MARY MAGDALENE DE PAZZI (1566-1607)

HISTORICO-LITURGICAL NOTE

This saint was a Carmelite nun in the monastery of St. Mary of the Angels in Florence, Italy, at a time when Italy was undergoing a severe religious crisis because of the humanistic Renaissance and the Lutheran Reformation. Feuds between the noble families had also involved the de Pazzi family. Less than a century before the saint's birth a member of her family had murdered a member of the Medici family during solemn Mass.

She made her First Communion and a vow of perpetual virginity when she was ten years old. Then, at the age of 16, she entered the Carmelite cloister against the wishes of her parents. It was the very year in which St. Teresa of Avila died in Spain (1582). Catherine eventually became subprioress of the monastery and, after enduring physical and spiritual trials for a period of 5 years, she died a holy death at the age of 41. She was canonized in 1669, together with St. Peter Alcantara, the Spanish Franciscan.

MESSAGE AND RELEVANCE

In the Opening Prayer of the Mass we read that God "filled St. Mary Magdalene de Pazzi with heavenly gifts and the fire of your love." The Latin version refers to her "consecrated virginity," which, as we have seen, was vowed by this saint in her pre-adolescent years, before she entered the Carmelite monastery. The "heavenly gifts" refer to the active and passive purgation that she endured during the five years that Pope Sixtus V was making radical reforms in the Church. The charism of continuous union with God was accompanied by her conscientious and faithful observance of the Carmelite Rule. For fifteen years prior to her death she was tormented by the fear that she would not be saved. In the last stage of her physical and spiritual sufferings she made a vow to renounce all spiritual joy and consolation. "O Lord," she prayed, "let me suffer or let me die; or rather, let me live on that I may suffer more."

The fruit of the foregoing petition is synthesized in the statement: "To contemplate you with purity of spirit and with ardent love." As regards "purity of spirit," the Office of Readings gives an excerpt from her treatise *On Revelation and on Trials*, in which we find the sublime petition addressed to the Holy Spirit: "Come, food of every chaste thought, fountain of all mercy, sum of all purity. Come! Consume in us whatever prevents us from being consumed in you."

As to her "ardent charity," it is manifested in the letters she wrote to cardinals, bishops, and even to the pope, to urge them to work for the reform of the Church. This she understood to be the personal mission received from God when she was 20 years old. In response to her promptings, Pope Sixtus V instituted radical reforms in many areas of Church life. It should be noted, however, that because of the animosity of some of her superiors, many of her letters never reached their destination.

St. Mary Magdalene's example of ardent love for the Church, even in most difficult times, should inspire us to make our love for the Church more authentic and disinterested.

Preface of the Mass (Carmelite Missal): *By the working of your Holy Spirit you kindled in St. Mary Magdalene de Pazzi a visible love for your Incarnate Word and*

a consuming zeal for the holiness of the Church. To
bring the Church she so ardently loved to the perfect
likeness of Christ the heavenly Bridegroom, she poured
out her life in heroic prayer and sacrifice.

May 26
ST. PHILIP NERI (1515-1595)

HISTORICO-LITURGICAL NOTE

Born in Florence, Italy, into a family of modest income, Philip frequented the Dominican church of St. Mark, where he acquired a great respect for Savonarola. Later, during a period in which he engaged in commerce at Cassino, he came into contact with Benedictine spirituality. Back in Rome in 1536, he became acquainted with St. Ignatius Loyola. For a time he studied at the University Sapienza but he soon gave that up and began to work as a lay apostle among the people of Rome. With the help of his confessor he founded the lay Confraternity of the Most Blessed Trinity to provide assistance for pilgrims. Advised that he could do much more good as a priest, he was ordained in 1551 at the age of 36. Through his apostolate in the confessional and his spiritual conferences, he attracted a group of followers who ultimately formed the Congregation of the Oratory.

St. Philip Neri was in contact with the outstanding figures of the day: Ignatius Loyola, Charles Borromeo, Francis de Sales, Camillus de Lellis, Felix of Cantalice and numerous popes such as Paul IV, Pius V, Gregory XIII, Gregory XIV and Clement VIII. For a time Pope Paul IV deprived him of his faculties to hear confessions, due to unfounded criticism of his activities and his formation of groups of pilgrims. In 1575, St. Philip received papal approval for the Congregation of the Oratory and the pope gave him the church of St. Mary of Vallicella for its headquarters. In 1578 Philip began the construction of a new church and to this day the Romans call it the *Chiesa Nuova*. In the last years of his life, between the ages of 75 and 80, St. Philip concentrated on the ministry of the confessional and spiritual conferences. He died in Rome with a reputation for cheerful goodness and optimism.

MESSAGE AND RELEVANCE

The three prayers of the Mass describe very well the spiritual traits of St. Philip Neri, who deliberately cultivated some eccentricities in order not to fall victim to the admiration of the people. He also declined all ecclesiastical honors. In the Opening Prayer we ask God, who "raises up your faithful to the glory of holiness," to "kindle in us the fire of the Holy Spirit, who so filled the heart of St. Philip Neri." The confidence that St. Philip had in supernatural means, and especially in the sacrament of reconciliation, was one of his outstanding characteristics. Moreover, his insistence on chastity based on humility and lived in joy was prompted by the ardor with which his heart was inflamed by the Holy Spirit. The motto of his Congregation of the Oratory is *Sola caritas* (Love alone).

In the Prayer over the Gifts another charism of Philip is mentioned: "Keep us always cheerful in our work for the glory of your name and the good of our neighbor." The cheerfulness that made Philip Neri appear ever young and attracted young men to him was the means by which he was able to make the things of God attractive to them. With the help of men like Palestrina, he made use of music and song as alternatives to vice and a means of promoting healthy joy. He was convinced that cheerful people, inclined to merriment, are more easily led along the ways of the Spirit.

The Prayer after Communion invites us to imitate St. Philip Neri by "hungering after this sacrament in which we find true life." The desire for things that are worth living for is one of the elements of St. Philip Neri's pedagogical method. It is also the basis of the programs of the Oratorians. The discovery of authentic values can provide a truly fascinating vision of holiness whereby one can experience the Christian joy of living. Few can resist the unbounded confidence and optimism of St. Philip Neri.

The Office of Readings contains an excerpt from a treatise by St. Augustine because there is nothing available from the pen of Philip Neri. He burned all his writings before he died. St. Augustine refers to the joy of being in Christ, and this helps us understand better a saying of St. Philip Neri: "A servant of God ought always to be happy." The spirituality of St. Philip Neri is relevant and available to all; it is beautifully summarized in the words of St. Augustine: "Wherever you are on earth, however long you remain on earth, the Lord is near, do not be anxious about anything" (Office of Readings). Consequently, the duties and involvements in the affairs of this life need never be an obstacle to the love and service of God.

> Preface: *In St. Philip, you have given us a vivid example that arouses our fervor for the following of Christ. His luminous witness prompts us to love you with joy and to serve you in the poor and the sick. His remarkable life shows us how to turn to you with undivided hearts and he reminds us that the fidelity of each day is the offering that is most pleasing to you.*

May 27
ST. AUGUSTINE of CANTERBURY (+604/5)

HISTORICO-LITURGICAL NOTE

Although there was a cult of St. Augustine (or Austin) of Canterbury in England since 747, he was not listed in the Roman Calendar until 1882. He died on May 26, in 604 or 605, but his feast is celebrated a day later because the feast of St. Philip Neri is celebrated on May 26.

The Council of Cloveshoe (747) ordered the name of St.

Augustine to be placed in the litany of the saints immediately after that of St. Gregory. After the restoration of the Catholic hierarchy in England in 1850, the name of this first evangelizer of England was placed in the liturgy of the universal Church.

We do not know much about Augustine's life before 596, when he was prior of the monastery of St. Andrew in Rome. In 596 Pope Gregory the Great commissioned Augustine and some 30 monks to evangelize southeastern England, where Christianity had been submerged by the paganism of the invading Saxons in the fifth and sixth centuries. After the conversion of Ethelbert, king of Kent, Augustine returned to France and was ordained a bishop. King Ethelbert gave him the ancient church of St. Martin in Canterbury. At Christmas in 597 Augustine had the joy of seeing a large number of Ethelbert's subjects baptized. After a second band of missionaries arrived in 601, Augustine received the pallium as first archbishop of England and was assigned to Canterbury with two suffragan sees, London and Rochester. At the same time Pope Gregory sent directives for the establishment of a hierarchy in England. The missionaries were not to destroy pagan temples, but convert them to use for Christian worship. Moreover, all pagan feasts were to be replaced by Christian feasts.

Augustine then turned his attention to the Catholic bishops who had fled from the Saxons into Wales and Cornwall. Cut off as they were, they had fallen into certain liturgical usages at variance with the universal Church. Augustine tried repeatedly to win them over, but without success. He died on May 26, 604 or 605, after having spent 7 years evangelizing England.

MESSAGE AND RELEVANCE

The new Opening Prayer for this Mass mentions the success of Augustine's preaching, by which God "led the people of England to the gospel." The missionary work of

Augustine was hampered by the fact that the English clergy were not following the reformed liturgy promulgated by Pope Gregory the Great. As long as this situation prevailed, it was impossible to achieve Church unity.

The letter of Gregory the Great to Augustine in the Office of Readings reminds the archbishop that the miracles he worked are a cause for fear as well as joy. "I know through your love for that people specially chosen for you," says Pope Gregory, "that almighty God has performed great miracles. But it is necessary that the same heavenly gift should cause you to rejoice with fear and to fear with gladness. You should be glad because by means of external miracles the souls of the Angles have been led to interior grace. But you should tremble lest, on account of these signs, the preacher's own weak soul be puffed up with presumption; lest, while seeming externally raised aloft in honor, it fall internally as a result of vainglory."

In view of the divisions in the Anglican Church, we should pray today that the ecumenical movement will eventually terminate with the reunion of the Anglicans with the Mother Church of Rome. This is the goal we seek and we should especially ask the intercession of St. Augustine of Canterbury for the success of the ecumenical dialogue.

Opening Prayer: *Father, by the preaching of St. Augustine of Canterbury, you led the people of England to the gospel. May the fruits of his work continue in your Church.*

May 31
VISITATION of the BLESSED VIRGIN MARY

HISTORICO-LITURGICAL NOTE

This feast has been transferred from July 2 so that it can be celebrated between the Annunciation (March 25) and the birth of John the Baptist (June 24). The feast itself originated in the Roman liturgy in the sixth century. It was introduced into the archdiocese of Prague in 1386, and in 1389 Pope Urban VI extended it to the whole Latin Church, fixing July 2 as the date for its celebration. The Franciscans had already been celebrating this feast in the thirteenth century. In the Eastern Church the feast is celebrated by the Melkites, the Maronites and the Malabarese of India.

MESSAGE AND RELEVANCE

The new prayers for the Mass celebrate the salvific event in which the Virgin Mary was inspired by God to visit Elizabeth and assist her in her need. Our petition is that we may always be open to the working of the Holy Spirit. The "fiat" of the Blessed Virgin at the Annunciation was a manifestation of her docility. Her journey to visit Elizabeth is reminiscent of David's journey when he carried the Ark of the Covenant to Jerusalem. The First Reading of the Mass, from the Book of Zephaniah (3:14-18) calls for joy and exultation at the visit of the Lord. The Old and the New Covenant are thus united in Mary, who is hailed as "Ark of the Covenant."

The conclusion of the Opening Prayer of the Mass asks that, with Mary, we may praise God forever, a sentiment repeated in the Prayer after Communion: "Let the Church praise you for the great things you have done for your people." The reference to the Canticle of Mary is evident and in the Office of Readings St. Bede provides a commentary on that Canticle.

Yet another theme for the feast is found in the Office of Readings, where an excerpt from the Song of Songs (2:8-14) can be applied to Mary, "springing across the mountains, leaping across the hills." Prompted by a "missionary spirit" to perform a work of mercy on behalf of her aged relative, Mary anticipates the *diakonia* of the Church, which is sent especially to the poor so that they may know that they too are loved by God and may therefore exult with joy as Mary did.

Finally, in the Prayer after Communion there is a direct reference to John the Baptist, who "hailed the presence of our Savior in the womb of Mary." In fact, we may say that this encounter between the two unborn infants, as that between their mothers, represents the epochal transition from the Law and the prophets of the Old Covenant to the Messiah and the New Testament (cf. Lk 16:16; Mt 11:12-13).

In celebrating the feast of the Visitation it is not necessary to wax sentimental, as if we were dealing only with a family of relatives, thus ignoring the salvific meaning of the feast. Each one of us can associate with Mary the Christ-bearer and experience the joy of her presence.

> Prayer After Communion: *Lord, let the Church praise you for the great things you have done for your people. May we always recognize with joy the presence of Christ in the Eucharist we celebrate, as John the Baptist hailed the presence of our Savior in the womb of Mary.*

Saturday after the Feast of the Sacred Heart
IMMACULATE HEART of MARY

HISTORICO-LITURGICAL NOTE

This feast springs from contemporary piety but has its roots in the Marian apostolate of St. John Eudes (+ 1680), an outstanding apostle of devotion to the Hearts of Jesus and Mary. After repeated requests and repeated refusals between 1669 and 1729, on December 8, 1942, the twenty-fifth anniversary of the apparitions at Fatima, Pope Pius XII dedicated the Church and the human race to the Immaculate Heart of Mary. He placed the feast on August 22 and extended it to the entire Latin Church. It has now been moved closer to the feast of the Sacred Heart of Jesus.

MESSAGE AND RELEVANCE

The Opening Prayer states that God prepared the heart of the Virgin Mary to be "a fitting home for your Holy Spirit." The Gospel text and the Communion Antiphon continue the same theme by saying that "Mary treasured all these words and pondered them in her heart." Recalling the words at the Annunciation, Mary was able to come to a fuller understanding of her divine motherhood, since she had not understood the response that Jesus gave when she found him in the Temple.

We too can be living temples of the Holy Spirit (1 Cor 3:16-17), and that is what we ask in the petition of the Opening Prayer: "May we become a more worthy temple of your glory." The indwelling of the Holy Spirit is not something static; rather, in the Prayer after Communion we ask that we may "experience the deepening of your life within us." Although the heart is at the center of this liturgy, we must avoid any devotional sentiment that is not based on Scripture, where the heart is seen as the basis of our moral and religious relationship with God. The heart of Mary is the cradle of all Christian meditation on the mysteries of Christ. St. Lawrence Justinian advises us in the Office of Readings: "Imitate her, O faithful soul. Enter into the deep recesses of your heart so that you may be purified spiritually and cleansed from your sins."

To meditate in our heart is the proper method for learning how to make the salvific events applicable to our own day and avoid the superficiality which prevents us from rejoicing abundantly in God's blessings (Prayer after Communion). But first we must pray for God's "help and forgiveness" (Prayer over the Gifts). This we ask of the Father of mercy through the Immaculate Heart of Mary.

Preface: *From the height of the cross, Christ entrusted his Mother to the beloved disciple to care for her in his stead. John is a symbol of the human race, and thus Mary becomes the Mother of all so that divine grace would be bestowed more abundantly on us who have believed and experienced the inexhaustible riches of her heart.*

JUNE

June 1
ST. JUSTIN (+166)

HISTORICO-LITURGICAL NOTE

This feast appeared in the Roman Calendar for the first time in 1882 and it is celebrated on the same date as in the Byzantine and Maronite Churches, having been transferred from the arbitrary date of April 14.

Justin was born near ancient Sichem, of Roman or Greek parents, at the beginning of the second century. In his studies he consulted various philosophies — Stoic, Peripatetic, Pythagorean and Platonic — but at Ephesus he met a wise man who directed him to the study of the Old Testament. He was told: "You are a lover of beautiful speech but you are certainly not a friend of action or of truth." He converted to Christianity around the year 130 and went to Rome, where he opened a school. Many of the early Christians were uneducated, but Justin believed that if the Christian teachings were properly explained, many more persons would embrace the faith. "It is our duty," he said, "to make known our doctrine."

Only three of his written works have come down to us: two *Apologies* and his *Dialogue with Trypho the Jew*. He is among the first to describe in detail for non-believers the rite of baptism and the eucharistic liturgy. He lived and died a layman. At his execution, six other Christians were martyred with him, five men and one woman.

MESSAGE AND RELEVANCE

The Opening Prayer of the Mass is derived from that of 1882 and it delineates the character of this "philosopher martyr," as Tertullian referred to him. There are two themes in the prayer, of which the first is that "through the folly of the cross" God "taught St. Justin the sublime wisdom of Jesus Christ." During his court trial, when asked which system of teaching he followed, Justin replied: "I have tried to learn about every system, but I have accepted the true doctrines of the Christians." When threatened with torture, Justin replied: "We hope to suffer torment for the sake of our Lord Jesus Christ, and so be saved."

The second theme of the Opening Prayer is that we too should "reject falsehood and remain loyal to the faith." As an intellectual, Justin was a searcher after truth, and he was converted as a result of following the advice of the venerable old man to study the Old Testament. The antiphon for the Canticle of Mary in the Liturgy of the Hours quotes the words of Justin: "Suddenly my soul caught fire, and I became filled with love for the prophets and those men who are the friends of Christ."

Justin's defense of truth was not based on a philosophical argument supported by reason but on the moral implications of truth. Yet he was perhaps the first person to build a bridge between pagan philosophy and the Christian teachings. By means of his writings he was able to dialogue with the pagans and the Jews, endeavoring to show that the complete revelation of truth has come through the incarnation of the Word.

In the Prayer over the Gifts reference is made to the liturgical mysteries which St. Justin "vigorously defended." He not only defended them; he explained them in great detail in order to silence those who spread false rumors about Christians because they celebrated their liturgy secretly. The antiphon for the Canticle of Zechariah states: "In every sacrifice let us praise the Creator of all things through his Son Jesus Christ and through the Holy Spirit."

St. Justin looked upon apologetics, the defense of Christian teaching, as a "preparation for the gospel." He is perhaps the first writer after St. Paul to grasp the universal implications of Christianity. At the same time, we should recognize the seeds of Christ's doctrine that are found in many non-Christian religions. This was explicitly stated by the Second Vatican Council in the document on evangelization (*Evangelii Nuntiandi*, no. 53).

Preface: *In the early days of your Church you chose Justin the martyr so that by his writings he could expound to Jews and pagans the mysteries of the prophets and the teaching of the apostles. Fearlessly he defended the gospel of Christ before the rulers. He faithfully completed his ministry, after bearing witness to you before the people, and you gave him the privilege of shedding his blood in order to receive the crown of eternal glory in the luminous company of martyrs.*

June 2
ST. MARCELLINUS and ST. PETER (+303?)

HISTORICO-LITURGICAL NOTE

This feast was inserted in the Roman Calendar by Pope Vigilius (555). According to the Jerome Martyrology and the liturgical records of the eighth century, these saints were beheaded during the persecution under Diocletian, after being forced to dig their own graves in a hidden spot. According to an account that dates from the sixth century, their bodies were miraculously revealed and were buried in the catacomb of St. Tiburtius. In 827 Pope Gregory IV sent the relics to Germany, where they were deposited at Seligenstadt, near Frankfurt. The names of Marcellinus and Peter are mentioned in the First Eucharistic Prayer.

MESSAGE AND RELEVANCE

The Latin version of the Opening Prayer invites us to recall our Christian heritage as manifested by Marcellinus and Peter, who were among the most honored of all the early Christian martyrs in the time of Pope Damasus (384). It states that through the martyrdom of these two saints God has given us a proof of his constant presence in the Church. Pope Damasus stated that when he was still a boy he had heard the details of the martyrdom from the executioner, who had later become a Christian. The Office of Readings contains an excerpt from Origen's *Exhortation to Martyrdom*, which was written 70 years before the death of Marcellinus and Peter. It says in part: "Jesus laid down his life for us; so we too should lay down our lives, I will not say for him, but for ourselves and also, surely, for those who will be helped by the example of our martyrdom." Our imitation of their constancy in the faith consists, as is stated in the responsory for the Office of Readings, in a struggle, "not against human enemies, but against the principalities and powers, against the evil spirits" (Ep 6:12).

> Opening Prayer: *Father, may we benefit from the example of your martyrs Marcellinus and Peter, and be supported by their prayers.*

June 3
ST. CHARLES LWANGA and COMPANIONS (+1886-1887)

HISTORICO-LITURGICAL NOTE

The martyrdom of these 22 saints from Uganda, Africa, occurred on May 26 and June 3, 1886, and January 27, 1887. Their feast was fixed on June 3 because on that day the leader of the group, Charles Lwanga, was burned to death after suffering terrible torture. They are the first group from 100 Catholics and Protestants who were murdered by the vicious King Mwanga. They are the first martyrs of black Africa and they were canonized during the third session of the Second Vatican Council, with the entire Catholic episcopate in attendance.

Uganda had been evangelized first by the White Fathers in 1879 but they were expelled in 1882. Two years later King Mwanga invited them to return, but later he became a fierce persecutor of the Christian religion. In 1885 he murdered a group of Christians together with their Anglican bishop Hannington, under the pretext that they were guilty of espionage. Later in the same year he had Joseph Mkasa beheaded, together with some of the court pages, because they "prayed from a book."

In 1886 Charles Lwanga and twelve companions were sentenced to death. The youngest in the group was Kizito, a lad of 13 years. Another member was Matthew Malumba, "the most beautiful flower of the crown," who had first converted to the Moslem religion, then to the Protestant, and finally became a Catholic.

Charles Lwanga has been declared patron of Catholic Action and of black African youth. Within a year after their martyrdom the number of catechumens rose from 800 to 3,000. In the decree of their canonization in 1964 Pope Paul VI hailed the martyrdom of Anglicans and Catholics in Uganda as strengthening the hope of Christian unity.

MESSAGE AND RELEVANCE

The Opening Prayer contains a famous statement by Tertullian: "Father, you have made the blood of the martyrs the seed of Christians." The Latin version of the prayer then asks that "the mystical field of the Church, which has been made fruitful by the sacrifice of these martyrs, may produce an ever more abundant harvest to the glory of your name."

During his pastoral visit to Africa in 1969, Pope Paul VI celebrated Mass on an altar above the urn containing the relics of the saints. In doing so, he was reviving the tradition of St. Cyprian, who celebrated Mass over the tomb of the martyrs of Carthage. In fact, the responsory for the Office of Readings is taken from a letter by St. Cyprian. In his homily, quoted in the Office of Readings, Pope Paul VI stated that these new martyrs of Africa are "a page worthy in every way to be added to the annals of that Africa of earlier times which we, living in this era and being men of little faith, never expected to be repeated."

In the Prayer over the Gifts there is an allusion to the refusal of the martyrs to accede to the request of the king to commit sins of impurity. The steadfast refusal of the young martyrs is rich in significance for the proper formation of youth in our day. The Prayer after Communion states that as the sacraments "helped them endure their sufferings," they can also "keep us steadfast in faith and love."

> Opening Prayer: *Father, you have made the blood of the martyrs the seed of Christians. May the witness of St. Charles and his companions and their loyalty to Christ in the face of torture inspire countless men and women to live the Christian faith.*

June 5
ST. BONIFACE (672/5-754)

HISTORICO-LITURGICAL NOTE

This saintly bishop and apostle to Germany was martyred, together with 52 companions, on June 5, 754. Immediately there was a cult in his honor, not only in Germany but also in England, where he was named co-patron, together with Gregory the Great and Augustine of Canterbury. His feast was introduced to the Roman Calendar only in 1874, at the request of the Fathers of the First Vatican Council.

Boniface was born around the year 673 at Wessex, England, received his education at the monastery in Exeter and entered the Benedictine abbey at Nursling. Desirous of preaching the gospel in a foreign land, he obtained that commission from Pope Gregory II, who changed his name from Winfrid to Boniface. He was so successful as a missionary that he was ordained a bishop in 722 and given jurisdiction over all of Germany, dependent directly on the Holy See. He succeeded in planting the Church firmly in western Germany, with the help of zealous monks and nuns, many of whom are saints.

The next pope, Gregory III, gave him Bavaria as a new mission territory and named him archbishop (732). During the next nine years Boniface founded numerous dioceses, among them Salzburg, Regensburg and Passau. In 741 he founded the famous abbey at Fulda and in 744 obtained pontifical exemption for the monastery, the first such privilege in the history of the Church. While preparing to administer the sacrament of confirmation on a group of converts, he was murdered by a hostile band that suddenly descended upon them. In accordance with his wishes, he was buried at the abbey in Fulda where, to this day, the bishops of western Germany hold their meetings.

MESSAGE AND RELEVANCE

The new Opening Prayer of the Mass is based on the Ambrosian and Parisian Missals and in it we ask that we may be loyal to our faith and profess it courageously in our lives. The missionary work of St. Boniface was supported and fostered in two ways; first, by the influence of the king and nobles, but without placing the Church under obligation to them; and secondly, by recruiting help from the monasteries in England. Boniface founded monasteries throughout western Germany and in due time they became centers of agriculture and the arts. He also uprooted the superstition and idolatry of the pagans, eventually cutting down their sacred oak tree.

Inspired by the example of St. Boniface, we pray that we may be "loyal to our faith" and have the "courage to profess it all our lives."

The Office of Readings gives an excerpt from a letter of St. Boniface to the abbess of the monastery in Bischofsheim. It contains advice that is applicable to Christians today: "Let us stand fast in what is right and prepare our souls for trial. . . . Let us be neither dogs that do not bark nor silent onlookers nor paid servants who run away before the wolf."

> Opening Prayer: *Lord, your martyr Boniface spread the faith by his teaching and witnessed to it with his blood. By the help of his prayers keep us loyal to our faith and give us the courage to profess it in our lives.*

June 6
ST. NORBERT (1080/85-1134)

HISTORICO-LITURGICAL NOTE

The feast of St. Norbert was listed in the Roman Calendar in 1620 to honor a man who worked for the reform of the Church in the twelfth century and was the founder of the Premonstratensians, an order of canons regular, also known as Norbertines. Born of a noble family in Lorraine, he was a subdeacon at the age of 30 and became the emperor's almoner. He was, however, very worldly and interested only in pleasure until a close brush with death during a violent thunderstorm led to his conversion. Ordained a priest in 1115, Norbert gave away all his possessions and retired to the valley of Premontré in northern France. Within a few months he had 40 companions, and on Christmas day, 1121, they made profession of vows. This was the beginning of the Canons of Premontré.

Norbert was in close contact with the Cistercian, St. Bernard, but his new order was inspired not so much by the monks of Citeaux as by the Benedictine monks of Siegburg and by the eremitical life that was greatly respected since the beginning of the twelfth century. While he was at the Diet of the Holy Empire at Speyer, Germany, the citizens of Magdeburg disagreed on the election of a new archbishop. In the end they elected Norbert by a unanimous vote. He appointed members of his own Order to posts in the archdiocese and struggled to promote reform and to repossess ecclesiastical properties. He died at Magdeburg in 1134 and was canonized by Pope Gregory XIII in 1582. His relics were transferred to the Premonstratensian abbey in Strahov, Bohemia, in 1627.

MESSAGE AND RELEVANCE

The new Opening Prayer of the Mass emphasizes St. Norbert's "preaching and pastoral zeal." Although he had favored a more contemplative life when he founded the Premonstratensians, when he became archbishop he needed their help in the reform of the Church in Magdeburg. Consequently, he assigned them a preaching mission for the evangelization of the people.

Norbert was always a contemplative at heart. The Office of Readings states that "he spent many hours in contemplation of the divine mysteries and fearlessly spread the spiritual insights which were the fruit of his meditation."

By adopting the Rule of St. Augustine for his Order, Norbert was the first founder to combine the monastic life with apostolic activity. He was especially devoted to the Holy Eucharist and the Blessed Virgin Mary. Like St. Bernard, he preached against those who denied the real presence of Christ in the Blessed Sacrament.

In the conclusion of the Opening Prayer we ask God: "Always grant to your Church faithful shepherds to lead your people to eternal salvation." The Office of Readings describes St. Norbert's reform of the clergy, leading them back to an apostolic and evangelical life. In this context we recall the statement that is a challenge to priests in every age: "You are not a priest for yourself; you are a mediator between men and

God. So what are you, priest? You are nothing and you are everything." This saint, who is the forerunner of the Franciscan and Dominican friars, and had served so well as a peacemaker that he was called the "angel of peace," was also a promoter of both personal and communal prayer for the priests of his diocese. He knew from experience that prayer is the soul of the apostolate.

> Opening Prayer: *Father, you made the bishop Norbert an outstanding minister of your Church, renowned for his preaching and pastoral zeal. Always grant to your Church faithful shepherds to lead your people to eternal salvation.*

June 9
ST. EPHREM (306-373)

HISTORICO-LITURGICAL NOTE

Ephrem died at Edessa in 373, according to a chronicle composed in 540, and his feast is celebrated on the day of his death. However, it is celebrated on a different date in the East, with a preference for January 28. His feast was inscribed in the Roman Calendar by Pope Benedict XV and he was named Doctor of the Church in 1920.

According to a disputed historical account, quoted in a panegyric by St. Gregory of Nyssa, St. Ephrem was born into a Christian family in Mesopotamia. However, it is more commonly believed that his parents were pagans and that they disowned him when he was baptized at the age of 18. The bishop assigned to Ephrem the task of founding a school, and Ephrem remained in that post during the attacks by the Persians. When they finally obtained control of the city in 363 through political negotiations, the Christians fled and Ephrem retired to a cave near Edessa. He did not, however, live as a hermit, but frequently went into the city to preach.

Since he is known as St. Ephrem the Deacon, it is likely that he never became a priest, and perhaps never wanted to. About the year 370 he travelled to Cappadocia to meet St. Basil but the last time he took part in any public activities was in the winter of 373. There was a great famine in the land and Ephrem prevailed on the wealthy to let him distribute their donations. Exhausted from his labors, St. Ephrem died in his cave in June, 373. His prolific writings are his heritage to succeeding generations of Christians.

MESSAGE AND RELEVANCE

The revised Opening Prayer of the Mass contains a theme that is dear to the Syriac Church: the Holy Spirit inspired St. Ephrem to sing the praises of God's mysteries. There is no mention, as in the previous prayer, of his preaching and writing against heretics. It was because of his hymns and poetry that he was called the "harp of the Holy Spirit." He was the first in the Syriac Church to organize boys' choirs and he is the only Doctor from that Church.

In his writings he defends the primacy of Peter and the popes and he speaks of Mary as being free from any taint of sin. "You and your Mother, Lord, are the only perfectly beautiful ones. . . . There was no stain of sin in your Mother." St. Gregory of Nyssa said of him: "The splendor of his life and his doctrine illumine the entire universe." There is no Eastern rite that does not use some of the hymns composed by St. Ephrem, and in the Syriac Church it was customary to read excerpts from his works after the proclamation of the Gospel.

The Office of Readings contains an excerpt from the writings of St. Ephrem: "Lord, in your sacrament we daily embrace you and receive you into our bodies; make us worthy to experience the resurrection for which we hope. We have had your treasure hidden within us ever since we received baptismal grace; it grows ever richer at your sacramental table." In these words St. Ephrem gives us a program of spirituality and liturgy that is relevant today for the whole Church, especially since he belonged to the Church when it was not yet divided between east and west.

> Opening Prayer: *Lord, in your love fill our hearts with the Holy Spirit, who inspired the deacon Ephrem to sing the praise of your mysteries and gave him strength to serve you alone.*

June 11
ST. BARNABAS

HISTORICO-LITURGICAL NOTE

The feast of St. Barnabas, who is mentioned in the First Eucharistic Prayer, together with Stephen and Matthias, was celebrated in Rome on this date in the eleventh century and also in the East. A native of Cyprus and a Jew of the tribe of Levi, he is also called an apostle (Ac 4:36). His name originally was Joseph but the apostles changed it to Barnabas. He sold his farm and gave the proceeds to the apostles (Ac 4:37). He then went forth to preach the gospel at Antioch, the third greatest city of the Roman Empire. It was Barnabas who presented Paul to the apostles and convinced them that Paul was truly converted (Ac 9:27). Moreover, it was at Antioch that Christians were first called by that name (Ac 11:26).

On the first missionary journey of Paul and Barnabas they went to Cyprus and later to Asia Minor (Ac 13:24); but on the second missionary journey Barnabas left Paul in order to join his cousin John Mark and return to Cyprus. He took part in the Council of Jerusalem to help settle the dispute about the observance of the Jewish law by Gentile converts.

According to ancient sources, Barnabas spent some time in Rome, but it is said that he was dead by the year 60 or 61. He was stoned to death at Salamis in Cyprus. His relics were discovered in the fifth century. Some persons believe that he composed the Letter to the Hebrews, and in the early

Church there was a Gospel attributed to him, but it has not come down to us.

MESSAGE AND RELEVANCE

The new prayers of the Mass are based on the biblical account of the apostolate of Barnabas. The Entrance Antiphon and the Opening Prayer refer to Barnabas as a man of faith filled with the Holy Spirit and sent to proclaim the gospel to the nations. He was chosen by God (Ac 13:2-4) to work with Paul, in success and in failure (Ac 13:45-46), and to suffer persecution (Ac 13:50-51). Paul and Barnabas failed to convert the Jews at Iconium and narrowly escaped death (Ac 14:6).

In the Prayer over the Gifts we ask God to "kindle in us the flame of love by which St. Barnabas brought the light of the gospel to the nations." We are thus urged to imitate two characteristics of this saint. First of all, to recognize the gifts of the Holy Spirit that enabled Barnabas to collaborate with Paul in the ministry of the word (Ac 14:12). Secondly, we note his readiness to carry the gospel message to the Gentiles and his defense of the Gentile converts at the Council of Jerusalem. Moreover, we note his patient mediation when he and Paul had a disagreement concerning John Mark and went their separate ways (Ac 15:36-38).

In the Office of Readings we have an excerpt from a treatise by St. Chromatius, who praises the preaching ministry of the apostles and then says: "We must not hide this lamp of law and faith. Rather, we must set it up in the Church, as on a lampstand, for the salvation of many, so that we may enjoy the light of truth itself and all believers may be enlightened." This advice is in complete harmony with the teaching of Vatican Council II concerning the ministry of the word as the primary function of bishops and priests.

Preface (Proper to the Barnabites): *The mysterious voice of your Spirit selected St. Barnabas from the Church of believers in Christ and associated him with*

*Paul and the college of the apostles, commanding him
to proclaim the truth of the gospel so that redemption
and salvation would be preached to all peoples. All this,
O Father, is a miracle of your grace and a gift of your
love.*

June 13
ST. ANTHONY of PADUA (1195-1231)

HISTORICO-LITURGICAL NOTE

St. Anthony died at Arcella, near Padua, Italy, on June
13, 1231, at the early age of 36 and he was canonized on
Pentecost of the following year by Pope Gregory IX. His cult
became widespread immediately after his death and the
Franciscan Order had already bestowed on him the title of
Doctor, although it was not made official until Pope Pius XII
proclaimed him "Evangelical Doctor."

Anthony was born at Lisbon, Portugal, and was baptized
with the name of Ferdinand. At an early age he attended the
school of the Canons of St. Augustine and after two years he
transferred to the Augustinians of Coimbra, where he remained for nine years. Deeply affected by the sight of the
bodies of five Franciscan protomartyrs of Africa that were
brought back from Morocco, and also because of his acquaint-
ance with a Franciscan friar in Coimbra, he joined the
Franciscan Order and took "Anthony" as his name in religion.

A few weeks later he embarked for Morocco, but after a
short stay he had to leave because of illness. However, due to
storms at sea, he was forced to disembark at Sicily and then
went on to the mainland of Italy. He took part in the General
Chapter of the Franciscans at Portiuncula in 1221, where he
met St. Francis of Assisi. He was ordained to the priesthood in
Italy and began a preaching ministry that took him through
northern Italy to southern France and into the stronghold of the
Albigensians. Returning to Italy in 1227, he reached his

zenith as a preacher at Padua. He was also the first Franciscan to teach theology and was named a lector by St. Francis himself. He died at Padua, where he had been assigned since 1230, and the city gave him a triumphal funeral. He is buried there in the basilica that bears his name.

MESSAGE AND RELEVANCE

The new Opening Prayer of the Mass recognizes Anthony as "an outstanding preacher" that God gave to his people. St. Anthony gave evidence of his preaching skill very early in his priesthood. Pope Gregory IX and Thomas of Vercelli rightly called him an "Ark of the New Testament," because of his biblical exegesis. He was also called the "Hammer of Heretics." Above all, he was an authentic Franciscan, faithful to the traditions established by St. Francis of Assisi.

In the Office of Readings we have an excerpt from a sermon preached by St. Anthony for the feast of Pentecost: "The man who is filled with the Holy Spirit speaks in different languages. These different languages are different ways of witnessing to Christ, such as humility, poverty, patience and obedience; we speak in those languages when we reveal in ourselves these virtues to others. Actions speak louder than words; let your words teach and your actions speak. We are full of words but empty of actions."

In the Opening Prayer we pray: "With his assistance may we follow the gospel of Christ and know the help of your grace in time of need." Popular devotion to St. Anthony as a helper of the oppressed is not fictitious. His name is attached to the law promulgated in Padua in 1231, exempting from imprisonment those who could not pay their fines or other financial debts. He is rightly invoked as "a ready helper in time of need." To this day "St. Anthony's bread" is still distributed to the poor by Franciscan friars throughout the world.

We are invited to imitate the saint whom St. Francis of Assisi called his "bishop." His knowledge of Sacred Scripture made him competent in theological disputes and a master of persuasion. He is pictured in art with a book, signifying his love of Scripture; with a flaming heart, signifying his zeal as a preacher; or holding the Infant Jesus in his arms, recalling a visit from the Infant during one of his raptures. But for us the relevance of St. Anthony is his fidelity to the gospel, his zeal in dialoguing with those in error, and his loving concern for the poor.

> Opening Prayer: *Almighty God, you have given St. Anthony to your people as an outstanding preacher and a ready helper in time of need. With his assistance may we follow the gospel of Christ and know the help of your grace in every difficulty.*

June 19
ST. ROMUALD (951/2-1027)

HISTORICO-LITURGICAL NOTE

Formerly celebrated on February 7, this feast has been moved to June 19. Romuald was born at Ravenna, Italy, of a noble family around the year 951. When his father killed another man in a duel, Romuald was so affected that he retired to a Benedictine monastery. He remained there for three years, but he was so observant of the rule that he aroused the animosity of the lax monks, especially when he tried to give them fraternal correction. With the abbot's permission, he moved to the vicinity of Venice and placed himself under the direction of a hermit.

For the next thirty years Romuald travelled extensively throughout Italy, founding monasteries and hermitages. He also suffered a prolonged period of spiritual dryness, and when it ended he obtained permission to join a group that was going to Hungary as missionaries. He tried several times to carry out his plan, but each time he entered Hungary he immediately became seriously ill. He took that as a sign that it was not God's will that he engage in that apostolate. In 994 he returned to Ravenna and eventually, in 1012, he founded what was to become the Camaldolese Order of hermits. After some years at Camaldoli, Romuald returned to his travels. He died, alone in his cell, at the monastery of Val di Castro. In 1595 Pope Clement VIII approved a feast for the translation of his relics to Fabriano.

MESSAGE AND RELEVANCE

The Opening Prayer refers to St. Romuald's mission in the Church, namely, to renew the life of solitude and prayer. He adapted the Rule of St. Benedict so that in addition to liturgical prayer and manual labor, the monks could devote themselves to solitude and private personal prayer. According to his plan, there were two classes of monks: the hermits and the recluses. The first lived in separate cells but prayed the Liturgy of the Hours in common at designated times; the recluses, however, did not leave their hermitages for any reason whatever. They even had their own private altars for the celebration of the Eucharist. The austerity of Camaldolese life was somewhat mitigated by the time the Constitutions were approved by Pope Alexander II in 1072.

Although a hermit by temperament and lifestyle, Romuald was also aware of the problems of the Church in his day. He responded to the request of the emperor to have his monks go forth to evangelize Poland, Bohemia and Russia, but without much success. As we have seen, he himself had wanted to be a missionary to Hungary.

In the Opening Prayer we ask that we may attain to the joy of heaven by following Christ through self-denial. The phrase "bring us the joy of heaven" strikes an eschatological note that is especially relevant to the Camaldolese style of life. Totally withdrawn from the world to a life of prayer and solitude, these hermits have their gaze fixed constantly on the life that is to come. Their holy founder St. Romuald, an outstanding reformer of the monastic life in his day, serves as an exemplary reminder to monks of today to be faithful to the observances of the monastic life.

> Preface: *In your kindness you filled St. Romuald, father and teacher of monks and hermits, with the joy of sublime contemplation; you illumined him with the light of prophecy and inflamed him with apostolic zeal. Thus, by the silence of his tongue and the eloquence of his life, he led many souls along the way of salvation.*

June 21
ST. ALOYSIUS GONZAGA (1568-1591)

HISTORICO-LITURGICAL NOTE

This saintly seminarian died in Rome in 1591 and was canonized in 1726. He was born of a noble family at Castiglione (between Brescia and Mantua, Italy) and his father earnestly wanted him to become a soldier, but that was not to be. At the age of 10 Aloysius consecrated himself to God with a vow of virginity. He received his First Communion at the age of twelve from the hands of St. Charles Borromeo.

In his early teens Aloysius and his brother Ridolfo served at the court of the Duke of Mantua and later at the court of the prince of Asturias in Spain. On his return to Italy in July, 1584, Aloysius was determined to enter the Society of Jesus. He transferred his right of succession to his brother Ridolfo and on November 25, 1585, he entered the Jesuit novitiate in Rome. He lived there for six years, with St. Robert Bellarmine as his spiritual director. He received the minor orders at St. John Lateran and continued to prepare himself for the priesthood, dreaming of the foreign missions and even martyrdom.

During the plague of 1591 he nursed the sick and, like several other members of the Jesuit community, he contracted the disease, but he never recovered from it. He died at midnight between June 20 and 21, with the name of Jesus on his lips.

MESSAGE AND RELEVANCE

The revised prayers of the Mass refer to three characteristics of this young Jesuit whom Pope Pius XI named patron of youth in 1926. First of all, the Opening Prayer states that in St. Aloysius God "combined remarkable innocence with the spirit of penance." We then ask that "we, who have not followed his innocence" may follow his example of penance. Although Aloysius accused himself of being a sinner, the fact is that he never stained his baptismal innocence. He followed a schedule of austerity and mortification from which he did not deviate even when he served at court. After he entered the Society of Jesus he became even more austere.

In the Prayer over the Gifts we find a second characteristic of Aloysius. We ask that we may "always come to the Eucharist with hearts free from sin." The Latin version of this prayer speaks of the "wedding garment of St. Aloysius" (cf. Mt 22:11-13). Hence, the second characteristic of St. Aloysius is that he was garbed in charity. So intense was his love of God that he frequently fell into ecstasy, not only in the chapel, but sometimes at meals or during the recreation period. This same charity prompted him to serve the sick and the needy and to have a preference for the poor and lowly, in spite of his noble heritage.

The third characteristic is in the Prayer after Communion, where, after referring to the "bread of life," we ask that we may serve God without sin and spend our lives in thanksgiving. The Communion Antiphon also refers to the Eucharist as "bread from heaven" and "bread of the angels." The description of Aloysius as "angelic" in the former liturgy has been omitted so that the young saint would appear more human and not ingenuously innocent. St. Aloysius had a premonition that he would die on the octave day of Corpus Christi and he asked for Viaticum, even though he did not seem to be in immediate danger of death. In a letter to his mother, in the Office of Readings, after speaking of his impending death, he concludes: "I write all this with the one desire that you and all my family may consider my departure a joy and favor, and that you especially may speed with a mother's blessing my passage across the waters till I reach the shore to which all hopes belong."

> Opening Prayer: *Father of love, giver of all good things, in Saint Aloysius you combined remarkable innocence with the spirit of penance. By the help of his prayers may we who have not followed his innocence follow his example of penance.*

June 22
ST. PAULINUS of NOLA (353/4-431)

HISTORICO-LITURGICAL NOTE

The feast of St. Paulinus is celebrated on the day of his death, according to his disciple Uranius and the Jerome Calendar. Born at Bordeaux, France, of a Roman senatorial family and well trained in rhetoric and poetry, he spent 20 years in political life. He travelled extensively in France, Spain, and Italy, and in 381 he became governor of Campania, Italy. Returning to France after the victory of the Goths at Adrianopolis, he married the Spanish lady Theresia, who shared with him her ideal of living a strictly evangelical life. They came into contact with some of the most important persons of the time, including St. Martin of Tours and St. Ambrose.

In 389 Paulinus was baptized and moved to Spain. After the death of his only child, Celsus, he gave away all of his patrimony and embraced a monastic style of life. Under pressure from the people, he was ordained a priest at Barcelona in 394, but he then retired to Nola, near Naples, close to the shrine of St. Felix, and founded a small monastic community. Together with his wife, both of whom now lived a life of celibacy, he set up a hospice for the sick and for pilgrims to the shrine of St. Felix. In 409 Paulinus was called by the people to be bishop of Nola, but we have few details of his episcopate except that he ruled with wisdom and generosity. Paulinus died at Nola at the age of 76, after serving for 20 years as bishop. His relics were transferred to Rome but were restored to Nola by order of Pope Pius X in 1909.

MESSAGE AND RELEVANCE

The new Opening Prayer of the Mass touches on two aspects of the spiritual profile of this saintly bishop. The first is his pastoral concern for his people. Although we have scant documentation on his episcopate, we do know that he had a gift for cultivating friendly relations, as is evident from his vast correspondence with well-known personages of his day, including St. Augustine of Hippo. In his letter to Alipius, bishop of Tagaste and friend of St. Augustine, which is contained in the Office of Readings, he expresses his friendship and sends a gift: "We have sent to you a loaf of bread in token of our unity; it symbolizes as well the substance of the Trinity. By accepting it you will make it a bread of blessing."

The second trait of his spirituality is his love of poverty and his love for the poor. In the Opening Prayer we ask that we may imitate "his love for others." In fact, Paulinus gave up all his possessions in order to live evangelical poverty. He wrote in a poem dedicated to St. Felix: "With all my wealth I pay for the hope of heaven, because hope and faith are of much more value than all the riches of this world." The spirituality of Paulinus was an ascetical spirituality in which the wealthy should be stewards of earthly goods for the benefit of the poor and the poor should pray to God for the benefit of the wealthy. The austere life of this great bishop, who with his wife lived the evangelical counsels and had a great concern for the poor, is a good model for us who live in a consumer society.

Opening Prayer: *Lord, you made St. Paulinus renowned for his love of poverty and concern for his
people. May we who celebrate his witness to the gospel
imitate his example of love for others.*

June 22
ST. JOHN FISHER (1469-1535) and
ST. THOMAS MORE (1477-1535)

HISTORICO-LITURGICAL NOTE

This feast honors two martyrs of the Catholic Church in
sixteenth-century England, one a bishop and the other a
layman. They were canonized in 1935 and their feast was
placed on the day of the martyrdom of St. John Fisher. Thomas
More died a few days later, on July 6.

John Fisher was born in Yorkshire, England, and was
ordained a priest at the age of 25, after a brilliant career at
Cambridge University. He distinguished himself by combat-
ting the Protestant heresies and especially the theses proposed
by Martin Luther. At the age of 35, while remaining Chancellor at Cambridge, he became bishop of Rochester. He was
confessor to the mother of Henry VIII, Elizabeth of York, and
was renowned for his humanistic as well as his theological
learning. He was a friend of Erasmus of Rotterdam, to whom he
gave a chair at Christ's College at Cambridge. Erasmus said of
Fisher: "There is not a man more cultured, more admired or
more holy." Fisher's episcopal residence was like a monastery
because of its austerity and the daily Liturgy of the Hours as
well as the discipline of the domestics. Because he defended
the validity of the first marriage of Henry VIII, he was imprisoned for the first time in 1533. Later, he was interned in the
Tower of London because he refused to take the oath of loyalty
after the king married Anne Boleyn and rejected papal author-

ity over the Church in England. He was beheaded a month after Pope Paul III had named him a cardinal.

Thomas More was born in London and studied at Oxford and in London. He was twice married and was a member of Parliament. Together with Pico della Mirandola (whose biography More had written in 1494) and Erasmus (who was More's close friend), More was an outstanding humanist. His most famous work, *Utopia*, is a book of political philosophy, showing a society based on the natural virtues. Eventually More became Chancellor to Henry VIII, succeeding Cardinal Wolsey. He was opposed to the king's divorce and after three years he resigned as Chancellor and refused to recognize the king's spiritual supremacy. After imprisonment in the Tower of London, he was beheaded on July 6 at the age of 57.

MESSAGE AND RELEVANCE

The new Opening Prayer of the Mass dates from 1969 and is based on St. Paul's Letter to Timothy (4:6-7) and two texts from the writings of St. Hilary. In the first part of the prayer we read that God "confirms the true faith with the crown of martyrdom." We then ask for "the courage to proclaim our faith by the witness of our lives."

John Fisher witnessed to and defended the faith when he declared that the royal marriage could not be dissolved by any power on earth or in heaven. He asserted that he was willing to give his life in defense of this teaching, as did John the Baptist. His martyrdom was like a liturgy of the word. He first read the passage from John 17:3 and then said to the people: "I have come here to die for the faith of the Catholic Church and of Christ." He then recited the *Te Deum* and Psalm 30. To the end he was concerned about the bishops who would yield to the king and he said, somewhat bitterly: "Courage has been betrayed by those who should have defended it."

Thomas More, who was described by Pope Pius XI as a "truly complete man," considered himself unworthy of martyrdom and feared for his weakness, as he wrote to his daughter Margaret: "Although I know well, Margaret, that because of my past wickedness I deserve to be abandoned by God, I cannot but trust in his merciful goodness. . . . I will not mistrust him, Meg, though I shall feel myself weakening and on the verge of being overcome with fear." Nevertheless, he was able to meet death with a smile and a humorous remark on his lips.

These two martyrs were firmly convinced that the Roman See is of divine institution, at a time when papal power was both spiritual and political. There was a conflict between papal authority and the divine right of kings. There was also the scandal of the Western Schism, with popes and anti-popes. It is understandable, therefore, why some bishops and clergy, universities and educated people had signed the Act of Supremacy.

The last paragraph of the letter of St. Thomas More to his daughter Margaret is well worth pondering: "Nothing can come but what God wills. And I am very sure that whatever that be, however bad it may seem, it shall indeed be the best."

> Opening Prayer: *Father, you confirm the true faith with the crown of martyrdom. May the prayers of Saints John Fisher and Thomas More give us the courage to proclaim our faith by the witness of our lives.*

June 24
BIRTH OF ST. JOHN THE BAPTIST

HISTORICO-LITURGICAL NOTE

This solemn feast dates from the fourth century and at one time it was preceded by a day of fasting as well as a Mass for the vigil. In the Middle Ages it was celebrated with three Masses. St. Augustine and some other theologians saw something symbolic in the fact that St. John the Baptist was born in the summer, when the days are beginning to shorten, and Christ was born in the winter, when the days are gradually getting longer. The revised liturgy has restored the vigil Mass in addition to the Mass for the feast. In many Catholic countries, especially in Spain and Latin America, June 24 is a day of popular celebrations. Byzantine Christians celebrate the feast of the *conception* of John the Baptist on September 24.

MESSAGE AND RELEVANCE

There are two themes in the Masses of the vigil and the feast, based on the role of John the Baptist as precursor of the Messiah. In the Latin version the Opening Prayer for the vigil refers to John as the one who "prepared the way of salvation," and the Prayer after Communion says that John is the prophet who "pointed out Christ the Lamb, sent to atone for the sins of the world."

The Preface for the Mass of the feast sums up the life and mission of John the Baptist. From all those born of woman, God chose John to prepare the way of the Lord. He was indeed more than a prophet because he not only preached repentance and conversion, but he actually pointed to Christ present in the midst of mankind. More than that, he baptized in the waters of the Jordan him who is the author of baptism.

John's action as a prophet was heroic, even to the point of death; he was also humble in stating that he was not worthy to tie the strap of Christ's sandal (Jn 3:30). He did not make himself equal to Christ, as St. Augustine points out in the Office of Readings: "John was a voice that lasted only for a time; Christ, the Word in the beginning, is eternal." There is a message here for us today, when so many Christians do not distinguish between tolerance and the integrity of the faith. The words of Christ to John are also relevant: "Blessed is the man who finds no stumbling block in me" (Mt 11:2-6).

Preface: *We praise your greatness as we honor the prophet who prepared the way before your Son. You set*

John the Baptist apart from other men, marking him out with special favor. His birth brought great rejoicing: even in the womb he leapt for joy, so near was man's salvation. You chose John the Baptist from all the prophets to show the world its Redeemer, the Lamb of sacrifice. He baptized Christ, the giver of baptism, in waters made holy by the one who was baptized. You found John worthy of a martyr's death, his last and greatest act of witness to your Son.

June 27
ST. CYRIL of ALEXANDRIA (370-444)

HISTORICO-LITURGICAL NOTE

The feast of St. Cyril, also celebrated on this date in the Byzantine and Coptic liturgy, but on June 7 by others, was extended to the entire Latin Church by Pope Leo XIII, who proclaimed St. Cyril a Doctor of the Church in 1883.

Born at Alexandria of an illustrious family and a nephew of the Patriarch Theophilus of Alexandria, he was prejudiced against St. John Chrysostom, Patriarch of Constantinople, and was present at the famous synod that deposed him (403). Cyril succeeded his uncle as Patriarch in 412; he fought against the heretics, closed the churches of the Novatians and expelled the Jews from the city. This provoked a reaction from the prefect Orestes, although the emperor had approved Cyril's actions.

The great esteem that the bishops of the East and Pope Zosimus had for Cyril is a testimony to his zeal for the faith and the expertise he exhibited in the first period of his episcopate, when he wrote the greater part of his exegetical works. But when Nestorius, who became Patriarch of Constantinople in 428, denied the divinity of Christ and, consequently, that Mary is the Mother of God, St. Cyril reacted vehemently. He wrote to Pope Celestine I about the matter and, after the

Roman Synod, Cyril was told to notify Nestorius of the papal decision. The letter sent by Cyril to Nestorius was badly interpreted and Cyril himself was accused of heresy. Hence the convocation of the Council of Ephesus by the emperor Theodosius (431), over which Cyril presided in the name of Pope Celestine I. He deposed Nestorius and commanded the reading of the Nicene Creed as well as his last letter to Nestorius, together with 12 anathemas. His triumph was complete.

After the Council, St. Cyril continued to defend orthodox Catholic doctrine and to administer his see. The Church is indebted to him for his defense of the mystery of the Incarnation and for the dogma of Mary's divine motherhood. Some have said that if he had exercised more patience and diplomacy he might have prevented the rise of the Nestorian Church, but the truth is that since the time of St. Cyril Nestorianism has never been a real threat to the Church.

MESSAGE AND RELEVANCE

The Opening Prayer states that the bishop Cyril "courageously taught that Mary was the Mother of God." We are thus reminded of the Council of Ephesus, attended by more than 200 bishops. The letter that he sent to all the monks of Egypt to justify the title "Theotokos," "Mother of God," as applied to Mary (Office of Readings) reveals the complete orthodoxy of St. Cyril. Consequently, we ask in the Opening Prayer: "May we who cherish this belief receive salvation through the incarnation of Christ your Son."

Although Cyril was somewhat inexact in his first exposition of doctrine at Ephesus, he was struggling to defend the dogma of the Incarnation, which is the basis for the doctrine on the divine maternity of Mary. We should also note that all of Christianity at that time sided with Cyril against Nestorius. We profess that Jesus Christ is the Son of God and Mary is the Mother of God. St. Cyril states it this way: "Surely she must be the Mother of God if our Lord Jesus Christ is God, and she gave birth to him! Our Lord's disciples may not have used those exact words, but they delivered to us the belief those words enshrine, and this has also been taught us by the holy fathers."

> Opening Prayer: *Father, the bishop Cyril courageously taught that Mary was the Mother of God. May we who cherish this belief receive salvation through the incarnation of Christ your Son.*

June 28
ST. IRENAEUS (120/140-202/3)

HISTORICO-LITURGICAL NOTE

This feast is listed in the Jerome Calendar for June 28 and it was first celebrated at Lyons, France; from there it spread to the East. It was inscribed in the Roman Calendar only in 1928.

Irenaeus was born at Smyrna and was a member of the Christian colony of Greek origin in Asia Minor. He was a disciple of Polycarp, who had heard St. John the Evangelist preach. He emigrated to southern France and eventually visited Rome. He became very well acquainted with various heresies and especially Gnosticism. His treatise against the Gnostics has come down to us in Latin and it contains a systematic presentation of Catholic doctrine. Around the year 177 he was back at Lyons, which was then still a mission territory and was suffering under the violent persecution by Marcus Aurelius.

Irenaeus became a priest at Lyons and eventually became bishop of the diocese. He sent missionaries to various parts of France and, according to Jerome and Gregory of Tours, he suffered martyrdom, but there is no other proof of this. His relics were contained in a crypt beneath the altar but were totally destroyed by the Calvinists in 1562.

MESSAGE AND RELEVANCE

The prayers of the Mass highlight the characteristics of St. Irenaeus. In the Opening Prayer we invoke God, who "called St. Irenaeus to uphold your truth," and we also refer to truth in the Prayer over the Gifts. The Church at Lyons gave him the title of "Doctor," since he destroyed the heretical teachings of the Gnostics. He is without a doubt one of the greatest theologians of the second century. His theology is based on Scripture and Tradition, as all theology should be.

Our petition in the Opening Prayer is that we may be renewed "in faith and love." St. Irenaeus had stated: "It is better and more profitable to be simple and less well educated but close to God through charity than to appear wise and gifted but to blaspheme the Master." Therefore in the Prayer over the Gifts we ask for an increase of the love of truth and that the Church will remain firm in faith and unity.

The Prayer after Communion states that "as the holy bishop Irenaeus reached eternal glory by being faithful until death, so may we be saved by living our faith." St. Irenaeus is truly a model of perseverance in the faith. His teaching is in accord with the apostolic tradition which, he said, "is made known throughout the world because it can be seen in every church by anyone who wants to know the truth." He also said that we can rely on the bishops who were installed by the apostles and their successors until our time. They have not taught anything that resembles the foolish teachings of the Gnostics.

Another note that emerges from the Opening Prayer and the Prayer over the Gifts is the request that "we may always be intent on fostering unity and peace in the Church." As a man faithful to tradition, Irenaeus acted as a mediator in the dispute concerning Easter, when Pope Victor threatened to excommunicate the Church in Asia Minor. Eusebius reports in his *Ecclesiastical History* that Irenaeus, representing the Church in France, agreed with Pope Victor that Easter should be celebrated on a Sunday, but he advised the pope not to excommunicate a whole Church because it was holding to an ancient custom.

The criterion for preserving unity and peace while tolerating diversity of traditions is stated by Irenaeus in his treatise *Against Heresies*. He asserts that Sts. Peter and Paul established the Church at Rome, and the apostolic tradition has come down to us through a series of their successors. Hence, the Church of Rome has supreme authority by reason of its origin and all the other Churches should be in union with the Church of Rome. The Church, says Irenaeus, should have "one heart, one soul, and one mouth." This is a great incentive for all Christian churches to review the tradition in order to find a basis for reunion with the Church of Rome, the mother of all the churches.

> Opening Prayer: *Father, you called St. Irenaeus to uphold your truth and bring peace to your Church. By his prayers renew us in faith and love that we may always be intent on fostering unity and peace.*

June 29
ST. PETER and ST. PAUL (+67?)

HISTORICO-LITURGICAL NOTE

This solemn feast was already celebrated in the *Depositio Martyrum*, as early as 354 and on this same date at a time when St. Peter's Basilica at the Vatican was still under construction. In the time of St. Ambrose (339-397), the solemnity was celebrated in three station churches and also with a vigil liturgy, but in the seventh century the liturgy was celebrated on two different days, with the feast of St. Paul assigned to June 30. In some of the Eastern Churches the double feast was celebrated on June 28.

According to ancient tradition, Simon, whose name was

changed to Peter (meaning rock), died by crucifixion with his head near the ground, as was the Roman custom for the crucifixion of slaves. Recent excavations confirm that the martyrdom of St. Peter, around the year 67, took place on the Vatican hill, where the basilica of Constantine was constructed.

Paul of Tarsus, whose name was originally Saul, was a Pharisee and a persecutor of Christians. He converted to Christianity after his extraordinary experience on the road to Damascus (Ac 9:1-19). After his second imprisonment at Rome he was beheaded (around the year 67, according to Tertullian) not far from the basilica that was given to the care of monks in the sixth century.

MESSAGE AND RELEVANCE

These two saints have always been coupled together in the devotion of the Christian people, as we read in the Preface: "Both shared a martyr's death." It is not absolutely certain, however, that they were imprisoned together.

In the new Opening Prayer of the Mass for the feast we read that through the apostles Peter and Paul the Church "first received the faith," and in the Opening Prayer for the vigil we refer to them as the "apostles who strengthened the faith of the infant Church." In the Prayer after Communion for the vigil we profess that this faith had its beginning in the teaching of these apostles. This apostolic faith is manifested, as it was at Jerusalem, in the breaking of the bread, the teaching of the apostles, the community that is of one heart and soul through charity, and the prayers of the apostles. Consequently, we pray for "love and unity" in the Prayer over the Gifts.

In Rome, the city of the two apostles, the monument on the Palatine hill from which Caesar Augustus issued his decrees is reduced to archaeological ruins, but the Apostolic See which, according to St. Ignatius of Antioch, "presides over the charity of all the churches," is rightly acclaimed as the Church of Rome, a Rome that was crimsoned by the blood of these two great leaders (cf. Office of Readings). Rightly, then, do we sing in the hymn for Morning Prayer of the Liturgy of the Hours:

> Rejoice, O Rome, this day; thy walls they once did sign
> With princely blood, who now their glory share with thee.
> What city's vesture glows with crimson deep as thine?
> What beauty else has earth that may compare with thee?

In the city of Rome the successors of St. Peter have governed the Church for two thousand years. And the history of the popes is both tumultuous and brilliant.

Finally, the martyrdom of St. Peter and St. Paul is also a symbol of the unity of the Church, as St. Augustine says in the Office of Readings: "Both apostles share the same feast day, for these two were one; and even though they suffered on different days, they were as one."

> Preface: *Father, all-powerful and ever-living God, we do well always and everywhere to give you thanks. You fill our hearts with joy as we honor your great apostles: Peter, our leader in the faith, and Paul, its fearless preacher. Peter raised up the Church from the faithful flock of Israel. Paul brought your call to the nations, and became the teacher of the world. Each in his chosen way gathered into unity the one family of Christ. Both shared a martyr's death and are praised throughout the world. Now, with the apostles and all the angels and saints, we praise you for ever.*

June 30
FIRST MARTYRS of the CHURCH of ROME (+64)

HISTORICO-LITURGICAL NOTE

Christians always kept in memory the famous fire in

Rome on July 16, in the year 64, and the subsequent martyrdom of a large number of Christians by Nero. We learn from
Tacitus that some were thrown to the wild beasts and others
were burned at the stake as human torches. However, only the
Roman Martyrology mentions June 24 as the day for the feast.
The Jerome Martyrology, on the other hand, mentions 979
martyrs on June 29, immediately after the eulogy in honor of
St. Peter and St. Paul. This feast was extended to the entire
city of Rome in 1923 but it was not celebrated universally in
the Church until 1969.

MESSAGE AND RELEVANCE

The significance of this feast is expressed in the Opening
Prayer of the Mass, in which we ask God, who "sanctified the
Church of Rome with the blood of its first martyrs," to help us
"find strength from their courage and rejoice in their triumph."
There has been an evolution in the biblical concept of martyrdom. In Judaism martyrdom was an act of obedience to the
Law, and there was a gradual development of hope in the
resurrection (1 and 2 M). For Christians, however, martyrdom
is understood in a Christological context, because the eschatological power of God works through the cross of Christ.
The passion of Christ was in part the result of the violent
opposition and hatred of Satan, but at the same time his
passion and death were oriented towards a glorious resurrection. Christian martyrdom is in a sense a continuation of the
warfare that Satan waged against Christ; at the same time it is a
manifestation of the divine power that was victorious through
the Cross (2 Cor 12:9). That is why martyrdom connotes the
presence of the Spirit, who can overcome all human weakness.
Through our fraternal devotion to the martyrs we are confirmed
in the faith because they are for us a sign of the Spirit of God.

In addition to the Christological and Trinitarian aspects
of Christian martyrdom, there is an ethical dimension. Here it
becomes a weighty argument in favor of the truth of Christianity when we contemplate the heroic courage of the martyrs

who are offered to us as examples. It is in this way that we "find strength in their courage and rejoice in their triumph" (Opening Prayer). The Office of Readings contains an excerpt from St. Clement's letter to the Corinthians, written between the years 96 and 98. After speaking of the martyrdom of Peter and Paul, he speaks of "a great throng of the elect who gave us the finest example of endurance in the face of many indignities and tortures." He concludes: "We ought to put aside vain and useless concerns and go straight to the glorious and venerable norm which is our tradition, and we should consider what is good, pleasing and acceptable in the sight of him who made us. Let us fix our gaze on the blood of Christ, realizing how precious it is to his Father, since it was shed for our salvation and brought the grace of repentance to all the world."

These nameless men and women martyrs that we honor today are expiatory lambs of anti-Christian hatred. They represent all who suffered or are suffering religious persecution throughout the world.

Opening Prayer: *Father, you sanctified the Church of Rome with the blood of its first martyrs. May we find strength from their courage and rejoice in their triumph.*

JULY

BLESSED JUNIPERO SERRA (1713-1784)

HISTORICO-LITURGICAL NOTE

José Miguel Serra was born in Petra, Mallorca, Spain, the son of a farmer, and joined the Franciscan Order in 1730, taking the name of Junipero. After ordination he received a doctorate in theology and taught philosophy at the Lullian University at Palma de Mallorca. In 1749 he sailed for Mexico and en route he preached his first sermon in the Americas at San Juan, Puerto Rico. From 1750 to 1758 he preached extensively throughout Mexico and held numerous administrative offices, including that of Commissary of the Holy Office of the Inquisition.

In 1767 Mexico expelled all the Jesuits and Junipero was chosen president of the missions in Lower California. When the Spaniards took over Upper California in 1769, Junipero accompanied the Spanish forces to San Diego, California, where he founded the first mission in that territory. In the following year he established his headquarters at Monterey-Carmel, California, and in subsequent years he established 9 missions in California.

Junipero followed the traditional Spanish method for the administration of the missions, but he frequently came into conflict with the civil and military authorities because of their mistreatment of the Indians. Contrary to legend, he did not walk from mission to mission but rode on a mule or horse, accompanied by a military guard. His dedication to the

- 169 -

Indians resulted in some 6,000 baptisms. He died at San Carlos Mission in Carmel, California, and was buried with military honors. In 1931 his statue was placed in the Hall of Fame in Washington, D.C. In 1935 the Serra Club was founded in Seattle, Washington, to foster vocations and to promote Catholicism throughout the United States. It was officially established as "Serra International" in 1938. Junipero Serra was beatified by Pope John Paul II in 1988.

MESSAGE AND RELEVANCE

When Junipero Serra requested permission to go to America as a missionary, he stated in his request: "All my life I have wanted to be a missionary. I have wanted to carry the gospel message to those who have never heard of God and the kingdom he has prepared for them. But I became proud and allowed myself to be distracted by academic studies. Now I am filled with remorse that my ambition has been so long delayed."

In his homily at the beatification ceremony, Pope John Paul II said that Junipero Serra was "a shining example of Christian virtue and the missionary spirit. His great good was to bring the gospel to the native peoples of America, so that they, too, might be consecrated to the truth." In the Opening Prayer of the Mass our petition is that we, too, may be inspired by his example to be "faithful witnesses to Jesus Christ." Indeed, the Second Vatican Council has called upon all Christians, regardless of their state of life, to be missionaries and evangelizers, especially by the example of their Christian lives.

> Opening Prayer: *God most high, your servant Junipero Serra brought the gospel of Christ to the peoples of Mexico and California and firmly established the Church among them. By his intercession, and through the example of his evangelical zeal, inspire us to be faithful witnesses of Jesus Christ.*

July 3
ST. THOMAS

HISTORICO-LITURGICAL NOTE

The feast of the apostle Thomas, formerly celebrated on December 21, has been transferred to July 3 in order to coincide with the translation of his relics to Edessa. The Syro-Malabar Rite in India, where the people call themselves "Thomas Christians," and the Syro-Malankara Rite also celebrate his feast on this day. Pope Paul VI proclaimed St. Thomas the patron of India in 1972.

This apostle is simply named Thomas in the Gospels of Matthew and Luke (Mt 10:3; Mk 3:18; Lk 6:15; Ac 1:13) but St. John's Gospel (11:15; 20-24) adds the Greek name "Didymus" (twin) because that is the meaning of "Thomas." He is also known as "doubting Thomas," because when Jesus appeared to the apostles to prove that he had truly risen, Thomas was not with them and so refused to believe that it was he whom they had seen. Later, Christ appeared again when Thomas was with the group, and he made his famous confession of faith: "My Lord and my God!"

The Antiochene tradition of his missionary journey to Persia, and especially his stay in India, is based on apocryphal literature that may well have a historical basis. Legend has it that he was martyred at Calamina in India, but no one has succeeded in identifying that place. Others maintain that he was martyred at Mylapore or present-day Madras. His relics were ultimately transferred to Abruzzi, Italy, where they are venerated.

MESSAGE AND RELEVANCE

The Communion Antiphon of the Mass quotes the words of Christ to the doubting Thomas: "Put your hands here, and see the place of the nails. Doubt no longer, but believe" (Jn 20:27). The Opening Prayer of the Mass and the Prayer after

Communion refer to the confession of Thomas that Jesus Christ is Lord and God (Jn 20:21-29). By his act of faith he made amends for his previous skepticism. In the Prayer after Communion we say that "with St. Thomas we acknowledge Christ to be our Lord and God." Our faith in the resurrection of Christ rests solidly on the testimony of the apostles, as we read in the responsory for the Office of Readings: "We have seen it with our own eyes and with our own hands we have touched the Word of life; what we have seen and heard we declare to you" (1 Jn 1:1). In the Office of Readings St. Gregory the Great says: "The disbelief of Thomas has done more for our faith than the belief of the other disciples" (cf. also the antiphon for the Canticle of Zechariah).

A second biographical note is found in the first antiphon for Morning Prayer and it is indicative of the mentality of Thomas. At the Last Supper, when Jesus spoke of his departure, Thomas spoke up: "Lord, we do not know where you are going; how can we know the way?" To this, Jesus replied: "I am the Way, the Truth and the Life." Yet another significant passage, omitted in the liturgy, is the one in which Thomas urges his companions: "Let us go along, to die with him" (Jn 11:16).

What is applicable to us is the petition in the Prayer after Communion: "May we show by our lives that our faith is real." And in the acclamation for the Gospel we read: "Blessed are those who have not seen me, but still believe." In the Office of Readings St. Gregory makes a very important observation: "Faith is the proof of what cannot be seen. What is seen gives knowledge, not faith. . . . There is here a particular reference to ourselves; we hold in our hearts one we have not seen in the flesh." Hence the words of Christ, "Blessed are those who have not seen and have believed" apply to us, but only, says St. Gregory, "if we follow up our faith with good works. The true believer practices what he believes."

Preface: *The risen Christ appeared to the apostles the first time when Thomas was absent, so that the incredulous apostle, having overcome his skepticism,*

*would strengthen our faith by his gesture. When he saw
the pierced hand of the Master, Thomas proclaimed
him his Lord and his God and was able to testify with
extraordinary certitude to the truth of the resurrection.*

July 4
ST. ELIZABETH of PORTUGAL (1271-1336)

HISTORICO-LITURGICAL NOTE

This saintly queen of Portugal was the daughter of King
Peter III of Aragon and was named after her great-aunt, St.
Elizabeth of Hungary. At the early age of 12 she was married to
Denis, king of Portugal, from whom she had two children:
Constance, future queen of Castile, and Alphonse, successor
to the throne of Portugal. She endured with heroic patience the
infidelity of her husband and even provided for the education
of his illegitimate children. King Denis died in 1325, and
Elizabeth tried unsuccessfully to enter the Poor Clares at
Coimbra. Failing that, she became a Franciscan Tertiary and
moved to a house adjacent to the monastery, where she followed a monastic schedule. Throughout her entire life she had
been faithful to the practice of prayer, including the daily
recitation of the Liturgy of the Hours. Her charitable works
included a hospital, a residence for wayward girls, a home for
foundlings and the monastery of the Poor Clare nuns at
Coimbra, where she was buried in 1336. St. Elizabeth was
canonized in 1625 and listed in the Roman Calendar in 1630.

MESSAGE AND RELEVANCE

The Opening Prayer of the Mass refers to the principal
activity of Elizabeth: "Father of peace and love, you gave St.
Elizabeth the gift of reconciling enemies. . . . Give us the

courage to work for peace among men, that we may be called the sons of God." The beatitude, "Blessed are the peacemakers," applies to this saintly queen in a special way. When she was accused of inciting her son to rebel against the king, all her goods were confiscated and she was sent into exile. She refused to use the troops and arms that her supporters offered her; rather, she urged them to remain loyal to the king. She endured this unjust punishment with consummate patience and was finally vindicated. On several other occasions she reconciled her husband with their son and also prevented the waging of war by Ferdinand IV of Castile and James II of Aragon. The discourse of St. Peter Chrysologus in the Office of Readings is a commentary on the beatitude of the peacemakers. One of Elizabeth's sayings was: "If you love peace, all will be well."

The responsory for the Office of Readings is a text from Isaiah, which describes St. Elizabeth's care of the sick and the poor: "Sharing your bread with the hungry, sheltering the oppressed and the homeless; clothing the naked when you see them and not turning your back on your own" (Is 58:7). Her chapel in honor of the Immaculate Virgin at the convent of the Trinity in Lisbon is perhaps the first sanctuary in which the Immaculate Conception was venerated. It is said that her last words before dying were: "Mary, Mother of grace." The example of this queen, who patiently resigned herself to a very unhappy marriage and devoted herself to the service of a family beset with tensions, is a source of edification and consolation to many married women in contemporary society.

Opening Prayer: *Father of peace and love, you gave St. Elizabeth the gift of reconciling enemies. By the help of her prayers give us the courage to work for peace among men, that we may be called sons of God.*

July 5
ST. ANTHONY ZACCARIA (1502-1539)

HISTORICO-LITURGICAL NOTE

This feast is celebrated on the date of the death of St. Anthony Zaccaria, who died in 1539 at the early age of 37 and was canonized in 1879.

He was born at Cremona, Italy, and was given a Christian education by his mother, who was widowed at the age of 18 and dedicated her life to the care of her only son. At an early age Anthony made a vow of virginity and renounced his inheritance. He studied medicine at Padua and returned to Cremona with the intention of working as a physician. But under the guidance of two Dominicans he prepared for the priesthood instead and was ordained in 1528. Moving to Milan in 1530, he founded a society called "Eternal Wisdom" and then, with two members of that society, he founded the Congregation of Clerks Regular of St. Paul, which had for its purpose the reform of the clergy and laity. The Congregation was approved by Pope Clement VII in 1533 and its members became known popularly as the Barnabites, since their headquarters were in the church of St. Barnabas. The Constitutions were definitively composed in 1579, after being reviewed by St. Charles Borromeo. With the assistance of Countess Torelli, St. Anthony also founded a congregation for women.

MESSAGE AND RELEVANCE

The revised Opening Prayer of the Mass gives the dominant characteristic of this saint, who began his studies during the time that Martin Luther was rebelling against the Church (1520-1524). Our petition is that God will give us "the sublime wisdom of Jesus Christ, the wisdom which inspired St. Anthony Zaccaria to preach the message of salvation in your Church." Mention is also made of "the spirit of St. Paul," to whom Anthony was so devoted that he placed his Clerks Regular under his patronage. Preaching the "message of salvation" as St. Paul had done (Ac 13:26), he was instrumental in the conversion of numerous sinners.

The only writings of St. Anthony Zaccaria are 12 letters, 6 sermons and the Constitutions for the Barnabites. In a sermon to his followers, which is in the Office of Readings, St. Anthony speaks of the consequences of that divine wisdom which makes us fools for the sake of Christ: "Since we have chosen such a great apostle Paul as our guide and father and claim to follow him, we should try to put his teaching and example into practice in our lives." Anthony intended to found an apostolic congregation dedicated to the ministry of the word and the ministry of the sacraments. In this way he was able to wage a counterattack against the followers of Luther. There are two Barnabite saints: Alexander Sauli and Francis Xavier Bianchi.

The sermon in the Office of Readings reminds us of the perennial relevance of the teaching of St. Paul, the apostle to the Gentiles: "Such a leader should not be served by faint-hearted troops, nor should such a parent find his sons unworthy of him." The example of St. Anthony Zaccaria is relevant to our times, when we are called upon to implement the teachings of the Second Vatican Council. Moreover, his promotion of the Forty Hours Devotion and his associations for married couples could also be imitated today.

Preface (Proper to the Barnabites): *You raised up our father Anthony Mary to work in your vineyard with such zeal that, arriving quickly at perfection, he travelled a long road on the path of sanctity. He raised up in your Church new religious families and, removing a large number of the faithful from the vanity of the world, he taught them to love above all things our Lord Jesus Christ, raised on the cross and hidden behind the eucharistic veil.*

July 6
ST. MARIA GORETTI (1890-1902)

HISTORICO-LITURGICAL NOTE

This young girl was scarcely twelve years old, when she died in defense of her chastity at Nettuno, Italy, on July 6, 1902. She was canonized by Pope Pius XII in 1950, and it is the first time in history that the mother of a saint was present at the canonization.

Maria Teresa Goretti was born of a poor family and was uneducated, but she manifested a maternal spirit in caring for her four little brothers and the neighbors' children while the adults were working in the fields. Her father died when she was ten years old, and one of the men who had worked with her father, Alexander Serenelli by name, had made several attempts to seduce Maria. Her refusal so angered him that he threatened to kill her, which eventually he did, stabbing her 14 times. Maria died in the hospital at Nettuno after forgiving her assassin. In 1910, during his 8th year in prison, Alexander was converted after a dream in which the young martyr presented him with a bouquet of flowers. He was released from prison in 1928 and after asking pardon of Maria's mother, he received Communion with her at the Christmas Mass. Alexander was also present for the canonization of Maria Goretti in 1950. He spent his last years as a Franciscan tertiary with the Capuchins and died in 1970.

MESSAGE AND RELEVANCE

In the Opening Prayer of the Mass we invoke God as the "source of innocence and lover of chastity," who gave St. Maria Goretti "the crown of martyrdom." Maria is a gift for the Church in our time and she gives witness to a great truth: it is possible to reach a high degree of sanctity even in what St. Ignatius of Loyola called "the first degree of humility," namely, to prefer death rather than commit a mortal sin. When Maria stated, "Alexander wanted me to do something evil and I did not want to," she was verifying her previous decision never to yield to his advances, although she had told her mother, "He will kill me." Pope Pius XII said in his sermon at the canonization, which is in the Office of Readings: "With splendid courage she surrendered herself to God and his grace and so gave her life to protect her virginity."

In the Opening Prayer we pray that we may be faithful to God's teaching, as Maria was. Her defense of her virginity makes no sense at all to many persons, but this adolescent had the courage and the purity of heart to say to Alexander: "Don't do it; it is a sin; you will go to hell." On her deathbed Maria not only pardoned Alexander but she said: "I hope that he too will join me in Paradise."

> Opening Prayer: *Father, source of innocence and lover of chastity, you gave St. Maria Goretti the privilege of offering her life in witness to Christ. As you gave her the crown of martyrdom, let her prayers keep us faithful to your teaching.*

July 11
ST. BENEDICT (480-547)

HISTORICO-LITURGICAL NOTE

The date of the death of St. Benedict, the Father of Western Monasticism, is given in the Calendar of Montecassino as March 21. Since this day falls in Lent, the feast is celebrated on July 11, when, in the seventh century, Benedict's relics were transferred to Fleury, France. In 1966 Pope Paul VI proclaimed St. Benedict the patron of Europe and in 1980 Pope John Paul II added the names of St. Cyril and St. Methodius.

Benedict was born at Nursia, Italy, and after completing

his studies in Rome, at about 20 years of age, he left the world for the monastic life. After experimenting with various types of monasticism, he spent three years at Subiaco, living an eremitical life. He attracted followers and soon had a colony of monks under his direction, but because of the jealousy of a local priest, Benedict moved south to Montecassino. There he founded a monastery of the cenobitic life, a "school for the service of the Lord." He composed the now famous Rule of St. Benedict, which ultimately became the standard legislation for all monastic life in the Western Church. His motto, according to Gregory the Great, was "Ora et labora" (Pray and work) and his insignia was a plough and a cross. St. Benedict placed great emphasis on personal love for Christ, humility and prudence. When his last hour approached, he was carried to the abbey church where, with his arms raised to heaven, he expired with a prayer on his lips.

MESSAGE AND RELEVANCE

The new prayers of the Mass delineate the spiritual traits of this "Father of Western Monasticism," who so successfully made the transition from the solitary life of a hermit to the community life of a monk. The Opening Prayer of the Mass refers to the Rule of St. Benedict when it states: "God our Father, you made St. Benedict an outstanding guide to teach men how to live in your service." The Rule of St. Benedict successfully harmonizes Eastern monasticism and Roman wisdom with evangelical prudence so that the Benedictine monastery becomes the new city of God. The abbot represents the paternal authority of God, but always mindful of the superiority of love over the law. Thus, in the Office of Readings an excerpt from the Rule states that the monk should first "put Christ before all else" and, secondly, follow Christ "by the guidance of the gospel." These instructions are valid not only for the monk, who dedicates his life to the "service of God," but for all Christians who are intent on pleasing God alone.

Yet another trait of Benedictine spirituality is found in the Prayer after Communion, taken from Chapter 72 of the Rule of St. Benedict: "May we be faithful in doing your work (*opus Dei*) and in loving our brothers and sisters in true charity." The Benedictine monastery is supposed to be a community of fraternal charity, in which the formation of the complete Christian transcends even manual labor and hospitality. The cross and the plough thus become symbols not only of spiritual culture but of human culture as well.

Finally, in the Prayer over the Gifts, which is inspired by the Apostolic Constitution of Pope Paul VI that proclaimed St. Benedict patron of Europe, we ask that "we may know unity and peace in your service." The word "service" is constantly repeated because it is something so typically Benedictine.

St. Benedict's spirituality is eminently Christocentric; in fact, throughout the centuries the Benedictine monks were the cultivators of the devotional life of the people, centered on Christ. This Christocentric spirituality is also an authentic humanism because it joins the practice of prayer (*ora*) with the tasks of the Christian in the temporal order (*labora*). Consequently, the ideal of Benedictine monasticism as both contemplative and active is very relevant to Christians today.

Preface (Monastic Supplement): *By your grace you significantly enlightened the soul of St. Benedict, who never put anything before his love of Christ and desired to put himself and his sons in your service. You made him renowned in holiness and outstanding in miracles; you perfected him as an eminent master of the monastic life; you gave him to all as a teacher of spiritual wisdom in his love for prayer and for manual labor. A luminous guide for people to the light of the gospel, raised to heaven by a shining path, he teaches people of all times to seek you, O Father, along the right path to the eternal riches prepared for them by you.*

July 13
ST. HENRY (973-1024)

HISTORICO-LITURGICAL NOTE

Henry II, duke of Bavaria, died at Bamberg, Germany, on this date in 1024 and was canonized in 1146. He was an unusually capable military leader and a prudent statesman. Above all, however, he was zealous in promoting the reform of the Church and fostering missionary evangelization.

Henry was the eldest of four brothers and sisters (Bruno became bishop of Augsburg, Gisella married Stephen of Hungary and Brigid became abbess of the monastery of St. Paul in Regensburg). He was educated in monastic schools, where he cultivated his love for the Church and for the monastic life. Pope Pius X named him patron of Benedictine lay oblates. He married Kunegunda of Luxemburg, who became a Benedictine nun after his death in 1024. They had no children, and legend has it that Henry lived a continent life.

After the death of Otto III, Henry was elected emperor and was crowned first at Magonza in 1007 and later by Pope Benedict VIII at Rome. He was the first emperor in the West to receive the golden globe surmounted by the cross. Henry wanted to have the seat of the empire in Germany rather than in Rome and for that purpose he established the diocese of Bamberg. Called to Italy by Pope Benedict VIII, he assisted in the reform of the Church (1021), in which Robert the Pious of France was also interested. He died at the age of 51 in the imperial palace near Gottingen, requesting to be buried in the cathedral that he had constructed at Bamberg.

MESSAGE AND RELEVANCE

The revised Opening Prayer of the Mass states that Henry, filled with God's love, was raised from an earthly kingdom to eternal happiness in heaven. He was head of the vast empire of Charlemagne, which was disorganized and divided. As far as the Church was concerned, he participated in synods, named bishops who were worthy of that office, and supported monasteries, including the famous Benedictine abbey at Cluny. Henry also erected numerous cathedrals, restored churches damaged by heretics, established dioceses and promoted monastic reform. He thought that monasteries were indispensable as centers of prayer and focal points for the civilization of the people.

St. Henry remains even today an example of zeal for Christ and his Church. The Office of Readings contains his letter establishing the new diocese of Bamberg. "Present glory is fleeting and meaningless while it is possessed," says Henry, "unless in it we can glimpse something of heaven's eternity." This sentiment is one that should be expressed repeatedly in modern society, but perhaps the most important lesson we can learn from St. Henry is fidelity to the duties of our state in life.

> Opening Prayer: *Lord, you filled St. Henry with your love and raised him from the cares of an earthly kingdom to eternal happiness in heaven. In the midst of the changes of this world, may his prayers keep us free from sin and help us on our way towards you.*

July 14 (United States)
BLESSED KATERI TEKAKWITHA (1656-1680)

HISTORICO-LITURGICAL NOTE

Kateri (Catherine) Tekakwitha is the first North American Indian to be proposed for canonization. She was born at Auriesville, New York, and died at the age of 24 at Caughnawaga, near Montreal, Canada. Her mother was an Algonquin who had been baptized at Three Rivers, Quebec, but during an Iroquois raid she was carried off to New York, where she was married to a pagan Mohawk chief. Two children were born of this marriage but only Kateri survived; her parents and her brother died in a smallpox epidemic when Kateri was 4 years old. Her face was permanently disfigured and her eyesight was impaired because of the disease. She was raised by an uncle who at one time had three Jesuit missionaries as guests. Kateri received instructions and was baptized on Easter Sunday, 1676.

The other Indians were so vehemently opposed to Kateri's conversion that a Jesuit missionary advised her to flee to a settlement near Montreal, where she could freely practice her religion. She reached the settlement in 1677 and for the next three years, under the guidance of a Jesuit spiritual director and an older woman named Anastasia, Kateri led a life of great austerity and charity. In 1679 she made a vow of virginity and a year later she passed to her eternal reward. Her death was the occasion for a great revival of religious fervor among the Christian Indians. She was beatified by Pope John Paul II in 1980.

MESSAGE AND RELEVANCE

Kateri Tekakwitha is the "Lily of the Mohawks" that was irrigated by the blood of French Jesuit martyrs. Her life is all the more remarkable when one reads the account of the martyrdom of those first missionaries. Once stirred to anger, the Indians practiced satanic cruelty on their enemies. Yet God raised up this saintly maiden in the midst of savagery and brutality.

Likewise remarkable is the fact that at the age of 23 she was able to make a vow of virginity. A celibate life was not held in high regard among the Indians, and being the only Christian in her lodge, Kateri was subject to constant abuse and insults. Because she refused to work on Sundays, she was branded as lazy and the Indians made fun of the Rosary. When at last she was able to escape to the colony near Montreal, she was able to follow her schedule of prayer and austerity unmolested. Her

Jesuit spiritual director wrote about her: "Every morning, winter and summer, she was in our church at four o'clock. She remained several hours in succession in prayer. . . . If sometimes asked, 'Catherine, do you love our Lord?'. . . . 'O Father! O Father!' she would say, and she could say no more." At the moment of her death she whispered: "Jesus, I love you!"

This first North American Indian to be raised to the altars of the Church is an outstanding example of perseverance in the faith in the midst of persecution. Her strength came from her close and constant union with God in prayer. She is a model for all those who are rejected by their own or are persecuted because of their fidelity to the practice of their religion.

> Opening Prayer: *Lord God, you called the virgin Kateri Tekakwitha to shine among the Indian people as an example of innocence of life. Through her intercession, may all peoples of every tribe, tongue and nation, having been gathered into your Church, proclaim your greatness in one song of praise.*

July 14
ST. CAMILLUS de LELLIS (1550-1614)

HISTORICO-LITURGICAL NOTE

Camillus de Lellis died at Rome near the church of the Magdalen, which now contains his body. He was canonized in 1746 and proclaimed patron of the sick and of hospitals in 1886 and of hospital staffs, together with St. John of God, in 1930.

Born in Chieti, Italy, of a noble family, he entered the military and served both in Venice and in Spain against the Moors. At that time he led a disorderly life, especially addicted to gambling and associating with persons of bad reputation. He spent some time as a patient in the hospital of St.

James in Rome and was shocked at the manner in which the patients were treated. At the age of 25 he converted and gave up gambling for good. Twice he tried to enter the Capuchins but was turned away because of bad health. With the help of St. Philip Neri, his confessor, he was ordained a priest at age 34 and dedicated himself to the care of the sick. He soon attracted other men to the same apostolate and that was the beginning of the community of Clerks Regular (now known as Camillians) whose apostolate is to care for the sick. The priest members devote themselves to the spiritual care of the patients and the lay members provide physical care. In 1607, because of internal dissension in the community, Camillus resigned as superior general and returned to the service of the sick.

MESSAGE AND RELEVANCE

The new Opening Prayer of the Mass expresses well the charism of Camillus, who was a giant in stature (more than six feet tall). Thus, we read that God "gave St. Camillus a special love for the sick." And in the Office of Readings, in an excerpt from his biography, written by one of his companions, it says that Camillus saw the person of Christ in the sick and to such an extent that as he fed and cared for them, he felt so strongly that he was serving Christ that he would ask pardon for his sins from the patients. He considered the sick to be his masters and he, their servant and minister (Mt 25:36). He wanted the hospital to be a house of welcome and he himself composed a welcoming rite for all the sick who entered.

The intercession of the Opening Prayer asks that by serving God "in our brothers and sisters we may come safely to [God] at the end of our lives." Once when a cardinal asked to see Camillus, the saint replied that he was with Christ and would see the cardinal when he finished. The Office of Readings reports that he once said: "If there were no poor people in the world, it would be necessary to dig to the center of the earth to look for them and rescue them, to show them compassion and do them good." This zealous servant of the sick is part of a trio of charitable saints, together with St. Vincent de Paul and St. John of God. He once said that he would like to have a heart as big as the world. His example should inspire us today to make necessary reforms in hospital care so that greater attention may be given to individual patients, thus replacing a perfunctory, impersonal care.

> Preface (Proper to the Camillians): *You have blessed our holy father Camillus with a singular spirit of fraternal charity so that, like his brethren in all things, he would dedicate himself entirely to the service of the sick and, seeing in them your suffering Son, would teach everyone the manner of serving them with utmost charity.*

July 15
ST. BONAVENTURE (1217/18-1274)

HISTORICO-LITURGICAL NOTE

This feast honors an outstanding Franciscan saint who was canonized in 1482 and proclaimed "Seraphic Doctor" in 1588. Born near Viterbo, Italy, he entered the Franciscan Order and was sent to Paris for his studies. Eventually he became a professor at the University of Paris. Between 1257 and 1274 he served as Minister General of the Franciscans and he promulgated the revised Constitutions of the Franciscans in 1260. The ringing of the Angelus bell in the evening grew out of a decision of the Franciscan general chapter while Bonaventure was minister general of the Order. He was greatly esteemed for his prudence in keeping peace between the relaxed friars and the observant ones. He refused the offer to become archbishop of York but eventually Pope Gregory X prevailed on him to accept the cardinal's hat and to be bishop of Albano, Italy. He was instrumental in preparing for the Second Council of Lyons (1274), which worked for reunion with the Greeks. A few weeks later, Bonaventure died at Lyons, with the pope at his deathbed.

MESSAGE AND RELEVANCE

The new Opening Prayer of the Mass highlights two traits of this Franciscan saint: "May we . . . always benefit from his wisdom and follow the example of his love." The motto of this Doctor of the Church was "To God alone be honor and glory." Although he was a contemporary and intimate friend of St. Thomas Aquinas, he preferred to follow the Augustinian theological system. In his masterpiece, *Journey of the Mind to God*, he states that one should give little place to understanding and much to unction; little to speech and much to interior joy; little to words and books and much to the gift of God, who is the Holy Spirit; little or nothing to creatures and all to the Creator, Father, Son and Holy Spirit.

In the Office of Readings one can appreciate the ardor of love of the Seraphic Doctor, whose spirituality is based on the sacred humanity of Christ and his passion and death. The mystical tone of his theology is also delineated in the Office of Readings when he says: "If you ask how such things can occur, seek the answer in God's grace, not in doctrine; in the longing of the will, not in the understanding; in the sighs of prayer, not in research."

Some persons have said that Bonaventure's ideas were not always in accord with the ideals of St. Francis of Assisi. He wrote the biography of St. Francis but made no mention of the "Testament" of Francis. It has also been said that the Constitutions promulgated in 1260 are only indirectly dependent on St. Francis of Assisi. However, that may be an indication of Bonaventure's balance and prudence in trying to mediate between the "spirituals" and the second generation of Franciscans.

St. Bonaventure offers a twofold example. First of all, to religious institutes that have been commanded by the Second Vatican Council to renew and adapt their life. Secondly, to theologians, who should "look not to the light but rather to the raging fire that carries the soul to God with intense fervor and glowing love" (Office of Readings).

> Opening Prayer: *All-powerful Father, may we who celebrate the feast of St. Bonaventure always benefit from his wisdom and follow the example of his love.*

July 16
OUR LADY of MOUNT CARMEL

HISTORICO-LITURGICAL NOTE

This is the patronal feast of the Carmelite Order. They take their name from Mount Carmel in Palestine, from which the Carmelite hermits later migrated to Europe. Legend states that Our Lady gave the brown Carmelite scapular to St. Simon Stock in England on July 16, 1251. Between 1376 and 1386 this feast was introduced in commemoration of the approval of the Carmelite Rule by Pope Honorius III in 1226. The feast was listed in the Roman Calendar in 1726 and is now celebrated universally throughout the Church.

MESSAGE AND RELEVANCE

The Latin version of the new Opening Prayer asks that through the maternal intercession of the Blessed Virgin, God will assist us so that "aided by her help along the pathway of life, we may arrive safely at the holy mountain, Jesus Christ." The mention of the "holy mountain" reminds us that Elijah the prophet lived on Mount Carmel with a colony of hermits. Throughout Carmelite history Mount Carmel has been the place of Mary's glory as Mount Tabor was the place of Christ's transfiguration. The antiphon for the Canticle of Zechariah is from Sirach 51:13-15: "When I was young and innocent, I sought wisdom. She came to me in her beauty, and until the end I will cultivate her. As the blossoms yielded to ripening grapes, the heart's joy, my feet kept to the level path because from earliest youth I was familiar with her."

The antiphon for the Canticle of Mary, from the Gospel according to Luke (2:51), presents Mary to us as one who heard the word of God and meditated on it in her heart. The discourse of St. Leo in the Office of Readings presents Mary to us as she who first conceived Christ in her mind and heart through faith and then in her body as his Mother. She is therefore an excellent model of Christian contemplation.

> Preface (Carmelite Missal): *Father, all-powerful and ever-living God, we do well always and everywhere to give you thanks, as we honor the Blessed Virgin Mary, the Mother of Carmel. Your Word filled her heart and inspired all her actions, making her constant in prayer with the apostles and, through her share in our salvation, constituting her the spiritual mother of all mankind. She watches unceasingly with a mother's loving care over the brethren of her Son, and lights us along our pilgrim way to the Mount of your glory, our beacon of comfort, and the embodiment of all our hopes as members of the Church.*

July 21
ST. LAWRENCE of BRINDISI (1559-1619)

HISTORICO-LITURGICAL NOTE

The feast of this Capuchin saint, who died at Lisbon on July 22, 1619, while on his way to the court of King Philip III to plead the cause of the oppressed people in Naples, has been transferred to this date because July 22 is the feast of St. Mary Magdalene. He was canonized in 1881 and proclaimed "Apostolic Doctor" by Pope John XXIII in 1959.

St. Lawrence was born at Brindisi, Italy, under the name Giulio Cesare Russo and entered the Franciscan Conventuals but transferred to the Capuchins in Verona. He studied at Padua and was conversant in French, German, Greek, Syriac and Hebrew. His ministry was preaching, but because of his administrative qualities he was successively Provincial of Tuscany, Venice, Switzerland and Genoa. In 1601 he was sent by the emperor Rudolph II to solicit the aid of the German princes against the Turks, who were threatening to overrun Hungary. He not only obtained their support, but he rode at the head of the troops as chaplain, armed only with the crucifix, and led them to victory at Szekesfehervar. From 1602 until 1605 he served as superior general of the Capuchins. He established the Capuchins in Austria, Moravia and the Tyrol. He died on his sixtieth birthday in Lisbon and was buried in the cemetery of the Poor Clares at Villafranca.

MESSAGE AND RELEVANCE

The Opening Prayer of the Mass recalls two outstanding virtues of St. Lawrence: fortitude and prudence. Undoubtedly he was one of the great defenders of Catholic doctrine against Lutheranism and also a leader in the military campaign against the Turks in Hungary. The Opening Prayer reads: "Lord, for the glory of your name and the salvation of souls you gave Lawrence of Brindisi courage and right judgment." We then ask: "By his prayers, help us to know what we should do and give us the courage to do it."

The writings of this humble but learned Capuchin were published only after his canonization; a more recent edition of 15 volumes appeared in 1956. Not only did his gift for languages enable him to dialogue with the Jews in Hebrew concerning the Old Testament, but also to converse with numerous heads of state as the pope's legate. He was also a successful peacemaker; even his last journey before his death was a peace mission.

St. Lawrence was also an outstanding preacher; he called

preaching an "apostolic duty" (Office of Readings). He preached in practically every country of eastern and western Europe. Since he was so well versed in Sacred Scripture, he could easily answer the objections of the Protestants.

St. Lawrence of Brindisi is an excellent model for preachers as well as a suitable patron for the ecumenical movement. In our day we may well emulate the fortitude and the prudence with which he performed his preaching ministry.

Opening Prayer: *Lord, for the glory of your name and the salvation of souls you gave Lawrence of Brindisi courage and right judgment. By his prayers help us to know what we should do and give us the courage to do it.*

July 22
ST. MARY MAGDALENE

HISTORICO-LITURGICAL NOTE

The feast of St. Mary Magdalene (from Magdala, near the Lake of Galilee) has been celebrated on this date since the tenth century, at Constantinople in the monastery of St. Lazarus. It was believed that her relics were transferred to that monastery in 899 from Ephesus. In the eleventh century the feast spread throughout the Church in the West and in the twelfth century the Lateran Missal identified Mary Magdalene as Mary of Bethany, whose feast was celebrated by the Greeks on March 18.

The identity of Mary Magdalene is disputed. Although many of the Western theologians maintained that Mary of Magdala and Mary of Bethany were one and the same person, others such as St. Jerome, St. Ambrose, St. Augustine and St. Thomas Aquinas leave the question unresolved. The Greeks, however, distinguish between the two Mary's and have separate feasts in their honor.

MESSAGE AND RELEVANCE

The liturgical texts assert that Christ "first entrusted to Mary Magdalene the joyful news of his resurrection" (Opening Prayer of the Mass, Entrance Antiphon, the Gospel of the Mass, the Alleluia). Mary received this testimony from the risen Lord and was told to carry the news to the apostles. "I have seen the Lord," she told them. She is therefore a model for all who are called to give witness to the risen Christ, as we ask in the Opening Prayer: "May we proclaim Christ as our living Lord."

In the Prayer over the Gifts and the Prayer after Communion there is another theme: Magdalene's "loving worship" and her "faithful love" that kept her close to Christ. St. Gregory the Great says: "Though the disciples had left the tomb, she remained. She was still seeking the one she had not found, and while she sought she wept; burning with the fire of love, she longed for him who she thought had been taken away. And so it happened that the woman who stayed behind to seek Christ was the only one to see him. For perseverance is essential to any good deed." In the Gospel according to John (chap. 20) we read that Mary Magdalene was so distraught that she did not even recognize the risen Lord when he stood before her.

Mary Magdalene, who had been liberated from seven devils, became such a faithful follower of Christ that her name is placed first in the list of women who accompanied Jesus (Lk 8:2; Mk 15:47; Mt 27:56). And even on Calvary, the faithful Mary Magdalene took her stand beneath the cross. According to the Eastern tradition, after Pentecost Mary Magdalene accompanied the Blessed Virgin and John to Ephesus, where she died and was buried.

The example of St. Mary Magdalene's ardent love for Christ, her courageous stance on Calvary, and her profession of faith in the risen Lord are relevant for us also, who have not yet fully understood the Scriptures (Jn 20:9).

> Preface: *You enkindled in her heart the fire of an ardent love for Christ that endowed her with freedom of*

spirit, and you infused in her the courage to follow Christ faithfully, even to Calvary. After his death on the cross, she sought her Master so zealously that she merited to meet the risen Lord and to be the first to announce the Easter joy to the apostles.

July 23
ST. BRIDGET (1303-1373)

HISTORICO-LITURGICAL NOTE

This Swedish saint died in Rome on July 23, 1373, and was canonized in 1391. Her feast was listed in the Roman Calendar in 1623. She lived at court for many years but she was also the foundress of a "double" monastery in which men and women religious lived in separate buildings but used the same church.

Bridget was born at Uppsala and at the age of 14 she married Ulf Gudmarsson, who was 18 years old. They had 8 children, one of whom, Karin, is also honored as a saint. In 1335 or thereabouts Bridget was summoned to the court by the young king of Sweden, Magnus II. There she served as lady-in-waiting to the young queen, Blanche of Namur. She tried unsuccessfully to curb the excesses of the king and queen.

By this time she was beginning to receive private revelations, and after the death of her youngest son Gudmar, Bridget and Ulf made a pilgrimage to Santiago de Compostela. On their return to Sweden, they decided to spend the rest of their lives in monasteries, but Ulf died in a Cistercian monastery in 1344. Bridget then donned the garb of a penitent and began to live the life of an ascetic. The visions and revelations became so insistent that Bridget became alarmed, fearing that she was being deceived by the devil. She was reassured after consulting a learned Cistercian monk, who made copies of the revelations in Latin.

It was at this time that Bridget, with financial help from

King Magnus, founded her double monastery and called the new institute the Order of the Most Holy Savior. Today there are no male members and, in fact, relatively few women, known as the Bridgettines.

In 1350 Bridget travelled to Rome for the Holy Year of 1350 and she remained there for the last 24 years of her life, except for a pilgrimage to the Holy Land in 1371. She worked energetically to bring the pope back to Rome from Avignon and she openly denounced the wickedness of the nobility at Naples and at Cyprus. She died in Rome at the age of 70 and her body was taken to the monastery in Vadstena, Sweden, for burial. She is the patroness of Sweden.

MESSAGE AND RELEVANCE

The revised Opening Prayer of the Mass states: "Lord our God, you revealed the wisdom of the cross in her loving contemplation of your Son." The English version, however, still has the previous formula: "Lord God, you revealed the secrets of heaven to St. Bridget." The revelations of St. Bridget fill 8 volumes and were received in four distinct periods: Sweden, 1344-1349; Rome, 1350-1363; various pilgrimages, 1364-1370, and the pilgrimage to the Holy Land, 1372-1373. However, Pope Benedict XIV was referring specifically to the revelations of St. Bridget when he wrote: "Even though many of these revelations have been approved, we cannot and ought not give them the assent of Catholic faith, but only that of human faith, when the rules of prudence present them as probable and worthy of pious credence." The Office of Readings contains a prayer by St. Bridget, addressed to Christ crucified. It reveals her tender devotion to the passion of Christ and is an inspiring summation of the meaning of the paschal mystery.

St. Bridget reports that Jesus said to her: "I am not speaking to you for yourself alone, but for the salvation of others." Because of that, she considered herself to be a messenger of the Lord. The Second Vatican Council has told us that we too must bring the gospel message to the world. In our day we are experiencing many of the same trials and scandals that were prevalent in the lifetime of this patron saint of Sweden.

> Opening Prayer: *Lord our God, you revealed the secrets of heaven to St. Bridget as she meditated on the suffering and death of your Son. May your people rejoice in the revelation of your glory.*

July 25
ST. JAMES

HISTORICO-LITURGICAL NOTE

The feast of St. James the Apostle, brother of St. John the Evangelist, has been celebrated in the West since the eighth century on July 25. In the Coptic and Byzantine Churches it is celebrated on a date closer to Easter. He was the first apostle to shed his blood for Christ; he was beheaded by Herod Agrippa I in the year 42 or 44, according to the Acts of the Apostles 12:2-3. He was buried at Jerusalem but tradition has it that around the year 830 his relics were transferred to Compostela, Spain, which became a popular center for pilgrimages throughout the Middle Ages. During the fourth and fifth centuries his feast was celebrated together with that of St. John on December 27 or 28, and this was the date of the feast in France until the seventh century.

James was the son of Zebedee and Salome (Mk 15:40; Mt 27:59) and he was one of the three privileged apostles, together with Peter and John. He witnessed the healing of Peter's mother-in-law (Mt 1:29-31), the resurrection of the daughter of Jairus (Mk 5:37-43), the transfiguration of Jesus (Mk 9:2-8), and the agony in the Garden (Mt 26:37). The tradition that he evangelized Spain has not been proven, nor do all scholars agree that the relics of St. James are at Compostela, Spain.

MESSAGE AND RELEVANCE

In the Mass the Prayer over the Gifts states that James was "the first apostle to share the cup of suffering and death." He and his brother John were also among the first apostles called by Christ, after Peter and Andrew. The Gospel tells us that on special occasions Jesus often called Peter, James and John to accompany him.

However it was the impetuous James who wanted to call down fire from heaven on the Samaritans for their lack of faith, and Jesus reprimanded him for this (Lk 9:51-56). In the Office of Readings St. John Chrysostom describes another incident in which Jesus corrected James, and also his brother John. They had asked Jesus to grant them the privilege of a high place in the kingdom, thus arousing the anger of the other apostles (Mk 10:35-45). "See how imperfect they all are," says St. John Chrysostom; "the two who tried to get ahead of the other ten, and the ten who were jealous of the two! But, as I said before, show them to me at a later date in their lives, and you will see that all these impulses and feelings have disappeared."

The lesson of this feast is: like St. James, we sometimes ask of the Lord more than we are ready or worthy to receive. We must become as little children and accept from the hands of our heavenly Father whatever he deigns to give us. Yet, the Opening Prayer reminds us that we must at the same time be strong and courageous in professing our faith.

Preface: *Jesus, our Redeemer, called St. James from humble labor with fishing nets and made him a fisher of men for their salvation. He responded to the divine call with a prompt and faithful spirit; therefore he merited to undergo the torment of martyrdom and to enter into glory before the other apostles of the Lord.*

July 26
ST. JOACHIM and ST. ANN

HISTORICO-LITURGICAL NOTE

The feast honoring the parents of the Blessed Virgin Mary is celebrated on the day that the basilica in honor of St. Ann was dedicated in Constantinople in the year 550. Her feast has been observed in the West since the time of the Crusades in the thirteenth century, but it was not placed in the Roman Missal until 1505. The feast of St. Joachim was introduced in the West only in 1584, and when the two feasts were combined, the date was originally set at March 20 by the Franciscans. In 1969 the date was fixed at July 26.

Details about Joachim and Ann are found only in apocryphal literature, such as the *Protoevangelium of St. James*, which dates back to approximately 165. It states that Mary's birth was miraculous because her parents were sterile, and that an angel predicted her birth to Joachim after he had fasted for forty days in the desert. St. Ann is greatly venerated in Canada, where there is an imposing basilica in her honor at Beaupré in Quebec.

MESSAGE AND RELEVANCE

The prayers in the Mass are taken from the Parisian Missal of 1738 and they emphasize two themes that are also repeated in the hymns and antiphons in the Liturgy of the Hours.

We first read in the Opening Prayer of the Mass: "God of our fathers, you gave Saints Joachim and Ann the privilege of being the parents of Mary, the Mother of your incarnate Son." In the Prayer over the Gifts we ask God to "give us a share in the blessing you promised to Abraham and his descendants." We are thus reminded of the continuity of the plan of salvation that extends from Abraham, through the prophets, and from

Joachim, Ann and Mary, to Jesus. Since God has been faithful to his promises through all those generations, we can pray with confidence that we may enjoy the blessings of eternal salvation. The Entrance Antiphon states: "Praised be Joachim and Ann for the child they bore. The Lord gave them the blessing of all the nations." Later on, when she visits Elizabeth, Mary will say in her *Magnificat*: "All generations shall call me blessed."

In the Eastern Church of the Byzantine Rite this feast is celebrated on September 9 in order to honor Joachim and Ann on the day after Mary's birth (September 8). In the Office of Readings St. John Damascene salutes the saintly parents in the following words: "Joachim and Ann, how blessed a couple! All creation is indebted to you. For at your hands the Creator was offered a gift excelling all other gifts: a chaste mother, who alone was worthy of him. . . . You have fashioned a jewel of virginity: she who remained a virgin before, during, and after giving birth. . . . You achieved with God's help something which transcends nature in giving the world the Virgin Mother of God as your daughter."

There is a second theme in the Prayer after Communion, where we read that God willed that his Son should be "born as a man so that men could be born again in you." As a member of the human race, Christ reveals to us the marvelous condescension of the heavenly Father towards mankind, which now enjoys solidarity with his incarnate Son. St. John Damascene touches on the same theme in the Office of Readings: "Thus nature remained sterile in Ann, until grace produced its fruit. For she who was to be born had to be a first-born daughter, since she would be the mother of the First-born of all creation, in whom all things are held together."

> Preface: *We praise you on this joyful feast of Saints Joachim and Ann, adoring the loving plan by which in your mercy you effected the redemption of the human race. With singular predilection you selected a chosen people so that they would be your people and from ancient times you established with them a covenant, prefiguring the new and perfect covenant to be offered to*

*all the peoples of the earth. And when the fullness of
time came, you gave to the couple we honor today a
most pure and holy daughter, the Virgin Mary, who by
your grace would give birth to the Savior of fallen
humanity.*

July 29
ST. MARTHA

HISTORICO-LITURGICAL NOTE

This feast in honor of the sister of Mary and Lazarus of
Bethany is now celebrated on the octave day of the feast of St.
Mary Magdalene, who is sometimes incorrectly identified as
Martha's sister. The error is due to a Franciscan tradition that
originated in 1262 and was widely promulgated in the Middle
Ages. It is unfortunate that all three intimate friends of Jesus
— Martha, Mary and Lazarus — are not honored on a common
feast. As it is, only St. Martha is so honored. This may indicate
that many persons still identify Mary Magdalene with Mary of
Bethany. Before this error became widespread, the feast of
Saints Martha and Mary was celebrated on the same day, either
January 19 or December 17. The Byzantine liturgy celebrates
the feast of Mary and Martha together on June 6.

MESSAGE AND RELEVANCE

The prayers of the Mass, the Entrance Antiphon and the
Communion Antiphon all refer to incidents in the relationship
of Jesus with his friends at Bethany. They also underline the
fact that Martha was the one who served table and for that
reason she has been chosen as patroness of innkeepers and
hostels. Several eminent theologians, for example, St. Gregory
the Great, St. Augustine and St. Thomas Aquinas, have used
Mary and Martha as examples of the contemplative life and the

active life respectively, but they assert that Christian perfection can be attained in either state of life.

In the Opening Prayer we pray: "Father, your Son honored St. Martha by coming to her home as a guest. . . . May we serve Christ in our brothers and sisters." In the house at Bethany Jesus was welcomed as a guest and as a friend (Jn 11:5), as is mentioned in the antiphon for the Canticle of Mary: "Jesus loved Martha and Mary and their brother Lazarus." Nevertheless, Jesus mildly rebuked Martha when she complained that Mary was not helping her with the domestic chores. With that incident in mind, we pray that we may be free from "undue attachment to this passing life" (Prayer after Communion).

There is a choice from two Gospel passages in the Mass. The Gospel according to Luke (10:38-42) emphasizes the priority of contemplative activity over involvement in temporal or domestic affairs without, however, placing one in opposition to the other. Each one should fulfill the role that falls to his or her lot. In the Office of Readings St. Augustine says: "Our Lord's words to Martha teach us that though we labor among the many distractions of this world, we should have but one goal. For we are but travelers on a journey without as yet a fixed abode; we are on our way, not yet in our native land; we are in a state of longing, not yet of enjoyment. But let us continue on our way, and continue without sloth or respite, so that we may ultimately arrive at our destination."

Yet another theme is found in Martha's profession of faith when Lazarus was ill and she hastened to Jesus. It is found in the Communion Antiphon of the Mass and in the antiphon for the Canticle of Zechariah as well as the alternate Gospel of the Mass: "You are the Christ, the Son of the living God" (Jn 11:19-27). It is undoubtedly of great importance because it is used in the Christian initiation of adults. It serves to revive one's hope and to provide consolation, as it did to Martha when she knelt at Jesus' feet with her petition (Jn 11:32-33).

> Preface: *It is truly right and just to exalt you, O God of infinite mercy, as we honor with fitting praise Christ,*

*the king of the universe, on the feast of St. Martha, who
was happy to welcome him into her house and served
him with devotion and loving zeal. By the generosity of
her heart she obtained the resurrection of her brother
Lazarus, who was four days dead, and she merited to be
united for all eternity in the kingdom of heaven with
him whom she had received as a guest.*

July 30
ST. PETER CHRYSOLOGUS (380-451)

HISTORICO-LITURGICAL NOTE

This bishop of Ravenna, Italy, died in 451 and was
proclaimed a Doctor of the Church in 1729. At that time
Ravenna, like Rome, Milan and Constantinople, was an imperial residence and therefore a very important city. It was also
at this time that the Council of Ephesus was held and there was
disagreement concerning Mary's title as Mother of God
(*Theotokos*). Some theologians, like Theodoret, wanted her to
be called simply Mother of Christ.

Peter was an important personage because of his contact
with the empress Gallia Placidia, who constructed the church
of St. John the Evangelist because of a vow she made while
travelling from Constantinople to Ravenna. Moreover, he had
close relations with numerous bishops, including Germain of
Auxerre and Pope Leo the Great. The title "Chrysologus,"
which means "golden word," was conferred on him because he
was an unusually gifted preacher. He frequently used Greek
terms in his sermons but he also endeavored to bring the
teaching of the New Testament to bear on the lives of Christians. St. Peter Chrysologus encouraged frequent Communion
and was a staunch defender of the primacy of the Church of
Rome. He especially preached against the annual carnival,
saying: "He who delights in the devil cannot rejoice in Christ."

MESSAGE AND RELEVANCE

The Opening Prayer of the Mass states that Peter Chrysologus was "an outstanding preacher of your incarnate Word." Always a defender of orthodox teaching, St. Peter advised the heretic Eutychus to be obedient to the pope: "In the interests of peace and of the faith, we cannot make a judicial inquiry into matters pertaining to the faith without the approval of the bishop of Rome. My advice is that you obediently heed what the most blessed pope of the city of Rome has written, because the apostle Peter, who lives and presides over that see, does not refuse to teach the truth to those who seek it."

The intercession in the Opening Prayer is that we may "cherish the mystery of our salvation and make its meaning clear in our love for others." St. Peter Chrysologus did just this in Sermon 103, which is found in the Office of Readings: "That the Creator is in his creature and God is in the flesh brings dignity to man without dishonor to him who made man. Why then, man, are you so worthless in your own eyes and yet so precious to God?. . . . Why do you ask how you were created and do not seek to know why you were made?. . . . And so Christ is born so that by his birth he might restore our nature. . . . The creature he had formed of earth he now makes heavenly; and what he had endowed with a human soul he now vivifies to become a heavenly spirit. In this way he fully raised man to God."

In Sermon 130 for the anniversary of his episcopal ordination, St. Peter Chrysologus paints the portrait of an ideal bishop: "He obeys the king, he collaborates with those in power, he respects the elderly, he is kind to youth, he loves his companions, he is affectionate towards children; he imitates Christ in his generous service to all."

Opening Prayer: *Father, you made Peter Chrysologus an outstanding preacher of your incarnate Word. May the prayers of St. Peter help us to cherish the mystery of our salvation and make its meaning clear in our love for others.*

July 31
ST. IGNATIUS of LOYOLA (1491-1556)

HISTORICO-LITURGICAL NOTE

Born in 1491 in Guipuzcoa in the Basque section of Spain, Ignatius Lopez of Loyola was the youngest of 11 children. He was trained for a military career, but it came to an abrupt end when he was wounded in the battle of Pamplona in 1521. During a long convalescence he read *The Life of Christ* by Ludolph of Saxony and a collection of the lives of the saints. These readings proved to be actual graces that led to his conversion in the same year that Martin Luther took up residence in the castle at Wartburg during his crisis.

After a vision of the Blessed Virgin Mary, Ignatius made a pilgrimage to the Benedictine abbey at Montserrat to venerate the famous Madonna. He then settled in nearby Manresa, where he was a guest of the Dominicans and made a rough draft of his *Spiritual Exercises* (1522). The following year he made a pilgrimage to Jerusalem, where he was a guest of the Franciscans. Returning to Spain, he began the study of Latin at the age of 33 and then went to the University of Alcalá for further studies. There he was imprisoned on suspicion of being an illuminist, so he moved to Salamanca, where he was again questioned and then imprisoned for a time.

In February of 1528 Ignatius made his way to Paris, where he received the Master of Arts degree. On the feast of the Assumption in 1534 Ignatius and six companions, including the future St. Francis Xavier, gathered in a chapel in Montmartre and vowed to live poverty and chastity and to go to Palestine to preach the gospel. That failing, they would offer themselves to the pope and go wherever he would send them. But on the advice of a physician, Ignatius returned to Spain in 1535 in order to regain his health.

Two years later the entire group met in Venice, intending to sail for Palestine, but hostilities between Venice and the Turks made it impossible. Consequently, they proceeded to

Rome, where Ignatius was ordained a priest in 1538 and the Society of Jesus was approved by the papal bull *Regimini Militantes Ecclesiae* in 1540. The definitive Constitutions of the Society were approved in 1550.

In 1556 St. Ignatius died suddenly in Rome at the age of 65, after fifteen years as Superior General of the Society. He was canonized in 1622 and Pope Pius XI named him patron of spiritual exercises and retreats.

MESSAGE AND RELEVANCE

The prayers of the Mass present several characteristics of St. Ignatius. First, in the Opening Prayer, we read: "Father, you gave St. Ignatius of Loyola to your Church to bring greater glory to your name." The motto of the Society of Jesus is: *Ad majorem Dei gloriam* (For the greater glory of God). The same sentiment is expressed in the First Reading for the Mass, taken from St. Paul's First Letter to the Corinthians.

In the Prayer over the Gifts we read that the Eucharist is "the source of all holiness." Ignatian spirituality is eminently Christocentric, for which reason the antiphon for the Canticle of Zechariah states: "Would that I might know Christ and the power of his resurrection and that I might share in his sufferings" (Ph 3:10). Hence, Ignatian spirituality proposes certain virtues as essential for the imitation of Christ: obedience, poverty and humility.

In the Latin version of the Prayer after Communion we ask God that we may direct our entire life to the everlasting glory of his name. The Entrance Antiphon of the Mass is from St. Paul's Letter to the Philippians: "At the name of Jesus every knee must bend, in heaven, on earth, and under the earth; every tongue should proclaim to the glory of God the Father: Jesus Christ is Lord." This is appropriate for the founder of the Society of Jesus.

The words of St. Paul in the First Reading for the Mass are a neat summation of Ignatian spirituality: "Whether you eat or drink — whatever you do — you should do all for the glory of

God. . . . I try to please all in any way I can by seeking, not my
own advantage, but that of the many, that they may be saved.
Imitate me as I imitate Christ" (1 Cor 10:31-11:1). The relevance of the life and example of St. Ignatius Loyola is expressed in the Communion Antiphon: "I have come to bring fire to
the earth. How I wish it were already blazing!" (Lk 12:49).
Finally, the antiphon for the Canticle of Mary offers much food
for thought to contemporary Christians: "Of what use is it to a
man to gain the whole world, if he pays for it by losing his
soul?"

Preface (Society of Jesus):   *You called St. Ignatius to
associate himself with your Son so that, inflamed with
love for him, he would inspire countless souls to seek
your greater glory, to promote greater service to you
throughout the world, and to offer your people a Company marked with apostolic love in Jesus Christ our
Lord.*

AUGUST

ST. ALPHONSUS LIGUORI (1696-1787)

HISTORICO-LITURGICAL NOTE

St. Alphonsus Liguori founded the Congregation of the Most Holy Redeemer (Redemptorists) in 1732. He was born at Marianella, near Naples, Italy, and died in Campagna, Italy, in 1787, at the age of 91. He was canonized in 1839 and declared a Doctor of the Church in 1871. He is recognized by the Church as a patron of moral theologians and confessors.

At the early age of 17 Alphonsus had acquired doctorates in both civil and canon law. After failing to succeed in a court trial between Duke Orsini and the Grand Duke of Tuscany, he abandoned the practice of law in 1723. He also rejected marriage and a worldly life; rather, he studied for the priesthood and joined a missionary society of diocesan priests as well as an ecclesiastical confraternity. He was ordained a priest in 1726 and had for a time entertained the idea of becoming an Oratorian, but in the end remained a diocesan priest.

In 1729, at the age of 33, Alphonsus became chaplain at a college for the training of missionaries. There he met a priest, Thomas Falcoia, who had founded a convent of nuns and later became a bishop. When giving a retreat to the nuns, Alphonsus investigated a vision received by one of the nuns and concluded that it was authentic. He changed the rule and the habit of the nuns and that was the origin of the Redemptoristines, who claim St. Alphonsus as their founder. Later, as bishop, Falcoia asked Alphonsus to establish a congregation of missionaries to work among the people in the rural districts. In spite of opposition and dissension among the first members, the Congregation of the Most Holy Redeemer was finally approved by Pope Benedict XIV in 1749.

From 1726 to 1752 St. Alphonsus preached in the area around Naples and became much sought after as a confessor. He once said of his preaching: "I have never preached a sermon which the poorest old woman in the congregation could not understand." In 1748 St. Alphonsus published his first book of moral theology, to be followed by others that were translated into many different languages. Because of his extensive writing he has been named a Doctor of the Church and patron of moral theologians, but it is as a preacher and confessor that he is a model for the Redemptorists and other priests as well.

After 13 years of administration of the Congregation, Alphonsus was named bishop of Sant' Agata dei Goti (Benevento) at the age of 66, much against his will. At the age of 79 he resigned from his episcopal duties and retired to Nocera dei Pagani, near Naples. Once again the Redemptorists entered upon a period of trials and dissension and Alphonsus himself went through a period of deep interior suffering. He died in 1787, but it was not until 1793 that peace and unity were restored to the Redemptorists.

MESSAGE AND RELEVANCE

The Latin version of the Collect of the Mass states: "O God, you give to your Church ever new forms of the Christian life," which we may understand as applying to the foundation of the Congregation of the Most Holy Redeemer. The beginning of this new religious institute was difficult indeed. In a period of religious pessimism and rigorism, St. Alphonsus proposed his own motto: "*Copiosa apud Deum redemptio*" (With God redemption abounds). In his moral theology he adopted what is known as a moderate probabilism, meaning that in case of a moral doubt, one can act in accordance with what seems to be the more probable or safe decision.

In the petition of the Opening Prayer we ask God to "give us the grace to follow St. Alphonsus in his loving concern for the salvation of men." The ease with which Alphonsus preached to the people assured the success of his ministry of the word. Many of his musical compositions were much loved by the people, as were his spiritual treatises; for example, *The Holy Eucharist, The Glories of Mary, The Way of Salvation and Perfection, The Way of Divine Love.* He also wrote a guide for the use of confessors, drawing on his long experience in the confessional.

In the Prayer over the Gifts the Latin version says that St. Alphonsus "offered himself as a holy victim." This saintly bishop, so completely dedicated to the Eucharist, had to suffer persecution from members of the Congregation he founded. Moreover, when he submitted the Constitutions for royal approval, someone had changed the wording, and Alphonsus signed it without reading it carefully. The whole affair caused a division of the Congregation, one group approved by the Holy See and following the original rule, and another group approved in the kingdom of Naples and accepting the modified rule. The pope then withdrew the first group of members from the authority of St. Alphonsus. He bore these trials with admirable patience, but he then entered into a "dark night" in which he was beset by temptations, doubts and scruples. This interior trial lasted for 18 months and was followed by light, ecstasies, prophecies and miracles prior to his holy death.

In the Prayer after Communion St. Alphonsus is described as "a faithful minister and preacher of this Holy Eucharist." We then ask: "May all who believe in you receive it often and give you never-ending praise." St. Alphonsus not only promoted visits to the Blessed Sacrament, but he also paid close attention to the manner in which priests celebrate Mass. In the convents of the Redemptoristines, adoration of the Blessed Sacrament was to hold an important place in the daily schedule.

In the post-Conciliar Church we need to emphasize the

centrality of the Eucharist in our Christian life and worship. Since the Second Vatican Council there has been a revival of devotion to the Blessed Sacrament in many parts of the world.

> Prayer after Communion: *Lord, you made St. Alphonsus a faithful minister and preacher of this Holy Eucharist. May all who believe in you receive it often and give you never-ending praise.*

August 2
ST. EUSEBIUS of VERCELLI (283?-371)

HISTORICO-LITURGICAL NOTE

The feast in honor of the first bishop of Vercelli, Italy, who died on August 1, 371, is celebrated a day later because August 1 is the feast of St. Alphonsus Liguori. In the martyrology of the Middle Ages he was classified as a martyr, but that has now been omitted. The fact is that he suffered the unbloody martyrdom of exile for many years.

Eusebius was a native of Sardinia, and he studied at Rome where he became a lector. He was later named bishop of Vercelli in northern Italy where he became the first bishop to introduce community life for diocesan priests. He was persecuted by the heretical Arians and after the Synod of Milan (355) he was sent into exile because he refused to sign the document condemning St. Athanasius. During his exile he travelled to Palestine, Egypt, Alexandria and Antioch, always promoting orthodox teaching. After some years he was permitted to return to Vercelli, where he died.

MESSAGE AND RELEVANCE

The new Opening Prayer for the Mass presents Eusebius as a defender of the divinity of Christ against the Arians: "St.

Eusebius affirmed the divinity of your Son." He manifested his courage by refusing to sign the condemnation of Athanasius and also by confronting the emperor Constantius, who could have condemned him to death. The Office of Readings contains an excerpt from a letter in which he exhorts the faithful: "I beg you to keep the faith with all vigilance, to preserve harmony, to be earnest in prayer, to remember me always, so that the Lord may grant freedom to his Church, which is suffering throughout the world."

St. Eusebius defended the Church's teaching not only by words but by personal witness in undergoing suffering and exile. He is rightfully proposed as an example of sound teaching and faithful witness, inspiring us to unite ourselves to the Lord Jesus without making any concessions to secularism.

> Opening Prayer: *Lord God, St. Eusebius affirmed the divinity of your Son. By keeping the faith he taught, may we come to share the eternal life of Christ.*

August 4
ST. JOHN VIANNEY (1786-1859)

HISTORICO-LITURGICAL NOTE

The feast of the Curé of Ars, model and patron of parish priests, is celebrated on the anniversary of his death. He was canonized in 1925 by Pope Pius XI, who also named him patron saint of the parochial clergy in 1929.

Born near Lyons, France, in 1786, of a very devout family, John Vianney was five years old when the reign of terror in Paris was exiling or murdering the Catholic clergy and religious. He received his First Communion at a time when the troops of the French Revolution passed through the region and closed the parish church. His vocation was stimulated by contact with a holy priest and two years later he received his father's permission to study for the priesthood. He was not an outstanding student, but he was finally ordained in 1815 at the age of 29. He was assigned to the parish at Ars, some distance from Lyons, and he remained there for 42 years because the people repeatedly opposed his transfer. He himself tried several times to leave Ars in order to follow a contemplative life. He refused the appointment as a canon of the diocese and when he received the medal of the Legion of Honor in 1843, he sold it in order to give the money to the poor. He died of exhaustion at the age of 74, as he had predicted, peacefully and without fear.

MESSAGE AND RELEVANCE

In the Opening Prayer of the Mass we read that God "made St. John Vianney outstanding in his priestly zeal and concern for your people." This model for parish priests, totally dedicated to his parishioners, had once said: "Leave a parish without a priest for 20 years and the people will begin to adore beasts." He literally wore himself out in serving the faithful and especially in being constantly available for confessions. Yet he always felt incompetent because of his ignorance, as he put it. At the beginning, his preaching evoked fear and was somewhat Jansenistic, but later in life he overcame his preoccupation with predestination and damnation. He was then able to manifest the sweetness of mercy and a simplicity that was nurtured by his constant practice of prayer. His definition of prayer was succinct: "Prayer is nothing else but union with God" (Office of Readings).

Our petition in the Opening Prayer is: "by his example and prayers, enable us to win our brothers and sisters to the love of Christ." John Vianney was constantly occupied with the religious education of his parishioners, instructing them in plain language that they could understand. They often commented that no other priest had ever preached as he did. He opened a free school for poor girls in 1824 and he gave daily catechism lessons.

St. John Vianney suffered attacks from the devil for 34

years (1824-1858) and he was persecuted by some of his fellow priests for 10 years. He was even the victim of malicious lies and calumny but was eventually cleared of all accusations. This dedicated parish priest successfully overcame the religious indifference of the people. Convinced of the importance of public liturgical prayer, St. John Vianney knew from experience what the Second Vatican Council taught concerning liturgical prayer. "Private prayer," he said, "is like straw scattered here and there; if you set it on fire it makes a lot of little flames. But gather these straws into a bundle and light them, and you get a mighty fire, rising like a column into the sky; public prayer is like that."

Opening Prayer: *Father of mercy, you made St. John Vianney outstanding in his priestly zeal and concern for your people. By his example and prayers, enable us to win our brothers and sisters to the love of Christ and come with them to eternal glory.*

August 5
DEDICATION of the BASILICA of ST. MARY MAJOR

HISTORICO-LITURGICAL NOTE

This feast was inaugurated by Pope Sixtus III (432-440) on August 5 and it was a local feast until the fourteenth century. There was a legend concerning an apparition of the Blessed Virgin, who designated the place where the basilica was to be constructed. It was miraculously outlined in snow that fell in the night between August 5 and 6. From this derives the popular name of Our Lady of the Snows. Since the seventh century it has also been called Blessed Mary at the Crib, because of a popular belief that the manger of Bethlehem was preserved in the basilica. The Jerome Martyrology states (erroneously) that the basilica was dedicated on this date by Pope

Liberius in 366 (hence it was also called the Liberian Basilica). Above the entrance arch one can still see the words *"Plebi Dei,"* meaning dedicated to the People of God, reportedly from the time of Pope Sixtus III. The central nave is decorated with mosaics that date back to the fifth century. This feast was entered into the Roman Calendar in 1586.

MESSAGE AND RELEVANCE

The Opening Prayer of the Mass is taken from the Gregorian prayer for the feast of the Assumption and it focuses on the divine maternity of Mary, to whom the basilica was dedicated in the days following the Council of Ephesus (431). We ask pardon for our sins and that the "prayers of Mary, the Mother of your Son, help to save us, for by ourselves we cannot please you."

On this feast we recall the fundamental basis for Marian devotion, namely, her divine maternity. Hence, the Office of Readings contains a statement by St. Cyril of Alexandria to the fathers of the Council of Ephesus: "Let the union of God and man in the Son of the Virgin Mary fill us with awe and adoration. Let us fear and worship the undivided Trinity as we sing the praise of the ever-virgin Mary, the holy temple of God, and of God himself, her Son and spotless Bridegroom." We note also that in the Roman Canon of the Mass we have one of the most ancient references to Mary's divine maternity: "the ever-virgin Mother of Jesus Christ, our Lord and God." Today we can read with great profit the beautiful Encyclical of Pope John Paul II: *Mother of the Redeemer (Redemptoris Mater).*

Opening Prayer: *Lord, pardon the sins of your people. May the prayers of Mary, the Mother of your Son, help to save us, for by ourselves we cannot please you.*

August 7
ST. SIXTUS II and COMPANIONS (+258)

HISTORICO-LITURGICAL NOTE

Pope Sixtus II was martyred on August 6, 258, after occupying the chair of Peter for a year, but his feast is celebrated on this date because August 6 is the feast of the Transfiguration. We know the date of his martyrdom from a letter written by St. Cyprian, who was also martyred in 258. Pope Sixtus II was seized while celebrating the liturgy in a catacomb and was beheaded immediately. His cult is of ancient origin and the church containing his relics was given to St. Dominic, who in turn gave it to the cloistered Dominican nuns. Today the church is part of the Pontifical University of St. Thomas Aquinas, conducted by the Dominicans, and is known as the church of St. Dominic and St. Sixtus.

MESSAGE AND RELEVANCE

The Opening Prayer of the Mass comes from the Parisian Missal of 1738 and it states that God "enabled St. Sixtus and his companions to lay down their lives for your word and in witness to Jesus." The letter of St. Cyprian, referred to above, advises the bishops to prepare Christians for persecution: "I ask you to make these facts known to our fellow bishops, in order that by the exhortation of their pastors the brethren everywhere may be strengthened and prepared for the spiritual combat."

In the petition of the Opening Prayer we ask that we may have "the grace to believe in you and the courage to profess our faith." This pope and martyr is a model for bishops, who should be willing to give their lives for their flock. Moreover, the death of four deacons with the pope is a symbol of the unity that should prevail among all the ministers of the Church.

Opening Prayer: *Father, by the power of the Holy
Spirit you enabled St. Sixtus and his companions to lay
down their lives for your word in witness to Jesus. Give
us the grace to believe in you and the courage to profess
our faith.*

August 7
ST. CAJETAN (1480-1547)

HISTORICO-LITURGICAL NOTE

This saint died at Naples in 1547 and was canonized in
1671. He was born of an aristocratic family at Vicenza, Italy,
and was 12 years old at the time of the discovery of America
(1492). He received a doctorate in canon law at the University
of Padua in 1505 and became protonotary apostolic and secretary to Pope Julius II in Rome. He was ordained to the
priesthood in 1517 and remained in Rome for 13 years, where
the cry of the Fifth Lateran Council was: "The Church needs a
universal and radical reform."

In 1517 Cajetan and John Peter Carafa transferred the
Company of Divine Love to Rome. It had been promoted by St.
Catherine of Genoa and was dedicated to works of charity for
the sick poor. At the same time, Martin Luther began his
polemic against the Catholic Church. The work of the Company soon included the incurable syphilitics who were cared
for by Hector Vernazza at the hospital of St. James in Rome.
Later the work spread to Vicenza, Verona and Venice.

Cajetan returned to Vicenza in 1520 to care for his sick
mother and became rector of the church of St. Mary. In 1523
he went back to Rome where, at the advice of his Dominican
confessor, he organized an institute of Clerks Regular. The
society had three functions: preaching, the administration of
the sacraments and celebration of the liturgy. The Congregation was known as the Theatines and John Peter Carafa, who

had been ordained a bishop some years before, resigned as bishop and became superior general. In 1536 Carafa assigned Cajetan to Venice to combat Lutheranism, and then to Naples as superior. He died there at the age of 67, worn out from his attempts to bring an end to the discord in that city.

MESSAGE AND RELEVANCE

The Opening Prayer of the Mass states that God "helped St. Cajetan to imitate the apostolic way of life." Yet his way of life differed from that of other religious institutes. The Theatines observed the common life, as did the monks, and they practiced strict poverty, as did the mendicant friars, but their apostolate was exceedingly varied, and this attracted the diocesan clergy to them. There was also an element of reform in their life and ministry.

A second note is found in the petition of the Latin version of the Opening Prayer, namely, "to trust completely in the providence of God." In fact, the name given to the Theatines was the Order of Divine Providence and that was not by accident. Cajetan had implicit trust in the gospel statement: "Seek first his kingship, his way of holiness, and all these things will be given you besides" (Mt 6:33). In the Office of Readings a letter written by Cajetan contains this statement: "Even if all the saints and every single creature should abandon you, he will always be near you, whatever your needs."

Cajetan was animated by the evangelical dynamism of the gospel and was blessed with extraordinary mystical gifts, as when the Blessed Virgin placed the Infant Jesus in his arms on Christmas night in 1517 during his visit to the crib at St. Mary Major. The moral climate of Rome at that time was such that he remarked: "Rome was once holy but now it is a Babylon." The same thing can be said of some areas of our secularized culture.

St. Cajetan's example was an inspiration to many other

saints, such as Jerome Emiliani, John Matthew Ghiberti, Camillus de Lellis, and Ignatius of Loyola. We, who live in a culture marked by religious indifference, can well meditate on his statement: "Not sentimental love but active love purifies souls . . . Christ is waiting but nobody responds."

> Opening Prayer: *Lord, you helped St. Cajetan to imitate the apostolic way of life. By his example and prayers may we trust in you always and be faithful in seeking your kingdom.*

August 8
ST. DOMINIC (1170-1221)

HISTORICO-LITURGICAL NOTE

Previously the feast of St. Dominic was celebrated on August 4, and by special indult it is still celebrated on that date in Bologna, Italy, the city in which St. Dominic died. It has now been transferred to the first free day in August, after the feasts of the Basilica of St. Mary Major, the Transfiguration and St. Cajetan.

Born of the noble Guzman family at Caleruega, Spain, Dominic received his early education at Palencia and then became an Augustinian canon at the cathedral of Osma. At the age of 24 he accompanied his bishop, Diego de Azevedo, on a mission to Denmark that took them through southern France. There they came face to face with the Albigensian, Catharist and Waldensian heresies. They immediately began an apostolate of preaching. Bishop Diego returned to Spain to recruit more preachers but he died while there, and Dominic was left practically alone to carry on the preaching ministry.

In 1215 he founded a monastery of cloistered nuns at Prouille, near Toulouse, who would support the preaching ministry by their prayers. By 1217, the year in which Pope Honorius III confirmed the name and mission of the Friars

Preachers, they had taken up residence at the church of St. Romain in Toulouse, thanks to the kindness of Bishop Fulk. The papal bulls approving the Order of Preachers were issued by Pope Honorius III in 1218.

Dominic adopted the Rule of St. Augustine as the rule of life and borrowed from the Premonstratensian Statutes for the primitive Dominican Constitutions. In those Constitutions he placed great emphasis on personal and community poverty, the ministry of preaching and the assiduous study of sacred truth. St. Dominic stipulated that the Constitutions as such do not bind under sin and that superiors have the power to grant dispensation. Although the friars lived a monastic life, Dominic stated that the purpose of the Order was preaching for the salvation of souls. Very soon there were Dominican friars in Paris, Madrid, Rome and Bologna. St. Dominic always preferred to make foundations in university cities but he was also greatly interested in the foreign missions.

By July, 1218, Dominic was in Italy, where he preached in numerous cities, organized the monastery of nuns at St. Sixtus in Rome, and received from the pope the basilica of Santa Sabina, which is still the headquarters of the Dominican Order. He was also designated as the Master of the Sacred Palace, and to this day a Dominican holds that office. While on a preaching mission in northern Italy, Dominic was stricken with his last illness. He died in the midst of his brethren at Bologna, promising them that he would be of more use to them in heaven than if he were to remain with them. It was the evening of the feast of St. Sixtus, 1221.

MESSAGE AND RELEVANCE

In the Opening Prayer of the Mass we ask God to "let the holiness and teaching of St. Dominic come to the aid of your Church." In the Latin version St. Dominic is described as an outstanding preacher of God's truth. In fact, the word *Veritas* (Truth) is one of the mottoes of the Dominican Order. Dominic was a preacher of truth, the truth of the gospel. He replaced the manual labor of the monks with the assiduous study of sacred doctrine in view of the preaching ministry. Hence we pray that St. Dominic will "help us now as he once inspired people by his preaching."

In the Prayer over the Gifts we ask God to "give us the grace to preach and defend our faith." Today we do not have the same heresies to combat in the Church, but we do have the ever-present temptation to materialism, secularism and religious indifference. The arms in this battle are basically the same as those used by St. Dominic, but adapted to present-day needs: detachment from created goods, zealous dedication to the defense of the faith, the ministry of preaching, and the assiduous study of sacred truth.

In the Prayer after Communion we refer again to the preaching of St. Dominic and ask that "his prayers help us to live for you." In the Office of Readings, taken from the history of the Dominican Order, we learn the secret of St. Dominic's success as a preacher: "Wherever he went he showed himself in word and deed to be a man of the gospel. . . . He seldom spoke unless it was with God, that is, in prayer, or about God. . . . He always carried with him the Gospel according to Matthew and the Epistles of St. Paul, and so well did he study them that he almost knew them from memory."

As he was dying, St. Dominic said to the friars that his heritage to them was fraternal charity, humility and voluntary poverty. Pope Gregory IX said of him: "I knew him as a steadfast follower of the apostolic way of life. There is no doubt that he is in heaven, sharing the glory of the apostles themselves." The relevance of St. Dominic to our age is the importance of the ministry of the word, whether preaching, teaching or writing. The Second Vatican Council has stated that preaching is the primary ministry of bishops and priests. It is also the command of Christ himself: "Preach the good news to all nations."

Preface (Dominican Missal): *We praise and bless you today because you called our Father Dominic to proclaim your truth. He drew that truth from the deep springs of the Savior, water for a thirsty world. Supported by the prayers of Mary, the Mother of your Son, and compelled by a concern for the salvation of all, Dominic accepted the ministry of the word for his family. Speaking always with you or about you, O God, beginning all his actions in contemplation, he advanced in wisdom. He brought many to Christ by his life and teaching; he devoted himself without reserve to building up the Church, the body of Jesus Christ.*

August 10
ST. LAWRENCE (+258)

HISTORICO-LITURGICAL NOTE

The feast of this martyred deacon is very ancient. According to the Jerome Calendar he was executed four days after the martyrdom of Pope Sixtus II and companions. During the fourth century the feast was celebrated as a solemnity with a vigil of prayer; in the sixth century at Rome the Veronese Sacramentary offered fourteen different Masses together with the privilege of a vigil and an octave. The feast spread throughout Italy and into northern Africa.

Lawrence was a Spaniard, called to Rome from Toledo by the pope. According to St. Ambrose, he was burned on a gridiron, contrary to the usual Roman practice of beheading. Some fifty years after his death Constantine had a basilica constructed over his tomb. At various times there were modifications made on the church, by Pope Pelagius in the sixth century and by Pope Honorius III in the thirteenth. The basilica is one of the seven major churches of Rome.

MESSAGE AND RELEVANCE

In the Opening Prayer of the Mass we pray: "Father, you called St. Lawrence to serve you by love and crowned his life with glorious martyrdom." His love was manifested by fidelity to his ministry as a deacon, as St. Augustine says in the Office of Readings: "Lawrence was a deacon of the Church of Rome. There he ministered the sacred blood of Christ; there for the sake of Christ's name he poured out his own blood." The second antiphon for Evening Prayer quotes the words of Lawrence: "I rejoice greatly because I have been considered worthy to be a sacrificial victim for Christ."

St. Lawrence is one of the most venerated saints in the Church of Rome; in fact, he follows immediately after Saints Peter and Paul, and his name is mentioned in the Canon of the Mass. Loved by all because of his generosity to the poor, this deacon reminds Christians today that fraternal charity should prompt them to assist the poor and needy. The words of St. Augustine are good material for meditation: "Let us understand, then, how a Christian must follow Christ even though he does not shed his blood for him, and his faith is not called upon to undergo the great test of the martyr's sufferings" (Office of Readings).

> Preface: *Christ, your Son, offering his life for our ransom, loved us until the end and thus taught us that there is no greater love than to lay down one's life for the brethren. In like manner, Lawrence, his true and faithful disciple, gave the supreme proof of his love by his martyrdom.*

August 11
ST. CLARE (1193/4-1253)

HISTORICO-LITURGICAL NOTE

The life of St. Clare, written by Thomas of Celano, was recently recovered, after being lost since the sixteenth century. St. Clare died on this date in 1253 at the age of 61 and was canonized by Pope Alexander IV in 1255. He had visited

Clare during her last illness while he was still cardinal protector.

Clare was of an aristocratic family and she had met Francis numerous times during her adolescence. She fled from her home on Palm Sunday, 1212, and went to the Portiuncula, outside Assisi, where Francis lived with his small community. He cut her hair, clothed her in a rough habit, and for the time being, placed her in a Benedictine convent. Later she was joined by her sister Agnes, who was only 15 years old, and still later by her own mother and several women of illustrious families. Francis then placed them in a house adjacent to the church of San Damiano and named Clare the superior. She was to hold the office of abbess for 40 years, 29 of which were years of sickness. That was the beginning of the cloistered Franciscan nuns known as the Poor Clares. They practiced such severe austerities that Francis and the bishop of Assisi found it necessary to mitigate their ascetical practices somewhat. Pope Gregory IX composed the first Rule for the "Poor Ladies of San Damiano" but in 1247 Pope Innocent IV promulgated another Rule permitting the ownership of community property, which Clare did not wish to accept, so she wrote yet another Rule. When Pope Urban IV promulgated another mitigated Rule in 1263, it resulted in two different observances among the Poor Clares.

MESSAGE AND RELEVANCE

The Opening Prayer of the Mass is taken from the Proper of the Franciscans and it states that God "inspired St. Clare with the love of poverty." No one followed the example of the poverty of St. Francis of Assisi more assiduously than St. Clare. She obtained from the pope "the privilege to not have privileges," that is, to live absolute poverty. Our petition is that we may "follow Christ in poverty of spirit and come to the joyful vision of your glory."

In the Prayer over the Gifts we are asked to "be transformed into ardent apostles of the love of God." Clare referred to herself as the "little plant of our holy Father Francis" and she promised to bless the nuns during her life and after her death. On her deathbed Clare said to her own soul: "Go in peace; you have followed the good way; go in confidence, because your Creator has sanctified you, has cared for you constantly, and has loved you with all the tenderness of a mother for her child. O God, blessed be you for having created me."

In the Prayer after Communion we ask God to give us victory over sin and health of soul and body. Although these petitions can be used in any Mass, on this feast we should here pray especially for victory over the egoism that comes from the possession of worldly goods.

> Preface (Franciscan Missal): *You wondrously inflamed your servant Clare to follow like Francis in the footsteps of your Son. To him you espoused her mystically through perpetual fidelity and love. Raising her to the summit of seraphic perfection through the highest poverty, you made her the mother of countless virgins.*

August 13
ST. PONTIAN and ST. HIPPOLYTUS (+235?)

HISTORICO-LITURGICAL NOTE

The feasts of these two martyrs were celebrated separately in the Middle Ages but they were combined for this date in 1969. Pope Pontian and the priest Hippolytus were both exiled to Sardinia by Emperor Maximinus and sentenced to hard labor in the quarries.

Hippolytus was a Roman priest who lived in the early part of the third century. He was a very learned man and an important theologian in the early Church. St. Jerome called him "a most holy and eloquent man." He was highly venerated in Rome and his name is in the canon of the Mass according to the Ambrosian rite.

Pontian succeeded Pope Urban I as pope in the year 230.

We have few details concerning his life and martyrdom. What is certain is that he was exiled to Sardinia to work in the mines and he resigned the papacy while there. Pope Fabian had the bodies of Pontian and Hippolytus brought back to Rome for burial.

MESSAGE AND RELEVANCE

In the Opening Prayer we ask that the suffering of these two saints will "fill us with your love and make our hearts steadfast in faith." The solidarity of these two martyrs is noteworthy; they were exiled together and they both suffered martyrdom in Sardinia. St. Cyprian says in the Office of Readings: "How blessed is this Church of ours, so honored and illuminated by God and ennobled in these our days by the glorious blood of martyrs. In earlier times it shone white with the good deeds of our brethren, and now it is adorned with the red blood of martyrs. It counts both lilies and roses among its garlands."

The significance of these two martyrs for us lies in the fact that St. Pontian defended the orthodox teaching against a theologian as eminent as Origen and that Hippolytus, the first anti-pope (against Pope Callistus), was reconciled to the Church and became a martyr.

Opening Prayer: *Lord, may the loyal suffering of your saints, Pontian and Hippolytus, fill us with your love and make our hearts steadfast in faith.*

August 14
ST. MAXIMILIAN KOLBE (1894-1941)

HISTORICO-LITURGICAL NOTE

This heroic Franciscan died at Auschwitz in Poland at the

hands of the Nazis on August 14, 1941, and was canonized as a martyr by Pope John Paul II in 1982.

Born in the little town of Zdunska Wola in Poland and given the name Raymond at baptism, he entered the Conventual Franciscans in 1907 and received the name of Maximilian. He studied philosophy and theology in Rome and received academic degrees; he was ordained a priest in 1919. Because of his great devotion to the Blessed Virgin, he added the name Mary to Maximilian when he made solemn profession in 1914. He was convinced that the Church was entering upon a Marian era and he founded the Militia of the Immaculate, whose members were called Knights of the Immaculate. He constructed an entire city which he called City of the Immaculate.

As a missionary in Japan he constructed a similar city near Nagasaki in 1930. When he returned to Poland in 1936 the Gestapo took over his City of the Immaculate and turned it into a concentration camp. Arrested in 1941, he was sentenced to the labor camp at Auschwitz. When, as a punishment for the escape of a prisoner, a group of nine prisoners were condemned to death, Maximilian voluntarily stepped forward and offered to take the place of a married man who had a family. He died of starvation on the eve of the feast of the Assumption at the age of 47. His body was cremated, together with the other eight corpses.

MESSAGE AND RELEVANCE

The prayers of the Mass emphasize the characteristics of this martyr of fraternal charity. The Opening Prayer begins with the statement: "God, you have given to the Church and the world St. Maximilian, ardent in his love for the Immaculate Virgin and totally dedicated to his apostolic mission and to the heroic service of his neighbor" (Latin version). The reference to St. Maximilian's Marian devotion and apostolate shows that he was striving not only to defend the faith and to contribute to the salvation of souls, but also to win one soul after the other for

the Immaculate Virgin. This he did by using all the communications media at his disposal: publications, radio, theater and
cinema.

In the petition of the Opening Prayer we ask that we may
imitate the life and death of Christ by dedicating ourselves to
the service of others. In the letter by St. Maximilian in the
Office of Readings we learn that for this apostolic Franciscan
the proof of our perfect charity is obedience, and it should be
practiced especially when we are asked to sacrifice our own
will. In the Prayer after Communion we ask that "the same fire
of charity which St. Maximilian Kolbe drew from this
eucharistic banquet may also inflame our hearts with heroic
love for others." He had always said: "Hatred is not a creative
force; only love is a creative power." He said to the commander
of the camp at Auschwitz: "I am a Catholic priest, and I am old;
I want to take his place because he has a wife and children."

After two weeks of starvation, an injection of carbolic
acid ended the life of Maximilian. He was found sitting against
the wall, his face radiant and his open eyes fixed on a certain
point. As one person reported, it was as if his entire body was
caught up in ecstasy. As early as 1920 Maximilian had written:
"I must become a saint as soon as possible." He had also said:
"Sanctity is not a luxury, but a simple duty. It is one of Christ's
first principles: 'Be perfect as your heavenly Father is
perfect'." This same doctrine was proclaimed by the Second
Vatican Council in its document on the Church (*Lumen
Gentium*).

St. Maximilian's Franciscan spirit of love and apostolic
service, accompanied by his intense devotion to Mary, remind
us today that whatever our state of life, we can, through the
intercession of Mary Immaculate, combine an intense active
life with a deep interior life of prayer.

Opening Prayer: *Gracious God, you filled your priest
and martyr, St. Maximilian Kolbe, with zeal for souls
and love for his neighbor. Through the prayers of this
devoted servant of Mary Immaculate, grant that in our*

efforts to serve others for your glory, we too may become like Christ your Son, who loved his own in the world even to the end.

August 15
ASSUMPTION of the BLESSED VIRGIN MARY

HISTORICO-LITURGICAL NOTE

The solemn Marian feast for August 15 is found in the Georgian Lectionary of the eighth century, although a different commemoration was indicated in the Armenian Lectionary of Jerusalem as early as 451. The feast of the Dormition of Mary, as it was called in the East, was established by the emperor Maurice (602) for the entire Roman Empire, where there already existed the feast of the *Theotokos* (Mother of God) on January 1. This feast was also celebrated at Rome under Pope Sergius (687-701) with the name *Pausatio*, together with other Marian feasts such as the Purification, the Annunciation, and the Birth of Mary. It was not until the eighth century that the feast was given the title "Assumption of the Blessed Virgin Mary" in the Gregorian Sacramentary. It was celebrated with a night procession from the church of St. Adrian to St. Mary Major, with a vigil and fasting, and with an Opening Prayer that was used until 1566.

The uninterrupted tradition of the Church, witnessed by Gregory of Tours (549) and other Fathers of the Church, is the basis for the celebration of Mary's assumption into heaven, body and soul. Ephesus is most likely the place where Mary died, according to the private revelations of St. Bridget and Catherine Emmerich and confirmed by recent archaeological findings. In 1946 Pope Pius XII polled the Catholic bishops throughout the world and after their affirmative response, he officially promulgated the dogma of Mary's assumption on November 1, 1950.

MESSAGE AND RELEVANCE

In the ancient Mass for the vigil of the feast, found in the Gregorian Sacramentary of the eighth century, the Opening Prayer relates Mary's assumption to her divine maternity. It reads: "God, turning your gaze to the humility of the Virgin, you raised her to the sublime dignity of Mother of your Son and crowned her with incomparable glory." The Opening Prayer for the vigil Mass in the revised liturgy is very similar.

There are three themes in the Mass for the feast, and they have both a personal and an ecclesial connotation. First, the Opening Prayer implies that Mary really died, because it says that God "raised" her. There is also a reference to her immaculate conception (the sinless Virgin Mary) and her divine maternity (Mother of your Son). The Opening Prayer reads: "God, you raised the sinless Virgin Mary, Mother of your Son, body and soul to the glory of heaven."

The second theme is found in the Preface of the Mass, recently composed from the document *Lumen Gentium* of the Second Vatican Council (no. 68) and from the Missal and Liturgy of the Hours in the Ambrosian rite. It states explicitly: "You would not allow decay to touch her body, for she had given birth to your Son, the Lord of all life." On this feast of Mary the paschal mystery of Christ is celebrated in a very special way because of the relationship between the Mother and Son, as is stated in the biblical texts of the Mass and the Liturgy of the Hours. Thus, we read in the first antiphon for Evening Prayer I: "Christ ascended into heaven and prepared an everlasting place for his immaculate Mother." The glorification of Mary is therefore the crowning of her journey of faith and singular grace; it is the feast of her predestination to eternal happiness and glory.

The third theme is that of the link between Mary and the Church, recalled in the reading for the Mass, taken from the

Book of Revelation. The intercession in the Opening Prayer is therefore eschatological. We ask to "see heaven as our final goal and come to share her glory." Again, in the Prayer after Communion, we ask to "be led to the glory of heaven by the prayers of the Virgin Mary." The Assumption of Mary is thus an eschatological sign of the Church.

In the Office of Readings the excerpt from the encyclical *Munificentissimus Deus* by Pope Pius XII states: "The august Mother of God . . . gained at last the supreme crown of her privileges — to be preserved immune from the corruption of the tomb and, like her Son, when death had been conquered, to be carried up body and soul to the exalted glory of heaven."

> Preface: *Today the Virgin Mother of God was taken up into heaven to be the beginning and the pattern of the Church in its perfection, and a sign of hope and comfort for your people on their pilgrim way. You would not allow decay to touch her body, for she had given birth to your Son, the Lord of all life, in the glory of the incarnation.*

August 16
ST. STEPHEN of HUNGARY (969/70-1038)

HISTORICO-LITURGICAL NOTE

Stephen, King of Hungary, died on August 15, 1038, after reigning for 42 years, and was canonized in 1083. Baptized at the age of 15, Stephen was the son of a pagan king and a Christian mother. He guided his people toward Christianity by admitting missionaries from Bavaria into his country. At the advice of Bishop Adalbert of Prague he married Princess Gisella of Bavaria, the sister of Henry II, and he evangelized his country with the help of the Benedictines from Cluny, France.

As king he faced important challenges and decisions.

First of all, he chose to be allied more with the West than with the East; secondly, he insisted on independence for Hungary rather than dependence on the Germanico-Roman or Byzantine empires; thirdly, he worked for national unity rather than favor the tribal system that was often divisive. He founded numerous monasteries and he received from Pope Sylvester II the royal crown, a processional cross, and the right to establish bishoprics and name ecclesiastical dignitaries.

After his death his relics, together with those of his son, Emeric, were venerated in a rite equivalent to canonization and in 1686 Pope Innocent XI extended the feast to the entire Church.

MESSAGE AND RELEVANCE

The Opening Prayer of the Mass refers to Stephen's role as an evangelizer of his country, saying that he "fostered the growth of your Church on earth." After the leader of the rebellious Magyars was killed in battle, Stephen worked in earnest for their conversion, sometimes using measures that to us seem repressive but were legitimate in his day. He consecrated the nation to Mary, whom he called "the Great Lady," and he himself gave religious instruction to the poor, whom he always treated justly. In view of his many good works and his spread of the faith, the pope bestowed on him the title of "Apostolic King."

In an age of iron, Stephen exercised clemency. Although he was a warrior king in order to obtain independence for his country, he was never cruel. Moreover, he established ten dioceses and named worthy men as bishops. He built numerous churches and monasteries and since he was always concerned about the pilgrims passing through Hungary en route to Jerusalem, Rome, Ravenna or Byzantium, he especially favored the Benedictine monks because of their hospitality towards guests.

In the Opening Prayer the petition is that St. Stephen "may continue to be our powerful helper in heaven." He is still for us a model of prudence and wisdom. This is evident from the advice he gave to his son, as reported in the Office of Readings: "Even now in our kingdom the Church is proclaimed as young and newly planted, and for that reason she needs more prudent and trustworthy guardians lest a benefit which the divine mercy bestowed on us undeservedly should be destroyed and annihilated through your idleness, indolence or neglect."

> Opening Prayer: *Almighty Father, grant that St. Stephen of Hungary, who fostered the growth of your Church on earth, may continue to be our powerful helper in heaven.*

August 19
ST. JOHN EUDES (1601-1680)

HISTORICO-LITURGICAL NOTE

This French saint died at Caen in Normandy, France, on this date in 1680 and was canonized in 1925. He fought vigorously against Jansenism and was one of the principal reformers of the Church in seventeenth-century France.

Born in Normandy, the oldest of seven children, he was educated by the Jesuits and later entered the Congregation of the Oratory founded by Berulle at Paris. Ordained a priest in 1625, he later was named superior of the Oratorians at Caen but still continued his apostolate of preaching popular missions and giving conferences to the clergy in Normandy and Brittany.

In 1643 John Eudes left the Oratorians in order to found the Congregation of Jesus and Mary (popularly known as Eudists), whose purpose was to preach missions in the rural districts and to conduct seminaries. In 1644 he founded the Work of Our Lady of Charity (or of Refuge), which eventually became the Institute of the Good Shepherd. He was an ardent promoter of devotion to the Sacred Hearts of Jesus and Mary. After 48 years of ministry, he died at the age of 79.

MESSAGE AND RELEVANCE

The revised Opening Prayer of the Mass states that God chose St. John Eudes "to preach the infinite riches of Christ." During his lifetime the Church in France was badly in need of reform. There was rampant superstition among the uneducated, repression of the lower class, ignorance among the lower clergy, and pomposity and special privilege among the prelates of the Church.

In the Office of Readings, an excerpt from his treatise on the Sacred Heart reveals his Christ-centered spirituality: "You are one with Jesus as the body is one with the head. You must, then, have one breath with him, one soul, one life, one will, one heart. And he must be your breath, heart, love, life, your all. These great gifts in the follower of Christ originate from baptism. They are increased and strengthened through confirmation and by making good use of other graces that are given by God. Through the Holy Eucharist they are brought to perfection."

Our petition in the Opening Prayer is that "we may know you better and live faithfully in the light of the gospel." There is no doubt that the final victory over Jansenism was due in great part to the promulgation of devotion to the Hearts of Jesus and Mary. Moreover, this devotion was most efficacious in correcting abuses in the French Church and in renewing the Christian life.

This "apostle and doctor of the Sacred Hearts," as he was called by Pope Pius X, is still today an example and teacher of the love that is charity. The following extract is from his treatise on the kingdom of Jesus, found in the Office of Readings for Friday of the thirty-third week of the liturgical year: "The mysteries of Jesus are not yet completely perfected and fulfilled. They are complete, indeed, in the person of Jesus, but not in us, who are his members, nor in the Church, which is his Mystical Body."

Opening Prayer: *Father, you chose the priest John Eudes to preach the infinite riches of Christ. By his teaching and example help us to know you better and live faithfully in the light of the gospel.*

August 20
ST. BERNARD (1090-1153)

HISTORICO-LITURGICAL NOTE

This great Cistercian saint died at Clairvaux, France, on this date in 1153, was canonized in 1174 and proclaimed Doctor of the Church in 1830. Because of him, the twelfth century is sometimes called the "Bernardine period."

Born in 1090 at Burgundy, France, of a noble family, he entered the abbey at Citeaux at the age of 23, taking with him thirty friends and relatives. This led to a revival of the Cistercian Order, and after three years Bernard became abbot at Clairvaux, a daughter house of Citeaux. But his life was not to be lived exclusively in the cloister; for example, he was commissioned by Pope Eugene III to preach the second Crusade. In addition, he founded numerous abbeys, from Spain to Syria and from Sicily to Sweden. He was also employed frequently as a peacemaker and venerated as much for his doctrine and interior life as for his numerous miracles.

MESSAGE AND RELEVANCE

The Opening Prayer of the Mass states that St. Bernard was "a radiant light in your Church." This is so true that Mabillon said of him that he is "the last of the Fathers but certainly not inferior to the first." Rather than enter the Benedictines at Cluny (the black monks), Bernard chose to enter the reformed Benedictines at Citeaux (the white monks, known today as Trappists). His literary output was impressive, comprising a treatise on grace and free will, the theology of Christian holiness, a commentary on the *Song of Songs*, and a treatise on the love of God. Bernard entered into controversy with Abelard, who had boasted: "I know everything in heaven and on earth, except the words 'I don't know'."

Also in the Opening Prayer we ask God that "we may be filled with this spirit of zeal and walk always as children of light." The reference to light is also found in the antiphon for the Canticle of Zechariah: "Blessed Bernard, your life, flooded by the splendor of the divine Word, illumines the Church with the light of true faith and doctrine." The affective tone of St. Bernard's theology is exemplified in the Office of Readings: "Love is sufficient of itself, it gives pleasure by itself and because of itself. It is its own merit, its own reward. Love looks for no cause outside itself, no effect beyond itself. Its profit lies in its practice." Bernard knew how to combat the proponents of false spirituality, who are often more dangerous than the declared heretic.

In the Prayer over the Gifts there is a second characteristic of Bernard, the "Mellifluous Doctor," namely, that "he strove in word and deed to bring harmony to your Church." When, in 1130, two popes were elected in Rome — Innocent II and Anaclete II — Bernard travelled all over Europe in order to urge Christians to obey the lawfully elected pope. Moreover, he battled so strongly against heretics that he was given the name "Hammer of the heretics."

In the Prayer after Communion we ask that "we, too, may burn with love for your Word, Jesus Christ." St. Bernard is above all a theologian enamored of the mystery of the Incarnation. His spirituality is eminently Christocentric and his devotion to Mary is inspiring. To him has been attributed the expression: *Omnia per Mariam* (All through Mary).

Finally, St. Bernard had a great appreciation for friendship. He once repeated the words of Job: "He who does not feel affection for his own friend has lost the fear of God." This Cistercian monk and devoted son of Mary teaches us how to approach God and neighbor along the pathway of love.

Preface: *You enable us to celebrate with joy the feast of St. Bernard. Endowed as he was with heavenly wisdom and fervent in the spirit of love and prayer, you constantly attracted him to your word. Outstanding in sanctity and in zeal, this admirable client of the Virgin Mary has spread throughout the world the light of faith and wisdom and has been in your Church a mediator of concord, unity and peace.*

August 21
ST. PIUS X (1835-1914)

HISTORICO-LITURGICAL NOTE

Pope Pius X died at Rome in 1914 and was canonized in 1954. He was born Joseph Sarto in Treviso, Italy, and after completing his studies at the seminary in Padua he was ordained a priest at the age of 23. After serving in various ministries in the diocese — chaplain, parish priest, chancellor and spiritual director of the seminary — he was ordained bishop of Mantua in 1884 and became a cardinal in 1893. He was elected pope in the conclave of 1903, much against his wishes.

The pontificate of Pope Pius X was extremely fruitful, not only because of the liturgical reforms that he inaugurated (the Breviary, the Mass, Gregorian chant, reception of Communion and a more active participation of the faithful in the liturgy), but also because of his pastoral work for the Church. In this area we should note his *Catechism*, his preaching every Sunday, the promulgation of the *Code of Canon Law*, the reform of the Roman Curia, the publication of the *Acta Apostolicae Sedis*, codification of the laws governing marriage, and regulations concerning study and the formation of the clergy. He was not interested in diplomacy and was intransigent in opposing every form of liberalism. As a result, he had serious conflicts with Russia, Germany, Spain, Portugal and the United States (he refused to grant an audience to Theodore Roosevelt). He was adamant in preserving the separation between Church and State and forbade the clergy to become involved in politics.

He died 22 days after the outbreak of the First World War, lamenting the loss of so many lives. His incorrupt body was venerated in St. Peter's basilica but in 1959 it was returned to Venice, thus fulfilling his promise when he left for the papal election in 1903: "Living or dead, I shall return."

MESSAGE AND RELEVANCE

In the Opening Prayer of the Mass we pray: "Father, to defend the Catholic faith and to make all things new in Christ, you filled St. Pius X with heavenly wisdom and apostolic courage." His courage was first manifested when he took away the privilege of certain Catholic nations to veto the election of a pope (Austria had vetoed the election of Cardinal Rampolla, which led to the election of Pope Pius X) and he threatened with excommunication anyone who would give out news during the conclave.

He also promoted Catholic Action, which would be further promoted by Pope Pius XI and Pope Pius XII. In 1905 he refused to agree to the concordat between France and the Church, thus totally separating Church and State and leading to the confiscation of Church property by the French government.

Especially noteworthy is his condemnation of Modernism, first with the decree *Lamentabili* and then with the encyclical *Pascendi*. Pope Pius X had proposed for himself the task "to defend the Catholic faith and to restore all things in Christ." The years of his pontificate were difficult ones, but he dedicated himself to his task with utter simplicity and fatherly love.

In the Prayer over the Gifts we ask that we may "come to these mysteries with reverence and receive them with faith." This petition brings to mind an outstanding achievement of Pope Pius X: the liturgical reform. In a sense he prepared the way for the liturgical renewal of the Second Vatican Council. He insisted that the people should not pray at Mass but should pray the Mass. He was opposed to concert-style liturgical music and promoted Gregorian chant. He rearranged the psalter of the Liturgy of the Hours and promoted biblical studies by founding the Biblical Institute in Rome and preparing a critical edition of the Vulgate Bible.

Finally, the Prayer after Communion, where we ask that the Eucharist will "strengthen our faith and unite us in your love," reminds us of his decree *Quam singulari*, in which he extended reception of Communion to children and advocated frequent Communion. He wrote in his will: "I was born poor, I have lived in poverty, and I wish to die poor."

The significance of St. Pius X is above all that even during his lifetime he was regarded as a saint. He seemed to have many of the same qualities that later appeared in Pope John XXIII. In addition to this, we can appreciate the immense good he did for the Church by his courageous reforms, similar in many ways to the changes advocated by the Second Vatican Council.

> Opening Prayer: *Father, to defend the Catholic faith and to make all things new in Christ, you filled St. Pius X with heavenly wisdom and apostolic courage. May his example and teaching lead us to the reward of eternal life.*

August 22
QUEENSHIP of MARY

HISTORICO-LITURGICAL NOTE

This feast was instituted by Pope Pius XII in 1955 for May 31, the last day of the month of Mary, but it has been transferred to the octave day of the Assumption in order to link her queenship to her glorification, as is stated in the document

Lumen Gentium of Vatican Council II: "The Immaculate Virgin . . . was taken up body and soul into heavenly glory when her earthly life was over, and exalted by the Lord as Queen over all things, that she might be the more fully conformed to her Son, the Lord of lords (cf. Rv 19:16) and conqueror of sin and death" (no. 59).

In some ancient icons the Virgin Mary is pictured together with Christ the *Pantocrator*, or Sovereign King. In the Middle Ages there were many hymns in which Mary was saluted as Queen; for example, *Salve Regina, Regina coeli, Ave Regina caelorum.* She is also addressed as Queen in the Litany of Loreto.

The title of Queen may seem to be incompatible with the modern preference for democracy and the emphasis on Mary as a Mother who serves us in our needs, but if we honor Christ as King (the feast that closes the liturgical year), there is a basis for this Marian title. The institution of this feast was requested at the Marian Congresses in Lyons (1900), Fribourg (1902), Einsiedeln (1906); it was again requested after the institution of the feast of Christ the King in 1925. By 1933 there were petitions from all over the world and in the centenary year of the proclamation of the Immaculate Conception (1954), Pope Pius XII made this feast a reality with his encyclical *Ad coeli Reginam.* The theological basis for the feast is found in the antiphon for the Canticle of Mary for the feast of the Assumption: "Today the Virgin Mary was taken up to heaven; rejoice, for she reigns with Christ for ever."

MESSAGE AND RELEVANCE

The Opening Prayer of the Mass states the basis of Mary's queenship: "You have given us the Mother of your Son to be our Queen and Mother." However, the title of "Queen" is not on the same level as the title of "Christ the King." Mary is invoked primarily as Mother, and it is in the sense of maternal care and service that her queenship should be understood; not in the sense of dominion and regal authority. Hence, Mary is Queen because she is the Mother of the King of kings (cf. Is 9:1-6).

The petition in the Opening Prayer is that "we may come to share the glory of your children in the kingdom of heaven." What was promised to the apostles is also promised to all Christians: "You are the ones who have stood loyally by me in my temptations. I for my part assign to you the dominion my Father has assigned to me. In my kingdom you will eat and drink at my table" (Lk 22:28-30).

The Communion Antiphon praises Mary for her firm faith that the promises of the Lord would be fulfilled (Lk 1:45). This is also stated in the antiphon for the Canticle of Mary in Evening Prayer: "Blessed are you, Virgin Mary, because you believed that the Lord's words to you would be fulfilled; now you reign with Christ for ever." For many centuries Christians have invoked Mary as Queen when they announce the fifth glorious mystery of the Rosary. Finally, the new rite for the crowning of statues of the Blessed Virgin states that there is no contradiction between the notion of the Queen of heaven seated next to her risen Son and that of the woman of the gospel, who is close to us.

> Preface: *You have willed to crown the Mother of Christ with a royal diadem so she could more clearly demonstrate to her children her benevolence and love. We rejoice today because of her singular dignity and, joyful for the gift received, we join all the citizens of heaven and with one voice we raise to you, O Father, our hymn of praise.*

August 23
ST. ROSE of LIMA (1586-1617)

HISTORICO-LITURGICAL NOTE

The first canonized saint of the New World died in Lima, Peru, on August 24, 1617. She was canonized by Pope

Clement X in 1671 and proclaimed patroness of the Americas, the Philippines and the West Indies. Her feast is celebrated on this date because August 24 is the feast of the apostle St. Bartholomew.

Born of humble Spanish parents, she was baptized as Isabel Flores y de Oliva, but because of her radiant beauty as an infant was given the name of Rose. She received the sacrament of confirmation from St. Turibius, archbishop of Lima. Three other contemporaries of Rose are also saints: the Dominicans, St. Martin de Porres and St. John Macias, and the Franciscan, St. Francis Solano. Rose refused to marry but became a Dominican Tertiary and, as was the custom at that time, she wore the Dominican habit.

In 1623 she was instrumental in making the foundation of the first monastery of cloistered nuns in Lima, dedicated to St. Catherine of Siena. With the help of her brother Ferdinand she built a small hermitage in the family garden, and there she spent most of her life. It was a life dedicated to penances that were so severe that they are incomprehensible to us today. Her mystical experiences and charismatic gifts were similar to those of another Dominican Tertiary, St. Catherine of Siena, but she also had to endure violent diabolical attacks and temptations. She experienced what is called the mystical espousal, at which time Jesus said to her: "Rose of my heart, be my spouse." When a fleet of Dutch ships sailed into the harbor of Lima and the entire city was paralyzed with fear, Rose rushed to the Dominican church, ready to die in defense of the Blessed Sacrament. The Dutch departed, however, and Rose did not die as a martyr, as she had wished. When she did die in 1671 at the age of 31, the entire city venerated her as a saint.

MESSAGE AND RELEVANCE

The Opening Prayer of the Mass gives us in one sentence the spirituality of this patroness of the Americas: "God our Father, for love of you St. Rose gave up everything to devote herself to a life of penance." She had made a vow of virginity early in life so that she could devote herself to prayer and penance. At the same time, however, she performed works of charity for the sick and the poor.

Our petition in the Opening Prayer is "that we may imitate her selfless way of life." So selfless was her love that she desired ardently to evangelize the Indians, some of whom were very savage. "If I were not a woman," she said, "I would devote myself entirely to the evangelization of the Indians." She serves well as a patroness of the Americas, giving an example of love for all the races. She likewise reminds us, as we see in the Office of Readings: "Let all men know that grace comes after tribulation. Let them know that without the burden of afflictions it is impossible to reach the height of grace. . . . This is the only true stairway to paradise, and without the cross they can find no road to climb to heaven."

> Opening Prayer: *God our Father, for love of you St. Rose gave up everything to devote herself to a life of penance. By the help of her prayers may we imitate her selfless way of life on earth and enjoy the fullness of your blessings in heaven.*

August 24
ST. BARTHOLOMEW

HISTORICO-LITURGICAL NOTE

This feast was celebrated on this date in France in the eighth century and in Rome in the ninth and tenth centuries. The Byzantine Church celebrated the translation of the relics of St. Bartholomew on August 25 and his feast on June 11, together with that of St. Barnabas.

Bartholomew, from Cana in Galilee, is identified by some as Nathanael because St. Matthew lists him together with Philip as one of the first apostles chosen by Christ. There is no agreement on where he preached the gospel. According to

Eusebius he preached in India; according to Rufinus, in Ethiopia and Arabia; but others mention places such as Mesopotamia and Phrygia. Most likely he went to Armenia, where he converted the king and, at the order of the king's brother, was skinned alive (according to the Persian custom) and then beheaded. His relics were transferred to various places: to Armenia in the seventh century; to Benevento in the ninth century, and finally to Rome in the tenth century. The skull of St. Bartholomew is venerated in Frankfurt, Germany, since 1238 and he has been named a patron of the sick.

MESSAGE AND RELEVANCE

The Gospel for the Mass is taken from John 1:45-51, which describes Nathanael's meeting with Jesus and his ultimate confession of faith: "You are the Son of God; you are the King of Israel." Therefore, in the Opening Prayer of the Mass we ask God to "sustain within us the faith which made St. Bartholomew ever loyal to Christ."

The petition of the Opening Prayer is that the Church may be "the sign of salvation for all the nations of the world." This is taken from the document *Lumen Gentium* of the Second Vatican Council (no. 48). The Office of Readings gives an excerpt from a homily by St. John Chrysostom in which he contrasts the works done by God and the weakness of the instruments used: "The good deeds which tax collectors and fishermen were able to accomplish by God's grace, the philosophers, the rulers, the countless multitudes cannot even imagine."

The remembrance of the apostle St. Bartholomew should be an occasion for us to renew our faith in Christ, our loyalty to his Church, and our desire to make the gospel known.

Opening Prayer: *Lord, sustain within us the faith which made St. Bartholomew ever loyal to Christ. Let your Church be the sign of salvation for all the nations of the world.*

August 25
ST. LOUIS (1214-1270)

HISTORICO-LITURGICAL NOTE

King Louis IX of France died of typhus in Tunis, Africa, during a crusade in 1270 and was canonized in 1297 by Pope Boniface VIII.

Born the son of King Louis VIII and Blanche of Castile, he was crowned king at the tender age of 12, and at the age of 19 he married Margaret of Provence, who bore 11 children. However, the greatest influence on King Louis IX was his mother, Blanche, who served as regent until Louis could assume full power.

One of his overriding ambitions was the liberation of the Holy Land, and to this end he embarked on several Crusades, but without success. In spite of his military failure, Louis IX was a good ruler and much loved by the people. He endowed the foundation of the Sorbonne University and was a personal friend of St. Thomas Aquinas.

Shortly after he landed at Tunis during his last Crusade, King Louis IX contracted typhus, as did his son Philip. Before his death he called for the Greek ambassadors and urged them to work for reunion with the Church of Rome. As he was dying, he extended his arms in the form of a cross and said: "I will enter your house; I will worship at your holy temple" (Ps 5:8). Then he lost his voice for a time, and when he regained it he spoke his last words: "Into thy hands I commend my soul."

MESSAGE AND RELEVANCE

The final part of the Opening Prayer of the Mass has been changed somewhat. Having stated that God "raised St. Louis from the cares of earthly rule to the glory of your heavenly kingdom," we ask that "we may come to your eternal kingdom by our work here on earth." Reflecting the excellent religious training he had received from his mother in his youth, King Louis IX wrote these words in a spiritual testament to his son: "My first instruction is that you should love the Lord your God with all your heart and all your strength. . . . You should permit yourself to be tormented by every kind of martyrdom before you would allow yourself to commit a mortal sin" (Office of Readings).

As a Franciscan Tertiary he often served the poor in person, and to such an extent that during the Crusades even the Muslims called him "a just Sultan." He also wrote in his testament to his son: "Be kindhearted to the poor, the unfortunate and the afflicted. Give them as much help and consolation as you can."

The deeply religious spirit of King Louis IX is evidenced also in the fact that he lived like a monk, praying the Divine Office daily. In this he resembles Philip II of Spain. He had the good fortune to receive as a gift from the Latin emperor at Constantinople the crown of thorns worn by Christ. He built the famous *Sainte Chapelle* in Paris to house the precious relic.

The message we receive from St. Louis is to avoid mortal sin, cost what it may, and to live in this world with our eyes fixed on our true home above.

> Opening Prayer: *Father, you raised St. Louis from the cares of earthly rule to the glory of your heavenly kingdom. By the help of his prayers may we come to your eternal kingdom by our work here on earth.*

August 25
ST. JOSEPH CALASANZ (1556/7-1648)

HISTORICO-LITURGICAL NOTE

This Spanish saint died at Rome in 1648 on this date and was canonized in 1767. He was born in the Province of Aragon, Spain, and became a doctor of civil and canon law at the University of Alcalá. Ordained a priest in 1584, he served as an apostolic visitor in his diocese and as vicar general. He then went to Rome, to serve as the theologian for Cardinal Colonna. Shocked at the condition of the abandoned children in the Trastevere, he opened a free school in that district of Rome. Eventually he attracted others to join him in the work and out of this he founded the Congregation of Clerks Regular of Pious Schools (known popularly either as Scolopians or Piarists). The members took a fourth vow to dedicate themselves to the education of poor youth. After many vicissitudes and troubles, of which some were caused by members of his own community, the Congregation was suppressed by Pope Innocent X in 1646, but restored in 1669. Joseph Calasanz died at the age of 92 in 1648, highly venerated by the people of Rome, and in 1948 he was declared patron of popular Christian schools.

MESSAGE AND RELEVANCE

The Opening Prayer of the Mass praises the virtues of this saint who, like St. John Baptist de la Salle, was a devoted educator of the young. Eventually he also admitted children from the upper classes and his work spread to Germany, Poland, Bohemia and Moravia. Yet he suffered many trials at the hands of the laity and some members of his own community, who accused him of being incompetent in governing the Congregation. His opponents prevailed because they had friends in high places in the Vatican. St. Joseph Calasanz endured these trials with heroic patience.

In the Office of Readings we find a statement of the goal of education according to St. Joseph Calasanz: "This ministry is directed to the well-being of body and soul; at the same time that it shapes behavior it also fosters devotion and Christian doctrine." How this ministry should be carried out is also explained in the Office of Readings: "All who undertake to teach must be endowed with deep love, the greatest patience and, most of all, profound humility. They must perform their work with earnest zeal."

This advice is still applicable to the education of youth in our day. Education must always include a religious orientation if it is to be fully human.

Opening Prayer: *Lord, you blessed St. Joseph Calasanz with such charity and patience that he dedicated himself to the formation of Christian youth. As we honor this teacher of wisdom may we follow his example in working for truth.*

August 27
ST. MONICA (332-387)

HISTORICO-LITURGICAL NOTE

St. Monica, mother of St. Augustine, died at Ostia, outside of Rome, in 387 but was not listed in the Roman Calendar until 1586. At one time her feast was celebrated on April 9, but was changed to May 4, the vigil of the conversion of St. Augustine, when her relics were transferred from Ostia to the church of St. Augustine in Rome (1430). The Augustinians celebrate the feast of St. Augustine's conversion on May 5. The present date for the feast of St. Monica, a day before the feast of St. Augustine, is much more significant.

Monica was born of Christian parents at Tagaste in northern Africa in 332. She was married to Patricius, a good man but of an irascible temperament and sometimes unfaithful. He was converted to Christianity in 371 and was baptized on his deathbed the following year. Monica was thus left with the care of her son, Augustine, who at the age of 16 was a catechumen but still a victim of his passions and involved in the Manichean heresy. Rather than distance herself from her son, Monica tried to stay close to him, but Augustine deceived her and escaped to Italy. It was only some time later, when Augustine was being influenced by the preaching of St. Ambrose at Milan, that Monica could rejoin him. She had the joy of attending his baptism at Easter in 387. Monica never returned to northern Africa but died at Ostia and was buried there. In 1946 a fragment of her original epitaph was discovered there.

MESSAGE AND RELEVANCE

In the Opening Prayer of the Mass we read: "God of mercy, comfort of those in sorrow, the tears of St. Monica moved you to convert her son St. Augustine to the faith of Christ." When Monica asked a bishop to try to influence Augustine, he responded with prophetic words: "Let him be, and continue to pray for him; it is impossible that a son of so many tears should be lost."

In the petition of the prayer we ask: "By their prayers, help us to turn from our sins." This is significant because St. Monica dedicated most of her life praying for the conversion of Augustine. In the Office of Readings we have Augustine's account of his mother's words to him just before her death: "Son, as far as I am concerned, nothing in this life gives me any pleasure. I do not know why I am still here, since I have no further hopes in this world. I did have one reason for wanting to live a little longer: to see you become a Catholic Christian before I died. God has lavished his gifts on me in that respect, for I know that you have even renounced earthly happiness to be his servant. So what am I doing here?"

The consolation experienced by St. Monica and her total abandonment to God can also be ours today if we persevere in patience and in trust. Moreover, her request in the Office of Readings reminds us to pray for the souls of the faithful departed: "One thing only I ask you, that you remember me at the altar of the Lord wherever you may be."

Preface (Augustinian Missal): *It is especially fitting for us on the feast of the saintly mother Monica to praise you for your gifts. Reborn in Christ, she lived in such a*

*way that her faith and her conduct were praise to your
name and she felt your presence in her heart. She
entrusted her husband to you and she nurtured her
children spiritually, being in labor again as often as
she saw them stray from you. And because of her daily
heartfelt tears, you granted that her son Augustine
should not be lost.*

August 28
ST. AUGUSTINE (354-430)

HISTORICO-LITURGICAL NOTE

This feast appears in the Sacramentary as early as the
eighth century, but it was not celebrated in Rome until after
the eleventh century. St. Augustine was ignored in the
Calendars of the Eastern Churches but is honored as one of the
great Doctors of the Western Church.

Born at Tagaste in modern Algeria on November 13, 354,
he studied the pagan classics but rejected the Scriptures,
considering them too demanding and uncultured. In 371 he
moved to Carthage, where he accepted the Manichean teaching of a double principle, one of good and another of evil. In
spite of the concessions to indulgence of the flesh permitted by
that doctrine, Augustine finally became a skeptic. Still un-
satisfied, he travelled to Rome, where he became deathly ill
but did not ask to be baptized. By the year 384 he was a teacher
of rhetoric in Milan and was reunited with his mother, Monica.

Hearing St. Ambrose give an explanation of Sacred
Scripture, Augustine was captivated. At the age of 32, while
shedding tears of anguish, he seemed to hear a child sing:
"Take and read." He opened the Bible at random and read the
words of St. Paul: "Let us live honorably as in daylight; not in
carousing and drunkenness, not in sexual excess and lust, not
in quarreling and jealousy. Rather, put on the Lord Jesus
Christ and make no provision for the desires of the flesh"

(Rm 13:13-14). After telling his mother what had happened, he made the necessary preparations and was baptized by St. Ambrose. He then went into seclusion, where he composed some works against the teaching of the Manicheans. After the death of his mother at Ostia, Augustine returned to Africa in 388 together with his friend Alipius and his son Adeodatus. He had already, at Monica's insistence, sent away his concubine, the mother of his son.

Some three years later Augustine was ordained a priest at Hippo, and in 395 he was ordained a bishop. For 35 years he preached in his cathedral, administered the affairs of the Church, answered letters that came to him from all parts, and defended the faith against heretics.

As bishop he lived a community life with some of his clergy and found time to write some of his major works, including his *Confessions*, a catechism for catechumens, and his great opus *Christian Doctrine*. When Alaric laid siege to Rome in 410, Augustine wrote another major work, *The City of God*; and finally, between 412 and 427, he wrote the treatise *On the Trinity*. After this, Augustine composed his books of *Retractions*, meaning that in going over his writings he found it necessary to edit some parts. He died at the age of 76, on August 28, 430, when the Vandals were at the gates of the city of Hippo. St. Bede states that Augustine's body was transferred to Sardinia to protect it from the Vandals. From there it was moved to Pavia, where it is venerated.

MESSAGE AND RELEVANCE

The new prayers of the Mass touch on the characteristics of this outstanding theologian who is rightly called "Doctor of Grace." In the Opening Prayer we ask that God will renew in his Church the spirit he gave St. Augustine, so that, filled with the same spirit, we "may seek you as the source of eternal love." The search for truth and for love was indeed the motivating force of Augustine's life. He had written: "What does the soul desire more ardently than truth? It is known by love." He realized that true wisdom is not found in the philosophy he had studied in his youth, but only when one transcends the level of the intellect and reaches the heart. Thus, he describes this wisdom as something "beyond the eye of the soul, beyond my spirit: your immutable light" (Office of Readings). In the responsory for Morning Prayer St. Augustine calls truth "the light of my heart." Then, in the antiphon for the Canticle of Mary and in the Office of Readings we find the beautiful exclamation: "Late have I loved you, O Beauty ever ancient, ever new; late have I love you."

St. Augustine's wisdom and prudence are also manifested in his *Rule*, followed not only by the Augustinians but by many men and women of other religious orders. In the first paragraph of the *Rule* he succinctly states the ideal of community life: "One heart and one soul in God," a phrase found in the Acts of the Apostles.

The Prayer over the Gifts is derived from St. Augustine's *Commentary on John's Gospel*; it asks that in celebrating the memorial of our salvation it may be for us "a sign of unity and a bond of love." Living as he did when there were factions in the Church, St. Augustine tried to promote unity. This was a constant theme in many of his writings. "Let us love God as Father," he said, "and the Church as mother."

St. Augustine understood very well that the focal point for unity in the Church is the Eucharist. Therefore in the Prayer after Communion we ask that we be made holy by "sharing at the table of Christ" and, as members of his body, may "become what we have received." Augustine is thus a teacher of liturgical spirituality based on the Eucharist. He developed this theme especially in his preaching at Easter, saying: "Sing and march; God is at the end of the march."

Preface (Augustinian Missal): *Father, all-powerful and ever-living God, we do well always and everywhere to give you thanks, and to praise you on this feast of Saint Augustine, our Father. His life was a constant quest to know you and rejoice in you, and in finding you to seek you with ever greater love. By his teaching he enlightened your Church. Moved by love for you and by zeal for your glory, he established communities of religious, setting before them the ideal of sharing all things in common. Tireless in proclaiming the good news of salvation by preaching and writing, he fostered unity and peace and built up the fellowship of the Church.*

August 29
BEHEADING of ST. JOHN the BAPTIST

HISTORICO-LITURGICAL NOTE

This feast in honor of the Precursor of the Lord has its origin in a crypt in Samaria, where his skull was venerated in the fourth century. By the fifth century the feast was celebrated in the East and by the seventh century it was celebrated at Rome under the title of the Beheading of St. John the Baptist. His martyrdom is reported in Mark 6:14-29. Eventually his skull was transferred to the church of St. Sylvester in Rome, although there is no documentation to prove this.

MESSAGE AND RELEVANCE

We read in the Opening Prayer of the Mass that God "called John the Baptist to be the herald of your Son's birth and death." This is further developed in the Office of Readings in the homily of St. Bede: "Through his birth, preaching and baptizing, he bore witness to the coming birth, preaching and baptism of Christ, and by his own suffering he showed that Christ also would suffer . . . John was baptized in his own blood, though: he had been privileged to baptize the Redeemer of the world."

In the Prayer over the Gifts reference is made to the preaching apostolate of John the Baptist: "Keep us faithful to your way of life, which John the Baptist preached in the wilderness, and to which he courageously witnessed by shedding his blood." The antiphon for the Canticle of Mary recalls his humility: "I am not the Christ; I have been sent before him to prepare his way. He must increase, and I must decrease." The responsory for Morning Prayer states: "You sent your disciples to John, and he gave witness to the truth. He was like a bright shining light."

The message of his feast is, first of all, that we should live our baptismal commitment for the rest of our lives. We have been reborn as children of God and heirs of heaven. Secondly, we should imitate the courage of St. John the Baptist by standing firm in our faith and resisting the temptation to compromise the gospel teaching.

> Preface: *We praise your greatness as we honor the prophet who prepared the way before your Son. You set John the Baptist apart from other men, marking him out with special favor. His birth brought great rejoicing: even in the womb he leaped for joy, so near was man's salvation. You chose John the Baptist from all the prophets to show the world its Redeemer, the Lamb of sacrifice. He baptized Christ, the giver of baptism, in waters made holy by the one who was baptized. You found John worthy of a martyr's death, his last and greatest act of witness to your Son.*

SEPTEMBER

ST. GREGORY the GREAT (540-604)

HISTORICO-LITURGICAL NOTE

This saintly pope died in Rome on March 12, 604, afflicted not only with physical suffering but dismayed at witnessing the desolation and ruin inflicted on the city by the barbarian invaders. The feast is celebrated on September 3, the date of his episcopal ordination in 590, to avoid having the feast fall during the Lenten season.

Gregory was born in Rome in 540, the son of a Roman senator and administrator of one of the seven regions of Rome. Gregory himself became prefect of the city from 573 to 578, and after the death of his father he distributed his great wealth among various monasteries and turned the family home into a monastery. In 579 he was sent to Constantinople as the emissary of Pope Pelagius II, after being ordained a deacon. But even at the court of the emperor, Gregory continued to live the monastic life.

He returned to Rome in 586 and was named abbot of the monastery of St. Andrew. He also served as secretary to Pope Pelagius II, whom he succeeded as pope in 590. He was the first monk to become a pope. One of the first things he did was to arrange for penitential processions to the seven churches of Rome in order to pray for the end of the plague, of which Pope Pelagius had died.

Pope Gregory the Great was both a contemplative and a man of action. He was the first pope to call himself "Servant of the servants of God." He sent missionaries to England and he was a peacemaker between nations. He served in the papacy for thirteen years, the last two of which were years of intense physical suffering. The title "the Great" was bestowed on him by Pope Boniface VIII. He is also one of the four Fathers of the Western Church, together with St. Ambrose, St. Augustine and St. Jerome.

MESSAGE AND RELEVANCE

Two of the prayers of the Mass are taken from the Gregorian Sacramentary. In the Opening Prayer we ask: "By the prayers of St. Gregory give the spirit of wisdom to those you have called to lead your Church." There is an implicit reference to the "rule of discipline" mentioned by St. Gregory in his *Pastoral Rule*, in which he lists the duties of bishops. He who had embraced the monastic life, had to sanctify himself through the works of his ministry and the pastoral care of the Church. This first of the medieval popes was truly a leader of his people, as is stated in the Office of Readings and in the antiphon for the Canticle of Zechariah: "Gregory, an outstanding pastor of the Church, has left us a splendid example and rule of life, a guide for all who shepherd God's people."

Not only did Gregory lead and serve the Church of Rome, but there are 854 letters to the Eastern Churches, which he tried to keep in union with Rome. The responsory for the Office of Readings says as much: "Through him the life-giving streams of the gospel flowed out to all nations." We read in the responsory for the Canticle of Mary: "Gregory put into practice all that he preached so that he might be a living example of the spiritual message he proclaimed."

In the Prayer after Communion we ask that we may "come to know your truth and live it in love for others." The responsory for the Office of Readings tells us that St. Gregory made this possible because "he drew his moral and mystical teaching from the source of Holy Scripture" and he served "both the great and the small with his all-embracing charity."

So important did he consider a knowledge of Scripture that he said that it enables one "to know the heart of God through the word of God." He also stated that "the word of God grows together with him who reads it." Occupied as he was with countless tasks, he said: "I know from experience that most of the time when I am with the brethren I learn many things about the word of God that I could not learn all by myself; it is you who impart to me what I should teach."

In the Prayer over the Gifts we see another dimension of this great reformer: "Lord, by this sacrifice you free the world from sin." His liturgical reforms touched three different areas. First, in the Roman Canon of the Mass he added the phrase: "Grant peace to our days." Secondly, he prescribed the singing of the Alleluia even outside paschal time, except in the penitential seasons. Thirdly, he unified the recitation of the Our Father at the end of the Canon of the Mass. His revision of the Sacramentary caused it to be called the "Gregorian" Sacramentary; and because he promoted the chant, it too is called "Gregorian."

The relevance of St. Gregory the Great to our times is that he greatly unified the Church by his disciplinary measures and was prudent in making necessary adaptations. His reforms touched every area of Church life and affected every group in the Church, including priests and bishops. His creative originality and administrative ability are an inspiration and a model for those who hold authority at any level of Church life.

Opening Prayer: *Father, you guide your people with kindness and govern us with love. By the prayers of St. Gregory give the spirit of wisdom to those you have called to lead your Church. May the growth of your people in holiness be the eternal joy of our shepherds.*

September 8
BIRTH of the BLESSED VIRGIN MARY

HISTORICO-LITURGICAL NOTE

This feast is connected with the basilica constructed in the fifth century on the site of the pool at Bethesda (cf. Jn 5:1-9). That was the supposed location of the home of Joachim and Ann, where the basilica of St. Ann stands today. The feast spread throughout the East in the sixth century and was introduced at Rome by Pope Sergius I (+701). But perhaps there was a feast before this date in the West, since it is likely that the faithful would want to honor the birth of Mary as well as the birth of John the Baptist, which feast dates back to the year 400. There are apocryphal accounts of Mary's birth, such as the gospel of pseudo-Matthew and another attributed to St. Jerome. This feast opens the liturgical year in the East and under Pope Innocent IV it was celebrated with an octave (1243) and later, under Pope Gregory XI, with a vigil (1378).

MESSAGE AND RELEVANCE

The first two prayers of the Mass are taken from the Gregorian-Adrian Sacramentary and they provide a biblical foundation for this feast. In the Opening Prayer we state that "the birth of the Virgin Mary's Son was the dawn of our salvation." The same theme is found in the Entrance Antiphon when we refer to Mary, "of whom was born the Sun of justice, Christ our Lord." Hence, the focal point of the feast is Jesus Christ, as we read in the antiphon for Mid-afternoon Prayer: "With heart and mind let us sing praise and glory to Christ on this holy feastday of the glorious Virgin Mother of God."

However, the Invitatory Antiphon for the Office of Readings is somewhat different: "Come, let us celebrate the birth of the Virgin Mary; let us worship her Son, Christ the Lord." The antiphon for the Canticle of Zechariah is taken from the

Byzantine rite and it says: "Your birth, O Virgin Mother of God, proclaims joy to the whole world, for from you arose the glorious Sun of justice, Christ our God."

In the Prayer over the Gifts we read that "the birth of Christ your Son increased the Virgin Mother's love for you." The implication is that if the birth of Christ preserved intact the temple of the Virgin, so also her birth was a salvific event. The second antiphon for Evening Prayer states that "God saw her beauty and visited her in her lowliness." The antiphon for the Canticle of Mary says that "the Lord has looked with favor on his lowly servant."

In the document on the liturgy the Second Vatican Council states that Mary "is inseparably linked with her Son's saving work." The mystery of the divine election of Mary as Mother of God is explicitly related to her humility. "My soul proclaims the greatness of the Lord, my spirit rejoices in God my Savior, for he has looked with favor on his lowly servant." That same sense of humility and lowliness is an indispensable condition for receiving the divine gifts.

> Preface: *Today we celebrate that happy day on which the glorious and immaculate Mother of God appeared in the world like a shining star. After the sin of the first woman, there was finally opened to us the long-desired gate of life and we have been called by the Son of the Virgin Mary out of the darkness into the joy of eternal light.*

September 9 (United States)
ST. PETER CLAVER (1580-1654)

HISTORICO-LITURGICAL NOTE

Born in Catalonia, Spain, Peter Claver entered the Society of Jesus at the age of 20, after completing his studies at the University of Barcelona. Assigned to Palma in Mallorca, Peter met the saintly Jesuit lay brother, Alfonso Rodriguez, who urged him to volunteer as a missionary to South America. He left Spain in April, 1610, and landed at Cartagena, Colombia, and was ordained to the priesthood there in 1615.

The slave trade had been flourishing in the Americas for almost 100 years and Cartagena was a central clearing house. In spite of condemnations by Pope Paul III and Pope Pius IV, this inhuman practice continued. Peter Claver began to work under the direction of a fellow Jesuit, Alfonso de Sandoval, who spent 40 years ministering to the slaves. Peter enlisted the help of catechists and interpreters and in the years that he ministered to the African slaves it is estimated that he baptized more than 300,000.

In 1650 Peter Claver fell victim to an epidemic that was raging through the city of Cartagena. He never fully recovered from the sickness and could no longer carry on his ministry. Abandoned and forgotten by most of the people, he died on September 8, 1654. Then the people remembered him and he was given a public funeral at the expense of the state. He was never again forgotten, and was canonized in 1888 by Pope Leo XIII, together with his former companion, Alfonso Rodriguez of Mallorca. Pope Leo XIII also named him patron of all those who minister to Negroes in any part of the world.

MESSAGE AND RELEVANCE

The Opening Prayer of the Mass states that God offers all peoples the dignity of sharing in his love. Although somewhat shy and withdrawn by temperament, Peter Claver was forceful in his insistence that the slaves from Africa were human beings and had human and religious rights. Very early in his ministry, as a young priest, he had declared that he would be "a slave of the Negroes for ever." As soon as a slave ship arrived, Peter would be there to minister to the Negroes, many of whom were sick or dying. It is estimated that out of every shipload one third of the Negroes died en route. Once the slaves were sent out to work in the mines or on the plantations it was impossible for Peter Claver to keep in touch with them, except for an occasional mission tour. Consequently, the majority of the Catholic slaves had received at most a rudimentary instruction in the faith.

The petition in the Opening Prayer is that we may be strengthened to overcome all racial hatreds and "to love each other as brothers and sisters." St. Peter Claver once said to an assistant: "We must speak to them with our hands before we try to speak to them with our lips." Consequently, he met every slave ship with medicines and whatever food he could beg. He nursed the sick personally, in spite of the stench of the pens in which the poor slaves were herded together with no hygienic facilities. Through his love and care for them, he hoped to lead them to a love for Christ. He taught them this prayer: "Jesus Christ, Son of God, you will be my father and my mother and all my good. I love you much. I am sorry for having sinned against you. Lord I love you much, much, much."

There is little need to seek for the relevance of St. Peter Claver to our contemporary society in which there are flagrant violations of human rights. This feast is celebrated in the United States as a reminder to all Christians to work for racial justice, not for the blacks alone, but for all minority groups and immigrants.

> Opening Prayer: *God of mercy and love, you offer all peoples the dignity of sharing in your life. By the example and prayers of St. Peter Claver, strengthen us to overcome all racial hatreds and to love each other as brothers and sisters.*

September 13
ST. JOHN CHRYSOSTOM (344/49-407)

HISTORICO-LITURGICAL NOTE

This Doctor of the Church died in Turkey on September 14, 407, and his body was transferred to Constantinople in 438.

His feast is celebrated on the vigil of the day of his death because September 14 is the feast of the Holy Cross. The Churches in Constantinople and Alexandria also observe this date. Born at Antioch around the year 349, John was educated by his mother, who was widowed at the age of 20, and by the famous Greek master Libanius. At the age of 18 he was baptized a Christian and at the age of 32 he was ordained a priest, after having lived the monastic life for six years. He spent 12 years as a preacher at Antioch, where his sermons won the admiration of the faithful, largely because he was able to incorporate both exegetical or dogmatic content with moral application. "Chrysostom" means "golden-mouthed."

It was largely because of his fame as a preacher that John Chrysostom was elected patriarch of Constantinople, but it was also because of his preaching that he aroused the hostility of the imperial court. Angered by one of John's sermons against pomp and luxury, the empress Eudoxia prevailed on Theophilus, bishop of Alexandria and an adversary of John Chrysostom, to have John sent into exile in 403. He was soon brought back by the emperor Arcadius, but two months later the empress had him exiled once more, first to the frontier of Armenia and then to the Black Sea. He died en route at the little town of Comana, saying: "Glory be to God for everything. Amen." It was the feast of the Holy Cross, September 14, 407.

MESSAGE AND RELEVANCE

The prayers of the Mass touch on the highlights of the life of St. John Chrysostom. First of all, in the Opening Prayer we pray: "Father, you made John Chrysostom renowned for his eloquence and heroic in his sufferings." This great orator, called by the Byzantines the "mouth of gold," and named Doctor of the Church by the Council of Chalcedon, is renowned not only for his writings (in which he rivals St. Augustine) but also for the pastoral and catechetical style of his preaching. In 1909 Pope Pius X proclaimed him the heavenly patron of preachers. He has left to the Church a legacy of scriptural exegesis that covers both the Old and the New Testaments, with special emphasis on the letters of St. Paul.

Secondly, the invocation in the prayer is that we may "gain courage from his patient endurance." His deportation by the empress was accepted by him as if nothing had happened, as we read in the homily he preached prior to his exile in 401: "I have only contempt for the world's threats, I find its blessings laughable. . . . If Christ is with me, whom shall I fear? Though the waves and the sea and the anger of princes are roused against me, they are less to me than a spider's web."

In the Prayer over the Gifts we say: "May the sacrament we receive . . . make us strong in your love and faithful in our witness to your truth." St. John Chrysostom's teaching on the Eucharist is found not only in his commentary on Scripture and his numerous letters, but also in his treatise *On the Priesthood.* Here we find the change that took place in John Chrysostom when he returned to the active life after being ordained a bishop. He devoted himself completely to his people. He was not intimidated in his efforts to bring wandering monks back to their monasteries, to reform the clergy, who were avaricious and self-centered, or to rectify the situation of virgins living under the same roof with priests under the pretext of being protected. During the suppression of the rebellion at Antioch in 387 he had said: "One man filled with zeal is enough to transform a people."

What is the relevance of this great bishop and preacher who was able to transform his love of the monastic life into zeal for the salvation of his people? His sermons are still powerful and instructive. Our present-day need for Christian re-evangelization in so many countries should prompt the clergy to imitate the fervor and courage of this great bishop and preacher who never faltered in proclaiming the gospel.

> Opening Prayer: *Father, the strength of all who trust in you, you made John Chrysostom renowned for his eloquence and heroic in his sufferings. May we learn from his teaching and gain courage from his patient endurance.*

September 15
OUR LADY of SORROWS

HISTORICO-LITURGICAL NOTE

This feast dates back to the twelfth century, although there are traces of it in the writings of St. Anselm and among the Benedictines of the eleventh century. However, it was especially promoted by the Cistercians and the Servites, so that in the fourteenth and fifteenth centuries it was widely diffused throughout the Catholic world. It is the patronal feast of the Servite Order. In 1423 the feast was celebrated in Cologne, Germany, by a decree of a provincial council. The date for the feast was the Friday after the Third Sunday of Easter.

In 1482 the feast was inserted in the Missal under the title "Our Lady of Compassion." Pope Benedict XIII placed it in the Roman Calendar in 1727, to be celebrated on the Friday before Palm Sunday. The Servites had introduced a feast in honor of the Seven Dolors of Mary in 1668 for the Sunday after September 14 (feast of the Holy Cross). It was placed in the Roman Calendar in 1814; in 1913 Pope Pius X fixed the permanent date of September 15 for the feast of Our Lady of Sorrows. The title "Our Lady of Sorrows" focuses on Mary's intense suffering during the passion and death of Christ; the previous title, "The Seven Dolors," referred to the seven swords that pierced her heart.

Falling as it does on the day after the feast of the Holy Cross, this feast reminds the faithful of the suffering of Mary during the passion and death of Christ. The famous statue by Michelangelo, the *Pietà*, and the hymn *Stabat Mater* are artistic representations of Mary's grief. Some liturgists, however, feel that a feast of the Sorrowful Mother in September does not fill the vacuum that is left in Passion Week.

MESSAGE AND RELEVANCE

This feast refers to all the sorrows of Mary, as indicated by the words of Simeon in the Entrance Antiphon: "And your own soul a sword shall pierce." The Communion Antiphon tells us that in uniting ourselves to Mary on this feast we are, with her, sharing in the sufferings of Christ. The Invitatory for the Office of Readings says the same thing: "Let us adore Christ, the Savior of the world, who called his mother to share in his passion."

In the Opening Prayer of the Mass we find the biblical basis for this feast: "As your Son was raised on the cross, his Mother Mary stood by him, sharing his sufferings." Mary's participation in the suffering and passion of Christ was different from that of other Christians; it was special because she was his mother.

In the Prayer over the Gifts we say: "While she stood beside the cross of Jesus, you gave her to us as our loving Mother." This is stated again in the Gospel for the Mass (Jn 19:25-27) and in the antiphon for the Canticle of Mary for Evening Prayer. Mary was not only intimately associated with the passion and death of Christ, but as our Mother she plays an active role as Mediatrix in our redemption by transmitting to us the fruits of Christ's passion.

In the Prayer after Communion we say: "As we honor the compassionate love of the Virgin Mary, may we make up in our own lives whatever is lacking in the sufferings of Christ for the good of the Church." This prayer is based on Colossians 1:24. The second antiphon for Morning Prayer states explicitly that "we have been made sharers in Christ's passion."

The responsory for the Office of Readings capsulizes the biblical references and adds: "A sword of sorrow pierced her blameless heart." In the Office of Readings St. Bernard says: "Truly, O blessed Mother, a sword has pierced your heart. . . . He died in body through a love greater than anyone had known. She died in spirit through a love unlike any other since his." St. Paul says in 2 Timothy 2:10-12, "If we have died with him, we shall also live with him; if we hold out to the end, we shall also reign with him." Consequently, the antiphon for the Canticle of Zechariah says: "Rejoice, O sorrowful Mother; after your great sufferings, you shine forth as Queen, enthroned beside your Son."

> Preface: *On Calvary the cruel sword of suffering pierced the heart of the Virgin Mary while the Savior of the world, nailed to the cross, freed the sons of Adam from the ancient condemnation and by his precious blood he opened the gates of the kingdom. In suffering death for our sins, Christ willed especially to associate his Mother with the redemptive passion so that she could obtain for her children more copious fruits of that sacrifice.*

September 16
ST. CORNELIUS (+253) and
ST. CYPRIAN (+258)

HISTORICO-LITURGICAL NOTE

According to the Office of Readings, St. Cyprian was beheaded at Carthage on September 14, 258. His feast was celebrated on that date in Rome in the crypt in which St. Cornelius was buried. St. Cornelius died in exile at Civitavecchia, the port of Rome, in September, 253, and was venerated as a martyr. The joint celebration is very ancient, going back to the Jerome Martyrology and the Sacramentary of Verona. However, when the feast of the Exaltation of the Holy Cross was introduced in the West in the seventh century, this feast was transferred to September 16. The two saints are also mentioned together in the Roman Canon of the Mass.

Cornelius was elected pope in 251 and he governed the Church until 253. During his short pontificate he was involved in the controversy over the sacrament of penance, with the heretic Novatian as his adversary. The question at issue was how public sinners and apostates are to be reconciled to the Church.

Before his conversion at the age of 25, Cyprian served as a rhetorician and a lawyer. He was elected bishop in 249 and became the metropolitan of approximately 150 bishops in northern Africa. During the persecution by Decius, in which Pope Fabian was martyred at Rome, Cyprian also became involved in the problem of the apostate Christians who had returned to the Church. He also took a negative stand on the validity of baptism conferred by heretics and in so doing he opposed the decision of Pope Stephen I.

Cyprian himself was a victim of the persecution by Valerian, first being exiled and later sentenced to be beheaded. His relics were transferred to Lyons, France, in the ninth century.

MESSAGE AND RELEVANCE

In the Opening Prayer of the Mass for these two saints we read: "God, our Father, in Saints Cornelius and Cyprian you have given your people an inspiring example of dedication to the pastoral ministry and constant witness to Christ in their suffering." We then ask that their prayers and faith will "give us courage to work for the unity of your Church." The bond of unity between the churches of Rome and of Carthage was very strong, partly because Carthage was the most Latinized province of the empire.

In Cyprian's letter to Cornelius, found in the Office of Readings, he writes: "After all, we have the same Church, the same mind, the same unbroken harmony. Why then should a priest not take pride in the praise given to a fellow priest as though it were given to him? What brotherhood fails to rejoice in the happiness of its brothers wherever they are?" For St. Cyprian the Church is the only way to salvation. "He cannot have God for his Father," he said, "who has not the Church for his mother." He even wrote a special treatise, *De unitate ecclesiae*, to promote unity in the Church.

In the Prayer over the Gifts, taken from the Parisian Missal of 1738, after stating that "the Eucharist gave them courage to offer their lives for Christ," we ask God to "keep us faithful in all our trials." In his letter to Pope Cornelius, Cyprian makes an indirect reference to the Eucharist when he says, "We are doing all we can to exhort our congregation, to give ourselves unceasingly to fasting, vigils and prayers in common."

In the Prayer after Communion we ask that "we may offer faithful witness to the truth of your Gospel." Cyprian was in good faith about the re-baptism of schismatics, but he was also totally committed to the primacy of the pope. "There is one God and one Christ," he said, "and but one episcopal chair, originally founded on Peter, by the Lord's authority. There cannot therefore be set up another altar or another priesthood." Similarly, as the Second Vatican Council teaches in *Lumen Gentium*: "The individual bishops are the visible source and foundation of unity in their own particular churches, which are constituted after the model of the universal Church; it is in these and formed out of them that the one and unique Catholic Church exists" (no. 23). The footnote on the foregoing text refers to two phrases of St. Cyprian: "The bishop in the Church and the Church in the bishop" (Letter 66); "One Church throughout the world divided into many members" (Letter 55).

The relevance of these two saints is first of all that through their prayers and example we should cultivate a deeper love for the universal Church as well as loyalty to our own local churches. Secondly, we can take to heart the responsory for the Office of Readings: "Let us arm ourselves in full strength and prepare ourselves for the ultimate struggle with blameless hearts, true faith and unyielding courage."

Opening Prayer: *God our Father, in Saints Cornelius and Cyprian you have given your people an inspiring example of dedication to the pastoral ministry and constant witness to Christ in their suffering. May their prayers and faith give us courage to work for the unity of your Church.*

September 17
ST. ROBERT BELLARMINE (1542-1621)

HISTORICO-LITURGICAL NOTE

Robert Bellarmine died on September 17, 1621, but was not canonized until 1930; he was declared Doctor of the Church in 1931. His feast has been transferred to this date from May 13.

Born at Montepulciano, Italy, of a noble family, he entered the Society of Jesus in 1560. He took his studies at the Roman College, at Padua, and finally at Louvain. Ordained to the priesthood in 1570, he remained as a professor at Louvain for seven years. For reasons of health he returned to teach theology at the Roman College (now the Pontifical Gregorian University), where he spent twelve years. There he wrote his famous four volumes of *Controversies*, which were almost placed on the Index because he denied the right of the pope to exercise direct temporal power. He was also a member of the commission for the revision of the Latin Vulgate under Pope Clement VIII and wrote the preface for that edition. He was so highly esteemed that he became the theologian for Pope Clement VIII, at whose request St. Robert composed two catechisms. It is said that these two catechisms were translated more frequently than any other book except the Bible and the *Imitation of Christ*.

In 1588 he became spiritual director at the Roman College and among his clients was St. Aloysius Gonzaga. He became rector of the Roman College and in 1594 was named provincial of the Jesuit Province at Naples.

In spite of his reluctance, he was named a cardinal in 1599 and as such he was involved in the dispute between the Jesuit Molina and the Dominican Bañez on the question of predestination. Next he was named archbishop of Capua (1602), where he was an exemplary pastor for three years. Finally he was called back to Rome by Pope Paul V, where he became the official theologian for the Holy Office. In 1616 he imposed silence on Galileo and in 1621 he retired to the Jesuit novitiate of St. Andrew near the Quirinale. There he died, after reverently reciting the Creed and receiving the blessing of Pope Gregory XV. It was the feast of the Stigmata of St. Francis, which he had promoted as a feast for the universal Church. His body lies in the church of St. Ignatius in Rome, next to that of St. Aloysius Gonzaga.

MESSAGE AND RELEVANCE

The revised Opening Prayer of the Mass no longer refers to the return of those in error to the Roman Catholic Church but states that God "gave Robert Bellarmine wisdom and goodness to defend the faith of your Church." In the period after the Council of Trent the Church was in the process of a reform that had been called for by numerous saints. St. Robert Bellarmine defended the faith at Louvain against Baius and in the first volume of his *Controversies*. Finally, his catechisms, which were written for the ordinary Christian, were used in many countries for many generations. His writings exerted a great influence on St. Francis de Sales.

Our petition in the Opening Prayer is that "we may always rejoice in the profession of our faith." St. Robert Bellarmine was "an inexhaustible fountain of doctrine," according to St. Francis de Sales. His ability to come immediately to the heart of a problem is exemplified in the Office of Readings: "If you are wise, then know that you have been created for the glory of God and your own eternal salvation. This is your goal; this is the center of your life; this is the treasure of your heart."

Opening Prayer: *God our Father, you gave Robert Bellarmine wisdom and goodness to defend the faith of your Church. By his prayers may we always rejoice in the profession of our faith.*

September 19
ST. JANUARIUS (+305)

HISTORICO-LITURGICAL NOTE

St. Januarius, popularly known as San Gennaro, was martyred with six companions at Pozzuoli, near Naples, sometime around the year 305. His feast is listed in the Jerome Calendar and also in the Calendar of Carthage (sixth century) and the Calendar of Naples (ninth century). The feast is likewise celebrated in the Eastern Churches, although the Byzantines celebrate it on April 20.

The most ancient reference to the existence of St. Januarius is in a biography of St. Paulinus of Nola. Describing the death of St. Paulinus, the author says: "Paulinus began to ask in a clear voice where his brethren were. One of the priests, thinking that he was referring to his brother bishops who had just celebrated [the Eucharist] with him in his bedroom, responded: 'Your brethren are all here with you.' But he answered: 'I am speaking of Januarius and Martin [of Tours], my brothers in the episcopate, who a little while ago were speaking to me and promising me that soon I would join them'."

San Gennaro, bishop and martyr, is a special patron of Naples. Connected with this feast is the liquefaction of his blood. Four times a year — the first Saturday of May, September 19, in the octave of the feast and sometimes on December 16 — the blood liquefies when the reliquary is exposed. There is historical proof of this event since the thirteenth century. Some popes have attached indulgences to the veneration of the relic.

MESSAGE AND RELEVANCE

The Opening Prayer of the Mass is taken from the Gregorian Sacramentary: "God our Father, enable us who honor the

memory of St. Januarius to share with him the joy of eternal
life." The feast serves to remind us of the importance of the
office and ministry of a bishop. The excerpt from a sermon of
St. Augustine in the Office of Readings contains a significant
statement: "This is why being set above you fills me with
alarm, whereas being with you gives me comfort. Danger lies
in the first; salvation in the second."

Apart from the seemingly miraculous liquefaction of the
blood, the veneration of San Gennaro has a firm foundation
because, as we read in *Lumen Gentium*, "We seek from the
saints example in their way of life, fellowship in their communion, and the help of their intercession." This constitutes the
relevance of this feast to our day.

> Opening Prayer: *God our Father, enable us who honor
> the memory of St. Januarius to share with him the joy of
> eternal life.*

September 20

ST. ANDREW KIM TAEGON,
ST. PAUL CHONG HASANG and
COMPANIONS (+1846)

HISTORICO-LITURGICAL NOTE

These two Korean martyrs, together with 111 companions, were canonized by Pope John Paul II during his pastoral
visit to that country in 1984. The priest Andrew was beheaded
on September 16 and the layman Paul was martyred on
September 22 in 1846.

The evangelization of Korea began early in the
seventeenth century with a group of fervent lay Christians. At
first they were without priests but eventually missionaries from
France entered Korea secretly. 103 members of this Christian
community were among the martyrs, as well as 3 bishops and 7

priests who belonged to the Foreign Mission Society of Paris. The persecution was carried on periodically between 1839 and 1867.

The information about St. Andrew the priest as well as several other martyrs is found in two letters. One was written from prison and in Latin. It was addressed to the Vicar Apostolic who had ordained Andrew to the priesthood in 1845. The other letter was addressed to Andrew's fellow Christians. The body of Andrew was carried from the river bank where he was beheaded and buried in the mountains.

MESSAGE AND RELEVANCE

There are two themes in the prayers of the Mass and the Liturgy of the Hours. The first is found in the Opening Prayer and it refers to the universality of God's salvific plan: "O God, you have created all nations and you are their salvation." The Church is missionary by its very nature, since Christ sent the apostles forth to preach the gospel to every nation.

In the Office of Readings one is impressed by the simplicity of the letter written by Andrew Kim. Being the son of a farmer who was also martyred for the faith (1821), Andrew uses a style that resembles the gospel parables: "Persecution, therefore, can only be regarded as the command of the Lord or as a prize he gives or as a punishment he permits." Thus, the true believer can see the hand of divine providence even in the most violent persecution.

The message contained in the final lines of the Opening Prayer, where we ask God for the strength to remain faithful to his commandments, is also the message of Andrew Kim to his fellow Christians: "We have received baptism, entrance into the Church, and the honor of being called Christians. Yet what good will this do us if we are Christians in name only and not in fact?"

Andrew brought to fruition his Christian education in his family and his later studies at Macao, from which place he had returned secretly to Korea. His message to us is that we should live an authentic Christian life and give Christian witness to the society in which we live. The modern amazing growth of the Church in Korea is undoubtedly the fruit of the martyrdom of these valiant witnesses to Christ.

> Opening Prayer: *O God, you have created all nations and you are their salvation. In the land of Korea your call to the Catholic faith formed a people of adoption, whose growth you nurtured by the blood of Andrew, Paul and their companions. Through their martyrdom and their intercession grant us strength that we too may remain faithful to your commandments even until death.*

September 21
ST. MATTHEW

HISTORICO-LITURGICAL NOTE

The veneration of St. Matthew at Rome goes back to the fifth century. By the eighth century there was also a vigil of the feast, as for the other apostles. The date, September 21, is found in the Jerome Calendar, although in the East the date of the feast is November 16 for the Byzantines and the Syrians and October 9 for the Copts.

The New Testament describes Matthew as Levi, the son of Alphaeus and a tax collector (Mk 2:13-14). He was born at Capernaum (Mt 9:9) and is the author of the First Gospel, which was written in Aramaic. Later accounts state that Matthew evangelized Persia (according to St. Ambrose and St. Paulinus of Nola) and probably Ethiopia (according to the Roman Martyrology). He was martyred in Ethiopia and his relics were eventually transferred to Salerno in the tenth century, according to Pope Gregory VII.

MESSAGE AND RELEVANCE

The prayers of the Mass are taken from the Parisian Missal (1738) and they portray three characteristics of this "talented scribe," as he is called in the responsory for the Office of Readings. In the Opening Prayer we invoke God who "chose a tax collector to share the dignity of the apostles."

The Gospel of Matthew is truly a manual of catechesis for the Christian faithful. It presents Christ as the Master who has replaced Moses in order to lead us to perfection (Mt 5:48). The teaching of Matthew has an eschatological note, it is true, but it always returns to the insistence on a continuing discipleship. Matthew addresses the Jews in a special way in trying to prove that Christ is the Messiah.

The final part of the prayer has us ask God that we may follow Christ and remain faithful in his service. In the Office of Readings St. Bede describes the calling of Matthew: "Our Lord summoned Matthew by speaking to him in words. By an invisible, interior impulse flooding his mind with the light of grace, he instructed him to walk in his footsteps."

The theme of the Prayer over the Gifts is an ecclesial one. We ask God to "continue to guide us in your love as you nourished the faith of your Church by the preaching of the apostles." It is in the Gospel according to Matthew that we find the word *ekklesia* (church; Mt 16:18; 18:17) as signifying a fraternal community (Mt 12:50). In the Church the one who presides is the one who serves (Mt 20:26) and special care is given to the little ones and the poor (Mt 18:1-10), even if they are weak in the faith (Mt 18:12-14).

In the Prayer after Communion we profess that "in this Eucharist we have shared the joy of salvation which St. Matthew knew when he welcomed your Son." Matthew was faithful to the Jewish traditions and did not wish to lose that continuity with Israel, but at the same time he was open to the new universal dimension of the gospel (Mt 8:11-12). In the intercession of this prayer we ask that the Eucharist will renew us in Christ, "who came to call not the just but sinners." Therefore, "many will come from the east and the west and will find a place at the banquet in the kingdom of God with Abraham, Isaac and Jacob, while the natural heirs of the kingdom will be driven out into the dark" (Mt 8:12).

The message to us is that we should dedicate our efforts to the "study of God's law so that with the Lord's guidance [we] might observe his precepts and teach them to others" (responsory for the Office of Readings).

> Preface: *In sending your only-begotten Son you have manifested your love for mankind and you have mercifully invited sinners to be seated at the banquet of the kingdom. Matthew, happy to welcome the Master into his home, generously accepted and, renewed by this encounter with grace, became a herald of your marvels.*

September 26
ST. COSMAS and ST. DAMIAN (+303)

HISTORICO-LITURGICAL NOTE

This feast commemorates the dedication of the basilica of Sts. Cosmas and Damian at the Roman Forum (a former pagan temple) by Pope Felix IV (526-530). The feast is anticipated by one day because tomorrow is the feast of St. Vincent de Paul, but previously it was listed in the Gelasian and Gregorian Sacramentaries for September 27. In the East it is celebrated on various dates: November 1, July 1 or October 17.

According to legend, these martyrs from Syria were twin brothers and physicians who served the sick free of charge. From ancient times they were venerated widely, according to testimony dating from the fifth century. There are various legends concerning their martyrdom, but most authors state that they were martyred in Cilicia, together with their three brothers, on September 27 during the persecution by Diocletian. Together with St. Luke, they are patrons of physicians, surgeons and pharmacists and their names are mentioned in the Roman Canon.

MESSAGE AND RELEVANCE

In the Opening Prayer of the Mass we thank God for giving us his fatherly care. The dedicated care of the sick by Sts. Cosmas and Damian was a reflection of God's divine providence. St. Gregory of Tours said that these two physicians cured as many people by their prayers as they did by their medical knowledge, and now in heaven they still cure the sick miraculously.

The Prayer over the Gifts contains a beautiful phrase, proclaiming that the sacrifice of Christ "gives all martyrdom its meaning." Hence we read in the responsory for the Office of Readings: "They loved Christ in life; they followed him in his death."

The Prayer after Communion is new and is inspired by the inscription on the mosaic in the basilica of Sts. Cosmas and Damian: "Martyribus medicis populo spes certa salutis." In other words, Sts. Cosmas and Damian were not only healers of bodily sickness but they also gave spiritual comfort and help to their patients. Therefore we ask in this prayer that "the Eucharist we receive in memory of Saints Cosmas and Damian will bring us salvation and peace."

The significance of this feast is found in the advice given in the Book of Sirach: "Hold the physician in honor, for he is essential to you, and God it was who established his profession. From God the doctor has his wisdom. . . . His knowledge makes the doctor distinguished, and gives him access to those in authority. . . . He endows men with the knowledge to glory in his mighty works, through which the doctor eases pain and the druggist prepares his medicines. . . . Then give the doctor his place lest he leave; for you need him too. There are times that give him an advantage, and he too beseeches God that his diagnosis may be correct and his treatment will bring about a cure" (Si 38:1-14).

In our day, when there are so many new instruments and techniques, we should remember and pray for the physicians, nurses, lab technicians and pharmacists. It is also well for the men and women in the field of medicine to know that Sts. Cosmas and Damian were motivated primarily by Christian charity and compassion for the sick and suffering.

> Opening Prayer: *Lord, we honor the memory of Saints Cosmas and Damian. Accept our grateful praise for raising them to eternal glory and for giving us your fatherly care.*

September 27
ST. VINCENT de PAUL (1581-1660)

HISTORICO-LITURGICAL NOTE

St. Vincent de Paul died at Paris on September 27, 1660, and was canonized in 1737. His feast was previously celebrated on July 19 so that seminarians taught by the Vincentians could celebrate the feast at the end of the academic year.

Born in Gascony, France, in 1581 of a poor family, he became a priest at the age of 19. Captured by pirates while on a sea voyage, he spent two years as a prisoner and slave in Tunisia, but he succeeded in converting his master to Christianity. By 1608 he was in Paris, searching for a benefice. His spiritual director, Peter de Bérulle (later a cardinal) advised Vincent to accept the charge of a parish at Clichy, in suburban Paris, where he gathered together a group of young men. Then for twelve years he served as chaplain to the aristocratic de Gondi family in Paris. During that time he suffered serious temptations against the faith, but after four years of crisis he engaged in an apostolate among the men who worked on ships.

For a few years he was pastor of a parish and then a chaplain to the galley-slaves in Paris, but it was in a catechetical apostolate to the peasants of the French countryside that Vincent found his particular vocation. In 1619 he met Francis de Sales and Jane Frances de Chantal, and in 1622 he became superior of the convents of the Visitation in Paris, a post he held until his death.

In 1625 he gathered together a group that would be the basis of the Congregation of the Mission (known later as Vincentians). Composed of both priests and brothers, the Congregation was to engage in parish missions among the poor and uneducated. The Congregation was approved by Rome in 1633 and its headquarters was established in the priory of Saint-Lazare (for which reason they are called Lazarists in France). Because of the need for priestly formation, the Vincentians soon added seminary teaching to their apostolate.

In 1633 the first members of the Daughters of Charity were gathered together under the direction of Louise Marillac, who died in 1660. These women were to be engaged in a social apostolate and works of charity. Consequently St. Vincent did not attempt to have them approved as a religious institute, which would have required observance of the cloister.

For 60 years France benefited from the charitable works of St. Vincent de Paul, the Congregation of the Mission and the Daughters of Charity. Vincent de Paul died in the autumn of 1660 and was canonized by Pope Clement XII in 1737. Pope Leo XIII named him patron of all charitable works throughout the Catholic world.

MESSAGE AND RELEVANCE

The prayers of the Mass are taken from the Missal of the Vincentians. The Prayer states that St. Vincent de Paul had "the courage and holiness of an apostle for the well-being of the poor and the formation of the clergy." The notion of service is central to the spirituality of St. Vincent, as is the virtue of simplicity. His apostolate can be summarized in two of his sayings: "It is not sufficient for me to love God if I do not love my neighbor . . . . I belong to God and to the poor."

Our petition in this prayer is that "we may be zealous in continuing his work." This great apostle of charity says in the letter quoted in the Office of Readings: "It is our duty to prefer the service of the poor to everything else and to offer such service as quickly as possible. . . . Do not become upset or feel guilty if you interrupted your prayer to serve the poor."

In the Prayer over the Gifts we pray: "Lord, you helped St. Vincent to imitate the love he celebrated in these mysteries. By the power of this sacrifice may we also become an acceptable gift to you." Vincent had said that the Church was going to ruin because of bad priests. Consequently, he constantly tried to promote the pastoral ministry and the celebration of the Eucharist. At the same time he corrected the exaggerated emphasis of the French School on the altar and sanctuary as the exclusive place for a priest. Rather, he followed St. Augustine's teaching that the priest is a "man for others."

In the Prayer after Communion we ask that the example and prayers of St. Vincent will "help us to imitate your Son in preaching the good news to the poor." The antiphon for the Canticle of Zechariah describes Vincent as one who "consoled the sorrowful, defended the rights of orphans and generously aided widows." He offered the services of the Daughters of Charity to the hospitals that he founded, to work as nurses in time of war and to make home visits to the sick poor. He had a keen sense of serving Christ in the poor and needy.

The relevance of St. Vincent de Paul is that his example urges us to respond to the need for evangelization in contemporary society and to promote authentic social values. Secondly, St. Vincent tells us in the Office of Readings: "Even though the poor are often rough and unrefined, we must not judge them from external appearances. . . . If you consider the poor in the light of faith, then you will observe that they are taking the place of the Son of God who chose to be poor." On his deathbed, when asked to bless all his works, Vincent responded: "He who began the work will bring it to completion" (2 Cor 8:6).

Preface (Proper to the Vincentians): *We do well al-ways and everywhere to give you thanks and praise on this feast of St. Vincent de Paul. You called him to dedicate himself totally to the service of the poor, in imitation of your divine Son; in him, filled with zeal for the spread of your kingdom, you have given us an example and model of apostolic zeal, so that we also, with the power of your Spirit and inflamed with your love, would expend our energies and our entire life in working for the salvation of the poor, through Christ our Lord.*

September 28
ST. WENCESLAUS (907/8-929)

HISTORICO-LITURGICAL NOTE

Wenceslaus, the ruler of Bohemia, was martyred near Prague on September 28, 929, and is the first Slav to be canonized. The account of his martyrdom was written shortly after it occurred and his feast was first introduced into the Roman Calendar in the fourteenth century.

After the death of his father, Wenceslaus was educated by his maternal grandmother, St. Ludmilla, who was murdered later through the machinations of his mother. He assumed power officially in 925 at the age of 15, but immediately met with the hostility of the pagan officials. When the young ruler married and had a son, his younger brother Boleslaus, realizing that he had no chance of succession to the throne, joined the opposition. In September, 929, he invited Wenceslaus to the celebration of the feast of Sts. Cosmas and Damian. Then, as Wenceslaus was entering the church, his brother struck him on the head with a sword; they struggled, and then friends of Boleslaus finished the assassination. In 932 his remains were transferred to the church of St. Vitus in Prague. By the year 984 the feast of St. Wenceslaus was being observed, and today the Czechs include his name in the litany of the saints. He is the patron saint of the cathedral at Cracow, Poland.

MESSAGE AND RELEVANCE

The new Opening Prayer of the Mass states that God taught St. Wenceslaus "to prefer the kingdom of heaven to all that the earth has to offer." In the account of his martyrdom, in the Office of Readings, we learn that Wenceslaus was exemplary in the practice of virtue: "He was charitable to the poor, and he would clothe the naked, feed the hungry and offer hospitality to travelers according to the summons of the gospel. . . . He loved all his people, rich and poor." In fact, Wenceslaus was such a devout and pious ruler that his enemies said he belonged in a monastery rather than on the throne. He did not take revenge for the murder of his grandmother nor did he permanently exile his own mother for her involvement with the anti-Catholic faction. He tried, rather, to soften the harsh penalties that were in use in his day.

The intercession of the Opening Prayer is that "his prayers free us from our self-seeking and help us to serve you with all our hearts." Shortly after he came to power, some of his advisors were urging him to take revenge on his mother for her treason. He told them: "Why do you want to prevent me from applying the divine law of Jesus Christ and to obey his commandments? I reject your advice because I want to serve God with all my heart."

The relevance of St. Wenceslaus is that he respected and followed God's law even under difficult circumstances. This saintly ruler, who died at the age of 22, exemplified the very realities that Pope Paul VI described in *A Call to Action*: "Christians who are invited to take up political activity should try to make their choices consistent with the gospel and, in the framework of legitimate plurality, to give both personal and collective witness to the seriousness of their faith by effective and disinterested service of men."

Opening Prayer: *Lord, you taught your martyr Wenceslaus to prefer the kingdom of heaven to all that the earth has to offer. May his prayers free us from our self-seeking and help us to serve you with all our hearts.*

September 28
ST. LAWRENCE RUIZ and COMPANIONS (+ 1637)

HISTORICO-LITURGICAL NOTE

The Filipino layman, Lorenzo Ruiz, and fifteen companions were martyred at Nagasaki by the Japanese in 1637 and were canonized by Pope John Paul II in Manila, October 18, 1987. Lorenzo was of Chinese origin and lived in Binondo, the Chinese section of Manila. He was the father of a family and he went to Japan with the Dominican missionaries in order to avoid arrest for a crime of which he was accused. All 16 martyrs were either members of the Dominican Order or in some way associated with it: 3 lay persons, 2 consecrated virgins, 2 cooperator brothers and 9 Dominican priests. When the news of their martyrdom reached Manila on December 27, 1637, a solemn *Te Deum* was sung in the church of Santo Domingo.

MESSAGE AND RELEVANCE

In the Opening Prayer of the Mass we ask that we may imitate the patience of these martyrs by fidelity to God's service and generous solidarity with our neighbors. The solidarity of these martyrs was manifested in their exhortations to one another to make the last heroic sacrifice when one or another at first hesitated. The variety of nations represented — Spain, Italy, France, Japan and the Philippines — constitutes an inspiring mosaic of the universality of the Church.

In the Office of Readings we find an excerpt from the homily preached by Pope John Paul II when he canonized them at Manila in 1987. The Holy Father stated that in the exercise of their baptismal priesthood or their priesthood of Holy Orders, these sixteen martyrs offered to God the greatest possible act of adoration and love by shedding their blood in union with the sacrifice of Christ on the altar of the cross. At the same time their martyrdom was the greatest possible act of love for their brethren, to which we also are called to give ourselves, following the example of the Son of God, who sacrificed himself for us.

The intercession of the Opening Prayer cites the seventh beatitude but substitutes the word "gospel" for "justice," with an implicit reference to Mark 8:35: "Whoever loses his life for my sake and the gospel's will preserve it." This is precisely what Lorenzo stated before the Japanese judges: "I am a Christian. I shall die for God, and for him I would give many thousands of lives. So do with me what you please." The Holy Father comments in his homily: "These words are a compendium of his life, an affirmation of his faith, the reason for his death. In the hour of his martyrdom the young father of a family proclaimed and brought to a close the Christian catechesis he had received in the school of the Dominican friars in Binondo."

The relevance of this feast of martyrs is found in the responsory for the Office of Readings: "Their love for life did not deter them from death. . . . You have suffered for a little while, but under God's covenant you have gained eternal life." To be Christians means to give each day to God in response to the promise of Christ, who came into the world so that all may have life and have it more abundantly.

Opening Prayer: *Lord God, in our service to you and to our neighbor give us the patience of the holy martyrs Lawrence and his companions; for those who suffer persecution for justice' sake are blessed in the kingdom of heaven.*

September 29
ST. MICHAEL, ST. GABRIEL, and
ST. RAPHAEL

HISTORICO-LITURGICAL NOTE

Previously each of these archangels had his own feastday: St. Michael, September 29; St. Gabriel, March 24; St. Raphael, October 21. Now, however one day is assigned to all three, and on the more ancient date of September 29, which commemorates the dedication of the basilica which was constructed in the fifth century in Rome. Documentation for this feast on September 29 can be found in the Jerome Martyrology and the Calendar of Verona as well as in the tradition of the East. Thus, in the Ethiopian Rite there is a commemoration on the twelfth day of each month; in the Byzantine Church the feast of St. Michael is celebrated on November 8. In the Latin Church, the feast of these three archangels was approved by the Lateran Council in 745.

The biblical references to *St. Michael*, whose name means "Who is like God?", are found in the Book of Daniel (chaps. 10 and 12), the Book of Revelation (12:7-9) and the Letter of Jude (9). The cult of St. Michael became widespread after the victory of the Lombards over the Saracens in 663 and was attributed to his intervention. Later the abbey of Mont-Saint-Michel in Normandy, France, became a center for pilgrims when the Benedictines took charge in 993.

St. Gabriel, whose name means "Power of God," is the archangel who stands in the presence of God (Lk 1:19). He is mentioned in the Book of Daniel (8:16; 9:21) as announcing the coming of the Messiah, in the New Testament as foretelling the birth of John the Baptist (Lk 1:10 and 19) and announcing to Mary that she would be the mother of Christ (Lk 1:26). He has been venerated since the second century, and in the Syriac Church he is considered the first among the angels. He is the patron of postal, telephone and telegraph workers.

St. Raphael, whose name means "God has healed," is venerated by both Jews and Christians. His name appears in the Book of Tobit (12:12 and 15), where he identifies himself as one of the seven who stand before God. He is the patron of travelers.

MESSAGE AND RELEVANCE

In the prayers and the Preface of the Mass these "princes of the angels" are portrayed as ministering spirits who exercise a watchful care over us. The Opening Prayer of the Mass invokes God our Father, who in a wonderful way guides the work of angels and men. Michael, who is a special protector of the Chosen People (Dn 10:13; 12:1) and is mentioned in the fight against Satan (Jude 9), is also identified as the archangel who will announce the final resurrection (1 Th 4:16). The prayer, however, refers to angels in general and does not mention the three archangels by name. The petition of the Opening Prayer is that "those who serve you constantly in heaven keep our lives safe from all harm on earth." This protective function of the angels is described by St. Gregory the Great in the Office of Readings, with special emphasis on Michael, Gabriel and Raphael. The antiphons for the Liturgy of the Hours also list the various functions of the three archangels as well as the role of angels in general.

In the Prayer over the Gifts we see another dimension of the mission of the angels: "Lord, by the ministry of your angels let our sacrifice of praise come before you." The same idea is expressed in the Roman Canon when the priest says: "We pray that your angel may take this sacrifice to your altar in heaven." In the Ambrosian Missal, however, the text is in the plural, "by the hands of your angels," because the angels are traditionally associated with divine worship (cf. Rev 8:3-5).

Finally, the Prayer after Communion has a reference to the Eucharist as viaticum or food for the journey. It reminds us of Elijah, who received bread from an angel during his journey to Mount Sinai (1 K 19:5) and of the manna given to the Jews on their journey to the Promised Land (Ex 16:5; Ps 77:24-25). Hence, we ask to be fed and strengthened by the bread of life, as we advance "along the way of salvation."

This feast is meaningful to us because in every Mass we are called upon to sing or recite the threefold "Holy, Holy, Holy" with the angels. Secondly, we should recall the words of Christ: "I solemnly assure you, you shall see the sky opened and the angels of God ascending and descending on the Son of Man" (Jn 1:51).

> Preface: *In your Word, the glorious Lord of the universe, you have also given life to the spiritual beings who in your kingdom have the joyful task of being for you an everlasting crown. The rebellious angels were cast down into the infernal abyss, but the choirs of angels and archangels sing to you for all eternity their hymn of fidelity and love. And we, hoping one day to share in their beatific existence, now join their eternal chorus of adoration and bliss, raising to you, O Father, our hymn of praise.*

September 30
ST. JEROME (347?-419/20)

HISTORICO-LITURGICAL NOTE

St. Jerome died at Bethlehem on September 30, in 419 or 420, at the age of 91. His feast was celebrated in France in the eighth century and from there it spread throughout the West between the ninth and eleventh centuries. He is the most erudite Latin writer of Christian antiquity, so much so that in the Ordinary of Pope Innocent III he is hailed as a Doctor.

Born in Dalmatia around the year 347, he studied at Rome, where he became proficient in Latin and Greek. He was a catechumen until the age of 18 or 19, when he was baptized by Pope Liberius (352-366). He next went to Trier, where he was entirely converted, and then moved to Aquileia in 370 to live with a community, but because of internal conflict he next moved to an island in the Adriatic Sea. Here he distanced himself from pagan culture and led an ascetical life.

In 374 he arrived in Antioch but went to live in the wilderness for the next 4 years, where he suffered from ill health and strong temptations of the flesh. One of the remedies he used was the study of Hebrew, which he called "the language of hissing and broken-winded words." On coming out of the wilderness he was ordained to the priesthood but on the condition that he could still live as a monk or recluse. Next he went to Constantinople, where he studied Scripture under St. Gregory Nazianzen, to whom Jerome was ever grateful.

When Gregory Nazianzen left Constantinople, Jerome accompanied the bishop Paulinus to Rome to attend a Council called by Pope Damasus. After the Council, the pope kept Jerome on as his secretary and also commissioned him to make a new edition of the Latin version of the Bible. At the same time he was serving as spiritual director to a group of devout noble ladies: Marcella, Paula and Eustochia.

When Pope Damasus died in 384, Jerome returned to the East, partly because he was greatly disliked by some of the Roman clergy, due to his harshness and sarcasm. He visited Palestine, Egypt and the desert of Nitria, and finally settled at Bethlehem, where he became spiritual director at a monastery built by Paula. There he was able to dedicate himself entirely to the translation of the greater part of the Old Testament from Hebrew. From 393 to 402 he was embroiled in a series of controversies in which he defended the orthodox doctrine of the Church.

After the death of Paula in 404, St. Jerome remained in the monastery, devastated and upset by news received from Rome, where Alaric was sacking the city. He also received the Roman refugees who had sought shelter in Bethlehem because of the incursions of the Saracens in Palestine (410-412), interrupting his work on the commentary on Ezekiel in order to do so.

We know nothing of the last days of St. Jerome, except

that he was buried in the confines of his hospice. He was greatly venerated in the Middle Ages and became the subject of a strange iconography, for example, presenting him dressed as a cardinal or with a lion lying at his feet. He was buried beneath the Church of the Nativity but later his body was transferred to Rome.

MESSAGE AND RELEVANCE

The three prayers of the Mass emphasize the characteristics of this Doctor of Sacred Scripture. The Opening Prayer refers to St. Jerome's "delight in his study of Holy Scripture." His work in this area is his greatest gift to the Church. The Office of Readings contains a famous sentence that was used by the Second Vatican Council in the document on Sacred Scripture, *Dei Verbum*: "For if, as St. Paul says, Christ is the power of God and the wisdom of God, and if the man who does not know Scripture does not know the power and wisdom of God, then ignorance of Scripture is ignorance of Christ."

The Prayer over the Gifts continues the theme of Scripture: "In reflecting on your word may we better prepare ourselves to offer you this sacrifice of salvation." The liturgy of the word is the first table in relation to the table of the Eucharist. Christian preaching should therefore be nourished by Sacred Scripture so that the divine word will be not only an interior illumination that serves as the rule of faith, but the hermeneutic criterion of that faith. We read in *Dei Verbum*: "The interpreter of Sacred Scripture, if he is to ascertain what God has wished to communicate to us, should carefully search out the meaning which the sacred writers really had in mind, that meaning which God had thought well to manifest through the medium of their words" (no. 12).

The Prayer after Communion once again emphasizes a knowledge of Scripture: "By studying your sacred teachings, may we understand the gospel we follow and come to eternal life." The monastic life lived by St. Jerome was the fruit of his meditation on Scripture. During the difficult times when Romans were fleeing to Bethlehem and Jerome was doing his best to assist them, he wrote: "I cannot help them all, but I grieve and weep with them. And, completely given up to the duties which charity imposes on me, I have put aside my commentary on Ezekiel and almost all study. For today, we must translate the words of Scripture into deeds, and instead of speaking saintly words we must act them."

The relevance of this exegete who could work as easily in Greek or Latin or Hebrew, consists in putting into practice the living word of Sacred Scripture. He once stated: "To *be* a Christian is a great thing, not merely to *seem* one. And somehow or other those please the world most who please Christ least. . . . Christians are made, not born."

Preface: *Today we proclaim you wise and wonderful because you have revealed your loving design by making your word known. Through your grace St. Jerome penetrated your divine revelation so profoundly that from this treasure he could dispense the old and the new wisdom, thus prompting us by his example to seek constantly in the sacred pages Christ, your living Word.*

OCTOBER

October 1

ST. THERESA of the CHILD JESUS
(1873-1897)

HISTORICO-LITURGICAL NOTE

St. Theresa, popularly known as the Little Flower, died at Lisieux on September 30, 1897, at the early age of 24 and was canonized in 1925.

Born at Alençon in Normandy, France, Theresa was the youngest of nine children born to Louis Martin and Zelie-Marie Guerin, but only four girls survived infancy. Marie Frances Theresa was educated at the Benedictine monastery in Lisieux. After being cured of a serious illness through the intercession of the Blessed Virgin Mary in 1883, she suffered from scrupulosity for a time but made a complete "conversion" in 1886 and tried in vain to enter the Carmel of Lisieux. She even pleaded personally with Pope Leo XIII during a pilgrimage to Rome, but to no avail. She finally succeeded in being admitted at the age of 15 in 1888. She was given the name Sister Theresa of the Child Jesus and the Holy Face.

In 1893 Theresa was named mistress of novices. In 1896 she had the first attack of tuberculosis, which would lead to her death in 1897. In the meantime the prioress, Mother Agnes of Jesus, a blood sister of Theresa, commanded her to write her memoirs, which were eventually published under the title *The Story of a Soul*. In this work Theresa expounds her doctrine of the "little way" of spiritual childhood and in a very short time it was known throughout the world. She died in 1897, and in

1944 was declared co-patroness of France, together with St. Joan of Arc. She is also co-patroness of the foreign missions, with St. Francis Xavier.

MESSAGE AND RELEVANCE

The liturgical texts portray the spirituality of St. Theresa, beginning with the Entrance Antiphon, which quotes Deuteronomy 32:10-11, a text dear to the young Carmelite: "The Lord nurtured her and taught her; he guarded her as the apple of his eye." The Opening Prayer of the Mass is based on Matthew 11:25: "God our Father, you have promised your kingdom to those who are willing to become like little children." Theresa had followed this teaching from an early age, when she promised never to refuse anything to the good Jesus. The theme of spiritual childhood is also contained in her name as a Carmelite, Theresa of the Child Jesus. It is likewise a constant theme in *The Story of a Soul*: "You can see that I am a very little soul and that I can offer God only very little things" (Chap. 11).

The antiphon for the Canticle of Zechariah is taken from Matthew 18:2: "Unless you change your lives and become like little children, you will not enter the kingdom of heaven." In Theresa the simplicity of total abandonment to God is associated with her complete holocaust. At the age of 15 she made her act of total oblation; during her novitiate she was submerged in a long period of aridity; at her profession she was assailed by disturbing doubts; and at the end of her life she suffered a terrible trial of faith. Yet, when Mother Agnes told her that her last agony might be prolonged, Theresa responded: "Well, all right. Ah! I would not want to suffer a shorter length of time."

In the Latin version of the Prayer over the Gifts reference is made to a second aspect of her spirituality, namely, her self-offering to God's merciful love. On the feast of the Blessed Trinity, 1895, she offered herself to God as a holocaust of love and she experienced a transport of love resembling the transverberation experienced by St. Teresa of Avila. Her fidelity in little things and her courageous spirit of sacrifice enabled her to transform even the periods of great suffering into times of joy and peace.

In the Office of Readings we learn from St. Theresa that the Church is composed of many members and not every individual can be an apostle, prophet or teacher. She finally found her own personal vocation in St. Paul's First Letter to the Corinthians (chaps. 12 and 13): "O Jesus, my love, my vocation, at last I have found it. My vocation is LOVE!"

The Prayer after Communion touches on a third trait of Theresa's spirituality: she prayed for the salvation of all mankind. For this reason Pope Pius XI named her co-patroness of the foreign missions. In the Office of Readings we find this statement: "In the heart of the Church, my mother, I will be love, and thus I will be all things, as my desire finds its direction." She even promised that after her death she would let fall a "shower of roses." During the interrogation at her entrance into Carmel she had stated that she entered Carmel for the salvation of souls, and especially to pray for priests. Later, she would have liked to go to Hanoi for a new foundation.

The relevance of St. Theresa of the Child Jesus is evident from the worldwide devotion to her immediately after her death. She gives witness to two outstanding virtues that are needed by all devout Christians: a radical humility that makes us aware of our weakness and our total dependence on God, and secondly, complete surrender to the infinite mercy of God in an act of perfect love. Pope Pius XI did not hesitate to say that "St. Theresa of the Child Jesus is the greatest saint of modern times."

Preface (Carmelite Missal): *Father, all-powerful and ever-living God, we do well always and everywhere to give you thanks. You reveal the secrets of your kingdom to those who become like little children. Among them you chose St. Theresa, hidden in Christ, to proclaim the good news of your merciful love. Your*

*Holy Spirit moved her to make her life a loving oblation
of prayer and self-denial for the salvation of all mankind through Christ and his Church.*

October 2
GUARDIAN ANGELS

HISTORICO-LITURGICAL NOTE

This feast dates from 1411, when in Valencia, Spain, it
was introduced in honor of the guardian angel of the city. In
1590 Pope Sixtus V granted Portugal a special Liturgy of the
Hours in honor of the guardian angels. The feast was added to
the Roman Calendar in 1608, when Pope Paul V placed it on
the first free day after the feast of St. Michael. However,
devotion to the guardian angels dates back to the Middle Ages
and the most common representation in art was that of Tobias
being led by the archangel Raphael.

MESSAGE AND RELEVANCE

There are three themes in the Mass. In the Opening
Prayer we say: "God our Father, in your loving providence you
send your holy angels to watch over us. Hear our prayers,
defend us always by their protection and let us share your life
with them for ever." The biblical foundation for belief in the
angelic protection of individuals is found in the two readings of
the Mass. The first is from Exodus 23:20-23: "See, I am
sending an angel before you, to guard you on the way." The
second is from the words of Jesus: "I assure you, their angels in
heaven constantly behold my heavenly Father's face" (Mt
18:5).

In the Prayer over the Gifts we ask that under the care and
protection of the angels, God will "keep us free from danger in
this life and bring us to the joy of eternal life." In the Office of

Readings St. Bernard tells us: "And so the angels are here; they are at your side; they are with you, present on your behalf. They are here to protect you and to serve you. But even if it is God who has given them this charge, we must nonetheless be grateful to them for the great love with which they obey and come to help us in our great need."

In the Prayer after Communion we ask that by the ministry of the angels we may be led along the way of salvation and peace. The first antiphon for Morning Prayer tells us: "The Lord will send his angel to accompany you and to guide you safely on your way" and the second antiphon states that God has sent his angels "to rescue his faithful servants." The same theme is repeated in the responsory in the Office of Readings. The antiphon for the Canticle of Zechariah reflects the sentiments in Hebrews 1:14, saying that "they are all ministering spirits, sent to care for those on the way to salvation." The readings for Daytime Prayer are taken from the Acts of the Apostles and they refer to the angel of the Lord who released the apostles from prison (Ac 5:17-20), the angel who liberated St. Peter (Ac 12:7), and the angel sent to Cornelius (Ac 10:3-5).

This feast serves as a reminder that divine providence has entrusted us to the custody of the angels. The angels eternally sing the praises of the Lord, and hence the antiphon for the Canticle of Mary states: "The angels will always see the face of my heavenly Father." If, as stated in John 1:51, the angels hover over the incarnate Word, then we can celebrate all the solemn liturgical feasts, from Bethlehem to the Ascension, in their company.

> Preface: *Heaven is the dwelling-place of the angels, mysterious and sublime creatures; consequently the loving hope of the faithful who dwell in the darkness of this earthly life dares to trust in the light and comfort of these select spirits who enjoy your beatific presence and never cease their service of praise and adoration.*

October 4
ST. FRANCIS of ASSISI (1181/82-1226)

HISTORICO-LITURGICAL NOTE

St. Francis died on October 3, 1226, and was canonized two years later by Pope Gregory IX. In 1939 he was named patron of Italy, together with St. Catherine of Siena. He is unique among the saints, not only because he received the stigmata, but especially because of his likeness to Christ in his lifestyle and apostolate.

Born at Assisi, the son of a wealthy wool dyer, Francis Bernardone spent a somewhat turbulent and adventurous youth, taking part in the war between Assisi and Perugia. After a mysterious dream he returned to Assisi where, in the church of St. Damian (1206), he heard three times the invitation from the crucifix to repair the Church, which was falling into ruins. As a result, at the age of 25 Francis renounced his patrimony and in the presence of the bishop and the citizenry he stripped himself of all his possessions and consecrated himself to God.

In the first phase of his life (1204-1209) he donned the garb of a penitent and led a rather secluded life. Finally, after hearing the passage from the gospel that describes the mission of the apostles (Lk 9:3-5), Francis realized that his vocation was that of an itinerant preacher. He gathered together a small group with the intention of following the teaching of the gospel as literally as possible. This was the beginning of the Order of Friars Minor (Franciscans) and the first Rule was approved orally by Pope Innocent III in 1209.

In the second period (1209-1224) Francis and his companions preached the gospel to people of every condition. Desirous of martyrdom, Francis even went to Morocco, Egypt and finally to Palestine. Five Franciscan friars were later martyred in Morocco by the Muslims. In 1212 Francis founded the cloistered Franciscan nuns with the assistance of Clare of Assisi. In 1220 he began work on a second Rule because of the desire of some of the friars to relax the rigors of strict poverty.

In 1223 Francis, who was a deacon, celebrated Christmas by presenting in tableau form a living crib and he himself sang the gospel.

In the last phase of his life (1224-1226), almost blind and suffering from various physical afflictions, Francis received the stigmata (September 14, 1224) on Mount Alverno. Wounded with love, he composed the famous "Canticle to the Sun." He died at the age of 45.

MESSAGE AND RELEVANCE

The prayers of the Mass are taken from the Franciscan Missal and they depict the spiritual traits of St. Francis of Assisi, beginning with the Entrance Antiphon: "Francis, a man of God, left his home and gave away his wealth to become poor and in need. But the Lord cared for him." The Opening Prayer of the Mass states that God "helped St. Francis to reflect the image of Christ through a life of poverty and humility." We ask that we may walk in the footsteps of St. Francis and imitate his joyful love.

By giving personal witness to the gospel teaching, Francis hoped to reconcile the ecclesiastical and civil powers. In his Rule, adopted in 1221, he exhorts his followers to live total poverty and littleness and to be travelling preachers. By being friars *minor*, without any privileges or authority, and renouncing stability as well as ecclesiastical offices, Francis symbolized the Church of the poor as well as a poor Church. By living gospel poverty, he was able to count himself among the least of the brethren and in so doing he found true freedom and joy.

In the Prayer over the Gifts mention is made of the "mystery of the cross, to which St. Francis adhered with such burning love." The Latin version says that the cross stamped itself on the soul and body of Francis, thus referring to the stigmata. His are the first authenticated stigmata in the history of the Church.

The Prayer after Communion refers to a third characteristic of St. Francis, namely, his "apostolic love and zeal." We ask that we who receive God's love "may share it for the salvation of all mankind." Francis sent his friars forth to preach the gospel of salvation, but he also recognized the need for periods of solitude and prayer. His introduction of the Christmas crib into popular devotion, with its emphasis on the poverty, humility and innocence of the Holy Infant, has been incorporated into the traditional celebration of Christmas. His spirituality was eminently Christ-centered, whether it focused on Christ in Bethlehem or Christ on the cross of Calvary. To this day the Franciscans are the custodians of the devotion known as the "Stations of the Cross." Hence, the exhortation in a letter addressed to all the faithful by St. Francis: "We must not be wise and prudent according to the flesh. Rather, we must be simple, humble and pure. We should never desire to be over others. Instead, we ought to be servants who are submissive to every human being for God's sake."

The apostolic zeal of St. Francis of Assisi should stimulate us to re-evangelize the Christians of our day. Moreover, his insistence on poverty should prompt modern Christians to place less emphasis on wealth and to live more simply. The antiphon for the Canticle of Zechariah states: "Francis left this earth a poor and lowly man; he enters heaven rich in God's favor, greeted with songs of rejoicing."

Preface (Franciscan Missal): *You exalted your servant Francis through sublime poverty and humility to the heights of evangelical perfection. You inflamed him with seraphic love to exult with unspeakable joy over all the works of your creation. Branding him with the sacred stigmata, you gave us the image of the crucified Jesus Christ our Lord.*

October 6
ST. BRUNO (1035-1101)

HISTORICO-LITURGICAL NOTE

St. Bruno died on this date in 1101 in Calabria, Italy. He was never officially canonized but was included in the liturgy of the Carthusians in 1514 with the verbal permission of Pope Leo X. He was included in the Roman Calendar in 1584, in the Roman liturgy by a decree from the Congregation of Rites in 1622, and Pope Clement X extended the feast to the whole Church in 1674.

Born at Cologne, Germany, of a noble family, Bruno Hartenfaust did his preliminary studies in that city and later entered the cathedral school at Rheims, where he became the director of the school. After his ordination to the priesthood he became a canon of the cathedral and chancellor of the archdiocese. He was described as "an eloquent man, expert in all the arts, and a doctor of doctors." He was also a strong supporter of Pope Gregory VII in his battle against simony and the low morals of the clergy. After refusing to be bishop of Rheims, Bruno retired in 1082 to a monastery founded by Robert of Molesmes, the reformer of the Cistercian Order. He constructed a hermitage at Langres, France, where he lived a semi-eremitical life with two companions, but later he left that locality and went to Grenoble, where the bishop gave him a solitary place called Chartreuse. That became the cradle of the Carthusian Order, whose members live as hermits in a community setting.

Bruno, however, was called to Rome by his former pupil, Pope Urban II, in order to be counsellor to the Pope. He left Rome in 1092 because of the election of an anti-pope and went to Calabria in southern Italy, where he founded a charterhouse of Carthusians. Before his death he made a profession of faith in the real presence of Christ in the Eucharist, against the heresy of Berengarius. The Carthusian Order is the only one in the history of the Church that has never had a reform, because it never needed one.

MESSAGE AND RELEVANCE

The Opening Prayer of the Mass invokes God, who "called St. Bruno to serve you in solitude." Robert of Molesmes founded the Trappists or Cistercians of the Strict Observance, but Bruno wanted even greater solitude and separation from the world. He was perhaps motivated in part by fear of the final judgment, as can be seen on one of the murals at Chartreuse: "The day of judgment is approaching and I count the hours." Again, in one of the monasteries at Rheims we read: "Bruno, fearing the examination at the judgment that is to come, rejected the glory of the world and went into the desert." Twice Bruno refused to become a bishop, at Rheims and in Calabria. His life of prayer was accompanied by the study of Scripture, following the example of the desert fathers. He did not impose on the monks the vow of stability, as St. Benedict had done, but he did insist on the solitude required for the life of a hermit.

In the conclusion of the Opening Prayer we ask that we may be faithful to God "amid the changes of this world." In a letter to his friend Raul Le Verd, Bruno says: "How greatly the solitude and silence of the hermitage contribute to the benefit and joy of those who love it. Only those who have experienced it can know it." His letter to the Carthusians in the Office of Readings contains a valuable message: "By your work you show what you love and what you know. When you observe true obedience with prudence and enthusiasm, it is clear that you wisely pick the most delightful and nourishing fruit of the divine Scripture." Bruno, a man of great culture, teaches us the lesson of true wisdom.

> Opening Prayer: *Father, you called St. Bruno to serve you in solitude. In answer to his prayers help us to remain faithful to you amid the changes of this world.*

October 6 (United States)
BLESSED MARIE ROSE DUROCHER
(1811-1849)

HISTORICO-LITURGICAL NOTE

This Blessed was born in Quebec, Canada, the tenth of 11 children. Starting at the age of 18, she spent 13 years as a lay apostle in a parish where her brother was pastor. She established the first parish sodality in Canada, with the help of the Oblates of Mary Immaculate. At the request of the bishop in 1843 she founded the Sisters of the Holy Names of Jesus and Mary, a religious institute modelled on one by the same name in Marseilles, France. In this project also she was assisted by the Oblates of Mary Immaculate. The purpose of this religious institute is to provide religious education to the poorest and most abandoned children. The community founded a mission in Oregon as early as 1859. Marie Rose Durocher was beatified on May 23, 1982.

MESSAGE AND RELEVANCE

This Canadian Blessed is described in the Opening Prayer of the Mass as a person in whom God enkindled "the flame of ardent charity and a great desire to collaborate, as teacher, in the mission of the Church." Her entire life was dedicated to the service of the Church, first in the parish and later in religious life. We ask that we may have "that same active love" so that we may respond to the needs of today's world. It is especially in the area of Catholic education that Blessed Marie Rose demonstrates the importance of the parochial and private schools for the formation of good Christians.

Opening Prayer: *Lord, you enkindled in the heart of Blessed Marie Rose Durocher the flame of ardent charity and a great desire to collaborate, as a teacher, in the mission of the Church. Grant us that same active love so that, responding to the needs of the world today, we may lead our brothers and sisters to eternal life.*

October 7
OUR LADY of the ROSARY

HISTORICO-LITURGICAL NOTE

This feast derives from the feast of St. Mary of Victory, instituted by the Dominican Pope Pius V after the defeat of the Turkish fleet at Lepanto on October 7, 1571. Pope Gregory XIII made it obligatory for Rome and for the Confraternity of the Holy Rosary in 1573. In 1716 Pope Clement XI inscribed the feast in the Roman Calendar for the first Sunday in October. The Dominicans also celebrated this feast on the first Sunday of October.

Counting one's prayers on beads is a very ancient form of praying, used by Muslims and the people of India. It seems that the repetition of the Hail Mary on the beads of the rosary goes back to the twelfth century. Around the year 1328 a treatise named *Rosarius* referred to St. Dominic as the promulgator of the rosary. In the fifteenth century the Dominican Alan de la Roche emerged as an outstanding preacher of the "Psalter of our Lady," a term he preferred to the term "rosary." The title of this feast was changed from Holy Rosary to Our Lady of the Rosary in 1960.

MESSAGE AND RELEVANCE

The Opening Prayer of the Mass was previously used for the feast of the Annunciation and it resembles the prayer of the *Angelus*. The Christological emphasis in the prayer is significant, since the rosary focuses on the events in the life of Christ. The antiphons for Morning and Evening Prayer mention the mysteries that apply specifically to Mary: the Annunciation and the birth of Christ (joyful mysteries), Mary beneath the Cross (sorrowful mysteries), and the Assumption and Coronation of Mary (glorious mysteries).

In the Prayer over the Gifts we ask that "by celebrating the mysteries of your Son, we may become worthy of the eternal life he promised." The Dominican rosary ends with a prayer in which we ask: "Grant, we beseech thee, that meditating on the mysteries of the most holy rosary of the Blessed Virgin Mary, we may imitate what they contain and obtain what they promise." Our model for the praying of the rosary is Mary, who, as we read in the antiphon for the Canticle of Mary, "heard the word of God and cherished it in her heart."

The significance of the rosary is found in the sermon of St. Bernard, in which he enumerates various events in the life of Christ and then says: "I have said it is right to meditate on these truths, and I have thought it right to recall the abundant sweetness, given by the fruits of this priestly root; and Mary, drawing abundantly from heaven, has caused this sweetness to overflow for us." By meditating on the mysteries of the rosary we are able to draw near to Mary and with her to recall the mysteries of our redemption. In the antiphon for the Canticle of Zechariah we pray: "Holy and immaculate Virgin Mary, you are the glorious Queen of the world; may all who celebrate your feastday know the help of your prayers."

Preface (Dominican Missal): *On this feast of the Blessed Virgin Mary we praise, bless and proclaim your name. Consenting to the divine word, Mary became the Mother of God; embracing your saving will, she became the handmaid of the Lord; devoting herself to the life and work of your Son, Mary cooperated in the mystery of redemption. Because of this she stands before us, mother and model of the Church.*

October 9

ST. DENIS and COMPANIONS (+250?)

HISTORICO-LITURGICAL NOTE

The bishop Denis was martyred at Paris in the middle of the third century, together with his companions Rusticus and Eleutherius. By the end of the ninth century his feast was celebrated at Rome but was not introduced into the Roman Calendar until 1568. St. Denis and companions were martyred in Montmartre, Paris, and their bodies thrown into the Seine, from which they were recovered and given decent burial. The great abbey of Saint-Denis was eventually built over his tomb on the outskirts of Paris.

There has been a great deal of confusion concerning the identity of St. Denis because there are three persons with that name. The first is Denis (or Dionysius) the Areopagite, who was converted by St. Paul (cf. Ac 17:34) and was the first bishop of Athens, Greece. It is not likely that he ever left Greece, and some have claimed that he suffered martyrdom at Athens.

The second Denis is the pseudo-Dionysius or the pseudo-Areopagite. He was a famous mystical writer of the fifth century and his works were translated by the abbot Hilduin of the abbey of St. Denis in Paris (835). Hilduin later wrote a life of St. Denis of Paris, but he erroneously identified St. Denis of Paris as Dionysius the pseudo-Areopagite. This mistake was perpetuated for 700 years.

The third Denis was born in Italy in the third century and was sent to evangelize France with a priest and a deacon. All three were martyred, but today's feast is that of this St. Denis who is the highly venerated patron of Paris.

MESSAGE AND RELEVANCE

The Opening Prayer of the Mass is from the French Sacramentary of the ninth century and it states that God "sent

St. Denis and his companions to preach your glory to the nations" and that God "gave them the strength to be steadfast in their sufferings for Christ." In the Office of Readings St. Ambrose comments on Psalm 118 and explains the value of an unbloody martyrdom. "As there are many kinds of persecution, so there are many kinds of martyrdom. Every day you are a witness to Christ. . . . Be faithful and courageous when you are persecuted within, so that you may win approval when you are persecuted in public."

The relevance of St. Denis and companions is found in that same commentary by St. Ambrose, explaining what he means by an unbloody martyrdom: "You were tempted by the spirit of fornication, but feared the coming judgment of Christ and did not want your purity of mind and body to be defiled: you are a martyr for Christ. You were tempted by the spirit of avarice to seize the property of a child and violate the rights of a defenseless widow, but remembered God's law and saw your duty to give help, not to act unjustly: you are a witness to Christ. . . . You were tempted by the spirit of pride but saw the poor and the needy and looked with loving compassion on them, and loved humility rather than arrogance: you are a witness to Christ."

Opening Prayer: *Father, you sent St. Denis and his companions to preach your glory to the nations, and you gave them the strength to be steadfast in their sufferings for Christ. Grant that we may learn from their example to reject the power and wealth of this world and to brave all earthly trials.*

October 9
ST. JOHN LEONARDI (1541-1609)

HISTORICO-LITURGICAL NOTE

This saint, canonized in 1938, was a contemporary of St.

Philip Neri and St. John Calasanz. He was also the founder of the Congregation of Clerks of the Mother of God.

Born at Lucca, Italy, in 1541, he was educated as a pharmacist, but at the age of 25 he left that profession and studied for the priesthood. He was ordained a priest in 1571 or 1572 and dedicated himself to the catechetical instruction of children and youth. He founded a Confraternity of Christian Doctrine in 1571 and in 1574 he founded the Congregation, which was approved by Pope Clement VIII in 1595. Under Pope Paul V the Congregation merged with the Clerks Regular of the Pious Schools. Persecuted in his own city, John went to Rome and was encouraged by his spiritual director, St. Philip Neri, to send the members of his Congregation to the foreign missions. In 1603 St. John Leonardi, together with the Spanish prelate G. B. Vives, founded the seminary *Collegium Urbanum de Propaganda Fide*, for the formation of priests from the mission countries. He died in Rome in 1609.

MESSAGE AND RELEVANCE

The new Opening Prayer of the Mass states that St. John Leonardi ardently desired to bring the gospel to all peoples so that the true faith of Christ could be spread always and in every place (Latin version). This holy priest, who was sent as an apostolic visitator by the Holy See to numerous religious institutes, was also a peacemaker among various factions. He was keenly aware of the need of a reform in the Church that would begin at the top and work down to the members.

The Office of Readings gives an excerpt from a letter that St. John Leonardi wrote to Pope Paul V. Speaking of those who want to work for moral reform, he says that they must present themselves as "mirrors of every virtue and as lamps on a lampstand. In this way they will gently entice the members of the Church to reform instead of forcing them, lest, in the words of the Council of Trent, they demand of the body what is not found in the head. . . . So let us work down from the highest cardinals, bishops and priests to the lowest, from superiors to inferiors."

Since St. John Leonardi was a co-founder of the seminary *Propaganda Fide*, the Opening Prayer of the Mass repeats the sentiments expressed in the Prayer after Communion in the Mass for the propagation of the faith. At a time when there is less emphasis on the foreign missions, the missionary zeal of St. John Leonardi reminds us of the importance of evangelization and re-evangelization. The Church is missionary by its very nature, in accord with the mandate of Christ: "Preach the gospel to every nation."

> Opening Prayer: *Father, giver of all good things, you proclaimed the good news to countless people through the ministry of St. John Leonardi. By the help of his prayers may the true faith continue to grow.*

October 14
ST. CALLISTUS (+222?)

HISTORICO-LITURGICAL NOTE

In the account of the martyrs published in 354, St. Callistus is mentioned together with Pontianus, Fabian, Cornelius and Pope Sixtus II. His feast was set on this date as early as the third century.

Callistus was a slave who was the founder of a bank in Rome where the baths of Caracalla now stand. Accused of a crime, he was condemned but later freed; still later, after a new accusation by his Jewish creditors, Callistus was again condemned and this time was sent to work in the salt mines in Sardinia (186). Liberated through the intercession of Pope Victor, he went to Anzio, Italy, where he was supported by the local church. He was ordained a priest by Pope Zephyrinus (198-217) and was placed in charge of the cemetery which eventually became the catacomb of the popes. He was elected pope in 217 but an opposing minority resisted and thus caused the first schism in the Church.

During the five years of his pontificate, Callistus was outstanding for his defense of traditional Catholic teaching and for his pastoral activity. He also made changes in the penitential practices and in marriage law. Although there was no persecution of the Church at that time, Callistus is listed as a martyr although there is no authentic account of his death. There is a legend that he was thrown into a well with a millstone around his neck; another legend states that he was lynched during a riot. His tomb was discovered in 1960.

MESSAGE AND RELEVANCE

The new Opening Prayer of the Mass is derived from a formulary attributed to Pope Marcellus and it reads as follows: "God of mercy, hear the prayers of your people that we may be helped by St. Callistus, whose martyrdom we celebrate with joy." An outstanding contribution of this pope was his defense of the doctrine of the Trinity. He excommunicated Sabellius, who taught that the Word, the second Person of the Trinity, is subordinate to the Father.

As regards the penitential regulations, Pope Callistus admitted to Communion those who had done public penance for such crimes as murder, adultery and fornication. Regarding marriage, he recognized as valid marriages some unions that were not so recognized by Roman civil law.

The relevance of this saint for us is that he rose from being a slave and a banker to the office and dignity of pope. Moreover, he had the courage to adapt ecclesiastical laws that are not of divine origin. Last of all, his zeal for the evangelization of all nations is worthy of imitation.

> Opening Prayer: *God of mercy, hear the prayers of your people that we may be helped by St. Callistus, whose martyrdom we celebrate with joy.*

October 15
ST. TERESA of AVILA (1515-1582)

HISTORICO-LITURGICAL NOTE

St. Teresa of Jesus (her name in religion) died at Alba de Tormes in the Province of Salamanca, Spain, on the historic night in which the Gregorian calendar replaced the Julian calendar. As a result, though she was born on October 4, her feast is celebrated on October 15. She was canonized in 1622 and named a Doctor of the Church in 1970 by Pope Paul VI.

Teresa was born at Avila, Spain, in 1515 with the family name of Teresa de Cepeda y de Ahumada and was of Jewish descent on her father's side. It was the golden age of Spain, because of the vast amount of that precious metal that poured into Spain from Latin America and also because of the large number of excellent spiritual treatises published during that period. As a child she was very devout and even wished for martyrdom at the hands of the Moors, but during adolescence her fervor cooled somewhat and she was for a time a typical vain and sentimental girl. At the age of 20, however, she was greatly moved by reading the letters of St. Jerome and she decided to become a nun at the Carmelite monastery of the Incarnation at Avila. Shortly after her entrance she became seriously ill and had to be sent away for treatment. She returned to the monastery after her cure but she was practically an invalid for several years. After reading the *Confessions* of St. Augustine and being deeply impressed by an image of the *Ecce Homo*, Teresa, at the age of 40, resolved to dedicate herself seriously to the practice of prayer.

She then began to work for the reform of Carmel and she obtained permission to found the convent of St. Joseph in Avila. With the help of St. John of the Cross, the reform was extended also to the friars. Eventually the Holy See recognized two distinct branches of the Carmelite Order, the Discalced and the Calced. Writing from her own personal experience, St. Teresa composed three major works on prayer and the mystical life: *The Life* (her autobiography), *The Way of Perfection*, and *The Interior Castle.* During her lifetime she made more than 40 new foundations of Carmelite nuns of the strict observance.

MESSAGE AND RELEVANCE

The prayers of the Mass touch on some of the high points of the life of St. Teresa of Jesus. In the Opening Prayer we read: "Father, by your Spirit you raised up St. Teresa of Avila to show your Church the way to perfection. May her inspired teaching awaken in us a longing for true holiness." St. Teresa carried out her mission at a time when Spain was entering upon a period of extensive colonialism. A new age was dawning, not only for Spain but for the Carmelite nuns. Rightly did Pope Paul VI acknowledge her authoritative teaching on prayer and its influence on the Carmelite Order, the praying Church and the world at large. In marking the fourth centenary of the death of St. Teresa, Pope John Paul II said that it was a powerful summons to the supreme values to which St. Teresa had dedicated her life.

The Prayer over the Gifts asks that God "accept the gifts we bring in your praise, as you were pleased with St. Teresa's offering of her life in your service." This valiant woman, who was as courageous and fearless as any man, was in bad health most of her life. In addition, she suffered intense spiritual trials, leading to the transverberation of her heart by an angel with a flaming lance.

Finally, in the Prayer after Communion we are invited to pray that God will "help us to follow St. Teresa's example and sing your merciful love for ever." Meditation on the sacred humanity of Christ is an essential element in the teaching of St. Teresa, as we see in the Office of Readings, where she writes: "God desires that these graces must come to us from the hands of Christ, through his most sacred humanity, in which God takes delight. . . . A person should desire no other path, even if he is at the summit of contemplation." The Entrance Antiphon and the Communion Antiphon are a canticle of love: "My soul longs for you, my God" (Ps 49:3); "For ever I will sing the goodness of the Lord" (Ps 89:2).

St. Teresa's message to us is, first of all, that "he who possesses God, lacks nothing; God alone suffices." Secondly, not only is it possible for an individual to attain to the heights of mystical contemplation, but our prayer should also have an ecclesial dimension. We too can experience the truth of St. Paul's statement: "We do not know how to pray as we ought; but the Spirit himself makes intercession for us" (Rm 8:22-27). The mystical life is offered to all, as St. Teresa teaches, but it must not be confused with the phenomena that sometimes accompany the mystical experience nor with the pseudo-mystical or pantheistic experiences of the religions of the East. Its source is love and its expression is a manifestation of love.

Preface (Carmelite Missal): *Father, all-powerful and ever-living God, we do well always and everywhere to give you thanks as we honor St. Teresa, on whom you bestowed such gifts of nature and grace. You espoused her to Christ, her divine friend, who taught her to be zealous in prayer and penance for the unity and the holiness of the Church. You endowed her with the wisdom of the saints to be our guide on the way of perfection and the spiritual mother of a new family in Carmel.*

October 16
ST. HEDWIG (1174-1243)

HISTORICO-LITURGICAL NOTE

St. Hedwig died in the Cistercian monastery at Trebnitz, Poland, on October 15, 1243, and was canonized in 1267. Her feast was listed in the Roman Calendar in 1689 but was transferred to this day because October 15 is the feast of St. Teresa of Avila.

Hedwig, Duchess of Silesia, was the daughter of Berthold IV of Bavaria. She had two brothers who were bishops and a sister who was an abbess. Another sister was queen of Hungary (the mother of St. Elizabeth) and she had a sister who married Philip II of France. She was educated in a monastery of Benedictine nuns, where she developed a love for Scripture, and at the age of 12 she married Henry I (1186) by whom she had seven children. She was a model wife and mother and was most generous in giving most of her income to charity. She prevailed on her husband to found a monastery of Cistercian nuns at Trebnitz and she retired there when her husband died, though she never became a nun in the strict sense of the word.

MESSAGE AND RELEVANCE

The new Opening Prayer of the Mass refers to St. Hedwig's "life of remarkable humility." This was especially evident in her service of the poor and the sick, whom she cared for personally. Because of her great devotion to the Eucharist, she had a special reverence for priests and she would assist at as many Masses as possible.

The Office of Readings gives an excerpt from her biography, written by a contemporary, and it describes her generosity to her neighbors and her concern for the poor and needy. "And because this servant of God never neglected the practice of all good works, God also conferred on her such grace that when she lacked human means to do good, and her own powers failed, the divine power of the sufferings of Christ strengthened her to respond to the needs of her neighbors. And so through the divine favor she had the power to relieve the bodily and spiritual troubles of all who sought her help." When one of her sons was killed in a battle against the Mongols (1241), she comforted her widowed daughter-in-law by saying: "It is God's will, and we must be pleased with what pleases God and what is his will."

The message of this feast is that although there are differences in culture, the European community must breathe with both lungs, the East and the West, as was pointed out by Pope John Paul II. Moreover, because of her dedication to works of charity, we see in St. Hedwig a model for those who have the means to relieve the suffering of the poor.

> Opening Prayer: *All-powerful God, may the prayers of St. Hedwig bring us your help and may her life of remarkable humility be an example to us all.*

October 16
ST. MARGARET MARY ALACOQUE (1647-1690)

HISTORICO-LITURGICAL NOTE

St. Margaret Mary died in the convent of the Visitation nuns at Paray-le-Monial in France on October 17, 1690 and was canonized in 1920. Born into a middle class family in Burgundy, France, her father died when she was 9 years old and she was badly treated in the family of an uncle who took her in. At the age of 24 she entered the monastery of the Visitation nuns at Paray-le-Monial. There she suffered greatly because of health problems but she was encouraged by the Lord to make profession (1672). The following year, on the feast of St. John the Evangelist, the Lord asked her to receive Communion on the first Friday of each month and to make reparation for the sins committed against him.

In June of 1675 Jesus asked that the first Friday after the feast of Corpus Christi be dedicated to his Sacred Heart, together with reception of Communion and acts of reparation. When her superiors were unwilling to cooperate, Margaret Mary received support and guidance from the Jesuit, Claude de la Colombiere. Nevertheless she still had to suffer more when the Lord instructed her to go contrary to her own

Visitation community. Finally, however, a friend of hers became superior (1640) and selected Sister Margaret Mary as an assistant and as mistress of novices. Thus, on June 21, 1686, the feast of the Sacred Heart was celebrated in the convent for the first time. The image of the Sacred Heart was painted on the standard of Louis XIV and was later adopted in France, Spain and the Tyrol.

In 1873 France was consecrated to the Sacred Heart and the basilica of Sacre Coeur was built in the Montmartre district of Paris. Later, Spain and Brazil also erected statues in honor of the Sacred Heart. In 1856 Pope Pius IX extended the feast of the Sacred Heart to the universal Church and in 1929 Pope Pius XI raised the feast to a solemnity.

MESSAGE AND RELEVANCE

The new Opening Prayer of the Mass omits any reference to the revelations of the Sacred Heart and asks only that the Lord "pour out on us the riches of the Spirit which you bestowed on St. Margaret Mary" so that we may "come to know the love of Christ which surpasses all understanding and be filled with the fullness of God." This prayer is based on St. Paul's Letter to the Ephesians (3:19).

St. Margaret Mary had been prepared for her mission by much suffering and contradiction in the various stages of her life. It was only when Fr. Colombiere's book, *Spiritual Retreat*, was read in the refectory in 1684 that the community accepted the messages from the Sacred Heart. In 1689 St. Margaret Mary was pleased to know that devotion to the Sacred Heart was being promulgated by the Jesuit, J. Croiset. All of this went a long way in breaking down the resistance of the Jansenists, who saw God as a vindictive judge and were reluctant to receive Communion more than once a year.

Christ revealed his love in 1675 during the octave of Corpus Christi, when he appeared to Margaret Mary and said: "Behold the heart that has so loved mankind but receives only ingratitude from most of them. . . . What is most sad is that many souls consecrated to me are the ones who treat me this way." In the Office of Readings there is a sentence taken from a letter of St. Margaret Mary which shows that the object of this devotion is not the physical heart but the person of Jesus Christ: "The Sacred Heart is an inexhaustible fountain and its sole desire is to pour itself out into the hearts of the humble so as to free them and prepare them to lead lives according to his good pleasure." In other words, the purpose of devotion to the Sacred Heart is to renew the effects of redemption in our souls, and Pope Pius XII said in his encyclical *Haurietis Aquas* that this is an obligatory devotion.

After the Second Vatican Council the renewed liturgy for the solemnity of the Sacred Heart has emphasized the biblical foundation for this feast, as found in John 19:31-37. Its significance for us today can be seen in another statement of St. Margaret Mary in the Office of Readings: "This divine heart is an abyss of all blessings, and into it the poor should submerge all their needs. It is an abyss of joy in which all of us can immerse our sorrows. It is an abyss of lowliness to counteract our foolishness, an abyss of love to meet our every need."

Opening Prayer: *Lord, pour out on us the riches of the Spirit which you bestowed on St. Margaret Mary. May we come to know the love of Christ, which surpasses all human understanding, and be filled with the fullness of God.*

October 17
ST. IGNATIUS of ANTIOCH (50-107?)

HISTORICO-LITURGICAL NOTE

This is the date assigned to this feast in the Calendar of Nicomedia in 360 and celebrated by the Syrian Church. According to St. Jerome and St. John Chrysostom, his tomb was venerated at the gates of the city of Antioch. The Byzantine

Church, on the other hand, celebrates this feast on December 20, which is the presumed date of the translation of the saint's relics to the basilica constructed over a pagan temple. This date was also adopted in the West, in accordance with the Jerome Calendar. The variety of dates for the feast is due in great part to the numerous translations of the relics of this martyr. The third transfer would have been from Antioch to Rome, to the church of St. Clement, when Antioch fell to the Saracens. The feast was not celebrated in Rome until the twelfth century.

Ignatius was the third bishop of Antioch, which had once been the scene of St. Peter's ministry. It is the city in which Christians were first called by that name. He was condemned to death by Trajan and was taken to Rome under military guard. On the way he stopped at Smyrna, from which he wrote four letters: to the churches at Ephesus, Magnesia, Tralles and Rome. From Troas he wrote three more letters: to the churches at Philadelphia and Smyrna and to St. Polycarp. He eventually arrived at Rome, where he was led to the amphitheater and was devoured by two fierce lions.

MESSAGE AND RELEVANCE

The liturgical texts are based on the letters of St. Ignatius and they highlight two themes: the ecclesiastical hierarchy and Christ's human nature.

In the Opening Prayer we say: "All-powerful and ever-living God, you ennoble your Church with the heroic witness of all who give their lives for Christ." The Latin version of the prayer refers to the Church as the Mystical Body of Christ and the ecclesial theme is also evident in the phrase used by St. Ignatius, who was perhaps the first person to speak of the Church as "the Catholic Church." The Church is a *communio* after the model of Christ's union with his heavenly Father (Ph 7:2); it is also a mystical and a hierarchical reality presided over by the bishop. As Ignatius stated in his letter to Smyrna:

"Where the bishop is, there is the Christian community, just as where Christ is, there is the Catholic Church."

In the Prayer over the Gifts we ask God to accept our offering "as you accepted St. Ignatius when he offered himself to you as the wheat of Christ, formed into pure bread by his death for Christ." Ignatius lived at a time when martyrdom was a witness to one's Christianity. Moreover, martyrdom is somehow related to the Eucharist, which is a memorial of the passion and death of Christ. Hence, in the antiphon for the Canticle of Mary we read: "I hunger for the bread of God, the flesh of Jesus Christ, born of David's seed; I long to drink of his blood, the gift of his unending love." This statement is significant, coming from a man who warned his fellow Christians against the Docetists, heretics who denied the human nature of Christ. In his letter to the Trallians he states flatly: "So turn a deaf ear to the talk of anyone whose language has nothing to do with Jesus Christ. . . . Those who believe in him will be raised like him by the Father."

The Prayer after Communion touches on a third theme, namely, that through the Eucharist we can be transformed into "loyal and true Christians." Mindful of the meaning of the title "Christian," St. Ignatius insists that they must be so not only in name but in their works (Rm 5:3). Thus, we read in the responsory for the Office of Readings: "Nothing will be hidden from you if you have perfect faith and love for Jesus Christ, since these are the beginning and end of life."

To carry this teaching into practice, we can turn again to the responsory just quoted: "Clothe yourself with gentleness, and be renewed in faith, which is the flesh of the Lord, and in love, which is the blood of Jesus Christ." The antiphon for the Canticle of Zechariah describes the Christian life as a constant search: "I seek him who died for us; I long for him who rose for our sake." However, courage in trial and suffering does not exclude holy fear: "Pray for me," says St. Ignatius in his letter to the church at Tralles, "so that I shall not fail the test."

Preface: *It is truly right and just always to give you*
thanks, omnipotent and eternal God, and to praise your

*greatness, which shone forth in a marvelous manner in
the martyr Ignatius. To express in deed the true meaning of the name Christian he willingly accepted the
bloody termination of his earthly existence, certain that
he would rise free and victorious after his torments and
would be reborn in you in the life of heaven. The
crucified Lord, his only love, so attracted him that no
power on earth could divert him from following the
divine Master as the model and reward of his
martyrdom.*

October 18
ST. LUKE

HISTORICO-LITURGICAL NOTE

According to the Jerome Martyrology, the feast of St. Luke was
celebrated in the Byzantine and Syriac Churches on this date
and it was introduced into the West in the ninth century. An
ancient tradition states that Luke was from Syria and he was a
doctor (cf. Col 4:14; Ph 24; 2 Tm 4:11). He was a companion of
Paul on his second journey and was also with him at Rome at
the end of Paul's life (cf. 2 Tm 4:11). It is probable that after
the death of Paul, Luke left Rome and went to Greece, where
he wrote his Gospel and wrote the Acts of the Apostles as a
kind of epilogue. He died a natural death at the age of 84. The
account of the translation of his relics from Constantinople to
Padua in 357 seems to be without foundation. He is the patron
of doctors, together with Cosmas and Damian, and also of
painters, because he is said to have painted an icon of the
Blessed Virgin Mary.

MESSAGE AND RELEVANCE

The new Opening Prayer of the Mass says that God "chose

Luke the Evangelist to reveal by preaching and writing the mystery of your love for the poor." Luke rejected the concept of Christianity as a religion for the elite and insisted that Jesus is the friend of publicans and sinners. He also presents the Church as a community in which all things are shared in common (cf. Ac 2:42-44).

The petition in the Collect cites the text from Acts 2:32 and Luke 3:6, asking that God will "unite in one heart and spirit all who glory in your name, and let all nations come to see your salvation." The Church is here presented as the fulfillment of God's plan, not as a model of utopian or privileged philanthropy, but as the joyous community of pardoned and converted individuals. From the theme of the poor to that of the Church as *communio*, Luke arrives at a universalistic vision of the Church in which the emphasis is not so much on the parousia as on the missionary aspect, preaching the gospel to all nations (cf. Lk 7:1-9; 13:28-30; Ac 1:8).

The Prayer over the Gifts accentuates two points. It asks that "the sacrifice we offer on the feast of St. Luke bring us healing and lead us to eternal glory." Luke the doctor has announced the glad tidings to all classes of persons and among them those who are sick in body or in soul (cf. Lk 10:9). He also refers to the Holy Spirit as the giver of new life (cf. Ac 13:48-52) and to the privileged place of Mary (cf. Lk 2:19, 51). The antiphon for the Canticle of Mary uses a phrase from Dante: "The holy Evangelist Luke is worthy of praise in the Church, for he has proclaimed the tender compassion of Christ."

The Prayer after Communion summarizes the entire message of Luke when it states: "All-powerful God, may the Eucharist we have received at your altar make us holy and strengthen us in the faith of the gospel." Luke's Gospel presents the mysteries of the life of Christ not only in some kind of chronological order but as the fulfillment of the plan of God that opens a new era in history. One should be open at each moment to the divine plan so that the tension caused by the delay of the parousia will be tempered by the good works performed by the Christian. For that reason we invoke the spirit of holiness that proceeds from the Eucharist.

The relevance of St. Luke for us is that both in the life of Jesus and in the life of the Church he places great emphasis on the practice of prayer (cf. Ac 2:42). Moreover, St. Gregory the Great states in the Office of Readings: "Whoever fails in charity towards his neighbor should by no means take upon himself the office of preaching." The gospel is not a form of propaganda nor a type of publicity; the Evangelist Luke reminds us that even the actions of Christ were a form of preaching, since all that he did, he did for our instruction. Consequently, we also should give witness to Christ in word and in deed.

> Preface: *You have willed that the mysteries of Christ your Son, the source of redemption and of life, should be made known through the Sacred Scriptures by the work of men illumined by the Holy Spirit. Thus the words and deeds of the Savior, recorded in the immortal pages of the gospel, were consigned to the Church and became the fertile seed that throughout the centuries produces fruits of grace and glory.*

October 19
ST. ISAAC JOGUES (1607-1646), ST. JOHN de BRÉBEUF (1593-1649) and COMPANIONS

HISTORICO-LITURGICAL NOTE

The feast of the French Jesuit martyrs is celebrated on the first free day following the date of the martyrdom of St. Isaac Jogues in 1646. The other 7 martyrs were John de Brébeuf, Charles Garnier, Anthony Daniel, Gabriel Lallemant, Noel

Chabanel, John de Lalande, and René Goupil. They were canonized in 1930 by Pope Pius XI.

French Jesuits were the first missionaries to go to Canada and North America after J. Cartier discovered Canada in 1534. Their mission region extended from Nova Scotia to Maryland. These 8 saints preached the gospel to the Iroquois and Huron Indians, and after being tortured, they were martyred in the area of what is now Auriesville, New York. The martyrdoms took place between 1642 and 1649. Ten years after the martyrdom of St. Isaac Jogues, Kateri Tekakwitha was born in the same village in which he died. These martyrs are co-patrons of Canada.

MESSAGE AND RELEVANCE

The Opening Prayer states that these Jesuits were the first missionaries and the first martyrs in the evangelization of North America. The missionaries arrived in Canada less than a century after its discovery by Cartier in 1534, in the hope of converting the Indians and setting up "New France." Their opponents were often the English and Dutch colonists. When Isaac Jogues returned to Paris after his first capture and torture, he said to his superior: "Yes, Father, I want whatever our Lord wants, even if it costs a thousand lives." He had written in his mission report: "These tortures are very great, but God is still greater, and immense."

In the intercession of the Opening Prayer we ask that the Christian faith will continue to spread throughout the world. The sufferings of the martyrs were not in vain because later on many of the Iroquois were converted and missionaries were welcomed by them. Moreover, from the blood of martyrs, which is the seed of the Church, came the Lily of the Mohawks, Kateri Tekakwitha.

In the Office of Readings we have an excerpt from the mission journal of St. John de Brébeuf, who had been a student of the great Jesuit spiritual writer, Louis Lallemant. He wrote: "For two days now I have experienced a great desire to be a martyr and to endure all the torments the martyrs suffered. . . . I vow to you, Jesus my Savior, that as far as I have the strength I will never fail to accept the grace of martyrdom, if some day you in your infinite mercy should offer it to me, your most unworthy servant. . . . On receiving the blow of death, I shall accept it from your hands with the fullest delight and joy of spirit. . . . My God, it grieves me greatly that you are not known, that in this savage wilderness all have not been converted to you, that sin has not been driven from it."

The relevance of this feast is found in the responsory for the Office of Readings: "Through faith the saints conquered kingdoms and did what was just." In the work of evangelization what is most effective is the desire that Christ be known by all peoples. We should ask the Holy Spirit to renew the evangelization of distant countries as well as the re-evangelization of our own nation. We should pray that he will raise up missionaries as courageous and zealous as were the North American martyrs whom we honor today.

> Opening Prayer: *Father, you consecrated the first beginnings of the faith in North America by the preaching and martyrdom of Saints John and Isaac and their companions. By the help of their prayers may the Christian faith continue to grow throughout the world.*

October 19
ST. PAUL of the CROSS (1694-1775)

HISTORICO-LITURGICAL NOTE

St. Paul of the Cross, founder of the Passionists, died at Rome on October 18, 1775, and was canonized in 1867. When first inscribed in the Roman Calendar his feast was celebrated on April 28, but it has been placed on the first free day after October 18, the feast of St. Luke.

Born Paul Francis Danei at Ovada, near Genoa, of a

family of merchants, he enlisted as a soldier at the age of 19, but the following year he left the army. From his youth Paul had been a devout Christian and had practiced austerity. In the summer of 1720 he had three extraordinarily clear visions in which he was instructed to found a religious congregation. After investigation, the bishop advised him to proceed with the project. Paul then retired into solitude for forty days and wrote a rule of life for what would eventually be the Congregation of the Passion. Later, he took up residence on Mount Argentario with his brother and two other companions for a life of prayer and penance. Paul and his brother John Baptist were ordained to the priesthood by Pope Benedict XIII in St. Peter's Basilica in 1727.

In 1737 the first Passionist Retreat (as they called their houses) was established; in 1769 Pope Clement XIV approved the new religious institute; in 1741 the Rule was approved, but with some mitigations. Paul added a fourth vow to promote devotion to the Passion of Christ. Pope Clement XIV gave the Passionists the church of Sts. John and Paul in Rome as their headquarters. Towards the end of his life St. Paul of the Cross founded the Passionist cloistered nuns, who established their first convent in 1771. He died in 1775 at the age of 80.

MESSAGE AND RELEVANCE

The prayers of the liturgy portray the characteristics of this penitential and apostolic saint who, in an age of rationalism and skepticism, founded a religious institute dedicated to the Passion of Christ. In the Opening Prayer we say: "Father, you gave your priest St. Paul a special love for the cross of Christ. May his example inspire us to embrace our own cross with courage." We are invited to understand the wisdom of the cross, as St. Paul stated in one of his letters (Office of Readings): "Indeed, when the cross of our dear Jesus has planted its roots more deeply in your hearts, then will you say: 'To suffer and not to die,' or 'Either to suffer or to die,' or better, 'Neither to suffer nor to die, but only to turn perfectly to the will of God'."

In the Prayer over the Gifts we ask, "May we who celebrate the mystery of the Lord's suffering and death put into effect the self-sacrificing love we proclaim in this Eucharist." Here we are reminded of the method of Passionist missions, introduced by St. Paul of the Cross in the baroque style of the eighteenth century. The sermon on the four last things was reinforced by the basic theme of the Passion of Christ. St. Paul sometimes took the discipline in the pulpit, had the church bells toll to remind the faithful that one day they would die, and gathered the men in the church while the women remained at home praying for them. St. Paul spent long hours in the confessional and was instrumental in the conversion of many sinners.

In the Prayer after Communion we pray: "Lord, in the life of St. Paul you helped us to understand the mystery of the cross. May the sacrifice we have offered strengthen us, keep us faithful to Christ, and help us to work in the Church for the salvation of all mankind." Accordingly, in the Office of Readings we find this statement: "When you become true lovers of the Crucified, you will always celebrate the feast of the cross in the inner temple of the soul, bearing all in silence and not relying on any creature." The responsory for the Office of Readings is taken from St. Paul the Apostle: "God forbid that I should boast except in the cross of our Lord Jesus Christ. Through it the world has been crucified to me, and I to the world" (Gal 6:14).

The message of St. Paul of the Cross to our day is found in the Office of Readings: "It is very good and holy to consider the Passion of our Lord and to meditate on it, for by this sacred path we reach union with God. In this most holy school we learn true wisdom, for it was there that all the saints learned it."

Preface (Passionist Missal): *You showed the wonders of your power in raising up St. Paul of the Cross to keep alive the memory of Christ's Passion. As he co tem-*

*plated the supreme love of your Son for us, you gave him
mystical insight and wisdom and special gifts of grace.
You marked him out by his spirit of penance, by his love
of poverty, and by his desire for prayer and solitude.
You made him a spiritual guide and a preacher of the
gospel. As he proclaimed the rich harvest of salvation,
his words and example brought back to you countless
sinners who had strayed from you. He kept before the
eyes of your people the Passion of Jesus Christ, our
Lord.*

October 23

ST. JOHN of CAPISTRANO (1386-1456)

HISTORICO-LITURGICAL NOTE

This saint died in Austria on this date in 1456, when the
Church was in the midst of schism and was threatened by the
Turks. He was canonized in 1630 and inscribed on the Roman
Calendar in 1890. He is well known by the people of the
United States because of the California mission " San Juan
Capistrano," to which the swallows return each year.

Born at Capistrano, near Aquila, perhaps of a Nordic
family that had emigrated to Italy, he studied law at Perugia
and eventually became governor there in 1412. He was taken
prisoner when Malatesta di Rimini conquered Perugia and is
said to have had a vision in which St. Francis of Assisi invited
him to enter the Franciscan Order. This he did, and he made
his religious profession in 1418. His master was Bernardine of
Siena and after his ordination in 1425 he dedicated himself to
preaching and being a promoter of the Franciscan reform.
Pope Martin V appointed him to resolve the conflict between
the Franciscans and the "Fraticelli" (1426). Later, John was
sent to the East as visitator of the Franciscans, and after the
Council of Florence he was named apostolic nuncio to Sicily
and then papal legate to France. He had been a missionary in

Germany, Austria, Poland and Hungary, where he preached the Crusade against the Turks.

After the conquest of Constantinople, the Turks attacked the fortress at Belgrade. The victory of the Christians was due in large part to the zeal and prayers of St. John, and the feast of the Transfiguration was instituted to commemorate the event. John died at the age of 70, leaving behind 19 volumes of his writings and more than 700 letters.

MESSAGE AND RELEVANCE

The new Opening Prayer for the Mass says that God "raised up St. John of Capistrano to give your people comfort in their trials." In fact, the victory over the Turks was attributed to St. John, who held high the standard with the monogram of the name of Jesus (drawn by St. Bernardine of Siena) and urged the 4,000 crusaders to invoke the name of Jesus. The city was saved and the enemy withdrew, as St. John had seen would happen in a previous vision.

So successful was St. John in his preaching that after one of his sermons more than 100 young university students entered the Franciscan Order. He also won many converts from among the Jews in eastern Europe. He spent long hours in the confessional and promoted works of charity by the Third Order Franciscans.

Another characteristic of the saint is found in the Opening Prayer: "May your Church enjoy unending peace and be secure in your protection." St. John was often named legate of the pope and he also defended his former teacher, Bernardine of Siena, who was criticized for preaching devotion to the Holy Name of Jesus. He was instrumental in bringing the Armenians to the Council of Florence. Finally, within his own Franciscan Order he tried, without success, to avoid the separation of the "Observants" from the "Conventuals." As a result of these many activities, John was called the "Apostle of Europe."

The Office of Readings offers an excerpt from St. John's

treatise, *Mirror of the Clergy*, which was addressed to those who exercise the ministry of preaching. It is still applicable to priests of our time: "Presbyters who are born leaders deserve to be doubly honored, especially those who labor in preaching and teaching. . . . They have been placed here to care for others. Their own lives should be an example to others, showing how they must live in the house of the Lord." As a reformer of the Franciscan Order and a travelling preacher, St. John of Capistrano teaches us to be prompt and zealous in promoting and upholding spiritual values.

> Opening Prayer: *Lord, you raised up St. John of Capistrano to give your people comfort in their trials. May your Church enjoy unending peace and be secure in your protection.*

October 24
ST. ANTHONY MARY CLARET (1807-1870)

HISTORICO-LITURGICAL NOTE

The founder of the Missionary Sons of the Immaculate Heart of Mary, Anthony Mary Claret died in the Cistercian monastery at Fontfroide in France on this date in 1870. He was canonized in 1950 and listed in the Roman Calendar in 1960.

Anthony was born at Salent in the Diocese of Vich in Catalonia, Spain, in the year in which Napoleon invaded Spain. He was trained for manual labor, since his father was a weaver, but in 1829 he entered the seminary at Vich. Ordained to the priesthood in 1835, he was assigned as pastor in his home parish. Later he went to Rome to work for the Propagation of the Faith. He also entered the novitiate of the Jesuits but had to leave because of ill health, so he returned to Spain and was assigned as pastor of a parish. His apostolate consisted of rural preaching, conferences for the clergy and publications (he wrote more than 150 books). Because of his successful apostolate he aroused the animosity of some of the clergy and as a result he left Catalonia for the Canary Islands (1848). After a year he returned to Catalonia and resumed his preaching apostolate.

In 1849 Anthony gathered together five priests who formed the basis of the Missionary Sons of the Immaculate Heart of Mary (popularly known as Claretians). At the suggestion of the Queen of Spain, Isabella II, Anthony was named archbishop of Santiago, Cuba (1850). For the next seven years he made pastoral visitations, preached against the slavery of the Negroes, and regularized numerous marriages. As a result of his activity he was frequently threatened with death and on one occasion an attempt was actually made on his life. In 1857 he was recalled to Spain as confessor to the queen. In this way he was able to exert some influence in the naming of bishops, set up a center of ecclesiastical studies at the Escorial, and work towards the recognition of religious orders in Spain. In 1869 he was in Rome, preparing for the First Vatican Council. He followed Isabella II into exile and at the insistence of the Spanish ambassador, was placed under house arrest in the Cistercian monastery at Fontfroide, where he died at the age of 63. His remains were ultimately returned to Vich.

MESSAGE AND RELEVANCE

In the new Opening Prayer of the Mass for this nineteenth-century apostle we pray: "Father, you endowed Anthony Claret with the strength of love and patience to preach the gospel to many nations." From his earliest years in the priesthood Anthony had a zealous missionary spirit that took him to Rome, the Canary Islands, and eventually to Cuba. Not only did he serve as rector of the seminary at the Escorial in Madrid, but he promoted Catholic publications and founded an academy of St. Michael for artists and literary persons. In Cuba he worked for the general uplifting of the population but did not succeed in founding a school of agriculture, as he had wished. He did, however, establish the Apostolic Institute of Mary Immaculate.

The patience of St. Anthony Claret was tested in the political upheavals of the nineteenth century, both in his native Spain and in Cuba. His efforts at reform stirred up a great deal of hostility. Therefore, we ask in the Opening Prayer that we may "work generously for God's kingdom and gain our brothers and sisters for Christ." In the Office of Readings, an excerpt from the writings of St. Anthony Mary Claret states: "The zealous man desires and achieves all great things and he labors strenuously so that God may always be better known, loved and served in this world and in the life to come, for this holy love is without end."

This great apostle, whose major work, *The Right Way*, reached millions of people, promoted fidelity to the gospel among all classes of people, and especially among the laity and religious. In this way he anticipated the teaching of the Second Vatican Council concerning the vocation of all the faithful to the perfection of charity.

> Opening Prayer: *Father, you endowed Anthony Claret with the strength of love and patience to preach the gospel to many nations. By the help of his prayers may we work generously for your kingdom and gain our brothers and sisters for Christ.*

October 28
ST. SIMON and ST. JUDE

HISTORICO-LITURGICAL NOTE

According to the Jerome Martyrology these two apostles are honored on October 28, but in the East the feast of St. Simon is May 10 and the feast of St. Jude is June 19.

According to St. Fortunatus, bishop of Poitier in the sixth

century, these two apostles were martyred in Persia. Between the sixth and eighth centuries there was a church dedicated to St. Simon on the shore of the Black Sea. According to tradition in the West, Simon, called "the Zealous," preached the gospel in Egypt and later joined St. Jude and went with him to Persia.

Jude, known also as Jude Thaddeus, is the author of a letter in which he warns the Christian converts against false teaching and immorality. Jude was probably crucified in Persia, after having evangelized Egypt and Mauritania. He is popularly venerated as the "patron of impossible cases."

MESSAGE AND RELEVANCE

The liturgical prayers for this feast are rather general in tone, since we do not have many biographical details for these two apostles. However, two themes do emerge: the missionary apostolate and the promise by Jesus of the indwelling of the Trinity in the souls of the just.

In the Opening Prayer of the Mass we say: "Father, you revealed yourself to us through the preaching of your apostles Simon and Jude. By their prayers, give your Church continued growth and increase the number of those who believe in you." In the Office of Readings St. Cyril of Alexandria explains that the apostles were sent by Christ, as he was sent by his Father: "Accordingly, in affirming that they are sent by him just as he was sent by the Father, Christ sums up in a few words the approach they themselves should take to their ministry. From what he said they would gather that it was their vocation to call sinners to repentance, to heal those who were sick, whether in body or spirit, to seek in all their dealings never to do their own will but the will of him who sent them, and as far as possible to save the world by their teaching."

The second theme is stated in the Communion Antiphon, which is the response given by Jesus to the question posed by Jude Thaddeus (Do you intend to show yourself to us and not to the world?): "If anyone loves me, he will hold to my words, and my Father will love him, and we will come to him, and make our home with him." This response by Jesus affirms one of the most consoling truths taught by Christ, namely, that the Trinity dwells in the souls of the just.

In the other two prayers of the liturgy we ask that our faith may be revived (in the Latin version) and that God will keep us in his loving care (Prayer after Communion).

The relevance of this feast for us hinges primarily on St. Jude Thaddeus, "patron of impossible cases." The power of his intercession has been acknowledged by countless persons who are devoted to him. Moreover, the significance of these two apostles can be gleaned from the First Reading for the Mass: "You are strangers and aliens no longer. No, you are fellow citizens of the saints and members of the household of God" (Ep 2:19).

Opening Prayer: *Father, you revealed yourself to us through the preaching of your apostles Simon and Jude. By their prayers give your Church continued growth and increase the number of those who believe in you.*

NOVEMBER

November 1
ALL SAINTS

HISTORICO-LITURGICAL NOTE

The solemnity of the feast of All Saints is probably of Celtic origin. The Martyrology of Tallaght, Ireland, lists April 17 as a commemoration of all the martyrs and April 20 as the feast of all the saints of Ireland, Britain and the rest of Europe. In England, Bede's Martyrology has no mention of this feast, but in the eighth or at the beginning of the ninth century November 1 is listed as the feast of All Saints. It is certain that in 800 Alcuin was accustomed to celebrate this feast and that his friend, Arno, Bishop of Salzburg, also acknowledged this feast.

At Rome the feast was celebrated with a vigil and fasting in the tenth century, but Rome borrowed from the East the date May 13. In Syria there was a feast in honor of all the Christian martyrs and St. Ephrem composed a hymn for the feast. On this same date in 609 Pope Boniface IV dedicated the Pantheon in Rome as a church in honor of "Mary ever Virgin and all the martyrs." The feast was celebrated in the Easter season to emphasize the paschal victory of the martyrs. We know from a sermon of St. John Chrysostom, however, that in the Byzantine rite the feast of All Saints was celebrated on the first Sunday after Pentecost.

MESSAGE AND RELEVANCE

The feast of All Saints applies not only to all the canonized saints, but to all the souls that are in glory. Every person in heaven is a saint because each one has reached the perfection of charity. There are three themes in the liturgy of the feast.

First, in the Opening Prayer we say that "we rejoice in the holy men and women of every time and place" and we ask that their prayers will bring us God's forgiveness and love. The first theme is therefore our belief in the combined intercession of the saints. The Preface of the Mass states that "the saints, our brothers and sisters," still have communion with us and give us inspiration and strength.

In the Prayer over the Gifts and the Prayer after Communion mention is made of the glory of the saints, in which all the blessed will share. The second theme is therefore the concept of the holy Jerusalem which is the goal of our earthly pilgrimage. We journey in hope and with an awareness of the saints' "concern to help and save us."

The third theme is found in the Prayer after Communion, where reference is made to the table of the Eucharist and the "joy of the kingdom, where Jesus is Lord for ever and ever." Our faith tells us that we can pass from the eucharistic table to the eternal banquet in heaven.

The liturgy for this feast is rich in biblical readings as can be seen in the 18 antiphons (of which only 6 are from the previous Breviary) and in the hymns, which date from the ninth and tenth centuries. The antiphon for the Canticle of Mary in Evening Prayer I mentions the various categories of saints: the glorious company of apostles, the fellowship of the prophets, the army of martyrs, and all the other saints. In the Latin of the hymn for First Vespers, on the other hand, the list begins with the prophets, then come the apostles, the martyrs, the confessors, the monks and virgins, and all the other saints. It is worth noting that the angels are also mentioned in the Latin version of the hymns, but only three persons are mentioned by name: the Blessed Virgin Mary, St. John the Baptist and St. Peter.

The significance of the feast is given in the Office of Readings, in the sermon by St. Bernard, which replaces the former reading from St. Bede. "Clearly," says St. Bernard, "if we venerate their memory, it serves us, not them. But I tell you, when I think of them, I feel myself inflamed by a tremendous yearning. Calling the saints to mind inspires, or rather arouses in us, above all else, a longing to enjoy their company, so desirable in itself. . . . In short, we long to be united in happiness with all the saints. But our dispositions change. The Church of all the first followers of Christ awaits us, but we do nothing about it. The saints want us to be with them, and we are indifferent. The souls of the just await us, and we ignore them."

> Preface: *Father, all-powerful and ever-living God, we do well always and everywhere to give you thanks. Today we keep the festival of your holy city, the heavenly Jerusalem, our mother. Around your throne the saints, our brothers and sisters, sing your praise for ever. Their glory fills us with joy, and their communion with us in your Church gives us inspiration and strength, as we hasten on our pilgrimage of faith, eager to meet them.*

November 2
ALL SOULS

HISTORICO-LITURGICAL NOTE

This feast is a commemoration of all the departed faithful of Christ. The feast dates back to the ninth century, although as early as the seventh century it was the custom in monasteries to set aside a day for prayers for the deceased. Actually it was a Benedictine abbot of Cluny who selected November 2 as the day for commemorating the faithful departed. Earlier, St. Augustine had praised the custom of praying for the dead outside their actual anniversary, since he felt that they needed suffrages to be admitted to heaven. The feast spread to Rome in the fourteenth century, and in the fifteenth century the Dominicans had the custom of celebrating three Masses on that day in order to fulfill all the requests for Masses. In 1915 Pope Benedict XV extended this privilege to the universal church, prompted by the large number of those who had died in the First World War. The Mass also received a proper Preface, taken from the Parisian Missal of 1738. Since 1969 the emphasis of the liturgy for this feast is on the paschal mystery and for that reason the Sequence *Dies Irae* was dropped. The feast of All Souls is always celebrated, even if it falls on a Sunday.

MESSAGE AND RELEVANCE

In the revised liturgy all the texts of the Mass have been changed in order to conform to the document on the liturgy that was promulgated by Vatican Council II. It states that even "funeral rites should express more clearly the paschal character of Christian death" (no. 81). Four new Prefaces have been added, under the titles "Hope of Resurrection in Christ," "Christ Died for Our Life," "Christ, Salvation and Life," and "Our Resurrection through the Victory of Christ." Moreover, the texts that expressed fear and anxiety before the terrible judgment of God have been omitted because they obscured hope in the resurrection.

The Opening Prayer for the first Mass states: "As we renew our faith in your Son, whom you raised from the dead, strengthen our hope that all our departed brothers and sisters will share in his resurrection." The Prayer over the Gifts acknowledges our mysterious contact with our dead and we ask God to "receive our brothers and sisters into the glory of your Son." The Prayer after Communion touches directly on the paschal mystery when it states: "Lord God, may the death and resurrection of Christ which we celebrate in this Eucharist bring the departed faithful to the peace of your eternal home."

The theme of the Opening Prayers of the second and third Masses for All Souls is faith. "Since our departed brothers and sisters believed in the mystery of our resurrection, let them share the joys and blessings of the life to come" (second Mass). "May all your people who have gone before us in faith share his victory and enjoy the vision of your glory for ever" (third Mass).

The Prayer over the Gifts for the second Mass refers to baptism as the source of the Christian life: "May this sacrifice wash away the sins of our departed brothers and sisters in the blood of Christ. You cleansed them in the waters of baptism." The same theme is found in the Prayer after Communion in the third Mass: "Bring the new life given to them in baptism to the fullness of eternal joy."

> Preface I: *Father, all-powerful and ever-living God, we do well always and everywhere to give you thanks through Jesus Christ our Lord. In him, who rose from the dead, our hope of resurrection dawned. The sadness of death gives way to the bright promise of immortality. Lord, for your faithful people life is changed, not ended. When the body of our earthly dwelling lies in death we gain an everlasting dwelling place in heaven.*

November 3
ST. MARTIN de PORRES (1579-1639)

HISTORICO-LITURGICAL NOTE

This saintly Dominican brother was canonized in 1962 and was listed in the Roman Calendar in 1969. Born in Lima, Peru, of a Spanish father and a freed black woman (they never married), this mulatto was a contemporary of four other canonized saints: the archbishop of Lima, St. Turibius, the Dominican brother John Macias, the Dominican tertiary Rose of Lima, and the Franciscan Francis Solano. Martin was given a Christian education by his mother and became a pharmacist and nurse. In 1603 he entered the Dominican Order as a lay brother, much against his father's wishes. He was assigned to be infirmarian in the priory but he soon became well known for his apostolate for the sick and the poor. He died at the age of 60, worn out from his intensive apostolate and his practices of penance. He was immediately venerated as a saintly man.

MESSAGE AND RELEVANCE

The Opening Prayer of the Mass is taken from the Dominican Missal and it states that God "led Martin de Porres by a life of humility to eternal glory." By reason of his mixed blood, Martin was in a lower class of society, although his father held high office and eventually became governor of Panama. Nevertheless, Martin himself chose the path of lowliness and humility. For many years he was simply a lay tertiary and it was only later that he was admitted as a cooperator brother in the Dominican Order. He was totally dedicated to the service of the poor but he was often sought out for counsel, even by persons of high rank.

In addition to his active apostolate and penitential practices, Martin spent long hours in private prayer, especially before the Blessed Sacrament. He has been acclaimed as the patron of social justice because he constantly worked for equal rights for all classes of people. He was also known as "Martin the charitable," and this was emphasized by Pope John XXIII in his homily at Martin's canonization: "He loved men because he honestly looked on them as God's children and as his own brothers and sisters. Such was his humility that he loved them even more than himself and considered them to be better and more righteous than he was." The Holy Father concluded his homily by urging us to follow the example of St. Martin de Porres: "It is deeply rewarding for men striving for salvation to follow in Christ's footsteps and to obey God's commandments. If only everyone could learn this lesson from the example that Martin gave us."

Opening Prayer: *Lord, you led Martin de Porres by a life of humility to eternal glory. May we follow his example and be exalted with him in the kingdom of heaven.*

November 4

ST. CHARLES BORROMEO (1538-1584)

HISTORICO-LITURGICAL NOTE

St. Charles Borromeo died at Milan on November 3, 1584, was canonized in 1610, and inscribed in the Roman Calendar in 1613. He was born at Arona, near Lake Maggiore, of a noble family (his mother was Margaret de Medici, the sister of the future Pope Pius IV). At the age of 21 Charles graduated from the University of Pavia with doctorates in canon and civil law. He was ordained a priest at the age of 24 and was called to Rome to serve in the Vatican, where he held several high offices. His uncle, Pope Pius IV, named him a cardinal and archbishop of Milan. However, his condemnation of the excesses and abuses in the offices of the Roman Curia aroused the animosity of many persons, and in 1565, after the death of the pope, Charles Borromeo returned at last to Milan, where he served as archbishop for 18 years.

This was the period of Spanish domination in Lombardy and St. Charles withstood all efforts to introduce the Spanish Inquisition into Milan. At this time religious wars were being waged in France, there were political and religious tensions in the Netherlands, and Queen Elizabeth in England was undoing the Catholic restoration initiated by Mary Tudor. In his own archdiocese Charles Borromeo reformed several religious institutes and, during the plague of 1576, he established hospitals and hospices for the victims. At the age of 46 he passed from this life.

MESSAGE AND RELEVANCE

The Offertory and Communion prayers of the Mass are taken from the Ambrosian Missal; the new Opening Prayer was inspired by the allocution of Pope Paul VI at the opening of the second session of Vatican Council II. The Mass prayers delineate the characteristics of this greatest Milanese saint after St. Ambrose.

In the Opening Prayer we ask God to preserve in his people "the spirit which filled Charles Borromeo" so that the Church can be "continually renewed and show the image of Christ to the world by being conformed to his likeness." St. Charles is here presented as a great reformer of the Church, for which reason he convoked a synod to implement the decrees of the Council of Trent.

In the Prayer over the Gifts St. Charles is proposed as "an example of virtue and concern for the pastoral ministry," and we ask that "through the power of this sacrifice we may abound in good works." Not only did he establish seminaries, sanctuaries, and schools for the young, but he also founded a confraternity for adoration of the Holy Eucharist. His popularity among the people kept pace with his countless good works, especially because he preached in the cathedral and in the parishes and assisted at the Divine Office in the cathedral. He was faithful to the practice of mental prayer and once told the clergy that nothing is more necessary for them than the practice of mental prayer; it should precede, accompany and follow their good works.

The Prayer after Communion mentions another characteristic of this saint, which caused St. Philip Neri to ask whether Charles Borromeo was made of iron. Hence, we ask God to "give us that courage and strength which made St. Charles faithful in his ministry and constant in his love." This was exemplified when St. Charles personally visited the victims of the plague of 1576, providing financial and medical assistance and arranging for Masses to be celebrated in the public squares. Moreover, he showed great courage in his struggle against the Spanish governors of Milan and in taking strong measures against witchcraft and the sensual license that accompanied the carnival.

The example of St. Charles is still relevant today, especially as regards dedication to his pastoral ministry and devotion to the Blessed Sacrament. In his sermon at the last synod he attended, he urged the clergy to strive that all that they do might be a work of love. "This is the way we can easily overcome the countless difficulties we have to face day after day, which, after all, are part of our work. In meditation we find the strength to bring Christ to birth in ourselves and in others."

> Preface (Ambrosian Missal): *Today we wish to praise you as we recall our saintly bishop Charles, who glorified you by his eminent virtues. You gave him to the Church as a solicitous shepherd who was a shining light in the darkness of the world and, inflamed with ardent charity, was for your flock a mirror of life and a model of justice. He led to you the people entrusted to his care and in moments of difficulty he was able to sustain his people with dedicated love.*

November 9

DEDICATION of
ST. JOHN LATERAN BASILICA

HISTORICO-LITURGICAL NOTE

The Lateran basilica was erected around the year 324 by the emperor Constantine and is the cathedral of Rome. In the twelfth century this feast was assigned to November 9, for reasons unknown. The basilica has as its patrons St. John the Evangelist and St. John the Baptist (because of the baptistry adjacent to the basilica), although since the seventh century it has also been known as the basilica of the Most Holy Savior. However, between the tenth and twelfth centuries many churches dedicated to the Savior chose November 9 to recall a miracle that occurred in Beirut before the Nicene Council in 787. Blood gushed from a statue of the Savior when a crazed man struck it with a sword. This feast was not celebrated universally until 1565.

MESSAGE AND RELEVANCE

Among the texts used for this feast, two of them pertain directly to the Lateran basilica. The first reading in the Mass (Ezk 47:1-12) and the responsorial psalm refer to the baptistry because they have a baptismal theme. Also implied is the Church as the people of God and as a temple, as expressed in the Book of Revelation 22:1-2. There is also a Christocentric theme because according to John 2:21, Christ is designated as the new temple.

The second reading of the Mass has an ecclesial theme: the faithful are seen as living stones which form a spiritual edifice built on Christ, who is the cornerstone. They are a "chosen race."

The Lateran basilica was the official seat of the bishop of Rome from the fourth to the fourteenth century. What remains today is the *triclinium* of Pope Leo III (816), the holy stairs from the papal palace (considered by some to have come from the palace of Pontius Pilate), and the "holy of holies," the ancient treasury of the Lateran basilica. Finally, the Lateran basilica is called "the mother of all the churches."

On Holy Thursday the Holy Father celebrates Mass in the Lateran as bishop of Rome surrounded by his clergy. For that reason this feast should remind all members of every diocese or local church that they have been generated by the Lateran basilica and that by reason of their baptism they are members of a particular local church. Moreover, they should realize that each local church or diocese has its origin in the mother-church of Rome, which is historically situated in the Lateran basilica.

The relevance of this feast is evident. As vital members of

our local church, we should relate to the mother-church in Rome, going beyond our geographical confines to a sense of the universal Church. Thus, we read in the second lesson of the Liturgy of the Hours: "Although the universal Church of God is constituted of distinct orders of members, still, in spite of the many parts of its holy body, the Church subsists in an integral whole, just as the Apostle says: 'We are all one in Christ,' nor is anyone separated from the office of another in such a way that a lower group has no connection with the head" (St. Caesarius).

> Opening Prayer: *God our Father, from living stones, your chosen people, you built an eternal temple to your glory. Increase the spiritual gifts you have given to your Church, so that your faithful people may continue to grow into the new and eternal Jerusalem.*

November 10
ST. LEO the GREAT (+461)

HISTORICO-LITURGICAL NOTE

This saintly pope died on November 10, according to the Jerome Martyrology, and this date has replaced the former date set by the Bede Martyrology, which was extant in the Middle Ages. In the East the feast was celebrated at Constantinople on February 18. Pope Leo was declared a Doctor of the Church in 1754.

Leo was probably born in Tuscany, Italy, between 390 and 400, but he was Roman in education and in mentality. In the year 440 he was in France in order to reconcile warring factions and from there he was called by the people and the clergy to succeed Pope Sixtus III.

As pope he defended the faith against heresy and in 443 convoked an assembly to expose the errors of the Manicheans (already condemned by Pope Innocent I in 416). He also opposed the Nestorians, who had been condemned by the Council of Ephesus in 431, the Priscillianists, and the Arians who had invaded northern Africa.

In the second period of his pontificate Leo defended the doctrine of the Incarnation through the Council of Chalcedon (451). His activities extended into various fields: liturgy, politics, preaching and writing. He is without doubt the most influential personage of the fifth century.

MESSAGE AND RELEVANCE

The prayers of the Mass, taken from the Sacramentary of Verona, touch on three aspects of the personality of St. Leo the Great. First, the Opening Prayer is based on the text "Thou art Peter," a text on which Pope Leo frequently commented in his discourses. We ask God: "Never allow the power of hell to prevail against your Church, founded on the rock of the apostle Peter." Living at a time in which the empire in the West was beginning to disintegrate, both internally and externally, Pope Leo developed the theology of the primacy of the pope and defended the continuity between the pontiff and St. Peter (the antiphon for the Canticle of Zechariah). In the second lesson for the Office of Readings there is a quotation from the sermon preached by Pope Leo on the anniversary of his episcopal ordination. It shows that his awareness of being a successor of St. Peter is very modern. "Sharing in this office, my dear brethren, we have solid ground for rejoicing; yet there will be more genuine and excellent reason for joy if you do not dwell on the thought of our unworthiness. It is more helpful and more suitable to turn your thoughts to study the glory of the blessed apostle Peter. We should celebrate this day above all in honor of him."

In the Opening Prayer we ask: "Through the prayers of Pope Leo the Great keep us faithful to your truth and secure in your peace." This is the second aspect. Not only did St. Leo establish peace in ecclesiastical matters, but he persuaded

Attila to retreat peacefully from Italy. A few years later he also persuaded the Vandal Genseric not to murder the civilians or burn the city. In the Prayer over the Gifts we ask that the Church "continue to grow everywhere under your guidance and under the leadership of shepherds pleasing to you." Pope Leo was a model for the flock in his defense of the weak and the persecuted. Even as he stoutly defended the Church against heresy, he was able to forgive and even to reconsider when necessary.

The third aspect is found in the Prayer after Communion, in which we pray: "Under your powerful guidance may the Church grow in freedom and continue in loyalty to the faith." Pope Leo instituted some new feasts, such as the Chair of St. Peter, and he gave greater emphasis to the feast of Christmas. He also replaced pagan celebrations with the penitential practice of fast and abstinence to mark the four seasons of the year. But above all, he is the great defender of the mystery of the Incarnation and a champion of peace and freedom for the Church.

The relevance of this feast is expressed in the antiphon for the Canticle of Mary: "Day after day Peter proclaims to the whole Church: You are Christ, the Son of the living God." The testimony of St Leo the Great, defender of the Incarnation and promoter of church unity, can be a stimulus for the fostering of peace and fidelity in our own day. As he stated in his allocution on his election as pope: "As what Peter believed about Christ is always valid, so also what Christ gave to Peter will always endure."

Opening Prayer: *God our Father, you will never allow the power of hell to prevail against your Church, founded on the rock of the apostle Peter. Let the prayers of Pope Leo the Great keep us faithful to your truth and secure in your peace.*

November 11

ST. MARTIN of TOURS (317-397)

HISTORICO-LITURGICAL NOTE

St. Martin died at Candes, near Tours, in France on November 8, 397. His feast was celebrated from the eighth century through the Middle Ages on November 11, the day of his burial.

According to the biography written by Sulpicius Severus, Martin was born in Hungary to a Roman official and was educated at Pavia in Italy. He enlisted in the imperial guard and it is said that he gave half of his cloak to a beggar in 334 and later Christ appeared to him in a dream, wearing the selfsame cloak. He was baptized a Christian in 337 after spending six years as a catechumen. He received the minor order of exorcist but after Hilary of Poitiers was exiled, Martin returned to Hungary, where he converted his mother. When Hilary returned to Poitiers, Martin also went there and took up the life of a hermit at a place that later became the site of the monastery of Liguge, the first monastery in France, revived in 1852 by the Benedictines of Solesmes.

After he brought back to life a catechumen, Martin had the reputation of a miracle worker and was elected bishop of Tours in 371, dedicating his efforts to evangelization. In 375 he founded a monastery at Marmoutiers and from there he sent forth priest-monks. The monastery attracted many vocations and for a long time it was the center of all monastic life in France.

He resisted the representatives of the Roman Empire and gained liberty for the Church. At the same time he was criticized by some bishops and priests who would not accept the austere life that Martin expected of them. He died at a rural parish where he was trying to pacify the divided clergy.

Martin is one of the best loved and most popular saints. The period in late autumn is called St. Martin's summer in popular tradition because when the leaves are falling from the trees, the people enjoy the new wine, which is a symbol of the fruit of Christian virtue.

MESSAGE AND RELEVANCE

The prayers of the Mass are new, except for the Prayer over the Gifts, which is from the Tridentine Missal. The reason for the change is that the previous prayers have been placed in the Common for a confessor.

The Opening Prayer of the Mass and the antiphons of the Liturgy of the Hours are based on the biography of St. Martin. After stating that "by his life and death Martin of Tours offered you worship and praise," we pray: "Renew in our hearts the power of your love, so that neither death nor life may separate us from you." Martin's holiness was many-sided: he was a monk and a bishop, an evangelizer and a miracle worker. He is above all a model for those who practice monastic asceticism in the midst of the apostolate.

The theme, "seeing Christ in our neighbor" (Mt 25:40), which is found in the Communion Antiphon, is related to the theme in the third antiphon for Evening Prayer: "Now he lives with Christ for ever," which is reminiscent of the words of St. Paul: "For me, to live is Christ." Hence, this "shining light among priests" (third antiphon for Evening Prayer) "did not fear death, nor did he refuse to live" (first antiphon for Evening Prayer). In fact, when he was dying he said: "Lord, if your people still need me, I am ready for the task; your will be done" (second antiphon for Evening Prayer). Thus, "with hands and eyes raised up to heaven, Martin never ceased praying" (second antiphon for Morning Prayer). He "left this life a poor and lowly man and entered heaven rich in God's favor" (third antiphon for Morning Prayer). For that reason the antiphon for the Canticle of Mary says: "This blessed bishop loved Christ with all his strength and had no fear of earthly rulers; though he did not die a martyr's death, this holy confessor won the martyr's palm." In the Prayer over the Gifts we pray: "May this

Eucharist help us in joy and sorrow." This saintly ascetic, zealous apostle and man of prayer is a model for us today.

> Preface: *It is truly right and just, our duty and a source of salvation, to give you thanks, omnipotent and eternal God, and to praise you for the holy life of Bishop Martin, who was a glorious disciple of Christ your Son. With ardent longing he prepared for baptism and already knew how to show his love for the poor with exemplary generosity. Abandoning the uncertain honors of military life, he put himself at the service of the King of the universe by monastic profession. And when in your benevolence you willed that he be a shepherd of your flock, his zeal for the true faith and his love for your Church made him a shining example for all and a model of every form of justice.*

November 12
ST. JOSAPHAT (1580-1623)

HISTORICO-LITURGICAL NOTE

St. Josaphat was martyred in Vitebsk in White Russia on November 12, 1623, canonized in 1867, and inscribed in the Roman Calendar in 1882. He is one of the most dramatic figures in the history of ecumenism. His efforts to unite the Slav-Ruthenian Church to the Church of Rome triggered a cruel and ruthless persecution. The religious question was further aggravated by political factors.

John Kuncevic was born into an Orthodox family but he joined the Uniate Ruthenian Church after abandoning a business career at Vilna, a religious and intellectual center for the Ruthenians. He was convinced that only the monks, who were ascetics and promoters of the liturgy, could unite the Orthodox Ruthenians to the Catholics who, since the fourteenth century, had established Latin dioceses in Catholic Poland. In fact, in 1595 a synod of the Ruthenian Church had voted for reunion with the approval of Pope Clement VIII. In 1604 John became a Basilian monk and took the name Josaphat; with another monk named Rutski he began to work for the reform of the Basilians.

Josaphat not only preached union to the separated brethren, but in 1617 he wrote a book in which he demonstrated from exclusively Slavic texts the unity of the Church. At the time there were three Churches among the Ruthenians: the Latin Church in union with Rome, the Orthodox Greek Church, supported by Constantinople and Moscow, and the Greek Uniate Church, disdained by the Poles because of its lengthy liturgy and its married, ignorant clergy. Josaphat was the first person to join the first Basilian monastery united to the Roman Catholic Church. Eventually he became archimandrite, the equivalent of an abbot in the Latin Church.

Ordained coadjutor to the archbishop of Polotsk and then successor in the episcopal see (1617), Josaphat decided that his ministry should be to spread the Catholic faith among the Ruthenians. For ten years he did this by means of synods, catechesis and sanctions against unworthy clergy. His efforts aroused violent opposition from the Ruthenian nobility, who would lose their control of ecclesiastical benefices; from the middle class, who preferred their national rite and feared the introduction of Latin; and from the ordinary faithful, who were largely indifferent to juridical questions and resisted changes in the liturgy.

In 1621 the Byzantine patriarch of Jerusalem visited the Ukraine and consecrated a metropolitan and some Orthodox bishops for the Ruthenian Church. He found an ally against Josaphat in Sapieha, the Grand Chancellor of Lithuania. They accused Josaphat of endangering civil peace at a time when Poland, threatened by the Turks and by Sweden, needed to curry favor with its Orthodox neighbors. As a result, Josaphat was murdered by a mob and his body was thrown into the Dvina River.

MESSAGE AND RELEVANCE

The three prayers of the Mass emphasize the sacrifice of this martyr for Christian unity. First of all, the Opening Prayer asks God: "Fill your Church with the Spirit that gave St. Josaphat courage to lay down his life for his people." His courage stamped all the works of his ministry — his sermons and writings, the formation of his priests, his restoration of monasteries, the various synods and his defense of Catholic orthodoxy. As he was dying of the wounds inflicted by his attackers, he said: "You hate me to the point of killing me, but I hold you in my heart and am willing to die for you."

In the Prayer over the Gifts we ask God to "make us strong in the faith which St. Josaphat professed by shedding his blood." His adversaries had misinterpreted his intentions, thinking that he wanted to latinize the Ruthenian Rite, but the truth is that he never wanted to deprive the faithful of the Slavonic language or the Ruthenian Rite. He was working for Catholic orthodoxy, which is not necessarily linked to Latin culture rather than the Greek or Slavonic. Thus, Pope Pius XI stated during the third centenary of the death of St. Josaphat: "He felt that God had called him to restore worldwide unity to the Church and he realized that his greatest chance of success lay in preserving the Slavonic rite and Saint Basil's rule of monastic life within the one universal Church. Concerned mainly with seeing his own people reunited to the See of Peter, he sought out every available argument which would foster and maintain Church unity."

The Prayer after Communion refers explicitly to the ecumenical theme, asking that "the example of St. Josaphat inspire us to spend our lives working for the honor and unity of your Church." St. Josaphat himself was faithful to the Ruthenian Rite. As a Basilian monk he followed the monastic observances of the Eastern Church.

The relevance of St. Josaphat to our day is found in his ecumenical efforts for Church unity under the successor of St. Peter. Today, under the leadership of Pope John Paul II, sincere efforts are being made to foster closer relationship between the Latin and the Eastern Churches. And since the Second Vatican Council there has been a more fruitful dialogue between the Orthodox and the Uniate Churches as well as respect for the diversity of rites and languages. Both Churches have to recognize that they do not have a monopoly on the liturgy.

> Opening Prayer: *Lord, fill your Church with the Spirit that gave St. Josaphat courage to lay down his life for his people. By his prayers may your Spirit make us strong and willing to offer our lives for our brothers and sisters.*

November 13 (United States)
ST. FRANCES XAVIER CABRINI (1850-1917)

HISTORICO-LITURGICAL NOTE

St. Frances Xavier Cabrini is the first citizen of the United States to be canonized a saint. The process began only 11 years after her death and she was canonized on June 7, 1946.

Born prematurely in Lombardy, Italy, and baptized Francesca, she fervently desired to be a missionary ever since she was a young girl. After applying to enter religious life in several communities, and always turned down because of frail health, she was advised by the bishop to start a religious community herself. As a result, she founded the Missionary Sisters of the Sacred Heart and ultimately received approval from Rome. Early in 1889 Pope Leo XIII asked her to go to the United States, where there were many Italian immigrants. Within a few months after the arrival of the first group of Sisters, Mother Cabrini had already opened an orphanage and a school. She became a naturalized citizen in 1909 and during the remainder of her life she founded a total of 67 charitable institutions and houses of her Congregation. During her lifetime she obtained a number of special favors through her prayers. She died in Chicago just before Christmas in 1917.

MESSAGE AND RELEVANCE

The Opening Prayer of the Mass makes specific reference to the fact that Mother Cabrini went from Italy to the United States to serve the immigrants. Her heart had been set on going to China but both Bishop Scalabrini, founder of the Society of St. Charles for serving Italian immigrants, and Pope Leo XIII had insisted that the Missionaries of the Sacred Heart should work in the United States. Mother Cabrini travelled back and forth to Italy more than 25 times, bringing back other Sisters for the ever-expanding apostolate.

Our petition in the Opening Prayer is that from the example of St. Frances Xavier Cabrini we may learn "concern for the stranger, the sick and the frustrated." In spite of her poor health, Mother Cabrini was a veritable dynamo of energy. At the same time she was a woman of deep prayer and union with God. Her motto was taken from St. Paul: "I can do all things in him who strengthens me." She wrote in her retreat notes: "O Jesus, I love you very much. . . . Tell me what you wish me to do, and do with me as you will."

The example of St. Frances Xavier Cabrini is especially relevant to Catholics in the United States today. Her devotion to the service of the poor, the underprivileged and the sick should prompt many individuals to become active in works of charity for the needy. Moreover, in view of the tensions and prejudice that foster racial injustice, Mother Cabrini can help us "to see Christ in all the men and women we meet" (Opening Prayer). This is especially necessary as the United States is once again receiving numerous immigrants from various lands.

> Opening Prayer: *God our Father, you called Frances Xavier Cabrini from Italy to serve the immigrants of America. By her example teach us concern for the stranger, the sick and the frustrated. By her prayers help us to see Christ in all the men and women we meet.*

November 15
ST. ALBERT the GREAT (1206-1280)

HISTORICO-LITURGICAL NOTE

St. Albert the Great died at Cologne, Germany, on this date in 1280, was canonized and proclaimed a Doctor of the Church in 1931, and was inscribed in the Roman Calendar in 1932.

Born at Lauingen in Bavaria, he studied at the University of Padua, where he entered the Dominican Order in 1222 or 1223. By 1228 he was teaching at the Dominican priory in Cologne and subsequently he taught at Freiburg-im-Breisgau, Regensburg, Strassburg and the University of Paris. At one time he had the young Dominican Thomas Aquinas as his student.

St. Albert the Great (*Albertus Magnus*) was a prolific writer on Sacred Scripture, theology, philosophy and the natural sciences. He contributed greatly to the adoption of Aristotle's philosophy for the study of theology, at a time when the systems of St. Augustine and Plato were in favor. He also wrote more on the Blessed Virgin Mary than anyone else in his day.

From 1254 to 1257 Albert was Provincial of the German Dominican Province and in 1260 he was named bishop of Regensburg, but he resigned two years later in order to preach the Crusade in German-speaking countries. He attended the Council of Lyons in 1274, and in 1278 he travelled to Paris to defend the teaching of St. Thomas Aquinas, who had died in 1274. St. Albert died at Cologne in 1280 and in 1941 Pope Pius XII named him the patron of students of the natural sciences.

MESSAGE AND RELEVANCE

The Opening Prayer of the Mass states that St. Albert had "the talent of combining human wisdom with divine faith." He had taught philosophy as a science distinct from but a "hand-maid" of theology, thus preparing the way for the Scholastic method. He used the study of the natural sciences as an efficacious means for correcting certain speculative theories that were confused with theology and he believed that the study of the liberal arts was indispensable for the study of Sacred Scripture. Convinced that there is a distinction between faith and science, but not a contradiction, Albert experimented in the natural sciences to such an extent that some persons called him a magician or an alchemist.

St. Albert is rightly called "the Great" because of his contribution to the Scholastic movement and his expertise in the natural sciences, especially in biology. In the Opening Prayer we ask that the advance of human knowledge will deepen our knowledge and love of God, a very appropriate petition in this age of technology and scientific research.

> Opening Prayer: *God our Father, you endowed St. Albert with the talent of combining human wisdom with divine faith. Keep us true to his teachings so that the advance of human knowledge may deepen our knowledge and love of you.*

November 16

ST. MARGARET of SCOTLAND (1046-1093)

HISTORICO-LITURGICAL NOTE

This queen of Scotland died at Edinburgh on November 16, 1093, and was canonized in 1250. She was born in Hungary, where her family was in exile while the Danish king Knute was on the English throne, but they returned to England when Edward returned to power. Later the family had to flee to Scotland because of the struggle between William of Normandy and Harold, the head of the Anglo-Saxon party.

In Scotland the cruel Malcolm III was in power and he

asked for the hand of Margaret in marriage. She accepted in 1070 at the urging of her family. As Queen of Scotland she patiently endured the savage manner of her husband and gradually turned him into a man of great virtue. Of her 8 children, two are honored as saints: David and Edith (who became Queen of England with the name Matilda).

Queen Margaret convoked a council in which she eliminated some of the ecclesiastical irregularities and reinstated certain Roman customs, such as beginning Lent on Ash Wednesday, the making of the Easter duty and the observance of Sunday as a day of rest. She constructed churches, monasteries and hospices. Immediately after her death she was venerated as a saint and Pope Clement X named her patron of Scotland in 1673. Her feast was extended to the universal Church in 1693.

MESSAGE AND RELEVANCE

The Opening Prayer of the Mass focuses on St. Margaret's "special love for the poor." She was a great promoter of works of charity and each day she served food to 24 poor persons, sometimes even washing their feet. During Advent and Lent she gave alms to 300 people. Whenever she appeared in public, she was immediately surrounded by beggars, to whom she always gave something.

The relevance of St. Margaret to our time is found in the Office of Readings, taken from the document *Gaudium et Spes* of the Second Vatican Council: "In earlier times God met his people in a covenant of love and fidelity. So now the Savior of mankind, the Bridegroom of the Church, meets Christian husbands and wives in the sacrament of matrimony. Further, he remains with them in order that, as he loved the Church and gave himself up for her, so husband and wife may, in mutual self-giving, love each other with perpetual fidelity" (no. 48).

This queen, wife and mother who influenced her husband for good and changed the manners at court, shows us that holiness is possible in all social conditions, however diverse.

Her deep humility in serving the poor and in asking others to point out her faults so she could correct them, stands as a luminous example of living according to the teaching of the gospel.

> Opening Prayer: *Lord, you gave St. Margaret of Scotland a special love for the poor. Let her example and prayers help us to become a living sign of your goodness.*

November 16
ST. GERTRUDE (1256-1302)

HISTORICO-LITURGICAL NOTE

St. Gertrude died in the Benedictine monastery at Helfta, Germany, on November 17 in 1301 or 1302. She was inscribed in the Martyrology in 1678 and in the Roman Calendar in 1738 without the formal process of canonization.

At the age of 5 Gertrude entered the Benedictine monastery, where she was educated under the care of the abbess, Gertrude of Hackeborn, the sister of St. Mechtilde. Eventually she was professed as a nun and at the age of 26 she received the first of the revelations for which she is famous. She was extremely devoted to the mystery of the Incarnation, expressed in the Sacred Heart of Jesus and the Holy Eucharist (she promoted frequent Communion). She authored several volumes of spiritual works although they were not discovered until 1536, after which her influence spread throughout Europe. Two centuries later, in France, the devotion to the Sacred Heart was promulgated by St. John Eudes and St. Margaret Mary Alacoque.

MESSAGE AND RELEVANCE

The Opening Prayer of the Mass, which has been partly changed, touches on the essential themes in the spirituality of this great German mystic. We read first of all: "Father, you filled the heart of St. Gertrude with the presence of your love." Her union with Christ was so intense that Jesus said to St. Mechtilde, the novice mistress: "If you want to find me, look for me in the heart of Gertrude."

A second theme in the spirituality of St. Gertrude is found in the petition of the Opening Prayer: "Bring light into our darkness." It is through her writings that St. Gertrude became widely known and venerated. In her treatise, *Herald of Divine Love*, she states that Christ said to her: "I want your writings to be indisputable evidence of my goodness." Numerous scholars have been impressed by her profound understanding of the theology of the Incarnation and the Trinity. She is rightly called "Gertrude the Great," not only because of her lofty mystical experiences but because she is a forerunner of devotion to the Sacred Heart of Jesus.

It is difficult to take literally her statement in the Office of Readings that she had been living "like a pagan among pagans" and that she was "hurrying to her eternal loss." Yet it is true, as she says, that "God shows infinite patience in bearing with the imperfect as long as they have not yet converted."

The relevance of this "herald of divine love," as Christ named her, is her intimate union with Christ and her devotion to the Sacred Heart of Jesus. In the Office of Readings we find her statement that God gave her "the inestimable gift of your intimate friendship, and in various ways allowed me to possess your Son's own heart, that most noble ark of God united with the Godhead."

Opening Prayer: *Father, you filled the heart of St. Gertrude with the presence of your love. Bring light into our darkness and let us experience the joy of your presence and the power of your grace.*

November 17
ST. ELIZABETH of HUNGARY (1207-1231)

HISTORICO-LITURGICAL NOTE

Although St. Elizabeth died on November 16, her feast was transferred to this date so that it would not conflict with the feast of St. Gertrude. St. Elizabeth died at Marburg, Germany, in 1231, was canonized in 1235 and was inscribed in the Roman Calendar in 1474.

Elizabeth was born in Hungary, the daughter of King Andrew II. At the age of 4 she was promised in marriage to Louis IV of Thuringia and the marriage was celebrated when she was 14. She was the mother of three children but her husband, who had joined the Crusade under Frederick II, died in an epidemic 18 days before the birth of the third child, Gertrude. Left a widow when she was scarcely 20 years old, Elizabeth left the castle at Wartburg and dedicated the rest of her life to extraordinary works of charity. After refusing to marry a second time, she founded a hospital in honor of St. Francis of Assisi at Marburg and donned the gray habit of the Franciscan tertiaries. During the last four years of her life she worked in the hospital she had founded and was greatly esteemed by the people. She died at the early age of 24. Since the thirteenth century she is a patron of Franciscan tertiaries, together with St. Louis IX.

MESSAGE AND RELEVANCE

The Opening Prayer of the Mass is new, and instead of emphasizing disdain for the world, it underlines the principal virtue of Elizabeth: "Father, you helped Elizabeth of Hungary to recognize and honor Christ in the poor of this world." In mid-winter of 1227 she asked the Franciscan friars at Eisenach to sing a *Te Deum* because she was considered worthy to share in the poverty of Christ. Then, on Good Friday in 1228, in that same Franciscan church, she voluntarily renounced all worldly pomp and everything else that Christ had commanded to be given up. The archbishop of Bamberg however prevented her from giving up all her goods because she would need them for the care of the sick and the poor. She herself lived an austere life in accordance with Franciscan poverty.

The intercession in the Opening Prayer is that we may serve our brothers and sisters in time of need. Elizabeth also visited the poor in their hovels; she sewed baptismal garments for infants and shrouds for the deceased. Once, on Holy Thursday she washed and kissed the feet of lepers.

The relevance of this saint is found in the Office of Readings, in the account written by her spiritual director: "Apart from those active good works, I declare before God that I have seldom seen a more contemplative woman." This exemplary Franciscan tertiary proved the possibility of combining the practice of poverty with the life of an aristocrat.

St. Elizabeth was canonized by Pope Gregory IX, who three years earlier (1228) had canonized St. Francis of Assisi. The Franciscan ideal is still of value today and St. Elizabeth is for us a model of compassion for the poor and needy. After her funeral, Frederick II wrote to Brother Elias, the successor of St. Francis: "The venerable Elizabeth, so dear to God and of an illustrious family, illumined the mist of this world like a morning star."

Opening Prayer: *Father, you helped Elizabeth of Hungary to recognize and honor Christ in the poor of this world. Let her prayers help us to serve our brothers and sisters in time of trouble and need.*

November 18

DEDICATION of the CHURCHES of ST. PETER and ST. PAUL

HISTORICO-LITURGICAL NOTE

This feast commemorates the dedication of the basilica of St. Peter in the Vatican in 350 and the dedication of the basilica of St. Paul in 390. The date for the celebration of the feast was already established in the eleventh century.

The construction of St. Peter's basilica was begun by Constantine and completed by his sons. It was built over what was formerly a pagan cemetery and later a burial place for Christians. Eusebius records in his history that just prior to the year 200 a priest named Caius stated that the relics of St. Peter were on the Vatican hill and those of St. Paul on the Ostian Way.

The excavations to discover the ancient basilica built by Constantine extended from 1940 to 1949. In 1950 Pope Pius XII announced the results. It is certain that they discovered the tomb of St. Peter, but it was not possible to make a definitive identification of the relics because there were other human bones in the immediate vicinity. It is also certain that the tomb had been visited after the time of Constantine and that the popes had distributed the relics (the head is venerated in the Lateran basilica). Since there are graffiti commemorating the apostles in the catacombs on the Via Appia, there is a possibility that some of the relics were placed there around the year 258. They did not discover the memorial that the author of the *Liber Pontificalis* (sixth century) attributed to Pope Anaclete (76-88). Finally, it was impossible to determine the exact shape and form of the original tomb. Today the tomb of St. Peter lies about 100 meters beneath the main altar in St. Peter's basilica. It is a symbol of the unity of the universal Church.

The basilica of St. Paul was re-consecrated in 1854 by Pope Pius IX because of repairs made after the fire of 1823.

Very likely it was constructed over the relics of St. Paul, as Caius maintains. Constantine may have built a small church at this site and it is certain that three emperors — Valentinian, Theodosius and Honorius — constructed a huge basilica on the site, resembling Constantine's basilica on the Vatican hill. It was consecrated by Pope Siricius in the fourth century and later restored by St. Leo. Since the eighth century the Benedictine monks have had charge of it. This feast was inscribed in the Roman Calendar by Pope Pius V in 1568.

MESSAGE AND RELEVANCE

The new prayers for the Mass of this feast focus on the fact that the relics of these two saints are in Rome. Thus, we read in the antiphon for the Canticle of Mary in the Liturgy of the Hours: "The bodies of the saints have been buried in peace, but their names live on forever."

The Opening Prayer is taken in part from the Sacramentary of Verona: "From them the Church first received the faith of Christ." The Communion Antiphon contains St. Peter's profession of faith: "Lord, you have the words of everlasting life, and we believe that you are God's Holy One." Finally, in the Office of Readings St. Leo the Great says: "As to their merits and virtues, which no words can describe, we should not think of any difference or distinction between them; their calling was the same, their labors were similar, theirs was a common death. . . . In all the labors of the present life, we shall always be helped by the prayers of our special patrons. Just as we are humbled by our own sins, so we shall be raised up by the merits of these apostles."

The Prayer over the Gifts is taken from the Parisian Missal of 1738; in it we ask God to "keep alive in our hearts the truth you gave us through the ministry of your apostles Peter and Paul." Similarly, the antiphon for the Canticle of Zechariah states that "Peter the apostle and Paul the teacher of the Gentiles taught us your law, O Lord." They planted the Church and watered it with their own blood. The Latin version of the Prayer after Communion, taken from the former Missal for January 25, asks that the People of God may "proceed securely along the path of unity and peace."

The relevance of this feast is seen in the hymn for Morning Prayer, which dates from the Carolingian period but is not included in the English translation of the Liturgy of the Hours. St. Peter is described as a "good shepherd who loosens the bonds of sin by the power of the keys with which he opens or closes heaven to the faithful by his word." St. Paul is invoked as a "master of life so that he will enable us to attain to the fullness of perfection after we have passed beyond the limits of our earthly life."

> Opening Prayer: *Lord, give your Church the protection of the apostles. From them it first received the faith of Christ. May they help your Church to grow in your grace until the end of time.*

November 18 (United States)
ST. ROSE PHILIPPINE DUCHESNE (1769-1852)

HISTORICO-LITURGICAL NOTE

Born at Grenoble, France, of wealthy, aristocratic parents, Philippine Duchesne manifested certain religious traits in her early teen years: zeal for the foreign missions, a strong attraction to religious life, a preference for ascetical practices and, above all, a deep-seated devotion to the Sacred Heart and the Blessed Sacrament. At the age of 18 she joined the Visitation nuns but because of the outbreak of the French Revolution the community had to disperse. Until peace was restored in France, Philippine dedicated herself to works of charity, always hoping that eventually the community of Visitandines could be re-assembled. When all efforts failed, Philippine joined the Religious of the Sacred Heart, founded by Madeleine Sophie Barat in 1800.

In 1818, at the age of 49, Philippine Duchesne landed at New Orleans with four other religious. The bishop sent the group to St. Charles, Missouri, to establish a school. A few years later they established an orphanage in St. Louis. There Mother Philippine came into contact with the first Jesuits assigned to Missouri and one of them said later that she saved the Jesuit mission from failure. She helped them in any way that she could, sharing with them the few resources that her own community had.

It was only at the advanced age of 72 that Mother Philippine was able to realize her own dream of being a missionary to the native American Indians. She went with three other sisters to open a school for Indian girls at Sugar Creek, Kansas. Unable to master the Indian language, Mother Philippine nevertheless exerted a tremendous influence by her practice of prayer. In fact, the Indians called her "The Woman Who Prays Always," and they loved and respected her. After only one year on the mission, Mother Philippine was called back to St. Charles, Missouri, where she spent the last 10 years of her life, and most of it in prayer before the Blessed Sacrament. She died peacefully and her relics are enshrined in St. Charles, Missouri. Her name is the first one inscribed on the Pioneer Roll of Fame in the Jefferson Memorial Building in St. Louis, Missouri. She was canonized by Pope John Paul II in 1988.

MESSAGE AND RELEVANCE

The outstanding characteristic of St. Rose Philippine Duchesne can be stated very simply: she was a woman of prayer. Even the native Indians perceived this. No doubt she achieved more for the ultimate success of the mission work of the Religious of the Sacred Heart than did those who were busily engaged in the teaching apostolate.

A second characteristic, equally evident, is her dedicated zeal and her perseverance in the face of the hardship and privations of mission life in the wilderness. The letter written by the bishop who had invited the Sisters to the United States says it all: "You have come, you say, seeking the Cross. Well, you have taken exactly the right road to find it. A thousand unforeseen difficulties may arise. Your establishment may grow slowly at first. Physical privations may be added, and those more keenly felt, such as lack of spiritual help under particular circumstances. Be ready for all. . . . You and I shall spend our lives in this thankless task; our successors will reap the harvest in this world; let us be content to reap it in the next."

There is still a need for evangelization under the same trying conditions. St. Rose Philippine gives an inspiring example to all who work for the salvation of souls under difficult circumstances. Even when one can do little or nothing in the active apostolate, there is always the apostolate of prayer.

> Opening Prayer: *Gracious God, you filled the heart of Philippine Duchesne with charity and missionary zeal, and gave her the desire to make you known to all peoples. Fill us who honor her memory today with that same love and zeal to extend your kingdom to the ends of the earth.*

November 21
PRESENTATION of the BLESSED VIRGIN MARY

HISTORICO-LITURGICAL NOTE

This feast dates from 1372 in the Latin Rite, when it was established by a decree of Pope Gregory XI, but it was celebrated in monasteries of southern Italy as early as the ninth century. The Eastern Church observed this feast in the sixth century (543) in connection with the dedication of a basilica in Jerusalem in honor of the Blessed Virgin Mary (destroyed by

the Persians in 614). The date of the feast in eleventh-century
England was November 21. It was included in the Roman
Missal in 1472 by Pope Sixtus IV.

According to the apocryphal *Protoevangelium of James*,
which dates from the second century, Mary was presented in
the temple at Jerusalem at the age of three, where she lived
with other girls and the holy women who had charge of them.

MESSAGE AND RELEVANCE

The Opening Prayer of the Mass is based on the Ambrosian Missal and it contains two themes. The first asserts that
the People of God are assembled in memory of the Blessed
Virgin Mary. She is the "daughter of Zion" and through her the
presence of the Lord is realized. This typology is of great
significance for the theology of Mary in the context of the
history of salvation as well as for interpreting the gospel
account of the infancy.

The second and central theme is found in the invocation
of the Opening Prayer, where we ask for "the fullness of God's
life and love" through the intercession of the Blessed Virgin
Mary. She is the new temple of God, as we read in the antiphon
for the Canticle of Mary: "Holy Mother of God, Mary ever-
Virgin, you are the temple of the Lord and the dwelling place of
the Holy Spirit. Beyond all others you were pleasing to our
Lord Jesus Christ." Mary is pleasing to God because she was
perfectly submissive to God's will. Hence, the antiphon for the
Canticle of Zechariah repeats the words of Elizabeth: "Blessed
are you, Mary, because you believed that the Lord's words to
you would be fulfilled."

The significance of this feast can be found in the fact that
on this day consecrated persons renew their vows to the Lord,
in memory of the offering of Mary to the Lord's service. Thus,
St. Augustine says in the Office of Readings: "The blessed
Mary certainly did the Father's will, and so it was for her a
greater thing to have been Christ's disciple than to have been
his mother, and she was more blessed in her discipleship than

in her motherhood. Hers was the happiness of first bearing in her womb him whom she would obey as her master."

St. Augustine is commenting on the words of Christ: "Blessed are they who hear the word of God and keep it." Hence, says Augustine, "Mary heard God's word and kept it, and so she is blessed. She kept God's truth in her mind, a nobler thing than carrying his body in her womb. The truth and the body were both Christ: he was kept in Mary's mind insofar as he is truth; he was carried in her womb insofar as he is man; but what is kept in the mind is of a higher order than what is carried in the womb."

> Opening Prayer: *Eternal Father, we honor the holiness and glory of the Virgin Mary. May her prayers bring us the fullness of your life and love.*

November 22
ST. CECILIA (+230 or 250?)

HISTORICO-LITURGICAL NOTE

In the year 545 Pope Vigilius celebrated this feast in the basilica of St. Cecilia in Trastevere (Rome), Italy. The Sacramentary of Verona states that Cecilia converted her husband Valerian and his brother Tiburtius to Christianity; she preserved her virginity even though married; and she was martyred for the faith. Her cult has been localized in two distinct places: in the catacomb of St. Callistus, where there is a picture of the saint, dating from the seventh century, and the basilica in Trastevere, which is mentioned in documents dating from the fifth century. The lack of information about St. Cecilia from the fourth to the sixth century, except for the graffiti on the walls of the catacomb, makes it difficult to explain her sudden popularity in the sixth century. She has been venerated as the patron of sacred music since the fifteenth century.

The basilica of St. Cecilia in Trastevere was constructed by Pope Paschal I (824). It contains a mosaic that shows St. Cecilia standing between her husband Valerian and his brother Tiburtius, both of whom were martyred. There is a question concerning her relics, which were found by Pope Paschal I, but not in the catacomb of St. Callistus, and he transferred the supposed relics to the church of St. Cecilia in Trastevere (Rome).

MESSAGE AND RELEVANCE

The Opening Prayer of the Mass is very general, without any reference to anything characteristic of St. Cecilia. The Italian version, however, makes explicit reference to her as patron of sacred music and song; it asks that we may "also be worthy to sing the praises of the Lord." The same reference to music is found in the Office of Readings, taken from a discourse by St. Augustine: "Words cannot express the things that are sung by the heart. . . . As if so happy that words can no longer express what they feel, people discard the restricting syllables. They burst out into a simple sound of joy, of jubilation."

The relevance of this feast can be found in the antiphons for the Canticle of Zechariah and the Canticle of Mary, in which we are urged to "cast off the works of darkness and put on the armor of light" and never to cease praying and speaking to God. In our secularized society we need to hear this call to conversion and be more faithful in our practice of prayer.

Opening Prayer: *Lord of mercy, be close to those who call upon you. With Saint Cecilia to help us, hear and answer our prayers.*

November 23
ST. CLEMENT (+97?)

HISTORICO-LITURGICAL NOTE

According to St. Jerome, this saint has been venerated since the end of the fourth century in the basilica of St. Clement in Rome, which is administered by the Irish Dominicans. His cult spread from Rome to northern Africa, Spain and France and even to Byzantium when his writings were translated into Greek. He was the third successor to St. Peter and in the mosaic in the basilica of St. Clement he is pictured with St. Peter and with an anchor, because according to legend, his body had been thrown into the sea so that the Christians could not recover it. He is not to be confused with the Clement mentioned by St. Paul (Ph 4:3), although Origen, Eusebius and St. Jerome identify him as such. He is the first of the early theologians known as the Apostolic Fathers.

MESSAGE AND RELEVANCE

In the Opening Prayer for the Mass there is a sentence taken from the Sacramentary of Verona. It refers to St. Clement as a "priest and martyr who bore witness with his blood to the love he proclaimed and the gospel he preached." No credence is given to the legend that Clement was condemned to forced labor in the marble quarries nor to the one that says he was thrown into the sea with an anchor around his neck. Rather, the text calls attention to the relationship between the mysteries of the liturgy and the preaching of the gospel.

A statement of Clement's in the Office of Readings is still applicable today: "The smallest parts of our body are necessary and valuable to the whole. All work together and are mutually subject for the preservation of the whole body. Our entire body, then, will be preserved in Christ Jesus, and each of us should be subject to his neighbor in accordance with the grace given to each."

St. Irenaeus called Clement an "apostolic man" because he had heard the preaching of the apostles. To him is attributed the greatest liturgical and canonical compilation from the earliest days of the Church. He is also important for stating in his letter to the Corinthians that the function and power of the priest come from the apostles and not from the community.

Opening Prayer: *All-powerful and ever-living God, we praise your power and glory revealed to us in the lives of your saints. Give us joy on this feast of St. Clement, the priest and martyr who bore witness with his blood to the love he proclaimed and the gospel he preached.*

November 23
ST. COLUMBAN (543-615)

HISTORICO-LITURGICAL NOTE

This Irish monk died at Bobbio, Italy, on November 23 and was greatly venerated in various parts of Europe during the eighth century. He was inscribed in the Roman Calendar in 1969.

Born in Ireland, he entered a monastery at Bangor. Later he left Ireland with 12 companions in order to evangelize France. Around the year 590 he received land for the construction of a monastery. When the number of monks reached 250, Columban wrote a Rule for the monks as well as a *Penitentiary*, a guide for confessors.

After some disagreements with the French bishops because of his Celtic usages, he was expelled from France. Passing through Switzerland with a group of monks, Columban finally settled in Italy, where he founded the monastery at Bobbio, between Genoa and Piacenza.

MESSAGE AND RELEVANCE

The Opening Prayer of the Mass is taken from the diocesan Missal of Bobbio, Italy, and it states that God "called St. Columban to live the monastic life and to preach the gospel with zeal." He was the first great missionary of those early days, crossing western Europe on his missionary journeys. He frequently pressured civil authorities to convert and, through them, he sought the conversion of their subjects. But he never compromised with the immorality and corruption of some of the rulers.

His blending of apostolic activity with the monastic life aroused the animosity of many bishops. The soul of Columban's apostolate was the monastic life, which was extremely austere and inflexible, together with harsh corporal punishment for infractions.

In the Opening Prayer we ask God that St. Columban's prayers will "help us to seek you above all things and to work with all our hearts for the spread of the faith." St. Columban was able to transform barbarian customs, consolidate the authority of bishops, reform the clergy and replace the canonical public penance with private auricular confession.

We venerate St. Columban as a master not only because his poetic compositions reveal the Irish love for nature, but because he inspires us resolutely to seek God above everything else. Because of his fervent zeal in evangelizing, he remains an excellent model for promoting the spread of the faith.

In the Office of Readings we find a statement from St. Columban that is especially relevant: "It is a glorious privilege that God should grant man his eternal image. . . . We must turn back our image undefiled and holy to our God and Father, for he is holy. . . . We must restore his image with love, for he is love. . . . We must restore it with loyalty and truth, for he is loyal and truthful."

Opening Prayer: *Lord, you called St. Columban to live the monastic life and to preach the gospel with zeal.*

*May his prayers and example help us to seek you above
all things and to work with all our hearts for the spread
of the faith.*

November 23 (United States)
BLESSED MIGUEL AGUSTIN PRO
(1891-1927)

HISTORICO-LITURGICAL NOTE

This Jesuit martyr gave his life for Christ during the
persecution of the Church in Mexico that began in 1910. He
died before a firing squad in 1927 and in 1930 the cause for his
beatification was introduced in Rome.

Born in Guadalupe, Mexico, Miguel entered the Jesuit
novitiate in 1911. By 1914 the revolution had become so
intense that all the young Jesuits were dispersed. They travelled to Laredo, Texas, to California, and then by way of
Nicaragua and Spain to Belgium. There Miguel completed his
studies and was ordained a priest in 1925. All those years he
suffered from a severe stomach ailment and his superiors
ultimately sent him back to Mexico. Within a month after his
arrival in Mexico City, the government banned all public
worship. For several years Father Pro ministered to the people
incognito but eventually an order was issued for his arrest and
he had to go into hiding. In November, 1927, a bomb was
thrown at the car of President Calles from an automobile that
had previously belonged to a brother of Father Pro. As a result,
the three Pro brothers were arrested and condemned to death.
The youngest brother received a pardon at the last moment and
was exiled to the United States. Father Pro faced the firing
squad with arms outstretched and at the last moment said in a
clear, strong voice: *"Viva Cristo Rey!"* (Long live Christ the
King!).

MESSAGE AND RELEVANCE

In the Opening Prayer we say that God gave Father Pro "the grace to seek ardently your greater glory and the salvation of your people." First of all, we note that the phrase "your greater glory" is a succinct expression of the motto of the Society of Jesus: "For the greater glory of God." Father Pro had previously offered his life to God for the Mexican people and by his martyrdom he glorified God. The blood of the martyrs is precious in the sight of God.

The thousands of people that passed by the casket of the martyr were well aware that he had given his life for them. President Calles had forbidden any public funeral, but the people defied his order. When one of Father Pro's sisters was overcome with emotion at the wake and began to weep hysterically, her father said to her: "Is that the way you act in the presence of a saint?" He well understood the words of Christ: "Greater love than this no man has but to lay down his life."

The death of a martyr for Christ is always relevant because in every age there are persecutions of the Church. The lesson we learn from the selfless dedication of Father Pro to his priestly ministry in the midst of great personal danger is expressed in the petition of the Opening Prayer: "May we serve you and glorify you by performing our daily duties with fidelity and joy."

Opening Prayer: *God our Father, you gave your servant Miguel Agustin the grace to seek ardently your greater glory and the salvation of your people. Grant that, through his intercession and following his example, we may serve you and glorify you by performing our daily duties with fidelity and joy and effectively helping our neighbor.*

November 24
ST. ANDREW DUNG-LAC (+1839) and COMPANIONS

HISTORICO-LITURGICAL NOTE

There are 117 martyrs in this group and although they died at different times, they were all canonized by Pope John Paul II on June 19, 1988. Of the group, 96 were Vietnamese, 11 were Spaniards, and 10 were French. There were 8 bishops, 50 priests and 59 lay Catholics in the group. Of the priests, 11 were Dominicans, 10 belonged to the Paris Mission Society, and the rest were diocesan priests plus one seminarian. Certain individual martyrs were mentioned by name in the process of canonization: Andrew Dung-Lac, a diocesan priest; Thomas Tran-Van-Thien, a seminarian; Emmanuel Le-Van-Pung, father of a family; the Dominican bishops Jerome Hermosilla and Valentine Berrio-Ochoa; and John-Theophane Venard, who had corresponded with St. Theresa of Lisieux.

MESSAGE AND RELEVANCE

The Opening Prayer of the Mass calls upon God, the origin and source of all fatherhood, who made Andrew and companions faithful to Christ even to the shedding of their blood. The tortures endured by these martyrs were indescribable but, as St. Cyprian says, the martyrs were stronger than their tortures.

The Prayer over the Gifts states that these martyrs showed unflinching fortitude in the face of adversity. A detailed description of their sufferings is found in the Office of Readings, taken from a letter written by Paul Le-Bao-Tinh to the seminary of Ke-Vinh in 1843. Nevertheless, Paul states that in the midst of his torments he was joyful because he was not alone; "Christ is with me." The petition in the Opening Prayer asks that we also may be missionaries and witnesses to the love of God. In the Prayer after Communion we say that "only the power of the Holy Spirit can sustain us so that we shall be able to suffer for the faith and thus merit an eternal reward."

The significance of the feast of these martyrs can be found in the words of Pope John Paul II in his homily at the canonization. After emphasizing that these martyrs were all obedient to civil authority in matters that were right and just, the Holy Father stated that in the face of the restrictions on the practice of the faith, they protested that they could not abandon their Christian religion and thereby disobey the supreme authority of God. Through the witness of these martyrs, said the Holy Father, the Church in Vietnam has proclaimed that it will not reject the cultural traditions and lawful institutions of the country but wants to be inculturated and thus contribute to the upbuilding of the entire country. This applies to Catholics in every country, who should strive to reconcile their cultural traditions and national loyalty with their life as Christians.

> Opening Prayer: *O God, source and origin of all fatherhood, you kept the blessed martyrs Andrew and his companions faithful to the cross of your Son even to the shedding of their blood. Through their intercession enable us to spread your love among our brothers and sisters, that we may be called and may truly be your children.*

November 30
ST. ANDREW

HISTORICO-LITURGICAL NOTE

The feast in honor of St. Andrew has been celebrated on November 30 since the beginning of the fifth century, according to the Jerusalem Calendar. Around the year 470 a church was dedicated to him in Rome, near St. Mary Major's, because he was the brother of St. Peter. He had been a follower of John the Baptist and was the first of the apostles to follow Christ; in fact it was he who led his brother Peter to Christ (Jn 1:35-42). For that reason the Greeks called him the "Protoclete" or first called. Tradition says that he preached the gospel in Greece and in the year 60 was crucified in Patras on an X-shaped cross (now known as St. Andrew's cross). His relics were transferred to Constantinople in 357 and later to Amalfi, Italy, in 1208, but his skull was sent to Rome in 1462. In 1964, as an ecumenical gesture, his relics were returned to Patras in Greece. There is great devotion to him in the Byzantine Church. He is patron of Russia and Scotland.

MESSAGE AND RELEVANCE

The texts for the Mass and the Liturgy of the Hours use the scarce details about St. Andrew that are found in the New Testament. The Entrance Antiphon and Communion Antiphon of the Mass refer to his vocation to follow Christ. The Opening Prayer, taken from the Gregorian Sacramentary, states that St. Andrew was called "to preach the gospel and guide your Church in faith." At the very outset he made his confession of faith, when he said to Peter: "We have found the Messiah" (Jn 1:41-42). Moreover, we read in Mark 1:18 that Andrew left his fishing nets at once and followed Christ.

Finally, in the Prayer after Communion we make a reference to the suffering of St. Andrew, asking that we may follow his example and, by sharing in Christ's suffering, live with him for ever in glory. He was closely associated with Christ and for that reason Philip asked Andrew to speak to Christ about some Greeks who wanted to see him (Jn 12:22).

The relevance of this feast is found in the Office of Readings, where St. John Chrysostom says: "After Andrew had stayed with Jesus and had learned much from him, he did not keep this treasure to himself, but hastened to share it with his brother." We today are also called to share our faith with others in order to build up the Mystical Body of Christ.

Opening Prayer: *Lord, in your kindness hear our petitions. You called Andrew the apostle to preach the gospel and to guide your Church in faith. May he always be our friend in your presence to help us with his prayers.*

DECEMBER

ST. FRANCIS XAVIER (1506-1552)

HISTORICO-LITURGICAL NOTE

On December 3, 1552, Francis Xavier died on the island of Shangchwan, near the Chinese port of Canton. He was canonized in 1662, inscribed in the Roman Calendar in 1663, and named patron of India and the Far East in 1748. Finally, in 1927 he was declared patron of foreign missions, together with St. Theresa of Lisieux.

He was born of a noble Basque family in Navarra, Spain, and in 1525 took up his studies in Paris. On the feast of the Assumption in 1534 he made his religious profession together with St. Ignatius Loyola in a church in Montmartre, Paris. At that time he also made a vow to go to the Holy Land, but being unable to do so because of a blockade by the Turkish Muslims, he went instead to Rome in 1538, where he placed himself at the disposition of the pope for work in the foreign missions. He and Ignatius Loyola had been ordained to the priesthood in Venice the preceding year. Consequently, when the King of Portugal asked for missionaries for India, Francis was able to take the place of a sick confrere.

Francis labored as a missionary in Goa, Malacca, Japan and China, and converted approximately 30,000 pagans. He died of exhaustion and fever on the island of Shangchwan.

MESSAGE AND RELEVANCE

The new prayers for this feast reflect the missionary activity of this saintly Jesuit. The Opening Prayer states that through the apostolic preaching of St. Francis Xavier, God called many people of the Orient to the light of the gospel. It ends by asking that every Christian community should burn with the same missionary fervor so that all over the world the Church will be gladdened with new sons and daughters.

Like many of the early Jesuits, Francis was imbued with a missionary spirit. Convinced as he was that salvation comes through belief in Jesus Christ, he was zealous in destroying the idols of the pagan religions. At the same time he was adept at inculturating Christianity in conformity with the mentality of the people. And even if he had not mastered their language, as happened in Japan, he was able to relate to them without an interpreter.

The Prayer over the Gifts tells us that the zeal of St. Francis Xavier for the salvation of souls "led him to the ends of the earth." He was drawn always to those who were far away and to such an extent that some of his fellow-Jesuits accused him of not being sufficiently interested in the affairs of the Society of Jesus. In a letter to St. Ignatius Loyola he expressed a desire to go around the universities in Europe to stimulate zeal for the missions: "I wish they would work as hard at this as they do at their books, and so settle their account with God for their learning and the talents entrusted to them. This thought would certainly stir most of them to meditate on spiritual realities, to listen actively to what God is saying to them. They would forget their own desires, their human affairs, and give themselves over entirely to God's will and his choice" (Office of Readings).

The Prayer after Communion asks God to "fill us with the same love that inspired Francis Xavier to work for the salvation of all. Help us to live in a manner more worthy of our Christian calling and so inherit the promise of eternal life." Thanks to the zeal of Francis Xavier, catechetical centers were established throughout Goa at a time when many of the

Portuguese colonists were anything but exemplary Christians. He reminded them how much God values a good will, accompanied by a humility that offers one's entire life to God for his greater glory.

> Preface (Society of Jesus): *Father, you inflamed St. Francis, son of the newborn Society of Jesus, with the ardor of charity and zeal for souls, so that, ignoring dangers, difficulties and fatigue, he would embark on numerous journeys and, acquainting people with the mysteries of salvation, would make them members of your Church.*

December 4
ST. JOHN DAMASCENE (675-749?)

HISTORICO-LITURGICAL NOTE

This feast is celebrated on the date on which the Byzantine Rite commemorates the transfer of the relics of St. John Damascene to Mar Saba, near Jerusalem (749 or 750). The feast was listed in the Roman Calendar in 1890, when Pope Leo XIII declared him a Doctor of the Church.

Born at Damascus around the year 675, of a Christian Arab family, he was educated by a monk who had been brought as a prisoner from Sicily to Damascus. For a time he served as finance minister for the Muslim caliph, but later he resigned his post and proceeded to Jerusalem, where he entered the Byzantine monastery at Mar Saba. He was ordained a priest in 726 and dedicated himself to study and writing. He was a poet as well as a theologian and in the latter field he wrote the famous work, *The Fount of Knowledge*, part of which was later translated into Latin under the title *De Fide Orthodoxa*. Together with the patriarch of Constantinople and Pope Gregory

II, John Damascene was one of the principal defenders of the use of images in religious worship. In this regard he made the following statement: "It is not the material that we honor but what it represents; the honor paid to images goes to the one who is represented by the image."

MESSAGE AND RELEVANCE

The new Opening Prayer of the Mass makes an indirect reference to the manual of dogmatic theology written by St. John Damascene. It asks that the true faith that he taught so well may be our light and strength. His famous dogmatic treatise was as highly regarded in the East as the writings of St. Augustine and St. Thomas Aquinas are regarded in the West. His teaching on the Assumption of the Blessed Virgin Mary was noted by Pope Pius XII when he defined the dogma of the Assumption in 1950. Finally, he composed numerous hymns that were incorporated into the Divine Office in the Byzantine Rite. In spite of all these accomplishments, he referred to himself as a "lowly and useless servant who would do better to confess his sins to God than to become involved in theological and political matters."

In the Office of Readings we find a passage from St. John Damascene that is especially significant: "And you, O Church, are a most excellent assembly, the noble summit of perfect purity, whose assistance comes from God. You in whom God lives, receive from us an exposition of the faith that is free from error, to strengthen the Church, just as our Fathers handed it down to us."

Opening Prayer: *Lord, may the prayers of St. John Damascene help us, and may the true faith he taught so well always be our light and our strength.*

December 6
ST. NICHOLAS (+350?)

HISTORICO-LITURGICAL NOTE

The feast of St. Nicholas, bishop of Myra in Turkey, falls on December 4 in the Eastern Church and has been celebrated at Rome only since the eleventh century. His relics were transported to Bari, Italy, in 1087. When Pope Urban II went to Bari in 1089 for the transfer of the relics of St. Eustachius to the cathedral, he also consecrated an altar in honor of St. Nicholas. An uncle named Nicholas was bishop of Myra and he ordained his nephew to the priesthood. The younger Nicholas then distributed all his possessions among the poor and entered a monastery, where he became abbot. In time he became bishop of Myra and was among those who signed the document affirming the divinity of Christ at the Council of Nicea (325). During a persecution of the Church he was imprisoned and tortured. He died in 345 or 350 at the age of 65.

According to legend, he was a great miracle worker and he provided a dowry for three poor girls whose father was forcing them into a life of prostitution. It is also said that he raised to life three youths who had been executed and saved three sailors from shipwreck. In the ninth century the folklore of northern Germany made St. Nicholas the *Weihnachtsmann*, the man of Christmas Eve; in the Anglo-Saxon world he is honored as "Santa Claus" (the name for Nicholas in German is *Klaus*). In the eleventh century the custom originated of distributing sweets to children on the eve of the feast of St. Nicholas.

Devotion to St. Nicholas has been widespread in the Greek, Slavic and Russian Churches. He is the patron of Russia, with St. Andrew, and is also honored as patron of Greece, Sicily and Lorraine, France. It is said that there are more than 2,000 churches named in his honor in Europe.

MESSAGE AND RELEVANCE

The new Opening Prayer of the Mass refers to St. Nicholas as a powerful helper: "By the help of St. Nicholas keep us safe from all danger." Throughout the centuries he has been considered a patron of difficult cases, similar to St. Jude Thaddeus and St. Rita of Cascia. Various groups such as sailors, prisoners, students, young girls, lawyers and pharmacists have looked to him as their patron. The Office of Readings quotes St. Augustine's teaching on the love that is required of bishops: "The love of Christ ought to reach such a spiritual pitch in his shepherds that it overcomes the natural fear of death which makes us shrink from the thought of dying, even though we desire to live with Christ in glory."

Although the cult of St. Nicholas as "Santa Claus" has been commercialized in modern times, he is nevertheless a model of charity, especially towards children. He is also a suitable patron for the ecumenical discussions between the East and the West. For this reason the institute conducted by the Dominicans at Bari, Italy, for promoting relations between the Eastern and Latin Churches is named after St. Nicholas.

> Opening Prayer: *Father, hear our prayers for mercy, and by the help of St. Nicholas keep us safe from all danger, and guide us on the way of salvation.*

December 7
ST. AMBROSE (339-397)

HISTORICO-LITURGICAL NOTE

St. Ambrose died on April 4 or 5 at Milan, and since the eleventh century his feast has been celebrated in Rome on December 7, the date of his ordination as a bishop. In 1298 he was listed as a Doctor of the Church, together with Augustine, Jerome and Gregory the Great.

He was born of a Roman Christian family in 339 (?) and his father was an official in Gaul. When his father died, Ambrose moved back to Rome with his brother and sister. There he became a lawyer and eventually a consul in the region of Milan, Italy. He was named bishop by popular acclamation, although he was still a catechumen. Eight days later he was baptized and, after receiving further instruction, was ordained a bishop. He frequently had to defend the rights and freedom of the Church, sometimes even against the emperor.

Ambrose was an apostle of charity, a reformer of the liturgy, a director of souls (he instructed and baptized St. Augustine), a defender of the vow of virginity and a commentator on the Old Testament and the Gospel according to Luke. Always weak in health, he died in 397.

MESSAGE AND RELEVANCE

The prayers of the Mass have been changed in part. The Opening Prayer states that Ambrose was "an outstanding teacher of the Catholic faith," with the courage of an apostle. He was well versed in the writings of the ancient Fathers as well as the classical pagan authors. He realized that his first duty as a bishop was to proclaim the word of God and he urged the clergy to dedicate their free time to reading and study. He insisted that one cannot understand fully the New Testament if he has not read the Old Testament.

In the Office of Readings we find this advice from Ambrose to a bishop: "Drink, then, from Christ, so that your voice may be heard. . . . He who reads much and understands much, receives his fill. He who is full, refreshes others." Unlike St. Jerome, he was able to make a harmonious synthesis between classical literature and the gospel teaching, insisting always that "Christ is everything for us."

The second reference in the Opening Prayer is to his apostolic courage. He made no compromises when it was a question of the rights of the Church. When the emperor Theodosius tried to enter a church after having been the cause of the death of 7,000 people, Ambrose prevented him. And when the emperor cited the example of David, Ambrose replied: "If you have imitated David in sinning, then imitate him in doing penance." Later, in 390, the emperor did penance and was reconciled to the Church. St. Ambrose insisted that the emperor is a member of the Church, but he is not over the Church.

In the Prayer over the Gifts we ask God to "give us the light of faith which guided St. Ambrose to make your glory known." Thus, Ambrose states in the Office of Readings: "The Church of the Lord is built upon the rock of the apostles among so many dangers in the world; it therefore remains unmoved. . . Although the elements of this world constantly beat upon the Church with crashing sounds, the Church possesses the safest harbor of salvation for all in distress."

Finally, in the Prayer after Communion we ask that we "may follow your way with courage and prepare ourselves for the feast of eternal life." St. Ambrose exhorted his priests: "Do not seek your own popularity but the good of others." He also told them that a priest should observe the rule of never harming anyone, even if provoked or attacked unjustly.

St. Ambrose has a message for our times in his strong defense of consecrated virginity. "The flesh," he said, "which was cast out of paradise, was again linked to God through a Virgin."

> Opening Prayer: *Lord, you made St. Ambrose an outstanding teacher of the Catholic faith and gave him the courage of an apostle. Raise up in your Church more leaders after your own heart, to guide us with courage and wisdom.*

December 8

IMMACULATE CONCEPTION of the VIRGIN MARY

HISTORICO-LITURGICAL NOTE

It seems that the English Crusaders brought the feast of the Immaculate Conception from the East in the middle of the eleventh century, together with the feast of St. Ann, which was celebrated on December 9. It originated in Greek monasteries, but the Pontifical of Exeter, England, is very similar to the Byzantine liturgy. It spread on the continent in the twelfth century and was adopted by the Franciscans, especially after Duns Scotus defended this dogma in 1263. It was listed in the Roman Calendar by Pope Sixtus IV in 1476, and the Sistine Chapel was dedicated to the Conception of Mary, after the Council of Basle decided to make it a universal feast (1439).

Prior to that, as early as 750, the feast of the conception of Mary by St. Ann, mother of the Theotokos, was celebrated in the East on December 9. It became an obligatory holy day by edict of Emperor Emmanuel in 1166. The ninth-century Calendar at Naples also listed the feast of the conception of Mary by St. Ann, and in 1050 Pope Leo IX recommended that the conception of the Virgin Mary should be honored.

However, this feast should not be confused with the feast celebrated in Spain on December 18 under the title "Conception of Mary," which referred to the conception of Christ by Mary. Since the feast of the Annunciation fell in Lent, the Spaniards transferred it to December.

Pope Clement XI made the conception of Mary a feast of obligation in 1708, and in 1855, after the definition of the dogma of the Immaculate Conception by Pope Pius IX on December 8, 1854, the name of the feast became the Immaculate Conception. Eight years before, in 1846, the bishops of the United States had made the Immaculate Conception the patronal feast of the Church in that country. The apparitions at

Lourdes in 1858 have been seen by some as a heavenly confirmation of the dogma.

MESSAGE AND RELEVANCE

The Opening Prayer of the Mass was composed at the time of Pope Sixtus IV in 1477 and it is a synthesis of the dogmatic definition: "You let her share beforehand in the salvation Christ would bring by his death, and kept her sinless from the first moment of her conception." Some of the Fathers of the East saw a parallel in the two conceptions; that is, the sterile Ann conceived Mary, and the virgin Mary conceived Jesus by the power of the Holy Spirit. Since the feast was celebrated many centuries before the dogmatic definition, we have a case in which the norm of belief (in the sense of a public proclamation) is based on the norm of prayer (*Lex orandi est lex credendi*).

The new Preface of the Mass is inspired by the Vatican II documents, *Lumen Gentium* and *Sacrosanctum Concilium*. It summarizes the dogma under four aspects. First, the Christocentric dimension relates not only to Mary's preservation from every stain of sin but also to her fullness of grace and her divine maternity. Secondly, the ecclesiological aspect is based on the text from Ephesians 5:27 because the Church is "the bride of Christ, radiant in beauty." Thirdly, the soteriological aspect relates the innocent Lamb of God to the purity of Mary. The fourth aspect is eschatological, in the sense that Mary was predestined to become the advocate of grace and the model of sanctity for the People of God.

In the Prayer over the Gifts we focus on the central point of this dogma, namely, that Mary was preserved from sin from the very first moment of her life. This was possible through the prevenient merits of Christ and not through the personal merits of the Virgin Mary.

The Prayer after Communion (in the Latin version) asks that "as we celebrate the singular privilege of Mary's preservation from sin, may we also be redeemed from the wounds of original sin." The existence of original sin and its effects on the descendants of Adam and Eve is presupposed; otherwise a feast of the Immaculate Conception would be meaningless.

The relevance of this feast is found in the first reading for the Mass (Gn 3:9-20) and the antiphon for the Canticle of Zechariah, which is taken from that same passage from Genesis. We should also note the mention of predestination in the second reading (Ep 1:3-12), and in the reading for Evening Prayer I (Rm 8:29-30). In the Office of Readings the words of St. Anselm place Mary at the very summit of all creation: "Lady, full and overflowing with grace, all creation receives new life from your abundance. Virgin, blessed above all creatures, through your blessing all creation is blessed; not only creation from its Creator, but the Creator himself has been blessed by creation."

> Preface: *Father, all-powerful and ever-living God, we do well always and everywhere to give you thanks. You allowed no stain of Adam's sin to touch the Virgin Mary. Full of grace, she was to be a worthy Mother of your Son, your sign of favors to the Church at its beginning, and the promise of its perfection as the bride of Christ, radiant in beauty. Purest of virgins, she was to bring forth your Son, the innocent Lamb who takes away our sins. You chose her from all women to be our advocate with you and our pattern of holiness.*

December 11
ST. DAMASUS (305?-384)

HISTORICO-LITURGICAL NOTE

This feast has been celebrated since the eighth century but it did not enter the Roman Calendar until the eleventh century because devotion to him was not widespread. He was elected pope by the clergy and the people and it was he who used the term "Apostolic See" in order to designate the primacy of the Roman See. Hence the axiom *Ubi Petrus, ibi ecclesia* (Where Peter is, there is the Church).

St. Damasus was the son of an official of Spanish origin and he lived at a time in which there were divisions between the East and the West in the Roman Empire. There was also an anti-pope named Felix, who claimed to be the rightful pontiff. These were violent times and Pope Damasus himself was falsely accused of terrible scandals and eventually exiled. He also had to defend the doctrine of the Church against various heretics such as the Arians, the Donatists, the Novatianists and others. He called St. Jerome back to Rome as his secretary and commissioned him to make a new translation of the Bible into Latin (the Vulgate). He was also the one who changed the liturgical language from Greek to Latin (except for the *Kyrie*). His relations with the Eastern Church were not cordial, and St. Basil criticized Pope Damasus as a man too proud to listen to those who told him the truth. He was a great promoter of devotion to the martyrs and it was through his efforts that Catholicism became the State religion under Theodosius I (379).

MESSAGE AND RELEVANCE

The Opening Prayer of the Mass is taken from the Sacramentary of Verona and it focuses on the great devotion of Pope Damasus to the martyrs. Rather than construct more basilicas in their honor, he made the catacombs sanctuaries where the faithful could venerate them. He was for that reason known as "the pope of the catacombs." In addition to this, he was zealous in locating the relics of the forgotten martyrs, not simply for archaeological reasons, but that these heroes of the faith could serve as models for the Christian faithful.

In the Office of Readings a passage from St. Augustine states: "We, the Christian community, assemble to celebrate the memory of the martyrs with ritual solemnity because we want to be inspired to follow their example, share in their merits, and be helped by their prayers. Yet we erect no altars to any of the martyrs, even in the martyrs' burial chapels themselves. . . . What is offered is offered always to God, who crowned the martyrs. . . . The veneration we call *worship* . . . is something we give and teach others to give to God alone."

Opening Prayer: *Father, as St. Damasus loved and honored your martyrs, so may we continue to celebrate their witness for Christ, who lives and reigns with you and the Holy Spirit, one God, for ever and ever.*

December 12 (United States)
OUR LADY of GUADALUPE

HISTORICO-LITURGICAL NOTE

Under the title of Our Lady of Guadalupe the Blessed Virgin Mary was named patron of Mexico by Pope Benedict XIV, who ordered a special Mass in her honor as well as a Liturgy of the Hours. Under the same title she is patron of Latin America and the Philippines. In 1945 Pope Pius XII stated that the Virgin of Guadalupe is the "Queen of Mexico and Empress of the Americas."

The focal point of the basilica at Guadalupe, Mexico, is the miraculous portrayal of the Blessed Virgin Mary as the Immaculate Conception. Juan Diego, a Catholic Indian aged 55, was hastening to Mass down Tepeyac hill on December 9, 1521. The Blessed Virgin appeared to him and told him to tell the bishop to have a temple built on that spot in her honor. After hearing the message, the bishop told Juan Diego to ask for a sign. At daybreak on December 12 Juan Diego was running to get a priest to give the last sacraments to an uncle who was dying. Again, Mary appeared, reassured Juan Diego about his uncle (who was cured at that moment), and bade him go to the bishop. Obedient to the bishop's previous request, Juan Diego asked for a sign, and Mary told him to go up into the rocks and gather roses. He knew that December was not the time for roses, but he did as commanded and filled his cloak with fresh roses. Appearing before the bishop he opened the cloak and let the roses fall out; then, to the bishop's amazement, he saw the figure of the Blessed Virgin Mary impressed on the inside of the cloak.

Today a magnificent basilica in honor of Our Lady of Guadalupe is one of the most frequented Marian shrines in the Catholic world. This feast is also celebrated in the United States because of the close link between the United States and Mexico. Juan Diego has been beatified and his feast is celebrated on December 9.

MESSAGE AND RELEVANCE

The Opening Prayer of the Mass states that God has blessed the Americas by the apparition of the Blessed Virgin Mary at Tepeyac, Mexico. As France was honored by the Blessed Virgin at Lourdes, and Portugal at Fatima, so also all the Americas, North and South, have been blessed by her appearance as Our Lady of Guadalupe. Her shrine should serve as a magnet to attract all who are devoted to the Blessed Mother.

Secondly, the Opening Prayer asks that her prayers will "help all men and women to accept each other as brothers and sisters." We have here a plea that racial justice will prevail throughout all the Americas, between the Hispanic-Americans and the Indians in Latin America, between the Afro-Americans and the whites in the United States, and between the English-speaking and French-speaking Canadians.

Finally, the prayer asks that "through your justice present in our hearts may your peace reign in the world." Justice is therefore emphasized as the foundation for peace, and the petition refers not only to the Americas, but extends to all nations. For that reason, this feast is particularly relevant to the situation in the world today, when so many tensions have resulted from ethnic, religious or nationalistic differences.

Opening Prayer: *God of power and mercy, you bles-*
sed the Americas at Tepeyac with the presence of the
Virgin Mary of Guadalupe. May her prayers help all
men and women to accept each other as brothers and
sisters. Through your justice present in our hearts may
your peace reign in the world.

Prayer in Honor of Blessed Juan Diego (December
9):   *Lord God, through blessed Juan Diego you made*
known the love of Our Lady of Guadalupe toward your
people. Grant by his intercession that we who follow the
counsel of Mary, our Mother, may strive continually to
do your will.

December 12

ST. JANE FRANCES de CHANTAL (1572-1641)

HISTORICO-LITURGICAL NOTE

This saint died on December 13, 1641, was canonized in
1767, and was inscribed in the Roman Calendar in 1769. Her
feast was placed on the eve of her death because December 13
is the feast of St. Lucy.

Born at Dijon, France, in 1572, of an aristocratic family,
she married the Baron of Chantal shortly after the age of 20.
She had six children, of whom only four survived. Her husband
died in a hunting accident in 1601, 14 days after the birth of
her last child. She then dedicated herself to the rearing of her
children and to the sick and the poor.

In 1604 Jane Frances met St. Francis de Sales, who was
preaching the Lenten sermons at Dijon, and she placed herself
under his spiritual direction. She consecrated herself totally to
God and was greatly inspired by her contacts with the Carmelite nuns of Dijon. After numerous spiritual purifications, she
attained to contemplative prayer.

In 1607 St. Francis de Sales revealed to her his intention to found a religious community of women who would not be cloistered and would admit older women and those of weak health. The Confraternity of the Visitation was finally established in 1610, after Jane Frances had arranged for the care of her youngest children. However, in 1615 the archbishop of Lyons insisted that these religious women be cloistered, contrary to the wishes of St. Francis de Sales, who wanted them to have an apostolate. After the death of St. Francis de Sales, St. Jane Frances published his writings and she herself died in 1641, after a long illness and numerous spiritual trials.

MESSAGE AND RELEVANCE

The revised Opening Prayer of the Mass refers to her twofold vocation: to marriage and to the religious life. It is said that the journal of her life served in part as a basis for *The Introduction to the Devout Life* by St. Francis de Sales. After his death she remained ever faithful to the Salesian spirit of the Visitation nuns. Towards the end of her life, however, she suffered a painful trial of faith.

The relevance of St. Jane Frances to our day is found in the Office of Readings, where one of the Sisters asked her what the martyrdom of love is like. She replied: "Yield yourself fully to God, and you will find out! Divine love takes its sword to the hidden recesses of our inmost soul and divides us from ourselves. I know one person whom love cut off from all that was dearest to her, just as completely and effectively as if a tyrant's blade had severed spirit from body."

Opening Prayer: *Lord, you chose St. Jane Frances to serve you both in marriage and in the religious life. By her prayers help us to be faithful in our vocation and always to be the light of the world.*

December 13
ST. LUCY (+304)

HISTORICO-LITURGICAL NOTE

This saint was martyred at Syracuse in Sicily, and her feast is listed in the Jerome Martyrology (sixth century). A Greek inscription found at Syracuse in 1894 testifies to the devotion to the saint by the end of the fourth or the beginning of the fifth century. A church was built above her tomb and dedicated to St. Agatha in the seventeenth century. It is likely that Pope Gregory the Great inserted her name in the Roman Canon of the Mass. There are also two monasteries — one in Syracuse and another near Rome — that are named Santa Lucia, as well as two churches in Rome that bear her name.

The account of her martyrdom dates from the fifth or sixth century and it states that while Lucy was on a pilgrimage to the tomb of St. Agatha, patroness of Catania, Italy, the saint appeared to her and promised her that the Lord would bless the city of Syracuse as he had Catania because of the virginal love of Lucy. Lucy then convinced her mother to give to the poor the money that had been set aside for her dowry. This so infuriated her fiancé that he had her brought before the judges so that she could be subjected to the violation of her body. This was impossible, however, because her body became so heavy that it was immovable. Lucy was then subjected to torture and although she suffered a deep gash in her throat, she continued to pray and to give testimony to Christ. She died after receiving Viaticum. Her relics are venerated in Venice, and she is the patroness of those who suffer afflictions of the eyes.

MESSAGE AND RELEVANCE

As with Cecilia, Agnes and Agatha, St. Lucy gives witness to both virginity and martyrdom. Since the third century virgins have been honored in third place in the liturgy, after the apostles and martyrs. When the persecutions ended, consecrated virginity represented a high degree of sanctity. Martyrdom gives witness to the heroism of one's faith and the power of God which conquers through the cross of Christ, but assaults against consecrated virginity are also attacks against the faith.

The combination of virginity and martyrdom in a young girl like St. Lucy should serve to rid us of the idea that women are weak and fragile creatures. Lucy manifested a remarkable courage throughout her trial and in the midst of her torments. This is stated in the antiphon for the Canticle of Mary: "Lucy, bride of Christ, by your suffering you have gained the mastery of your soul. You have despised worldly values and now you are glorious among the angels. With your own blood you have triumphed over the enemy."

Finally, the words of St. Ambrose in the Office of Readings are significant: "You are one of God's people, of God's family, a virgin among virgins; you light up your grace of body with your splendor of soul. More than others you can be compared to the Church. . . . Embrace him, the one you have sought; turn to him, and be enlightened; hold him fast, ask him not to go in haste, beg him not to leave you."

Opening Prayer: *Lord, give us courage through the prayers of St. Lucy. As we celebrate her entrance into eternal glory, we ask to share her happiness in the life to come.*

December 14
ST. JOHN of the CROSS (1542-1591)

HISTORICO-LITURGICAL NOTE

St. John of the Cross died at Ubeda in Andalusia, Spain, on December 14, 1591, was canonized in 1726 and declared a Doctor of the Church in 1926. Together with St. Teresa of Avila, he is an outstanding teacher of the ascetical and mystical life.

He was born John de Yepes at Fontiveros, a town between Salamanca and Avila. His father had been disowned by his family for marrying beneath his social class and it is possible that he was of Jewish descent, as was St. Teresa of Avila. However, John's father died before John was one year old and as a result his mother moved to Medina del Campo in order to earn a living. There, John studied under the Jesuits and also served as an apprentice for various trades, ending up as a male nurse.

John entered the Carmelite Order in 1563, and after his novitiate was sent to Salamanca for further studies. When he returned to Medina del Campo for his first Mass, he met St. Teresa of Avila, who convinced him to join her movement for the reform of the Carmelite friars and nuns.

John changed his name from John of St. Matthias to John of the Cross and threw himself wholeheartedly into the work of the reform, which eventually resulted in the separation of the Discalced Carmelites from the Calced Carmelites. He suffered persecution from the Calced Carmelites, even to the point of being kidnapped and held prisoner at Toledo. After holding numerous important positions among the Discalced Carmelites and after writing his major treatises and poems in mystical theology — *The Ascent of Mount Carmel, the Dark Night of the Soul, The Spiritual Canticle, The Living Flame of Love* — he died at Ubeda, as he had predicted, just as the friars were beginning the midnight Office.

MESSAGE AND RELEVANCE

The prayers of the Mass refer to the basic characteristics of the spiritual doctrine of St. John of the Cross. The Latin version of the Collect is explicit: "Father, you led St. John of the Cross to your holy mountain through the dark night of renunciation and the ardent love of the cross." St. John had stated in *The Ascent of Mount Carmel* that it is necessary to mortify every attachment to sensate things because in comparison with God, these things are pure darkness. And he said in *The Spiritual Canticle* that "the gate that gives entrance to these riches of his wisdom is the cross; because it is a narrow gate, while many seek the joys that can be gained through it, it is given to few to desire to pass through it."

Towards the end of his life, while praying before the crucifix at Segovia, a voice asked him what reward he wanted for his service for the Lord. John replied that he desired to endure suffering for the Lord and to be despised and counted as nothing. From the events that followed, it is evident that his request was granted. In the petition of the Opening Prayer we ask that "by following his example we may come to the eternal vision of your glory."

The Prayer over the Gifts has us ask that "we may imitate the love we proclaim as we celebrate the mystery of the suffering and death of Christ." In the sacramental sacrifice of the cross and resurrection John found the power to give witness to the sanctity of his life. He told God that he was ready and willing to do whatever God would ask of him.

The Prayer after Communion states that God has "shown us the mystery of the cross in the life of St. John." There is no doubt that this saint experienced the cross in various ways: sickness and mortification, persecution and calumny, aridity and mystical trials. All this may cause some to think of St. John of the Cross as a man of excessive austerity, but the truth is otherwise. His spiritual doctrine was based on charity, and one of his admonitions was that in the evening of life we shall be judged by love. St. John's charity extended also to the ministry of the word, for he spent most of his time in preaching to the people and giving spiritual conferences to the friars and the cloistered nuns. Moreover, like St. Francis of Assisi, this saintly Carmelite had a special love for the beauties of nature, since through them one could experience something of the beauty of God.

The teaching of this mystical doctor has special significance for our sensate society in which it is so easy to become attached to pleasure and to created goods. The path of detachment and self-denial is still the path that leads to union with God.

> Preface (Carmelite Missal): *Father, all-powerful and ever-living God, we do well always and everywhere to give you thanks as we honor St. John of the Cross. His life and teaching set before us anew the mystery of Christ's Cross and victory. He has taught us to make up what is wanting in Christ's passion, and to share and proclaim the joy of his resurrection. Inwardly strengthened by the living flame of your Spirit, he ascended in darkness to the heights of divine union as he sang canticles of your love, the Church's greatest treasure.*

December 21
ST. PETER CANISIUS (1521-1597)

HISTORICO-LITURGICAL NOTE

This Jesuit saint died at Fribourg, Switzerland, on this date in 1597, was canonized and declared a Doctor of the Church in 1925, and was inscribed in the Roman Calendar in 1926. Pope Leo XIII called him the second apostle of Germany, after St. Boniface.

Born at Nijmegen, Holland (then part of the German Empire), Peter was educated at Cologne and at Louvain. At the age of 23 he entered the Society of Jesus and published treatises on the Fathers of the Church. He also took part in the Diet of Worms in 1545. Ordained to the priesthood in 1546, he became the theologian to the cardinal of Augsburg at the Council of Trent. Called to Rome by St. Ignatius Loyola, he was sent to Messina, Sicily, to teach rhetoric. He made his solemn religious profession at Rome in 1549.

St. Peter Canisius then returned to Germany and spent the next thirty years there, working for the renewal of Catholic life. He held several important posts and eventually became

Jesuit Provincial of territory that included Germany, Austria and Bohemia. He also founded numerous Jesuit colleges that became decisive factors in the Catholic reform. Once relieved of his duties as provincial, St. Peter composed his famous *Catechism*, which in ten years went through 55 editions in 9 languages. He was next assigned to found a college at Fribourg in 1581 and there he died peacefully in 1597.

MESSAGE AND RELEVANCE

The slightly modified Opening Prayer of the Mass presents St. Peter Canisius as a defender of the faith. Versed as he was in the theology of the Fathers of the Church and in Sacred Scripture, he was a most suitable person to defend and expound the teaching of the Church. Even his *Catechism* was written from this perspective; not in an aggressive and polemic manner, but by way of persuasion and logical demonstration. The petition in the prayer is ecumenical; we pray for "all who seek the truth."

The Office of Readings describes a mystical experience that St. Peter had in Rome, before leaving for Germany. "It was as if you opened to me the heart in your most sacred body; I seemed to see it directly before my eyes. You told me to drink from this fountain, inviting me, that is, to draw the waters of my salvation from your wellsprings, my Savior. I was most eager that streams of faith, hope and love should flow into me from that source. I was thirsting for poverty, chastity, obedience. I asked to be made wholly clean by you, to be clothed by you, to be made resplendent by you."

As to the relevance of St. Peter Canisius, we first note the apparition of the Sacred Heart because that devotion became widespread in the seventeenth century and was later called an "obligatory devotion" by Pope Pius XII. Secondly, given the contemporary interest in the ecumenical movement, St. Peter Canisius is an excellent example of how to dialogue with persons outside the Roman Catholic Church.

Opening Prayer: *Lord, you gave St. Peter Canisius wisdom and courage to defend the Catholic faith. By the help of his prayers may all who seek the truth rejoice in finding you, and may all who believe in you be loyal in professing their faith.*

December 23
ST. JOHN of KANTY (1390-1473)

HISTORICO-LITURGICAL NOTE

This feast was formerly celebrated on October 20. St. John Kanty was canonized in 1767 and listed in the Roman Calendar in 1770.

He was born in a small village near Kanty in Poland, south of modern-day Auschwitz. The area had been annexed by Emperor Charles IV after it was renounced by King Casimir of Poland. John became a doctor of philosophy at the University of Cracow in 1418, and after teaching for 8 years in a conventual school, taught at the University of Cracow and ultimately became dean of the faculty. He also engaged in the pastoral ministry for some time but gave it up to return to teaching, and among his students were the children of the king. He transcribed more than 18,000 pages of theological treatises. At a time when John Hus was exerting great influence, St. John Kanty distinguished himself by his fidelity to orthodox doctrine and his kindness in his dealings with his adversaries. He is buried in the Church of St. Ann in Cracow and from the moment of his death he enjoyed the reputation of a saint and a miracle worker.

MESSAGE AND RELEVANCE

The Opening Prayer of the Mass asks that "we may grow

in the wisdom of the saints," and rightly so, since St. John Kanty could be considered a patron of schools. In the letter of Pope Clement XII in the Office of Readings we read: "Saint John Kanty deserves a high place among the great saints and scholars who practice what they preach and defend the true faith against those who attack it. When [the Hussite] heresy and schism were gaining ground in neighboring territories, his teaching at the University of Cracow was untainted by any error. At the pulpit he fought to raise the standard of holiness among the faithful, and his preaching was reinforced by his humility, his chastity, his compassion, his bodily penance and the other qualities of a dedicated priest and apostle. . . . With his humility went a rare and childlike simplicity: the thoughts of his heart were revealed in his words and actions. . . . The God in his heart and the God on his lips were one and the same God."

The second note in the Opening Prayer is that St. John manifested "understanding and kindness to others." His charity towards others is legendary, and therefore the antiphon for the Canticle of Mary is most appropriate: "What you did for the least of my brethren, you did for me" (Mt 25:45). He always set aside a portion of his income, and sometimes part of his food, for the poor, whom he welcomed as he would Christ.

The significance of this saint for us is his dedication to the study of sacred doctrine and his charity towards the poor and needy. At a time when there were numerous saints in Poland, St. John Kanty stands in the front line.

> Opening Prayer: *Almighty Father, through the example of John of Kanty may we grow in the wisdom of the saints. As we show understanding and kindness to others, may we receive your forgiveness.*

December 26
ST. STEPHEN

HISTORICO-LITURGICAL NOTE

The feast of St. Stephen, which is listed in the Martyrology of Nicomedia (361), the Syriac Martyrology (411) and the Lectionary of Jerusalem (415-417), has been celebrated in the West since the fifth century. However, the date of the feast at Constantinople was fixed at December 27 because the feast of the Mother of God was celebrated on December 26.

St. Stephen was a deacon in the early Church and he had been assigned by the apostles to distribute food to the poor. We read in the Acts of the Apostles that he worked great signs and wonders among the people and that certain Jews would engage him in argument but he always confounded them with his wisdom. Ultimately, they made false charges against him, brought in false witnesses, and succeeded in having him stoned to death.

According to the priest Lucianus, the relics of St. Stephen were discovered near the north gate of the city of Jerusalem, and the bishop of Jerusalem had the relics transferred to Saint Sion, near the Cenacle. Later a basilica was constructed in his honor and the relics were transferred there in 439. The basilica was destroyed by the Persians in 614 and was eventually replaced by an oratory. It was again destroyed in 1187. After the excavations in 1882, the church was rebuilt and consecrated in 1900. It stands near the *Ecole Biblique* of the Dominicans. The distribution of St. Stephen's relics to Prague, northern Africa, Constantinople and Rome has served to foster devotion to this saint. The church of St. Stephen in Rome is one of the Lenten station churches.

MESSAGE AND RELEVANCE

In the Opening Prayer of the Mass we ask that we may love our enemies, in imitation of St. Stephen, who prayed for his persecutors. St. Augustine pointed out that this saint had the privilege of having his martyrdom described in the Acts of the Apostles (chapters 6 and 7). In many ways his court trial and martyrdom were similar to what Christ experienced during his passion. The first antiphon for the Office of Readings states that during his martyrdom Stephen "looked to heaven and saw the glory of God, and Jesus standing at the right hand of the Father." (Ac 7:55)

Likewise in the prayer we find the theme of forgiving one's enemies, as Jesus did as he was dying on the cross. Stephen is therefore a representative of the original martyr, Jesus. His charity extended not only to the poor whom he served as a deacon, but also to his persecutors.

In the Latin version of the Prayer over the Gifts we ask God to "confirm us in the faith to which Stephen gave witness by his martyrdom." He had the courage to confront his accusers with proof of his testimony and to accuse them of "opposing the Holy Spirit just as your fathers did before you" (Ac 7:51).

The Prayer after Communion relates the martyrdom of Stephen to the Christmas season, and this is further developed in the Office of Readings in the sermon of St. Fulgentius: "The love that brought Christ from heaven to earth raised Stephen from earth to heaven. . . . Love was Stephen's weapon by which he gained every battle. . . . Love inspired him to reprove those who erred, to make them amend; love led him to pray for those who stoned him, to save them from punishment. . . . Christ made love the stairway that would enable all Christians to climb to heaven. Hold fast to it, therefore, in all sincerity, give one another practical proof of it, and by your progress in it, make your ascent together."

Stephen is thus a patron of all deacons, teaching them to serve others out of love and to remain ever faithful in the defense of Christ's teaching.

> Opening Prayer: *Lord, today we celebrate the en-*
> *trance of St. Stephen into eternal glory. He died pray-*
> *ing for those who killed him. Help us to imitate his*
> *goodness and to love our enemies.*

December 27

ST. JOHN, Apostle and Evangelist

HISTORICO-LITURGICAL NOTE

This feast is listed in the Calendar of Nicomedia (fourth century) together with that of his brother St. James, in the Syriac Breviary, in the Calendar of Carthage and also in the Eastern Calendar (celebrated in Palestine on December 29 and by the Armenians on December 28). In his funeral oration for his brother Basil, St. Gregory of Nyssa mentions the following feasts celebrated between Christmas and the feast of the Circumcision: Stephen, Peter (later transferred to June), John and Paul (also transferred to June). The feast of St. John is listed in the Western Calendar of the sixth and seventh centuries and at Rome in the Sacramentary of Verona (sixth century).

According to the biblical account, John was the son of Zebedee, a fisherman from Bethsaida, and of Salome who later served Jesus (Mk 1:20; Mt 15:40; 27:56). He had been a disciple of John the Baptist (Jn 1:39), but then he followed Christ, together with Andrew, the brother of Peter, and he became the beloved disciple of Jesus. John was usually invited, together with Peter and James, to share in some of the more significant events in the life of Christ. He preached the gospel in Samaria with Peter, and according to a legend he preached also at Antioch and later at Ephesus, where his tomb is venerated. He visited Rome but was exiled to the isle of Patmos, where he wrote the Book of Revelation. Previously he had written his Gospel and three letters. He died at Patmos towards the end of the first century.

MESSAGE AND RELEVANCE

The Entrance Antiphon for this feast, "In the midst of the assembly," was proper to the feast of St. John before it was assigned to the Mass for a confessor. The new Opening Prayer is taken from the ancient Roman Sacramentary and it focuses on the mystery of the Incarnation, which is proclaimed in the Fourth Gospel and in the prologue to the First Letter of John.

The alternate Entrance Antiphon relates that John reclined close to the Lord at the Last Supper. For that reason we ask in the Opening Prayer that we "may come to understand the wisdom he taught." Likewise in the Prayer over the Gifts we ask to "share in the hidden wisdom of your eternal Word." This beloved disciple is the theologian of love *par excellence*, as is evident from his letters. It is the same theology of love that was proclaimed by Jesus at the Last Supper and recorded by John.

In the Prayer after Communion we affirm that "St. John proclaimed that your Word became flesh for our salvation" and we ask that he may always live in us. St. John saw the tragic events on Calvary as a victory and he was able to transform those events into a moment of glory. The antiphons for Morning Prayer recall three events in the life of this apostle: he was a virgin, chosen by the Lord and loved above the other apostles; to this virgin Christ entrusted his Virgin Mother; and it was he who recognized the Lord when he appeared on the lake.

The relevance of this feast is found in the words of St. Augustine, quoted in the Office of Readings: "The disciples saw our Lord in the flesh, face to face; they heard the words he spoke, and in turn they proclaimed the message to us. So we also have heard, although we have not seen. . . . They saw, and we have not seen; yet we have fellowship with them, because we and they share the same faith."

Opening Prayer: *God our Father, you have revealed the mysteries of your Word through St. John the apostle. By prayer and reflection may we come to understand the wisdom he taught.*

December 28
HOLY INNOCENTS

HISTORICO-LITURGICAL NOTE

The first testimony we have concerning this feast comes from St. Peter Chrysologus in the fifth century, from the Calendar of Carthage and the Jerome Martyrology. The feast was celebrated as a solemnity after 1568. In Constantinople the feast was celebrated on December 29.

The biblical basis for this feast is found in Matthew 2: 13-18 (the Gospel of the Mass): "Once Herod realized that he had been deceived by the astrologers, he became furious. He ordered the massacre of all the boys two years old and under in Bethlehem and its environs, making his calculations on the basis of the date he had learned from the astrologers. What was said through Jeremiah the prophet was then fulfilled: 'A cry was heard at Ramah, sobbing and loud lamentation: Rachel bewailing her children; no comfort for her, since they are no more'." It is estimated that if the population of the Bethlehem area at that time was approximately 1000, perhaps 20 infant boys were slain.

MESSAGE AND RELEVANCE

The text of the prayers, taken from the Roman Missal, points out that the massacred infants were true martyrs even though they could not have known that they were being slain because of Christ. The Latin version of the Opening Prayer states that God was glorified in the Holy Innocents, not in words but by the shedding of their blood. Their martyrdom was a gift from God. They are, as Prudentius said, "the first victims for Christ." St. Bede compared them to those who "have washed their robes and made them white in the blood of the Lamb" (Rv 7:14).

The Prayer over the Gifts states that God gives the gift of

the supernatural life of grace to newly baptized infants even before they can understand. To the Holy Innocents, however, God gave not only the gift of supernatural life but the gift of martyrdom.

The Prayer after Communion refers again to the "wordless profession of faith" by the infant martyrs. By shedding their blood, the Holy Innocents gave witness to the mystery of the Word made flesh, the mystery of the Incarnation.

The relevance of the feast of the Holy Innocents is found in the Office of Readings, where the saintly bishop Quodvultdeus says: "How great a gift of grace is here! To what merits of their own do the children owe this kind of victory? They cannot speak, yet they bear witness to Christ. They cannot use their limbs to engage in battle, yet already they bear off the palm of victory." In our contemporary society the martyrdom of the Holy Innocents cannot but make us think of the killing of countless unborn infants by means of abortion. These infants, however, are not massacred by the soldiers of Herod but by their own mothers!

> Opening Prayer: *Father, the Holy Innocents offered you praise by the death they suffered for Christ. May our lives bear witness to the faith we profess with our lips.*

December 29
ST. THOMAS BECKET (1118-1170)

HISTORICO-LITURGICAL NOTE

Thomas Becket, archbishop of Canterbury, was murdered in the cathedral on December 29, 1170. He was canonized in 1173.

Born in London around 1118, he studied at Paris and returned to England after the death of his mother. At the age of 25 he became a cleric under the archbishop of Canterbury and spent some time in Rome and Bologna before going to Auxerre in France to study law. He became an archdeacon at the age of 36 and in 1154 was promoted to the office of chancellor under King Henry II, whose favor he enjoyed for 7 years. He took part in the war against King Louis IV of France and distinguished himself in the assault on Toulouse. He was ordained priest and bishop in 1162 and was the first person in England to celebrate the solemnity of the Blessed Trinity.

After becoming archbishop, his personality changed and he became more ascetical. At the same time his relationship with the king deteriorated, and Foliot, the bishop of London, added fuel to the king's growing dislike for Becket. The relationship grew worse when Becket resisted the king in the matter of Church property and the right of clerics to be tried by the ecclesiastical courts. Becket refused to sign the document that severely limited the rights of the Church and he was abandoned by the bishops who wanted to maintain good relations with the king. Condemned for disobedience to the king, he fled to France and spent 6 years in exile.

Pope Alexander II, meanwhile, needing the support of the king of France and King Henry II of England against the anti-pope, wrote three letters, seeking reconciliation with the king of England, but received no response. Through the efforts of the pope in 1170 a partial reconciliation was effected, and Becket decided to return to England. He carried with him the documents of suspension against the prelates who had counseled the king and the excommunication of Foliot of London.

The implacable hatred of Foliot and the bishop of Salisbury reached the point at which they arranged for four knights to murder Becket. Although the clergy wanted to barricade the doors of the cathedral, Becket refused, saying: "I am ready to die for the name of Jesus and the defense of the Church." In 1170 he was struck down at the altar of the Blessed Virgin and St. Benedict. King Henry II was placed under personal interdict by the pope and was absolved after his repentance in 1172. The death of St. Thomas Becket resulted in the reconciliation of the king of England with the Church, the king of France and the church at Canterbury. The story of the assassination of Thomas Becket spread throughout Europe and the East and became the subject of a drama by T.S. Eliot: *Murder in the Cathedral.*

MESSAGE AND RELEVANCE

The Opening Prayer of the Mass is one that is proper to the Church in England. It states that St. Thomas Becket gave his life for justice and for the freedom of the Church. In fact, Becket always fought for justice and freedom, as chancellor in defense of the king, and as archbishop in defense of the Church. Although there were periods of uncertainty in his life, he had the courage to persist in his efforts even when abandoned by other bishops.

In a letter written by Thomas Becket (the Office of Readings) we find an inspiring passage on the office and duty of bishops. "As successors of the apostles, we hold the highest rank in our churches; we have accepted the responsibility of acting as Christ's representatives on earth; we receive the honor belonging to that office, and enjoy the temporal benefits of our spiritual labors. It must therefore be our endeavor to destroy the reign of sin and death, and by nurturing faith and uprightness of life, to build up the Church of Christ into a holy temple in the Lord. There are a great many bishops in the Church, but would to God we were the zealous teachers and pastors that we promised to be at our consecration, and still make profession of being. The harvest is good and one reaper or even several would not suffice to gather all of it into the granary of the Lord. Yet the Roman Church remains the head of all the churches and the source of Catholic teaching."

Of particular significance to bishops and priests is the following statement made by Becket to a friend: "Hereafter, I want you to tell me, candidly and in secret, what people are saying about me. And if you see anything in me that you regard as a fault, feel free to tell me in private. For from now on people will talk about me, but not to me. It is dangerous for men in power if no one dares to tell them when they go wrong."

> Opening Prayer: *Almighty God, you granted the martyr Thomas the grace to give his life for the cause of justice. By his prayers make us willing to renounce for Christ our life in this world so that we may find it in heaven.*

December 31
ST. SYLVESTER (+335)

HISTORICO-LITURGICAL NOTE

The feast of St. Sylvester dates back to 354. His feast was listed both in the Jerome Martyrology and in the Sacramentary of Verona. The Greeks, Syrians and Armenians celebrated his feast on January 2.

Little is known about St. Sylvester except that he was elected pope in 314. It is possible that he became a Christian in the last great persecution by Diocletian. He contributed greatly to the expansion of the Church after the peace of Constantine. He reigned as pope from 314 until 335. He was represented by delegates at the Ecumenical Council of Nicea (325), possibly because he felt that he should not preside at a Council convoked by the political authorities. He did, however, make numerous regulations concerning Catholic observances, such as making Wednesdays, Fridays and Saturdays days of fasting.

Legend has it that Constantine had originally persecuted Pope Sylvester and when he contracted leprosy he was planning to go through a pagan ritual in order to be cleansed. But in a dream St. Peter and St. Paul commanded the emperor to go to Pope Sylvester for a cure. Constantine therefore requested baptism, which was conferred in the Lateran basilica, and simultaneously he was cured of leprosy. That was the moment in which Constantine made his peace with Christians and favored the Christian religion. Another legend states that he then moved the imperial seat to Byzantium because he did not consider it fitting that the emperor should have his head-quarters in the same place as the sovereign pontiff.

The foregoing legends contributed to the diffusion of the cult of St. Sylvester. His relics are preserved in the church of St. Sylvester in Rome. He is the first saint not a martyr to be venerated in the Church. In the Lateran basilica a mosaic shows Christ giving the keys to St. Sylvester and the symbol of civil power to Constantine.

MESSAGE AND RELEVANCE

The new Opening Prayer of the Mass does not provide any particulars concerning the life of St. Sylvester. However, the Office of Readings, taken from the history of the Church written by Eusebius, does give some details concerning the peace of Constantine. "We pray that this peace may be preserved for us stable and unshaken for ever. . . . Every place that a short time before had been laid waste by the tyrants' wickedness we now saw restored to life. . . . Churches were once again rising from the ground high into the air. . . . Our bishops performed religious rites with full ceremonial, priests officiated at the liturgy, the solemn ritual of the Church, chanting psalms, proclaiming the other parts of our God-given Scriptures, and celebrating the divine mysteries. Baptism was also administered, the sacred symbol of our Savior's passion."

The Church needs the freedom to proclaim the teaching of Christ and to promote human progress, but this is accomplished through the power of the Holy Spirit, as we read in the antiphon for the Canticle of Zechariah: "What you say of me does not come from yourselves; it is the Spirit of my Father speaking in you."

After 75 years of atheistic oppression of the people under

Communist rule, we may see today a repetition of what occurred during the pontificate of St. Sylvester, when the Church
emerged from persecution and suppression to the glorious
liberty it enjoyed after the peace of Constantine.

Opening Prayer: *Lord, help and sustain your people
by the prayers of Pope Sylvester. Guide us always in this
present life and bring us to the joy that never ends.*

ALPHABETICAL INDEX
OF NAMES